MEDIEVAL STUDIES AND THE GHOST STORIES OF M. R. JAMES

PATRICK J. MURPHY

MEDIEVAL STUDIES *AND* THE GHOST STORIES OF *M. R. JAMES*

The Pennsylvania State University Press | University Park, Pennsylvania

Portions of the material in this volume appeared, in an earlier form, in the following publications: Patrick J. Murphy and Fred Porcheddu, "The Antiquarian Diaries of Thomas Hearne and Mr. Poynter in the Fiction of M. R. James: Duty Unfulfilled," *English Literature in Transition, 1880–1920*, 55, no. 3 (2012): 339–60; "Amateur Error, Templar Terror, and M. R. James's Haunted Whistle," *Philological Quarterly* 92, no. 3 (2013): 389–415; "Renovation and Resurrection in M. R. James's 'An Episode of Cathedral History,'" *Studies in Medievalism* 22 (2013): 86–113; and "Lay of a Last Survivor: Beowulf, Great War Memorials, and M. R. James's 'A Warning to the Curious,'" *Review of English Studies* 66, no. 274 (2015): 205–22.

Library of Congress Cataloging-in-Publication Data
Names: Murphy, Patrick J., 1977– , author.
Title: Medieval studies and the ghost stories of M. R. James / Patrick J. Murphy.
Description: University Park, Pennsylvania : The Pennsylvania State University Press, [2017] | Includes bibliographical references and index.
Summary: "Examines the ghost stories of writer and academic Montague Rhodes James (1862–1936). Focuses on the intersection between his scholarly work and his fiction, arguing that his two careers are intriguingly intertwined"—Provided by publisher.
Identifiers: LCCN 2016044344 | ISBN 9780271077710 (cloth : alk. paper) | ISBN9780271077727 (pbk. : alk. paper)
Subjects: LCSH: James, M. R. (Montague Rhodes), 1862–1936—Criticism and interpretation. | Ghost stories, English—History and criticism. | Medievalism in literature.
Classification: LCC PR6019.A565 Z79 2017 | DDC 823/.912—dc23
LC record available at https://lccn.loc.gov/2016044344

Copyright © 2017 The Pennsylvania State University
All rights reserved
Printed in the United States of America
Published by The Pennsylvania State University Press,
University Park, PA 16802–1003

The Pennsylvania State University Press is a member of the Association of American University Presses.

It is the policy of The Pennsylvania State University Press to use acid-free paper. Publications on uncoated stock satisfy the minimum requirements of American National Standard for Information Sciences—Permanence of Paper for Printed Library Material, ANSI Z39.48–1992.

THIS BOOK IS FOR FRED

CONTENTS

Acknowledgments　ix

Introduction　1

1　Terror and Error　28

2　Recasting the Antiquary　52

3　Ex Cathedra　88

4　A Desideratum of Wings　125

5　To the Curious　165

Afterword: Professions of Reticence　185

Notes　189
Selected Bibliography　239
Index　243

ACKNOWLEDGMENTS

This book is dedicated to Fred Porcheddu-Engel, my longtime mentor and friend. Fred taught me Old English as an undergraduate at Denison University and he was the director of my senior thesis on ghost stories in 1999–2000. It was during that project that I came across M. R. James for the first time. After attending graduate school in Wisconsin, returning to Ohio for a job at Miami University, and publishing my first monograph (on medieval riddling, also for PSUP), I suggested to Fred that we edit or write a book together on James. Fred took to the idea with characteristic enthusiasm, and for the first couple years of research we intended the book to be a co-authored collaboration. As work progressed, however, it became increasingly clear that I was in a better position to pursue the idea to fruition on my own. Though Fred's influence on this book (and on my life and career) has been enormous, I wish to be clear that the final text of this study represents my own work and writing, with two notable exceptions. The section on the Gothic Revival at Rochester Cathedral in chapter 3 was originally researched and drafted by Fred, as was the discussion of Cambridge's Round Church and the "fylfots" of its windows in chapter 1. It was also Fred who tracked down the manuscript of "Oh, Whistle, and I'll Come to You, My Lad," allowing us to notice that the original form of the whistle's inscription had been overlooked. Investigating James with Fred was tremendously fun and a real privilege. For nearly two decades he has been to me a supremely generous friend and teacher, and I would like to think that something of the spirit of his keen, curious, and welcoming approach to scholarship might be felt in these pages. Of course, any of the book's limitations and shortcomings are entirely mine to own.

Reworked versions of arguments originally published in several academic journals are incorporated into this book. I would like to thank the editors and publishers of *Philological Quarterly, Review of English Studies, Studies in Medievalism,* and *English Literature in Transition, 1880–1920* for permission to reprint revised versions of this work. I would also like to thank Ellie Goodman and Hannah Hebert at Penn State University Press and my anonymous readers for their encouragement and insight. The sharp eye of copyeditor Suzanne Wolk saved me from many an error. Completion of the book was aided by an assigned research appointment in 2015–16 through the College of Arts and Science at Miami University and a research apprenticeship granted by the Miami Humanities Center and carried out by the incomparable Andrew Hofmann. Two other truly excellent undergraduate scholars, Michelle Taylor (in 2008) and Matt Browne (in 2015), completed summer projects on James that enriched my understanding of the subject. Research on this book would not have been possible without travel support provided by the Department of English at Miami in 2015 as well as a CFR summer research appointment at Miami in 2013. Many thanks are due to all those librarians and archivists who assisted me at King's College, Cambridge University Library, the Fitzwilliam Museum, Eton College, the British Library, and at Denison University, the University of Wisconsin, and Miami University. Erin Vonnahme, the humanities librarian at Miami, helped track down a rare source when hope was growing thin.

Innumerable others provided me with assistance and support along the way: at Denison, Garrett Jacobsen, Richard Hood, Marlene Tromp, Linda Krumholz, Erin Donovan, Stephen Weber, Francis Donelly, and the Grey Malkin Society; at Wisconsin, Jack Niles, Nick Doane, Kirsten Wolf, Brian O'Camb, Andrea Benton, and Lisa H. Cooper, whose support for this project has been kind and constant; at Miami, many friends, colleagues, and students, including Debbie Morner, Rachel Treadway, Sarah Broome, Melanie Vaughn, Jerry Rosenberg, LuMing Mao, Keith Tuma, Tim Melley, Katharine Gillespie, Jody Bates, Jim Bromley, Greta Smith, and Stephen Hopkins; fellow Jamesians, including Rosemary Pardoe, Robert Lloyd Parry, and Will Ross and Mike Taylor of *A Podcast to the Curious;* and many others among my friends and family who have directly or indirectly contributed to (or put up with) this project, including Michael Dahlstrom, Kristian de Flon Arntsen, and James Russell Akers, as well as my sister, father, mother, daughter, son, and wife. I love you all madly, even when you shy away from my academic writing. As for this book, read it and weep.

INTRODUCTION

Montague Rhodes James (1862–1936) is the author of some of the most highly regarded ghost stories of all time, thrilling fictions that have never passed out of print or lost their popular appeal. In a 2012 article in the *New Yorker,* Anthony Lane notes James's "talent—modestly offered, but as yet unsurpassed—for applying the very highest calibre of jolt."[1] But James was also the provost of King's College and vice-chancellor of Cambridge University (as well as provost of Eton, later in life) and a celebrated and influential scholar, whose name is still well known among academics indebted to his pioneering and wide-ranging research. James's biographers characterize him as "essentially a medievalist," though his interests extended to a number of related periods and fields, including the study of premodern religious texts—hagiography and biblical aprocrypha in particular—where his contributions continue to be deemed exemplary.[2] James was passionate about church architecture and decoration, and published both popular and scholarly works on the subject. His research in general often bridged disciplinary divides between art history and textual studies, especially in his study of book illustration and illumination. In fact, it is the broader and systematic study of medieval manuscripts—their form, production, and history—that constitutes James's most enduring scholarly legacy. Most notably, his series of descriptive catalogues, painstakingly produced between the 1890s and

1930s, helped set a new standard in his field and laid a central foundation for a subsequent century and more of ongoing scholarly effort.[3]

In the same year that James published his first descriptive catalogue (1895), his first ghost story also appeared in print: "A Curious Book," later retitled "Canon Alberic's Scrap-Book," a tale of haunted biblioclasty that recoils at the dismantling of medieval manuscripts—even as it plunders James's dearest scholarly interests as a rich vein of imaginative material. The protagonist, Dennistoun, is a "Cambridge man," serious in his pursuit of recreational archaeology at the medieval cathedral of Saint-Bertrand-de-Comminges, while his less inquisitive friends relax in nearby Toulouse.[4] It is thus the first of many autobiographical fictions, paralleling a trip James took in 1892 with friends to the same spot, and yet it is also somewhat parodic in its evocation of prefabricated Gothic chills—to which the protagonist is comically immune, at least at first, as his local guide cringes and winces about the nave.[5] This haunted sacristan is keeping an eye on him, the young man suspects, lest he make off with the cathedral's treasures, including, colorfully, a "dusty stuffed crocodile" (a local terror slain by Saint Bertrand, or else a souvenir of the Crusades) that adorns the stone wall above the baptismal font and that is still in place today to be glimpsed by Jamesian pilgrims.[6] Dennistoun's suspicions are misplaced, though, for, on the contrary, the verger is looking not to safeguard antiquities but rather to unload a dangerous treasure: a "scrap-book" of excised manuscript fragments and ransacked illuminations, the priceless but shameful handiwork of "the unprincipled Canon Alberic," a seventeenth-century cleric who has "doubtless plundered the Chapter library of St. Bertrand" some two hundred years back.[7] A certain scrap in particular catches Dennistoun's eye, a terrifyingly vivid sketch of the devil executed by Alberic himself: "One remark is universally made by those to whom I have shown the picture: 'It was drawn from the life!'"[8] Nevertheless, Dennistoun scruples only slightly to relieve the verger of this burden at a steep discount, and later that night pays a frightful price as he takes stock of his spoils.

In the story, we can already see many of the most characteristic features of James's fiction: the protagonist obsessed with the past; the dry, donnish tone and wry sense of humor; the distancing devices and ingenious narrative frames; the casual layers of arcane allusion; the historical pastiche and eye dialect; and, most of all, the silent creep of growing unease crowned by the characteristic "Jamesian wallop," a jack-in-the-box shock of terror as the narrative suddenly lurches into the supernatural.[9] In this instance, the jump arrives as Dennistoun leafs through the album and becomes aware of something just at the periphery of his vision: "A penwiper? No, no such thing in the house. A rat? No, too black. A large spider? I trust to goodness not—no. Good God! a hand like the hand in that picture!"[10]

Over the next few decades James would write more than thirty such "antiquarian" tales of terror, most of them first performed for friends at King's College as Christmastime entertainments. Among enthusiasts of ghost stories, they have earned for James the reputation as a matchless practitioner of the art. In the present-day opinion of Mark Gatiss, he is the "undisputed master of the form," while H. P. Lovecraft praised him in 1927 as "a literary weird fictionist of the very first rank."[11] In general, this consensus view of James as one of the greatest writers of ghost stories, among the living and the dead, is an enduring and commonplace assessment by those most heavily invested in the genre. Nevertheless, James's work has typically been valued primarily for its stylistic mastery and affective power rather than for any thematic interest it might hold. Two excellent and otherwise very thorough biographies of James, both of which focus on his scholarly and institutional achievements, offer discouragement to those who would attempt to find meaningful patterns in his fiction. Michael Cox maintains that James's imaginative writings, while "amongst the very best things of their kind," would not hold up under "a weight of critical analysis," while Richard W. Pfaff declares that there is "no evidence" that the stories had significance beyond delivering a feeling of pleasing unease.[12] Glen Cavaliero, one of James's least sympathetic critics, sees his tales as illustrating the limited value of the ghost story when pursued only as an empty, formal exercise.[13] James's own avowals on this score tend to reinforce the point. He never seems to have deviated from the stance taken in the preface to his first collected volume: "The stories themselves do not make any very exalted claim. If any of them succeed in causing their readers to feel pleasantly uncomfortable when walking along a solitary road at nightfall, or sitting over a dying fire in the small hours, my purpose in writing them will have been attained."[14]

Yet it would be curious indeed if such self-deprecations held researchers permanently in check. And although the present volume represents the first monograph on the subject, there have appeared over the decades a good many important and insightful investigations into James's fiction, studies to which my own is much indebted. Many of the critics who have engaged most thoroughly with his stories, however, have naturally tended to approach the subject primarily from the perspective of the rich critical traditions that trace the development of ghostly, horror, and gothic writings in English.[15] James, of course, cannot be understood apart from these traditions—he was, in particular, an ardent fan of Dickens and an enthusiastic editor of Sheridan Le Fanu—and yet what nettles Cavaliero most is that James quite self-consciously distanced his work from that of other contemporary writers of supernatural fiction, tales he found infected by a lurid, tasteless excess (those who crossed a line of "legitimate horridness").[16] This aloofness is best explained not simply as elitism, though class is undeniably a factor. It seems likely that James would have felt the incongruity of "a man in his position" (to paraphrase James's stuffy academic Professor Parkins) to be writing amateur ghost stories, however reticent or restrained.[17] Such anxiety is centered around a sense of academic professionalism, and it is the mixing of professional scholarship with sensational thrills and chills that is arguably the most striking thing about James's fiction.

For this reason, the study of his tales cannot remain separate from his scholarly work, either in particulars or in thematic concerns. To be sure, there have been many individual, not to say scattershot, attempts to clarify allusions in the ghost stories and even to identify isolated links between James's two intertwined achievements. The heroic efforts of the editor Rosemary Pardoe and the other contributors to her long-running journal *Ghosts & Scholars* must be credited for laying the groundwork of any attempt to make sense of James's stories.[18] Some of the finest work from that publication and others appears in a volume Pardoe co-edited, *Warnings to the Curious: A Sheaf of Criticism on M. R. James*. Crucial contributions to the study of the stories have come also from James's many devoted and expert editors, including Michael Cox, S. T. Joshi, Christopher and Barbara Roden, and, most recently, Darryl Jones.[19] For all this activity, though, it would be fair to say that most critical evaluations of James's work have tended to keep his imaginative writings largely chained off from his academic fields—and vice versa. An important volume dedicated to his academic legacy barely mentions his ghost stories, while James's scholarly biographers, especially Pfaff, give relatively scant attention to his creative work.[20]

And yet, once we begin to look for connections to James's scholarly interests, they are not found wanting. It is clear, for instance, that Canon Alberic's demon inhabits a scene from the Testament of Solomon, an early apocryphal text that recounts how the titular biblical king attained (and eventually lost) the power to command demons, forcing them to act as servants in the construction of the Temple.[21] But there is reason to suspect that the creature's particular codical framing—as a crouching devil vividly "drawn from the life" within a scrapbook of medieval illuminations—draws inspiration also from the Codex Gigas in the National Library of Sweden, a book famous not only for its prodigious size (it is often cited as the world's largest surviving medieval manuscript) but also for its garish full-page portrait of a squatting devil.[22] So unusual and arresting is this image that legends have arisen to account for it, typically involving a condemned monk who calls in desperation upon the devil to aid him in the production of this enormous copy of the Bible within the span of a single night. The demon obliges, but leaves behind a ghastly, sinewy, heavily taloned self-portrait, which has given the "Devil's Bible" its alternative name and may well have helped inspire Canon Alberic's bogey. As James notes in his book *The Wanderings and Homes of Manuscripts,* the Codex Gigas is often associated with another renowned manuscript, the Codex Argenteus, which—like the Devil's Bible—arrived in Sweden as war plunder.[23] The man who brought it there was "Count Magnus" Gabriel De la Gardie (1622–1686), a rather prosaic historical figure mainly notable today for having been portrayed in James's fiction as an outlandishly monstrous feudal tyrant.[24] These observations only begin to scratch the surface, but it is telling that so many such connections have gone undiscussed in the otherwise rich commentary James's tales have received. It was possible recently for a very well informed commentator to remark on the discovery of "a surprisingly rare link between [James's] ghost stories and his other career as one who by the mid-1890s 'in knowledge of MSS [was] already third or fourth in Europe.'"[25] The points of contact are not few, however, once we go looking for them.

Nor are they trivial. For instance, the rare link to which the medievalist A. S. G. Edwards refers is that Dennistoun's name is borrowed from the real-life figure James Dennistoun (1803–1855), the compiler of a noted album of cuttings and illuminations sliced from medieval manuscripts.[26] James thus quietly but unmistakably implies a parallel between what the fictional Dennistoun does and the way the biblioclast Canon Alberic has dispossessed texts and illuminations of their proper place within medieval originals. By removing the book from Saint-Bertrand—as the Codex Gigas was plundered from Prague—does Dennistoun visit upon it a deracination as destructive as Alberic's mutilations? Are there other ways in which the modern scholar dismantles, rather than recovers, the past? Dennistoun, no doubt, would deny these implications; he finds Alberic's actions "unprincipled," while his own ethical qualms seem eased by the centering gravity of his institutional affiliations. After all, the scrapbook will come to rest at Cambridge in the "Wentworth Collection" (alias the Fitzwilliam Museum, of which James was the director from 1893 to 1908): "his mind was made up; that book must return to Cambridge with him."[27] But notice how the effect of this phrasing is to attribute to the book the scholar's return: Canon Alberic's scrapbook has never been to Cambridge; it cannot "return" there. Admittedly, the usage here is idiomatic, and hardly intended by James as significant, and yet it does encapsulate an unspoken feature of much medievalist culture: the hope that academic study and curation have the power to redeem the past by reclaiming it professionally from scattered provincial homes.

The anxious line between legitimate and illegitimate engagements with historical materials is James's theme from the beginning, and many of his most famous fictions hazard uncomfortable connections between errant scholarly impulses of the past and practices authorized by an emergent academic profession. James's era has often been identified as a defining moment in the formation of what is now generally known as medieval studies, the early practitioners of which "increasingly cordoned themselves off as exclusive of any self-reflexive, subjective, emphatic or playfully non-scientific discussion of medieval culture," in the words of Richard Utz, charting the way in which supposedly undisciplined and rashly imaginative engagements with the Middle Ages came to be identified by and dismissed under the catchall term "medievalism."[28] James's own double legacy is a dramatic example of the distinction: his descriptive catalogues are considered an important contribution to medieval manuscript studies, while his ghost stories are eclectic, even somewhat eccentric, medievalizing fictions.[29] Nor did James always keep these enterprises strictly separated, even in performance. In one lecture, for instance, we find him following up a scholarly discussion of medieval sources of magical belief with a reading of one of his supernatural tales:

> And now I really think you must have had enough of dark fables for one night. Still, I cannot avoid adding for it will probably be brought to my notice if I do not volunteer the statement, that I undertake

if necessary in addition to the paper I had small hopes of writing, to read an effort in fiction which I concocted for last Christmas Eve.... I honestly think you might be let off with what you have had: if you agree with me I do trust you will say so. The alternative is that you will have to resign yourselves for a further period of I think rather over half an hour of listening.[30]

Given these close contacts between James's scholarly and imaginative writings, as well as his stature as a revered academic medievalist, it is rather surprising that his tales have received relatively little attention from those scholars who have in recent decades remade "medievalism" as its own special subject of inquiry, defined by the field's recognized founder, Leslie Workman, as "the study not of the Middle Ages themselves but of the scholars, artists, and writers who ... constructed the idea of the Middle Ages that we inherited."[31]

Lately, though, there has been an increased willingness among many medievalists to soften or even collapse the distinction between the categories of medieval studies and medievalism, with the recognition that even the most restrained engagements with the past inevitably bear the vivid imprint of the scholar's present. It is possible to speak of "academic medievalism," after all, and to detect powerful and pressing interests in the most disinterested of scholarly performances. James's work is no exception, though his academic writings tend to be as studiously cautious and restrained as they come. They are in fact profoundly reticent, in keeping with scholarly currents of the time as well as his own academic style, tastes, and research ideals. Those looking for heterodox statements, overt romantic fantasies, or extended theoretical speculation on the purpose or promise of historical or antiquarian research will be largely disappointed. Nor have James's methods, though often self-taught, aged poorly or done anything but enhance our knowledge of the past—with the possible exception of his recommended use of chemical reagent for the resuscitation of illegible texts, a now-shunned practice at which "modern scholars will shudder."[32] James's abhorrence of the destructive restorations of the Gothic Revival (a theme examined in detail in chapter 3) is much more representative of his conservative approach to scholarship. We might conclude, then, that James's medieval studies have not disintegrated into mere medievalisms in the eyes of present-day academics. But that is not to say that his scholarship escapes all criticism; despite expressing great admiration, the editor of *The Legacy of M. R. James* feels bound to address the question, "Were aspects of [his] erudition misplaced?"[33] The issue had been raised of James's errant dabblings even during his boyhood at Eton, where his masters perennially worried about the "streak of slight perversity" behind James's "peripheral scholarly interests."[34] The concern never fully dissipated and is, arguably, what fuels much of the fright in his ghostly tales.

This, then, is the chief method of the present volume: to trace the potential significance of James's many intricate medievalisms, with the related aim of illuminating the way they may reflect aspects of what it meant to be a scholar in his era, a remarkable "middle" period in the history of the humanities often understood today in terms of an undisciplined amateurism yielding to enduring institutions established by university professionals. James himself is a fascinatingly liminal figure in this narrative, and not only on account of his shadow career writing ghost stories. For although most horror fans (present and past) have assumed James's scholarly stature to be beyond reproach, his position in academic fields has always been more complicated, his reputation and legacy as a researcher more open to question. In particular, the paradoxical sense that James was both the quintessential professional and yet also something of an amateur has had a long afterlife, so that the four-volume history of Cambridge University characterizes him as a "scholar and dilettante . . . literary, whimsical, unpractical, yet in his own way a great technician with medieval manuscripts."[35] A great technician *and* a dilettante? The blurred line between a professional's work and a hobbyist's dabbling—the "avocational nature of the knowledge industry"—is one of the key elements that, as Shane McCorristine has recently (and convincingly) argued, "produces the ambient basis for the supernatural situation" in James's work.[36] Yet that fairly select set of critics who have profitably connected his two careers often neglect this tension. Martin Hughes, for example, rightly argues that James's fiction reflects his meditating "seriously about both the usefulness and the dangers . . . of his absorption in the past," but detects a fairly distinct line in James's fiction between "shallow enthusiasm" and "the restraint and balance of mind which comes from genuine scholarship."[37] Much of the best recent work on James has begun to trouble that enthusiast-professional divide, perhaps most notably in the writings of the distinguished medievalist Carolyn Dinshaw, who remarks that "in his amateur fiction . . . James reflected deeply and critically on his own professional preoccupations as manuscript scholar, philologist, archaeologist."[38] This dynamic that Dinshaw identifies, with all its attendant questions and complexities, forms the curious matter of my book.

THE ANTIQUARY AND HIS GHOST STORIES

Despite the titles of his collections, the ghosts of James's "ghost stories" do not tend to be of the sheer and sheeted variety. The distinctive Jamesian haunt, Lovecraft remarked, is "lean, dwarfish, and hairy—a sluggish, hellish night-abomination midway betwixt beast and man—and usually *touched* before it is *seen*."[39] The demon of Dennistoun's scrapbook is of this type, matching the Gigas-like drawing of Canon Alberic: "Imagine one of the awful bird-catching spiders of South America translated into human form, and endowed with intelligence just less than human, and you will have some faint conception of the terror inspired by this appalling effigy."[40] But even this figure of exotic revulsion leads us nowhere so much as back to James's own late nineteenth-century Cambridge and its heady atmosphere of professional self-invention, for our reaction to the image is filtered through the gaze of a "lecturer on morphology" who is horrified when shown the drawing. As Michael Cox has observed, the terrified morphologist is likely a fictionalized Arthur Shipley (1861–1927), a specialist in biological morphology and one of James's two companions on his 1892 trip to Saint-Bertrand.[41] Just months before James first read "Canon Alberic" for the Chitchat Society (a weekly gathering of Cambridge undergraduates and young academics), Shipley had published a successful textbook, *Zoology of the Invertebrata,* whose section on arachnid variety opens with a description of spiders who do not weave webs but rather dig burrows and "sit at the entrance of these holes waiting for their prey, which, in the case of the gigantic South American *Mygale avicularia,* often takes the form of small birds."[42] We may be tempted to imagine James, a well-known arachnophobe, blanching as he glances over his friend's new book. Perhaps he read no further!

Yet an intertextual trifle like this reminds us that James's earliest stories were largely produced for and read within close-knit college circles, spaces in which professional identities might be safely rehearsed and performed— and disciplinary misgivings aired. Present at the Chitchat Society that evening were men like Charles Waldstein (1856–1927), James's predecessor at the Fitzwilliam and Cambridge's first reader in the fledgling field of classical archaeology, and Walter Headlam (1866–1908), a young scholar whose emphasis on establishing a linguistic corpus to contextualize Greek texts set him in opposition to the "gentlemanly compositional classics" of past generations.[43] Shipley was equally a young pioneer in morphology, while James was an up-and-comer in his own inchoate fields. Whether Shipley was actually present in the room for this ribbing, James seems gently jocular in describing "a person of, I was going to say, abnormally sane and unimaginative habits of mind."[44] But he is also opening an implicit conversation between his own disciplines and Shipley's, a safely systematic one that successfully avoids conjuring its specimens from the imagination or straying from the strict limits of the morphologist's area of specialty.[45]

What was indeed unique about the new university specialists was not simply their minute knowledge of narrow fields but rather, as James Turner stresses, the sense that a single professional researcher could no longer be free to wander from one demarcated discipline to another. Disciplinary specialization implied isolated realms of expertise into which one could not cross without a "strenuous feat of reacculturation."[46] The "pitiable exhibition" of the amateur Karswell in "Casting the Runes" is condemned at least partly on account of its omnivorous scholarship: "there was nothing that man didn't swallow."[47] Yet the manuscript studies that most interested James (and his alter ego Dennistoun) also tended to encourage forays into a number of increasingly self-enclosed fields as well as to consider subjects not tamely residing in any one domain. Investigations into "the wanderings and homes of manuscripts" tended indeed to soften hardening boundaries separating the study of literature, biblical studies, historical linguistics, and art history (as well as requiring great skill in ancillary arts such as paleography and codicology). Beyond this, there was the material fact of the medieval manuscript itself. James was fascinated by books in every dimension—their place in time, their space on the shelf, the way the sheepskin codex engages senses other than sight.[48]

Personal relationships and local loyalties grounded such potentially dubious interests. The most noteworthy exception to the Jamesian ghost of hair and flesh is the sheeted specter of "Oh, Whistle, and I'll Come to You, My Lad," and it is significant that its victim, ambitious in the fatuous (and fictional) field of "ontography," sniffs at anything so mundane as material evidence.[49] But for all his professional polish, Parkins is a social failure, as incapable of closeness with colleagues as he is of fully translating the Latin inscriptions on the haunted whistle: *quis est iste qui uenit* (who is this who is coming?).[50] James revisits the motif in "A School Story," a much simpler tale he spun for the boys of the King's College Choir School, in which a schoolmaster receives threats from beyond the grave through the Latin exercises of unwitting pupils: *Si tu non veneris ad me, ego veniam ad te* (If you don't come to me, I'll come to you).[51] The chiasmus of the conditional locks the fate of its victim in a tight embrace, and indeed the schoolmaster and his tormenter end up at the bottom of an abandoned well, their bodies suggestively intertwined. But what would it mean for men to come together under proper conditions? James signals to his audience of young choristers that schoolboy rites of initiation—particularly the mastering of Latin constructions—are the correct path to an intimacy that outlasts knowledge of the Future More Vivid itself.[52]

That story more or less explicitly concerns institutions. As the narrator notes, "boys seldom allow that their schools possess any tolerable features," and James's tale is careful to inculcate in the choristers the full weight of their importance.[53] James himself spent nearly the whole of his life within the walls of elite educational foundations. Born in 1862, the youngest child of an Anglican clergyman (and the grandson of a Jamaican slaveholder), James was raised in Great Livermere near Bury St. Edmunds in Suffolk before entering private school at the age of eleven at Temple Grove, just outside London (the model setting for "A School Story"). From there it was on to Eton, where he stayed until the ripe age of twenty, becoming, as Tim Card notes, possibly "the oldest boy ever in the school."[54] After James returned to Eton in his sixties, Lytton Strachey was to remark tartly, "It's odd that the Provost of Eton should still be aged sixteen. A life without a jolt."[55] The strange sense that James was at once preternaturally advanced in his studies and yet arrested in his development was from the beginning tied to his precocious antiquarian interests. As a heartsick boy at Temple Grove, he wrote his father, "I desire above all things to make an archaeological search into the antiquities of Suffolk to get everything I can for my museum, and last but not by any means least, to get home."[56] School was to become his home, but fascination with the past endured. As H. E. Luxmoore, his beloved tutor at Eton and a later fixture at James's ghost-story sessions, wrote in an 1879 progress report, "The only other thing I note is to repeat the old warning . . . against prematurely transplanting medieval studies into a time when the grounding ought to be ensured which will make them all the better afterwards."[57]

After Eton, King's College in Cambridge was the next step, and there James was to stay on for nearly forty years, until finally leaving to become provost of Eton around the close of the Great War: "The bitter drops in the cup will make themselves felt in due time: but of course it is easier to contemplate quitting this place while it is empty than it would be in normal times."[58] The exception of this trauma notwithstanding, many—including James himself—have been struck by the long, almost abnormal uneventfulness of his scholarly existence and unattached lifestyle. During his own boyhood, age-old statutes mandating celibacy for college fellows had been lifted, allowing for the first time married men (not yet, of course, women) to make lifelong academic careers at Oxford and Cambridge. James himself was encouraged by friends to marry, but he preferred to remain a confirmed bachelor, thereby conforming to a rather outdated type of isolated and indolent "donnishness"—traditionally associated, not incidentally, with "antiquarian history or eccentric hobbies."[59] As Paul R. Deslandes has argued, married or unmarried, the permanent Oxbridge scholar was perceived by many in this era as a kind of immature relic, "a particular type of weakened or tarnished manhood."[60] That is not to deny that innumerable undergraduates respected James deeply as a mentor and as a man, but the course of his career did seem to run with a notably unmomentous flatness from undergraduate to fellow, from provost to vice-chancellor—all the while "without a jolt" up until the great exception of the war and his apparent retrogression, thereafter, to Eton. The many statements we read from contemporaries concerning James's "childishness" may be at least partly understood through this lens. Even James's most recent editor characterizes him as "a curiously incomplete man."[61]

The related question of James's sexuality has occasioned much speculation, especially in regard to his feelings for James McBryde (b. 1874), the friend whose illustrations for the first edition of *Ghost Stories of an Antiquary* became its pretext for publication. James had agreed to publish the collection on the condition that the younger man illustrate it, but before the artwork was completed, McBryde underwent an emergency appendectomy, dying the day after.[62] James writes in the book's preface, "Those who knew the artist will understand how much I wished to give a permanent form even to a fragment of his work; others will appreciate the fact that here a remembrance is made of one in whom many friendships centred."[63] In this commemorative context, the circumscription of James's affection for McBryde within a sphere of mutual friendship feels appropriate, but private correspondence hints at a deeper intimacy: "I think you know how much I value you, my dear thing," James writes to McBryde in a rare surviving letter, "and that anything that affects you is of very great interest to me."[64] James was the young man's close friend and beloved mentor, a role that (in the pedagogical tradition with which James identified) could at times involve a sense of intimacy verging on the erotic.[65] There is no concrete evidence, however, that this relationship—or any that James ever shared with another man—had a sexual dimension.[66] On the other hand, it should be said, we can have no definitive evidence to the contrary. Even Jones's cautious remark, "Whatever sexuality [James] did have was very probably unrecognized and certainly never articulated," seems to exceed what we can safely affirm. There are many unanswerable questions here that lie largely outside the scope of this book.

What can be stated with more confidence is that several members of James's first audience, the inner circle that gathered to listen to his tales, were quietly open with each other on this subject. The extensive diaries of A. C. Benson (1862–1925) make this clear. For instance, two of the younger men in the group, Percy Lubbock (b. 1879) and Oliffe Legh Richmond (b. 1881), seem to have had obvious sexual interest in men, including each other; Benson witnessed Lubbock receiving a "long and loverlike kiss" from Howard Sturgis (who shared a house in Windsor with A. C. Ainger, another ghost-session regular), while Richmond "sat regarding Howard with looks of love."[67] These men were all intimate friends and students of James's and members of his original enthusiastic audience.[68] In fact, it is a passage from Richmond's own unpublished reminiscences that serves as our most important source for what James's ghost-story sessions were like (cited below). Toward the end of this document, Richmond reflects on James's withdrawal to Eton: "As Provost of Eton he swam into peaceful waters. . . . He sat, studying what he willed, in a room surrounded by the admirable portraits, by the best artists, of the boys of the seventeenth and eighteenth centuries, whose leaving gifts they were. Were they *all* as handsome as that at eighteen years of age? They throw some light on Shakespeare's seeming-passionate admiration for a youth of that age in the century before."[69] This "seeming-passionate admiration" is, of course, not directly attributed to James, and at most the passage probably reflects only speculation on what a former mentor might find pleasing (at one point during the war years, Benson records Richmond and another man deliberating over "the mysterious love-life of Monty James").[70] Nevertheless, the point remains that same-sex desire was a personal question for a number of the bachelors who regularly gathered in James's rooms to hear him read (and afterward to play "animal grab," a game of groping at which Monty was famously adept: one listener recalls lying "writhing on the floor with Monty James's long fingers grasping at his vitals").[71] Though committed to celibacy, Benson in his diaries frequently confesses romantic interest in the youthful members of his acquaintance ("God knows how tremulously I try to interest these young Apollos," he writes in reference to Richmond and Stephen Gaselee, a young scholar who would one day pen James's obituary in the *Proceedings of the British Academy*). In another passage, Benson writes of being in love as an adolescent with an older boy: "I adored him at a distance. . . . But I never spoke to him till the blissful day when I had gone to Henley, and tired of heat and noise, made my way to the station to return. He got into the same carriage and told me ghost stories."[72]

The sense that supernatural tales might provide an almost erotic thrill is certainly evident in James's own fiction. The suggestive bed-clothed specter and beckoning title of "Oh, Whistle, and I'll Come to You, My Lad" is only the most obvious example (on the December night in 1903 when this tale was first performed, two other ghost stories were also read to the group, one by Benson and one by Percy Lubbock. Yet another sexual confidant of Benson's, Hugh Walpole, would purchase the manuscript of "Oh, Whistle" when it went on sale at Sotheby's in 1936).[73] Other instances are easy to adduce. "The Residence at Whitminster" opens with an "abominable" act between two boys witnessed by an outraged guardian, and whatever necromantic secret the youths share includes an element of sinister tenderness felt in the guilty moment: "he very gently laid his hand on Frank's head."[74] Black magic in James is often associated with such temptations. The pagan dabblings of two men in "An Evening's Entertainment" are made all the more illicit by their cohabitation off the beaten path:

> And one day he came back from market, and brought a young man with him; and this young man and he lived together for some long time, and went about together, and whether he just did the work of the house for Mr. Davis, or whether Mr. Davis was his teacher in some way, nobody seemed to know. . . . Well, now, what did those two men do with themselves? Of course I can't tell you half the foolish things that the people got into their heads, and we know, don't we, that you mustn't speak evil when you aren't sure it's true, even when

people are dead and gone. But as I said, those two were always about together, late and early, up on the downland and below in the woods; and there was one walk in particular that they'd take regularly once a month, to the place where you've seen that old figure cut out in the hillside.[75]

The landmark the two men frequent is probably the Cerne Abbas Giant, a possibly ancient and certainly eye-catchingly priapic figure sprawled on a chalky slope in Dorset.[76] More unmistakable still, once we investigate his sources, is the way James interweaves the horrors of "The Diary of Mr. Poynter" with the personal history of the antiquary John Poynter, a man who was expelled from Oxford in 1732 for "sodomitical practises."

As I detail in chapter 4, James's knowledge of Poynter can be traced to the writings of Thomas Hearne, an eighteenth-century medievalist of "black-letter" notoriety, whose scholarly efforts were a forerunner of James's own. James's fascination with such antiquarian precursors is probably partly to be explained by his own rather liminal position within shifting academic institutions, identities, and fields. In this regard the term "antiquary"—which James of course uses to describe himself in his first two volumes of fiction—takes on particular interest, for by 1904 the word had a very distinct history and complex relationship to professional medieval studies as it was developing. As Philippa Levine and others have detailed, the study of the material and textual past was an enormously popular avocation in Victorian England; societies and printing clubs flourished, while amateur scholars shared manuscripts and compared field notes through robust networks of antiquarian learning.[77] Although typically genteel and university-educated, the traditional antiquary had little formal training for his hobby, and no consistent methodology guided his researches. In fact, many contemporaries understood that what primarily distinguished this species of scholar was his refusal to specialize, often taken as a point of pride: "The true antiquary," Charles Roach Smith wrote in 1844, "does not confine his researches to one single branch . . . but in a comprehensive view surveys every fact."[78] Yet it was frequently charged that such scholarship failed to synthesize these broadly personal interests into a unified, detached vision of the past.[79] With an insatiable enthusiasm for all things old, the antiquary was rather known for scattered eclecticism. Roaming researchers could draw on the evidence of ancient artifacts as freely as they could textual records; their interests might encompass prehistoric, classical, and medieval art, history, literature, and languages, as well as architecture and other, less monumental, material remains of the past. Often, in fact, the scholar's "field" was defined not by subject matter, time period, or methodology so much as by the quite literal local fields and archives to which he had access; the antiquary is thus a figure associated with a kind of scrapbooking provincialism, local fragments and unbalanced enthusiasms pasted in and over everything else.

With the popularity of such pursuits came also an entrenched tradition of satire and scorn directed at perceived antiquarian excess, enervation, and eccentricity, a long-standing and widespread sense that the antiquary's undiscriminating scholarly appetites were misguided, his energies misapplied, his trivial objects of study unworthy of such devotion. The Dryasdust, it was thought, lavished attention on rare but worthless texts, prized trivial artifacts, eagerly consumed and regurgitated the detritus of history's dustbin. At best, this very curious kind of person was considered the handmaiden to the more masculine work of historical synthesis.[80] At worst, he was deemed to be suffering from a kind of temporal disease, a theme that merges with the antiquary's common association with deviant or underdeveloped sexualities.[81] The received narrative of James's "life without a jolt"—the antiquarian vita constructed by his many fans and critics, as well as by James himself—could easily be seen to echo these themes. The narrative is only partly redeemed, perhaps, by the prestigious if "anachronistic" academic institutions that lent James's life a sense of place and purpose. In a 1901 diary entry, A. C. Benson expressed his frustrations: "The whole place [King's College] seems to me deplorably empty of men of weight, purpose and vigour ... M. R. J[ames] absorbed in antiquarian things, sociable, amusing—it all seems to me rather *feeble*."[82]

In his fiction, James himself seems acutely aware of such dangers for antiquarian hobbyists. One of his haunted men is even named "Mr Dillet," a dilettante collector of dollhouses who witnesses within a miniature "Strawberry Hill Gothic" mansion the scaled-down revival of a grisly crime.[83] (One reductive reading would be that amateurs play with dolls at their own risk.) "The Haunted Dolls' House," in fact, was actually transcribed by James into a tiny tome to sit on the library shelves of Queen Mary's Dolls' House, a royal display piece viewed by more than a million visitors to the British Empire Exhibition of 1924–25. This story is in some respects a slighter "replica" of James's better-known tale "The Mezzotint," in which a museum curator observes a manor house by way of a haunted mezzotint (that is, a kind of print made by scraping and polishing copper plate). Across the moonlit lawn, in terrifying stages, we witness a cadaverous and vengeful spirit carry off a cruel aristocrat's only heir, the *"spes ultima gentis."*[84] A notable thing about this earlier version, though, is the way it resists the obvious plot twist of identifying the curator as a long-lost representative of the demon-shadowed line.[85] Instead, the engraved specter stays put within the mezzotint, and the professional antiquary remains a sterile bystander.

As these and many other examples attest, James was keenly interested in his profession's uneasy relationship to other scholarly, occupational, and hobbyist modes of engaging with the past. In many ways, indeed, the dilettantish "antiquary" might seem a ready-made figure against which the university specialist might define his work. The relationship, though, could be more complicated than simple opposition. As a new generation of academics worked to define their fields, it was not antiquarianism alone they sought to repudiate but any and all "unscientific" approaches to the past. Quite in contrast to dry antiquarianism, popular, journalistic, or belletristic writings would arrive at loose, premature conclusions, indulging in seductive storytelling calculated to appeal to a commercial and nonspecialist audience. A sharp rhetorical contrast was increasingly drawn between such writings and specialist history as "a science, no less and no more," in the words of J. B. Bury, speaking at Cambridge in 1903.[86] The exquisitely patient examination of primary sources was the professional's proper task, and many felt that restrained preliminary work was all the more urgent for a field still finding its footing. Yet for those opposed to the ascendancy of this highly dry style of scholarship, it too was haunted by the specter of academic errancy, "threaten[ing] to degenerate from a broad survey of great periods and movements of human societies into vast and countless accumulations of insignificant facts, sterile knowledge, and frivolous antiquarianism."[87] Was professional rigor nothing more than a recrudescence of the antiquarian impulse?[88]

Such observations may begin to help clarify the shadowy valence of what it would mean for James, in 1904, to publish a book of fiction under the title *Ghost Stories of an Antiquary*. James's unimpeachable institutional standing as a member of the Cambridge establishment no doubt made it easier to adopt a pose that was at once self-effacing and yet associated with privileged aristocratic leisure. The inherent self-deprecation also provided cover for the eccentricity of a professional medievalist publishing "a book of very gruesome grues," in the words of Oxford undergraduate Dorothy Sayers, writing to her parents in 1913.[89] And of course James did not just write weird fiction; he published tales that drew explicitly and intricately on the very subject matter of his academic expertise. A contemporary advertisement for the stories registered the curiosity of such an enterprise, and associated it with James's reputation for scattershot scholarly pursuits: "Those who know the extensive and miscellaneous character of Dr. James's researches in various fields of learning will not be surprised to find him appearing as the author of a volume of 'Ghost Stories.'"[90] It is perhaps safe to say, at the least, that "antiquarian" in 1904 was a potentially anxious, if somewhat accurate, description of James's wide-ranging research interests and an apt description of amateur fictions that both plunder scholarly materials and invoke as their central theme this increasingly anachronistic identity.

For such an antiquary, moreover, King's College offered a rare patch of vanishing habitat. Cambridge in the prime of James's career was undergoing a rather shiftless, shambling process of reform (a "transitional phase when new roles and old expectations often failed to mesh," in the words of Christopher Stray).[91] Reorganization to bring England's medieval institutions more in line with other contemporary universities faced resistance from many—including James—and took several decades, and more than one royal commission, to unfold. The intricate story has been well told elsewhere, but the general trend was—haltingly—toward the development of a more centralized and formal organization of teaching and governance, with more emphasis on specialized training in an expanded range of distinct fields, and, generally, the promotion of a more ambitious national, educational, and research mission for a university that had formerly functioned as a quasi-monastic way station for future clergy and idle gentlemen. Kingsmen a generation before James had sauntered to their degrees without examination. James, however, was one of the first to undergo a Tripos exam expanded to included specialized subjects; he studied archaeology under Waldstein and William Ridgeway, both specifically hired as readers in these fields, a new rank within an increasingly stratified academic hierarchy. At the green age of thirty-one, James would successfully supplicate for a doctorate in letters, a degree that (at the time) was viewed more as an honorific for lifetime achievement than as a basic qualification for academic posts.[92] He never did, though, join the slowly developing professoriate, which had previously enjoyed slender influence in the university. Nor did he do much formal teaching in the course of his career; "his College once appointed him Lecturer in Paleography," J. H. Clapham writes, "—but to carry on his Fellowship, not to make him lecture."[93] The many college and academic positions James occupied—fellow, director, dean, tutor, provost—tended to be administrative and ceremonial, his relationships with students fostered through informal guidance and mentoring rather than by way of systematic training and instruction.

In these various roles, James often stood in opposition to reform efforts, including those that would have opened Cambridge and its degrees to women (his opposition is discussed in chapter 4). In other matters, too, he dragged his feet. It was only following the crisis of the Great War that a sluggish process of professionalization accelerated at Cambridge, and James himself was a reluctant member of the Asquith Commission (1919–22), which reconstituted Cambridge government, reorganized the faculty system, and adopted measures to open the university to a greater social range of students. By this time, however, James had left his residence at King's, a move that probably had as much to do with wartime upheaval as with the changing face of Cambridge. The provostship at Eton offered a quieter life. After all, he had acceded to the vice-chancellorship of Cambridge in 1913, so that his years in that office were characterized by unprecedented crisis. Aside from administrative duties, James's long-standing role as undergraduate mentor was rendered immeasurably more difficult and painful, and it was often his somber responsibility to comfort the living with wartime sermons and words of commemoration. "No-one of his time," Anthony C. Deane recalls, "could match his felicity in composing a ceremonial address or an inscription for a memorial."[94] Following the war, in fact, James became a principal organizer, author, and designer of war memorials at Eton. His rank and eloquence led him to these roles, but his status as an eminent medievalist may have— in the minds of many—made him a man particularly well suited to the work. An authority on the past is thought to be positioned to contextualize such events, to incorporate them within larger frameworks of historical meaning, though James of course was not a historian in the common sense of the word. As I discuss particularly in chapter 5, these wartime experiences complicate the meaning of his antiquarianism as it finds expression in his later fiction. In fact, as he writes in his 1926 memoir, James himself would come to characterize the ghost story as an old-fashioned, and specifically prewar, genre:

And then, perhaps, a game of cards: then possibly an adjournment of a few of the company, and a ghost story composed at fever heat, but not always able to ward off sleep from some listener's eye (this rankles a little still): and so to bed with what appetites we might.

All very pedestrian and Anglican and Victorian and everything else that it ought not to be: but I should like well enough to have it over again.[95]

Indeed, framing each one of James's stories, whether or not it was actually performed at prewar King's, is the shadow of the Antiquary himself. James dedicated his first volume of stories to "all those who at various times have listened to them," and the image of the formidable Oxbridge don casting narrative spells over an awed gathering has informed the way these tales have been received ever since publication: "The discomfort of a nightmare was well worth the pleasure of knowing that a ghost story could still produce one," writes one reader in a letter to James, "but I doubt whether there are any ghost stories beyond those of an Antiquary which could still do so."[96] The antiquarian aura remains even for those who have never watched Christopher Lee channel James on the BBC, or attended one of Robert Lloyd Parry's performances impersonating an affable and engaging antiquary in his darkened study. The shadow of Monty the erudite entertainer has served as a hospitable paratext for many a reader, and it is not altogether an inaccurate one. By all accounts, James himself was a gifted performer, having acted in many amateur productions as a Cambridge undergraduate (including a starring role in an Attic Greek-language production of Aristophanes's *The Birds*), and the comic provincial voices of his fiction would likely have been enlivened by his knack for impersonation. No doubt, too, his talent for the spoken word would electrify in performance the "nicely managed crescendo" he so valued in ghostly tales; S. G. Lubbock notes that his delivery was "entirely untheatrical and immensely effective."[97] Richmond's account of these evenings gives a sense of James's talent for understated execution: "Monty disappeared into his bedroom. We sat and waited in the candlelight. Perhaps someone played a few bars on the piano, and desisted, for good reason. . . . Monty emerged from the bedroom, manuscript in hand, at last, and blew out all the candles but one, by which he seated himself. He then began to read, with more confidence than anyone else could have mustered, his well-nigh illegible script in the dim light. It was the ghost story of the year, begun that morning."[98]

Later paraphrases paint his audience as nervous, awestruck, and hesitant, awaiting James, who finally arrives to read, "his clear, confident voice cutting through the dim, flickering light of candle and fire."[99]

No doubt some such atmosphere was playfully cultivated, but the retrospective amplification of his charismatic presence may tend to obscure the collegial and familiar nature of these gatherings. The core of James's first audiences consisted of some of his closest friends, men who offered a comfortable sounding board for new work. The earliest reading, after all, took place at a meeting of the Chitchat Society, where compositions were read and afterward discussed and critiqued among close associates with "engaging frankness."[100] By 1893, James was a senior member of the club and only two years away from receiving his doctorate. But even as a schoolboy at Temple Grove he had already begun dabbling in the genre, and by Eton days we find him plying friends with such entertainments: "I must depart for awhile as I am engaged for a 'dark séance' i.e. a telling of ghost stories in which capacity I am rather popular just now. Some one will soon come to fetch me."[101] The transition from such schoolboy activities was apparently seamless. In fact, the tradition as it developed at King's was very much an Etonian affair, so that nearly all the "regular ingredients" (as James once put it) were former students or current masters of the elite school. Few of James's guests, though, were his age.[102] His listeners tended to be either former masters of his own (H. E. Luxmoore [b. 1841], A. C. Ainger [b. 1841], Walter Durnford [b. 1847]) or younger graduates of Eton he had befriended and mentored at Cambridge (Owen Hugh Smith [b. 1869], A. B. Ramsay [b. 1872], S. G. Lubbock [b. 1873], Percy Lubbock [b. 1879], Oliffe Richmond [b. 1881]). This generational dynamic may have suited the role James was to play on these evenings as the boyish-donnish focus of a "charmed and charming circle," his performances punctuated by rough horseplay within the stately rooms of the Gibbs Building: "chaff & extravagant fancy & mimicry & camaraderie & groups that gather and dissolve in this room and then that like the midges that dance their rings in the sunshine," in the breathless words of his indulgent and admiring tutor.[103]

Traces of these occasions remain in the stories, perhaps in ways that go beyond tone and the occasional allusion to an inattentive attendee.[104] In this regard, it is important to remember that the men who gathered in James's rooms were in the festive habit of entertaining one another with other kinds of creative productions for the holidays as well.[105] For Christmas 1895 and

1896, respectively, James wrote the plays *The Dismal Tragedy of Henry Blew Beard, Esq.* and *Alex Barber*, the latter a parody of the tale of "Ali Baba and the Forty Thieves," which he performed with a cast of the same men who were to become the audience for his ghost-story sessions.[106] Within a year or two of these performances, the ghost tradition seems to have edged out other creative efforts, but the association of the holidays with such parodies and spoofs may offer insight into the methods of invention that James employed in many of his supernatural tales. For example, "The Story of a Disappearance and an Appearance" (the only story actually set at Christmastime) is centered around a nightmarish transformation of the popular Punch and Judy play, the comic slapstick replaced by the sickening crack of actual skulls being crushed. Although the Punch tradition dates back to the sixteenth century, this story might be considered less "antiquarian" than those tales repurposing aspects of James's scholarly culture. Still, as the readings of this book suggest, James often took such a "parodic" approach to horror, and many of his transformations were reworkings of medieval texts, subjects, and genres—all grist for his mill of antiquarian terror.

It is common, especially among readers in awe of the institutions he represented, to imagine that James's learned associates might have followed along easily to such patterns, meeting each winking reference with knowing nods. A high level of Latinity might be taken for granted, yes, but much of the appropriateness of James's many allusions—and their potent resonance—was likely lost on his first listeners. James was a tastemaker among his friends and inspired a good many of them to write supernatural stories of their own, often with a derivative and superficially "antiquarian" air.[107] These men were not professed medievalists, however, though a few did have an amateur interest. F. E. Hutchinson (a literary scholar) was to publish a book on medieval glass in 1949. Ramsay, who probably witnessed more of James's readings than anyone else, had many casual antiquarian interests and once read to the Chitchat Society a paper on English mystery plays, an important inspiration—as we shall see in chapter 3—behind James's story "An Episode of Cathedral History."[108] But for the most part these listeners would have looked to their host as the genial expert on such matters. Among fans of his fiction to this day, in fact, James's uncanny knowledge of specialist subjects is a source of the stories' power and pleasure. The author was indeed, as Peter Ackroyd puts it, a "miniaturist in horror," and tracing the coherence and significance of James's antiquarian style is one of the chief aims of this book.[109] But the highly reticent patterns we find in his tales are probably better explained in terms of James's own inner sense of suitability, rather than as in-jokes among knowing peers. Authenticity would matter for one performing a version of his professional self, even (or especially) among colleagues in other fields. The very eccentricity of this medievalizing diversion may have entailed a certain self-applied pressure to get the details right, or at least to establish patterns that come very close, if not all the way, to adding up.

This near coherence, in fact, comes rather close to James's own aesthetic, as he once wrote: "The reading of many ghost stories has shown me that the greatest successes have been scored by the authors who can make us envisage a definite time and place, and give us plenty of clear-cut and matter-of-fact detail, but who, when the climax is reached, allow us to be just a little in the dark as to the working of their machinery. We do not want to see the bones of their theory about the supernatural."[110] Most famously, James declared his allegiance to the principle of "reticence" in ghost stories, which "may be an elderly doctrine to preach, yet from the artistic point of view I am sure it is a sound one. Reticence conduces to effect, blatancy ruins it, and there is much blatancy in a lot of recent stories."[111] It is not only paranormal matters, however, that are darkly patterned within his stories. As this book endeavors to show, James's medievalizing goes well beyond "antiquarian window-dressing," and its significance can transcend what James chose to acknowledge: "As for the fragments of ostensible erudition which are scattered about my pages, hardly anything in them is not pure invention."[112] As I hope to show, this statement requires qualification. James's inventiveness with his materials is affectively brilliant, but other implications are also worth considering.

There is evidence, for example, that James's ghosts are often "medieval" in the sense of conforming to narrative patterns and conceptions of the supernatural dating back to the Middle Ages. As Jacqueline Simpson has richly demonstrated, James often draws on traditional materials to, as he once put it, "make my ghosts act in ways not inconsistent with the rules of folklore."[113] "The Rose Garden," for instance, is centered around a stake haunted by ominous whisperings: "Pull, pull. I'll push, you pull" (uttered by some foul thing eager to be freed).[114] These distinctive details are widespread in Danish folklore, a subject familiar to James through sources such as the compilations of Evald Tang Kristensen (1843–1929), who documents many variations of the story of the "ghost-post," in which a spirit is pinned in place to prevent it from walking: *Ryk, så skal jeg trykk* (Pull, and I'll push), a voice invites those who stumble upon the not-to-be-removed stake.[115] Other tales rooted in traditional motifs include "A Neighbor's Landmark," wherein we encounter a spirit who knows not "why it walks or why it cries."[116] The reader, if not the walker, is to learn the reason. The ghost is being punished for the fraudulent appropriation of prime pastureland, and Simpson has convincingly shown that James probably modeled his shrieking wanderer on the "boundary ghosts" of Danish folklore, who traditionally suffer for similar transgressions.[117] We reach the highest pitch of horror as the narrator crosses through Betton Wood: "And just then into my left ear—close as if lips had been put within an inch of my head, the frightful scream came thrilling again."[118] James himself notes, in an academic article on the fourteenth-century supernatural tales of Byland Abbey, "there are many tales, Danish and other, of persons who answer the shrieking ghost with impertinent words, and the next moment they hear it close to their ear."[119] (Perhaps in James's tale, the scholar's curiosity stands in place of such impertinence?)[120] At any rate, permeable boundaries separate James's academic publications from his own tales. The article on the Byland hauntings, "Twelve Medieval Ghost-Stories" (published in the *English Historical Review*), was mistaken by the author of James's *Times* obituary for a collection of original fiction.[121]

In fact, James's article approaches the Byland Abbey stories partly in an academic spirit, partly as one who simply enjoys a good ghost story. "I did not find them disappointing," he remarks while documenting their codicological context in Royal MS 15. A. xx of the British Museum.[122] Does James's reputation as a ghost enthusiast precede him, even in this venue? Many of the qualities he stresses here—the tales' "local colour," their "picturesque touch[es]" and humorous details—line up with the hallmarks of his own storytelling.[123] Perhaps most striking, though, is the way in which these Byland haunts exemplify the peculiar corporeity of many medieval ghosts, their status as at once both walking corpse and immaterial *spiritus*, the contradictory product—some have argued—of Augustinian theology draped lightly over underlying Germanic traditions of the *draugr*, walking cadavers, and other uprisings of the undead.[124] The briefest of the Byland Abbey ghost stories memorably embodies this mixed quality. A woman is witnessed grappling with a ghost: "vidit manus mulieris demergentes in carne spiritus profunde, quasi caro eiusdem spiritus esset putrida et non solida sed fantastica" (he saw the woman's hands plunging deeply into the ghost's flesh, as if its flesh were rotten, and not solid but illusory [*fantastica*]).[125] Similar rotting spirits also populate several of the "courtiers' trifles" of Walter Map (ca. 1130–ca. 1208), a text James edited and translated. It is tempting to suspect that, in general, James's lasting influence on the genre may have played a role in resurrecting a rather medieval style of ghost for modern readers.[126] As I have noted above, James's ghosts certainly share this emphasis on physical yet illusory flesh: "In that moment the door opened, and an arm came out and clawed at his shoulder. It was clad in ragged, yellowish linen, and the bare skin, where it could be seen, had long gray hair upon it."[127] This extremity, from James's "Number 13," is the more tangible extension of a ghost we see elsewhere only as a shadow projected on a wall, viewed from across the street by the reddish light of a room adjacent to that of our unfortunate antiquary. It remains a shadowy idea of a demonic spirit for most of the story—dimly recalling Plato's allegory of the cave—until reaching forth to claw at us a bit in the climax.

It would be possible to multiply such examples, but the present study is not particularly focused on the question of how James's hauntings may conform to medieval patterns of apparitions, demonology, or black magic. In fact, many of James's most interesting "medievalisms"—the term can also refer to a particular instance of a modern author imaginatively appropriating or repurposing an element of medieval culture—are much more unexpected. As I have suggested, James often engages with and remakes medieval texts, modes, and genres not commonly or primarily associated with supernatural fear: manuscript textuality; biblical drama, liturgy, and church architecture; pastoral, enigmatic, and heroic poetry, to name just a few. Moreover, many of the most striking medievalisms in James's tales seem to have been borrowed from fields only obliquely related or adjacent to the main lines of his professional research. To take one example, examined in more detail in later chapters, the well-known Old English poems *Beowulf* and *The Dream of the Rood* are important sources of inspiration for two of his more well known stories. James was not a published authority on Anglo-Saxon poetry, though his chapter on Latin writings in the first volume of the *Cambridge History of English Literature* (1907) appears immediately following three sections on contemporaneous vernacular texts by medievalist colleagues, including substantial explications of both of these poems and a long discussion of medieval runes, another source of creative medievalizing for James. There can be no question, needless to say, that James was deeply knowledgeable in a wide range of such related areas. Yet while there are notable exceptions, discussed in the following chapters, in general one might observe that James *tends* to keep the central subjects of his scholarly publications separate from the materials reworked into ghost stories, an inclination that might be interpreted as drawing a line between frivolous fictions and serious research. And yet the two professions are inextricably linked, as the chapters of this book seek to show.

The first of these chapters is focused on scholarly errors, highly meaningful mistakes that mark not only the climactic moment of terror in two of James's earliest and most celebrated stories, but also their thematic preoccupation with scholarly errancy, disciplinarity, and specialization. Emending an erratum at the center of James's most famous haunted object—the whistle of the Templar preceptory—allows us to perceive how scholarly and companionate commitments are intertwined for James. The keeping of one is linked to the other, while fears of sexual wandering are associated with going astray academically. Misgivings of amateurism yield to darker pleasures of professionalism in the second chapter, however, where we find James recasting runological and pastoral traditions to great effect. The resonant medievalisms of the stories studied here tend to expose, by contrast, a freshly constricted academic culture, its emergent institutions of anonymous review and professional restraint. Something of a sanctuary from these anxieties, however, is arguably offered by James's "cathedraly" tales, the focus of chapter 3. Here, haunted Gothic structures shelter not only shadows of barren revival but an expansive sense of how present energies—creative and scholarly, local and unattached, sacred and secular—might engage with a multivalent past. From these cathedral episodes, I turn in chapter 4 to other kinds of time, and in particular to a consideration of how James's own signature scholarly contribution, his extensive cataloguing of medieval manuscripts, is figured in his fiction. What we might characterize as an "antiquarian temporality" tends to be the implicit menace of these stories, their central source of dread, but it is also entangled with other timelines—of both professional advance and institutional retreat. A fraying of these ties might be expected wherever medieval institutions fail, however, and that is also perhaps part of what we find in James's late tale, "A Warning to the Curious." An investigation into this story—and its relationship to James's roles memorializing and medievalizing loss in the Great War—concludes my study.

As this short summary suggests, I have attempted to structure this book both thematically and chronologically, so that we begin with some of James's earliest tales, laying a thematic foundation on which subsequent chapters build, concluding with James's postwar masterpiece. No attempt, however, has been made to give equal weight to every story, and for obvious reasons I focus most attention on those tales that I perceive as having particular ties to James's professional interest in medieval studies. As it so happens, this includes many of James's most celebrated works, but my focus on his medievalisms is determined by, as much as anything else, my own academic interests and background. Needless to say, I must leave many dimensions of James's fiction to the explorations of future researchers, but I do hope that this book is able to advance and enrich an ongoing conversation. To paraphrase James's preface to *Ghost Stories of an Antiquary*, the present study does not make any very exalted claim. If I succeed in drawing the attention of readers and critics to certain understudied aspects of his fiction—and in encouraging other medievalists and students of medievalism to investigate these tales—my purpose in writing will have been attained.

I

TERROR AND ERROR

Lee Patterson once remarked that "medieval studies has traditionally policed itself with the specter Error, every medievalist's nightmare: better to be dull than 'unsound.'"[1] The detection and correction of error has indeed been central to the field from its beginnings. In the introduction, I noted the emergent profession's need to disinfect itself of amateur sloppiness in James's day: many felt that antiquarian publications "swarm[ed] with errata" and were "riddled with misinterpretations."[2] This scholarly concern predates professionalization, but the development of medieval studies as an occupational vocation added urgency to a perennial fear. The formulation known as Sayre's Law posits that "in any dispute the intensity of feeling is inversely proportional to the value of the issues at stake"; a corollary might be the inverted relationship between a discipline's embattled claim for relevance and its toleration for minor miscues. Yet it is not only horror that defines error's relationship to the field. In fact, the correction of variance has long constituted a central and productive aspect of the medievalist enterprise. Whether through Lachmannian stemmatics, editorial recension, or peer review, the detection of error is a methodologically and professionally fundamental activity through which medievalists engage with their materials— and a central means by which historical distance might be bridged. Error marks the arrow of time, after all, and one of the foundations of historical philology is Erasmus's principle of *lectio difficilior*, the counterintuitive premise that the more awkwardly "difficult reading" is more probably original, less likely the product of a copyist's overly corrective mind.[3]

As this chapter will show, a related logic may trigger terror in some of James's earliest and most effective ghost stories. These hauntings, however, give imaginative form to a sense of errancy extending beyond the normal corrigenda slips of academic writing. Scholarly errancy in these stories encompasses as well an etymological sense of the word: to wander (Latin *errāre*) across disciplinary boundaries, to overstep academic imperatives, to dabble as an enthusiastic amateur in professional circles.[4] James's career spanned a formative era in the rise of medieval studies as a subject for university specialists. As James Turner has stressed, academic specialization in the humanities, as it developed in the late nineteenth and early twentieth centuries, was not novel or unique in its insistence that scholars develop exquisite expertise in narrow fields of study. What was truly distinct about this new disciplinary specialization was the notion that its boundaries were not to be crossed by individual scholars. Authority was increasingly isolated and restricted to "a distinctive cadre of methodologically acculturated experts" who mastered their subject but were also discouraged from pursuing interests elsewhere: "What was changing was whether a scholar could seriously aspire to roam from one site to another far away."[5] In this way, disciplinary specialization is not just about keeping amateurs out; it is also about keeping experts in—a principle antithetical to antiquarianism as it was traditionally conceived. As one long-running joke went, the members of the Society of Antiquaries were once asked to interpret a stone inscription: "KEE PONT/HI SSIDE." In the ensuing debate, the overheated scholars exert great learning but fail to recognize that the inscription is not medieval but modern, its message mundane.[6] "Keep on this side" is a simple rule to follow, yet in the course of James's early career, disciplinary lines were still very much in flux as historical scholarship was reinvented as a university-based profession.[7]

The notion, then, that James was a scholarly "dilettante" must be heavily qualified by the contexts in which his career developed. Certainly his wide-ranging interests in both texts and artifacts—in art and architecture, archaeology, apocrypha and saints' lives, textual transmission and early manuscripts—make it rather difficult today to define his academic identity precisely according to current norms of disciplinary specialization. From his days at Eton, masters worried about his "wandering in strange pastures,"[8] but even his most enduring scholarly achievement, the descriptive cataloguing of thousands of medieval manuscripts (to elucidate their "wanderings and homes," as he put it),[9] has been faulted for their many momentary lapses and slips. James himself catalogues his own misgivings in a volume published the same year as *Ghost Stories of an Antiquary*:

> Absence of references to printed editions of texts, failures to detect the identity of a nameless treatise, omissions of what prove to be important details in the descriptions of miniatures, ignorance of famous heraldic bearings, will all merit and perhaps meet with sharp reproof. If the cataloguer writes a bad hand and is, to say the least, an indifferent corrector of printed proofs, he has yet more to fear. To these errors and failings I plead guilty; but I have deliberately preferred risking mistakes and producing the best catalogue I could within five years, to consulting all the available experts and postponing publication until the ninth.[10]

In his obituary for James, Stephen Gaselee would accept this plea and in fact declare that "no true scholar would have it otherwise," for what made James's work erratic also made it great.[11] Indeed, the confessions of James the indolent proofreader may serve, somewhat counterintuitively, to maintain the integrity of his own scholarly performance. As Erving Goffman notes of the self-presentation of professional life, "telltale signs that errors have been made and corrected are themselves concealed. In this way, the impression of infallibility . . . is maintained."[12] Fallibility is never denied but rather is attributed to misprints and distractions. More than anything else, in fact, James's cataloguing work has been faulted for being unevenly applied, the impulse to lavish attention on pet interests overmastering the imperative to keep a disinterested distance from his material.[13] This failure inevitably sets him adrift: Pfaff reports of James's catalogue of the Fitzwilliam manuscripts, "Once again there were a great many errors of detail, some of considerable amusement."[14]

The issue of errant academic impulses, then, is at the heart of my thinking in this opening chapter, and the analysis offered here is indebted to the recent work of medievalists such as Seth Lerer, who emphasizes the centrality of error to academic selves, and Carolyn Dinshaw, who brilliantly explores the relationship between scholarly amateurism and nonnormative sexual identities and desires. As Dinshaw writes, amateur scholarship "is itself a bit queer, defined by attachment in a detached world," and one would be hard pressed to find better expression of the queerness of avocational medievalism than the weird fiction of James, in many ways a liminal figure in the history of his profession.[15] Indeed, the shade of errant antiquarianism, along with both the anxieties and the allure of academic errancy, shape James's fiction in characteristically complex fashion, and I propose here to approach error in a pair of Jamesian tales on two distinct but complementary levels. In the first instance, I hope to offer corrective solutions to several quite literal puzzles James has posed in his fiction, riddles that invite readerly errors as well as more "difficult readings." Some of these enigmas are explicit and have been the subject of keen interest and debate, while in other cases what I view as quite intentional puzzles have been either overlooked or (mis)interpreted as mere authorial blunders. I argue that this assumption is a mistake, though I maintain that how these riddles are posed invites the proliferation of significant errors, lapses that illuminate the "antiquarian impulse" as James imagined it: the emotional experience of errant scholarship, its perils and social utility, as well as a persistent longing for scholarly commitment and professional connection.

KEEP THAT WHICH IS COMMITTED TO THEE

That error plays an outsized role in James's ghosts stories should come as no shock, though critics of James may have missed some of its manifestations, including its role in "Oh, Whistle, and I'll Come to You, My Lad," a story Anthony Lane characterizes as "his finest and most anxiety-shrouded work, of which I will say nothing more. Readers should be led into temptation."[16] Before discussing this story, however, I would like to consider a tale that immediately follows in the same volume. "The Treasure of Abbot Thomas" is fiction inspired by James's very real and original discovery, in early 1904, that stained glass adorning the chapel of Ashridge Park in Hertfordshire came originally from the Premonstratensian church of Steinfeld in Germany, a home James deduced simply enough from the inscription "Abbas Steynfeldensis" on one of the panes.[17] Within months (and two years before publishing his academic pamphlet), James had partially revealed the discovery in fictional form, spinning his discovery of the wandering glass into a tale to fill out *Ghost Stories of An Antiquary,* brought out for the Christmas season that same year.[18] The two publications could hardly be more different. The dry form and style of the pamphlet are a study in disciplined reserve to contrast sharply with the extravagant fiction of "The Treasure of Abbot Thomas," while the tale is a remarkable example of medievalism that outpaces both in publication date and in its imaginative enthusiasm the committed scholarship upon which it is based.

It is also in many ways an archetypal Jamesian fiction: A learned gentleman (something of a doppelganger of James himself) is pursuing rather scattered scholarly interests when a routine moment of serendipity sparks investigation, international travel, and eventually an unnerving moment of terror. The antiquarian riddles are wrapped in biblical enigmas bundled in baffling puzzles, for even after identifying the provenance of the medieval windows, Somerton the protagonist is faced with three puzzling snippets adapted from the Vulgate Bible and glazed into the stained glass for all to see. But it is not until after accidentally scratching a line of light into a patch of black paint that Somerton realizes that an additional puzzle lies beneath in the form of an elaborate cryptogram, a code consisting of three groups of thirty-eight letters that, once cracked, will reveal—in a glass darkly, as it were—the location of the Abbot Thomas's secret hoard.[19] It is, Somerton learns, deposited in a chamber accessible only by descending the shaft of a medieval well. Yet when Somerton travels to Steinfeld, he mistakes for a sack of treasure the tentacled, writhing form of the gold's guardian, an error he can only overcome with the aid of a companion summoned from home. That friend obliges by resealing the chamber, but notices in the process a final enigmatic admonition inscribed into the stone of the wellhead: *depositum custodi* (Keep that which is committed to thee).[20]

The key observation for all these riddles, I will argue, is that Somerton has potentially gotten them wrong. James's notorious stylistic reticence as a writer may have led many readers to overlook the subtle errors tempted by these biblical lines, the first of which is the simplest and most easily caught: *Auro est locus in quo absconditur* (There is a place for gold where it is hidden).[21] Of this text, Somerton concludes that it is "undeniable" that it "might be taken to have a reference to hidden treasure."[22] But, as Somerton will painfully discover, the syntax of the statement gulls the reader into assuming that the subject of *absconditur* is an "it" to be identified with the gold, rather than the guardian: "it is hidden," yes, but as we'll learn, *it* is the abbot's "it." The hidden substitution of one "it" for another is to return in time as central both to the cryptogram and to the dramatized moment of error.

The second scriptural text also presents a puzzle, but one that James's critics have interpreted as unintentional: *Super lapidem unum septem oculi sunt* (Upon one stone are seven eyes).[23] James's choice to pose as a riddle this detail from Zechariah 3:9 is an interesting one, considering that identical imagery informs one of the great mysteries of medieval enigmatography: Exeter Riddle 90. The solution to this text (the sole Latin riddle of the medieval "Exeter Book" manuscript of Old English poetry) is famously uncertain, but the last clue describes wolves that *cum septem oculis videbant* (saw with seven eyes), imagery that has led modern solvers to speculate on Riddle 90's relationship to Revelation 5:6 as well as to the Zechariah passage.[24] Arguably, then, the quotation comes already bearing a strong association with insoluble medieval enigmatics as well as dark overtones of apocalypse. Nothing like this, though, crosses the mind of Somerton, who "very quickly concluded" that the second text "must refer to some mark on a stone which could only be found *in situ*,"[25] and these suspicions are later seemingly confirmed as he examines the inner wall of the well: "I snatched the lantern out of your hand, and saw with inexpressible pleasure that the cross *was* composed of seven eyes, four in a vertical line, three horizontal. The last of the scrolls in the window was explained in the way I had anticipated. Here was my 'stone with seven eyes.' So far the Abbot's data had been exact."[26] Once again, James winks at the quick confidence of Somerton, but sharp readers have balked at the cross of seven eyes, noting that a cross of "four in a vertical line, three horizontal" adds up to six total eyes, not seven, for the eyes of the intersection must presumably coincide. Thus an illustrator of this image resorts to five vertical eyes and three horizontal to get the seven, while annotators of the tale have implied that James was simply in error.[27] And yet the text makes perfect sense in terms of a sly visual trick, with Somerton concluding—in his cross-eyed haste—that four plus three always equals seven. The implication, in that case, is that there is one more uncounted eye "on" that stone, one that Somerton has missed. Perhaps the abbot himself has been keeping an eye on it? That, at least, is exactly what Somerton will come to realize, as his servant Brown narrates: "Master was busy down in front of the 'ole, and I was 'olding the lantern and looking on, when I 'eard somethink drop in the water from the top, as I thought. So I looked up, and I see someone's 'ead lookin' over at us."[28] Linguistic slips and puns of this kind are a classic riddling move,[29] and considering that the other biblical inscriptions are all recast as clever enigmas, we might be inclined to assign the error to Somerton rather than to James (whose data in the tale have been otherwise exact!).[30]

And yet there is a complication that cautions against jumping to quick conclusions. Michael Cox has noted that in a corrected copy of *Ghost Stories of an Antiquary* in Cambridge University Library (Adv.d.110.1), "MRJ deleted the word 'four' and wrote 'five' in the margin, but then apparently crossed out the correction. The configuration of the 'eyes' strictly needs five in a vertical line, flanked by two others, making seven altogether."[31] It is difficult to know what to make of this correction of a correction, made (perhaps) by James at least fifteen years, if not more, after "The Treasure of Abbot Thomas" was first published. Has the elder James forgotten, then recalled, the original trick of the cross? If not, why leave the line unchanged in later editions? The question becomes even more complicated when we take into account an unnoted additional bit of marginalia on the same page where Cox found the noncorrection. In the lower margin on this page, also written in pencil, is this design (fig. 1).

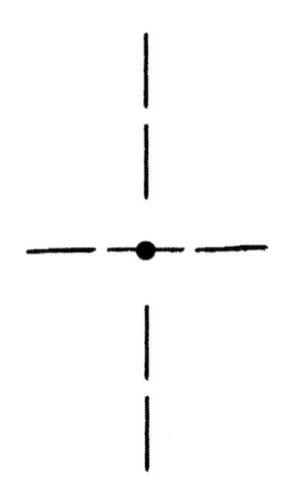

The center horizontal dash has a round dot in the middle of it. All the dashes are of equal length. Does this figure reveal that the seven-eyed cross actually does work, provided that the (oval-shaped) eyes of the transom are laid horizontally, while the vertical eyes of the center beam are tilted ninety degrees? This would have the effect of separating the two lines of eyes, blocking the overlap (the implication of the dotted center dash?), and lending a new precision to Somerton's observation of "seven eyes, four in a vertical line, three horizontal." Perhaps this solves the puzzle. And yet what kind of authority can we assign to this marginal solution in a printed book? Does it represent James's recollection of the original solution, or perhaps an attempt to devise a "fix" in retrospect? Can we even be sure that it was James who added this marginal solution to a book that has subsequently rested in the open stacks of Cambridge University Library for nearly a century? In fine, does the enigmatic diagram allow us to squint at James's original intention, or do our eyes remain shut—slitted something like those horizontal and vertical dashes?

However we answer these questions or respond to the literal riddle, the stone of seven eyes seems to represent something more than a straightforward "X" to mark the spot of subterranean treasure. The slab of stone invites error; its removal sets the stage for a terrifying correction. And, as I will show, it is the third biblical text that leads Somerton most dramatically to this moment by pointing him to the abbot's fiendish cryptogram: *Habent in vestimentis suis scripturam quam nemo novit* (They have on their raiment a writing which no man knoweth).[32] Although this writing that no man knows is the cryptographic centerpiece of the tale, it is probably not important here to explain every turn of Somerton's complex cracking of the "hopeless jumble of letters" found on the stained-glass garments. To do so would serve very little purpose, for Somerton's third error comes not in unscrambling the letters but in subtly misinterpreting the grammar of these deciphered words:

"Decem millia sunt auri reposita sunt in puteo in at . . . rio domus abbatialis de Steinfeld a me, Thoma, qui posui custodem super ea. Gare à qui la touche."

(Ten thousand pieces of gold are laid up in the well in the court of the Abbot's house of Steinfeld by me, Thomas, who have set a guardian over them. *Gare à qui la touche.*)[33]

Somerton remarks of the closing warning in French ("Let those who touch it beware") that the abbot "drafted it bodily into his cipher" from "a device which Abbot Thomas had adopted" as a kind of personal motto. He also notes, in passing, that "it doesn't quite fit in point of grammar."[34] Here is our "it," again, and in fact it is the "it" that does not seem to fit. For upon reflection we might recognize that Somerton's perception of a grammatical miscue is his own error, as he apparently assumes that the *la* (it) refers to the gold, rather than to the *custodem* (guard) that has been set *super ea* (over them [the plural gold pieces]).[35] In other words, Somerton assumes that Abbot Thomas has slipped up in a matter of grammatical number, whereas it is the antiquary who misconstrues the enigmatic antecedent.

This error of the "it" corresponds exactly to the miscue of the first clue: *Auro est locus in quo absconditur* (There is a place for gold in which it is hidden).[36] And this confusion of the guardian for the gold is dramatically recapitulated and amplified in the story's chilling climax:

> "Well, I felt to the right, and my fingers touched something curved, that felt—yes—more or less like leather; dampish it was, and evidently part of a heavy, full thing. There was nothing, I must say, to alarm one. I grew bolder, and putting both hands in as well as I could, I pulled it to me, and it came. It was heavy, but moved more easily than I expected. As I pulled it towards the entrance, my left elbow knocked over and extinguished the candle. I got the thing fairly in front of the mouth and began drawing it out. Just then Brown gave a sharp ejaculation and ran quickly up the steps with the lantern. He will tell you why in a moment. Startled as I was, I looked round after him, and saw him stand for a minute at the top and then walk away a few yards. Then I heard him call softly, 'All right, sir,' and went on pulling out the great bag, in complete darkness. It hung for an instant on the edge of the hole, then slipped forward on to my chest, and *put its arms round my neck*."[37]

In this chilling phrase (the italics are James's own), Somerton's error is translated into its rhetorical equivalent, what we might call a complex *syllepsis of perception* in which the retrospectively shifted meaning of "it" (now animated, active, uncanny) drags with it our sense of the meaning of the actions "hung" and "slipped," as well as verbs found earlier in the passage: "I pulled it to me, and it came." Come again? The cataphoric double take marks a jumble of bundled errors: errors of grammar, of translation, of counting, of perception of agency. The abbot has staged a dramatic moment of concentrated error and he is there to keep an eye on the spectacle.

But why has James, by way of the abbot's malevolent cunning, constructed such an ingenious mechanism of error, all the tumblers of correction clicking into place as Somerton swoons on the thirty-eighth step? Somerton's errors surely do not mark him as insufficiently erudite; on the contrary, the tale itself begins with the sprezzaturaic performance of an antiquary who can spot slight variants in the Vulgate from memory. James's audacious choice to begin the story with a lengthy block quote in Latin, effectively walling off the casual reader from entering easily into the tale, may in fact be read as symptomatic of the isolating nature of profound antiquarian learning. Perhaps, indeed, what this moment of error implies most immediately is that, with or without local error, study of the past is a potentially errant pursuit in itself—a wasteful, nihilistic, prideful, and petty activity that finds its dark reflection in Abbot Thomas, a man as obsessed with secret languages and the occult as his principal real-life model, the medieval abbot Johannes Trithemius (1462–1516), author of the *Steganographia*, a book of cryptography and ill repute that Somerton consults in his researches.[38] In James's fiction generally, the wicked power of black magic often overlaps with an obsession with what is most obscure, irrelevant, and academically marginal.[39] But the question of scholarly errancy cuts even deeper, so that the moment of converging errors at the antiquarian wellhead amplifies and dramatizes the anxieties, experiences, and pleasures of medieval studies as a discipline and as a daily practice.

To argue this is not to ignore the comic quality of the tale; James seems to express a benign version of Abbot Thomas–like glee in the game he is playing, and was surely very capable of laughing off error. A neatly appropriate example rounds out Nicolas Barker's retrospective celebration of James's towering talents as a professional paleographer and cataloguer: "All this was allied to an imaginative quality of mind (a quality that makes his ghost stories so much the best thing of their kind) which could convey a visual impression in succinct vivid words. But there was not too much philosophy about it either; cheerfulness was always breaking in. None rejoiced more than James when a printer's error made Abbot Thomas von Eschenhausen, whose treasure was—is?—buried at Steinfeld, put up a painted widow in the south aisle of his abbey church."[40] The "painted widow" was restored to "painted window" in later editions, but the cosmetic correction might serve to warn against finding "too much philosophy" in a cheerful slip of a storyteller's pen. Yet there does seem to be rather weighty resonance in the final

Latin citation of the tale, carved into the ornate base of the abbot's well. Overlooked until the tale's resonant conclusion, James allows the Latin phrase to slip just over the edge of the tale's ending as an unexplained and enigmatic coda: "One thing I did notice in the carving on the well-head, which I think must have escaped you. It was a horrid, grotesque shape—perhaps more like a toad than anything else, and there was a label by it inscribed with the two words, 'Depositum custodi.'"[41] The cognate language of this command ("Keep that which is committed to thee") recalls the *custos* (keeper) of the gold, but the imperative seems directed beyond the monstrous guardian's duty. *Depositum custodi* turns out to be another quotation from the Vulgate, from 1 Timothy 6:20 in particular, an observation that further links it with the other riddlic snippets of scripture posed by the abbot. It stands, then, as a kind of open-ended epimythium for a strange fable with no obvious moral.

In trying to understand this final inscription, we might stress that it is Gregory who makes the discovery (Somerton scrutinizes the same stone but mysteriously misses it completely). He does so while fulfilling his friend's desperate request that he reinter the "it" and reseal the open compartment, though Somerton does not fully reveal the nature of the favor to his friend until after the aid is accomplished: "The only word I will say about it is that you run no risk whatever by doing it, and that Brown can and will show you to-morrow what it is. It's merely to put back—to keep—something—No; I can't speak of it yet."[42] Here, Gregory is curiously asked first to put something back, but then, haltingly, "to keep" that which is committed to him. What is Gregory to keep? In what sense of protection or possession, preservation or resistance, concealment or constraint—a keeping in or a keeping back—is he to act? Somerton does not have words for what he needs done, or even for the enigmatic object in need of keeping. The only thing that is clear is the intense sense of commitment between the men—Gregory will keep Somerton, while Somerton must keep that which is committed to him. Such devotional urgency outweighs any other motive in the tale.

And indeed, the decided lack of interest the antiquary shows in the actual treasure would belie any grasping attempt to implicate greed as Somerton's sin: his itch is far more for the "long scratch" of light that betrays the window's hidden inscription (executed in "yellow stain") than for any literal golden hoard. If anything, one wonders if the finger of accusation points more precisely at temptations of intellectual appropriation—a scholar's tendency to feel a creeping sense of ownership over objects of study. If so, an instance of this might be identified as Somerton's subtly arrogant arrogation of the stained glass, which he begins to partially "restore" even before receiving permission from its owner. But the stentorian force of *depositum custodi* seems to me to reflect something more fundamental about the hardening sense of academic discipline that characterized James's era of medieval studies. For the antiquary-cum-medievalist in particular, the ambiguity of the custodial act of "keeping"—its oscillating implications of both protection and possession—implies a quite anxious imperative to maintain professional distance from objects of scholarly devotion. The wandering antiquary allows himself to be carried away by the clinging tentacles of undisciplined and uncircumscribed inquiry; perhaps he even diverts raw, as yet unpublished research into amateur fiction? But the professional keeps that which is committed to him.

Such a reading might be strengthened if we were to consider the exegetical contexts of the enigmatic admonition. Vincent of Lérins, for example, comments on 1 Timothy 6:20:

> Keep "that which is committed to thy trust," he says. What is that deposit? It is that which is entrusted to thee, not what is invented by thee: that which thou hast received, not what thou hast thought out for thyself: a matter not of ingenuity, but of doctrine; not of private usurpation, but of public tradition: a matter brought down to thee, not brought out by thee. . . . Let that which has been entrusted to thee remain with thee, and be handed down by thee. Gold thou hast received: render gold. Substitute not one thing for another.[43]

A version of this, secularized, is the kernel of Somerton's error: the amateur impulse to follow a stray, indulgent, overextended line of research without system, without discipline, without a professional's profound sense of caution. For without such detachment, the glaring error seems to warn, a scholar risks substituting his own guardianship for the treasures entrusted to him. In that light, the contrast between the exuberant medievalism of James's tale and the dryly cataloguic quality of his subsequently published *Notes of Glass in Ashridge Chapel* speaks volumes. The latter is hardly uncharacteristic of James's prodigious, meticulous academic output: the reticent notations, the restrained lack of speculation or theoretical excess, the discipline of bland identification and stone-faced observation, each entry neatly divided with a plastered space of antiseptic white. For all his worrying attachments, James was surely an academic who strove to keep that which was committed to him. But as the incongruent forms of his fiction and scholarship in very different ways attest, the specter of scholarly errancy never ceases to creep.

"OH, WHISTLE, AND I'LL COME TO YOU, MY LAD"

But if academic errancy long haunted James's professional career, the protagonist of his most celebrated tale comes a cropper, seemingly, for quite opposite reasons. Professor Parkins, a prim young expert in a trendily abstract field ("ontography")[44] receives a nasty shock when his rigid skepticism of spooks is thrust back in the famous form of a "face *of crumpled linen*" (another italicized Jamesian wallop) pressed up against his own.[45] This ghostly visitant comes only after being inadvertently summoned when Parkins blows a note "with a quality of infinite distance in it" through a whistle artifact he extracts from an altar niche in the ruins of a round Templar's preceptory.[46] Parkins would never have done anything of the sort, or gone anywhere near an archaeological site, were it not for his desire to oblige an acquaintance who has heard that he is headed for a working holiday of golf, isolation, and academic writing at the seaside resort town of Burnstow.[47] The socially awkward, "rather henlike" professor appears, however, to have as little inherent interest in golf as he does in archaeology; instead, he is attempting (rather paradoxically) to prepare himself for potential friendships by solitarily improving his game.[48] The whistle itself, enigmatically inscribed in a way I will discuss below, is pulled from a hole in the circular antiquarian green after Parkins has finished his round on the regular links with a newfound companion, Colonel Wilson, who comes to view the haunting in terms of his anti-Catholic prejudices. The activities of golf and antiquarianism are thus linked by their homosocial utility, though as early as the story's opening dialogue between colleagues in the "hospitable hall of St. James's College," Parkins has "rather sniffed at the idea that planning out a preceptory could be described as useful."[49] One might guess that, under normal generic conditions, such antiquarian inquiry only poses the atmospheric danger of kicking up ancient ghosts, but I will be arguing that James's tale implies quite a bit more: not only the peculiar social utility and institutional perils of being an "antiquary," but also the related risk of scholarly "attachment in a detached world," in Dinshaw's words. "Oh, Whistle," then, is a story that further explores the implications of Abbot Thomas's inscription. Commitments of academic discipline and all-male collegiality are again intertwined.

Indeed, the most famous image in the story, the specter's face of crumpled linen, not only breathes new life into the threadbare image of the sheeted ghost; it bundles together what most critics have seen as the twin concerns of the story: sex[50] and the shattering of Parkins's rigid sense of "apple-pie order."[51] The latter curious phrase arrives upon our first glimpse of the very sheets that later rise and become "twisted together in a most tortuous confusion": "[Parkins] was made welcome at the Globe Inn, was safely installed in the large double-bedded room of which we have heard, and was able before retiring to rest to arrange his materials for work in apple-pie order upon a commodious table which occupied the outer end of the room."[52] Apple-pie precision on the academic's desk is thus aligned with an ordered life between the sheets. By 1904 the etymology of this sense of "apple pie" had long been the subject of considerable speculation, the most favored etymons being a corruption either of the French words for "folded linen" (*nappes pliées*) or of a knight's tidy *cap-à-pie* (head-to-toe) armor. Entries on the subject often neighbored or subsumed discussion of the so-called apple-pie bed, a schoolboy prank also known as "short-sheeting" in which one of the victim's sheets is folded back on itself, so as to baffle entry.[53] One might expect a stuffy person like Parkins to have faced many an "apple-pie bed" in the dormitories of his youth, though the bedlam of his linens goes well beyond hidden folds: "'Excuse me, that isn't my bed,' said Parkins. 'I don't use that one. But it does look as if someone had been playing tricks with it.'"[54]

But whether or not the famous "face *of crumpled linen*" leers in retrospect at a folk etymology, the twisted sheets certainly represent a wrinkling of Parkins's neatly pleated, professionally detached existence: "'A man in my position,' he went on, raising his voice a little, 'cannot, I find, be too careful about appearing to sanction the current beliefs on such subjects.'"[55] Here, "such subjects" involve specifically the existence of ghosts, but the underlying force of the denial is far less about the occult per se than it is about the anxiety of a man in Parkins's sanctioned position to avoid professional errancy of any kind. An unease over trivial error manifests itself at several points in the story, as for example when Parkins suppresses a rejoinder that risks the misidentification of the biblical sect of the Sadducees.[56] Perhaps the most curious moment of error comes in the extended opening banquet scene, as Parkins expounds on his devout disbelief to a group of colleagues who seem to be in the habit of sending him up through an exploitation of his own "strictly truthful" manner:

> ". . . But I'm afraid I have not succeeded in securing your attention."
> "Your *undivided* attention, was what Dr. Blimber* actually said," Rogers interrupted, with every appearance of an earnest desire for accuracy. "But I beg your pardon, Parkins: I'm stopping you."[57]

The asterisk on "Blimber" is James's own, signaling a footnote where we read that "Mr. Rogers was wrong, *vide* 'Dombey and Son,' chapter xii."[58] Strangely, though, there is no corresponding moment in Dickens, leading later editors to correct with footnotes James's footnoted correction of Rogers's rude correction. Arguably, what this hall of mirrored errors ultimately reflects (aside from James's highly dusty sense of humor) is their thematic centrality to the story. Footnotes, after all, are the traditional mark and proof of academic soundness.

Likewise, at the center of the tale is an artifact drawn by an amateur from the historically charged site of a ruined Templar preceptory. Critics have noted, often in passing, that the haunted whistle seems specifically designed as a Templar artifact, and this is usually taken as darkly indicative of the whistle's vague association with idolatry and black magic.[59] It is worth also stressing that the spectacular suppression of the Order in the early fourteenth century, and its reputation for centuries thereafter, included a variety of other transgressions, from heresy, blasphemy, and treason to a range of sexual crimes—accusations that have so dogged the history of the Order that it would be easy to view the ruined preceptory as a symbol of sodomitical destruction.[60] Given the pursuant spirit's implied membership in an all-male order, the recontextualized lyrics of Robert Burns sound a shrilly phobic note of sexual transgression and same-sex desire:

Tho' father an' mother an' a' should gae mad,
O, whistle an' I'll come to ye, my lad![61]

When one also notes that it was widely believed in James's day that homosexuals lacked the ability to whistle (with their lips alone), Parkins's transgression seems overloaded with potential innuendo.[62] We may feel drawn to connect this find to other failings: the way Parkins lacks the capacity to call upon other men, to summon them for easy and uncomplicated companionship.

And yet to draw a line, unproblematically, from Templar history to Parkins's sexualized night terrors would amount to a reading as undisciplined as Colonel Wilson's blanket attributions of the whistle's threat to "the Church of Rome." In fact, writers of the nineteenth century had begun in earnest to counter the rampant myths of Templar excess—several of them because they were affiliated with neo-Templarian Masonic orders,[63] but others on more generalized historical grounds. Especially in the later decades of the century, scholars began producing works of enduring value based on careful description and analysis of original materials, and at least two of James's close acquaintances wrote fresh and pioneering works on the Templars. W. H. St. John Hope, for one, re-excavated Temple Bruer in Lincolnshire in order to investigate "lurid" claims of immurement by the Templars,[64] and the remarkable Léopold Delisle devoted fully half of his pioneering economic study to printing original inventories, expenditures, and other clerical documents that he and later scholars would use to assess the actual investments and activities of the Order.[65] James himself wrote, in another context, that "accusations of child-murder, of cannibalism and of other horrid practices, are among the first that any set of uneducated peoples is likely to bring against a tribe or sect whose practices they do not understand. Charges of this kind we know were made . . . against the Templars by their contemporaries."[66] As readers of James, then, we need not assume that his tale of horror is an uninformed expression of rumored Templar perversion.

In fact, if anything, the evidence rather suggests that Parkins, cap-à-pie in his apple-pie "golfing costume," has something to learn about sociability from the ideals of the order.[67] There are a number of medievalizing nods to chivalric culture that position Parkins as a kind of knight errant in training, from the narrator's characterization of him as "dauntless," to the story's opening "feast" in the "hospitable hall of St. James's College," to his reaction to a troubled night in the double-bedded room at the Globe Inn: "Parkins set forth, with a stern determination to improve his game."[68] Perhaps more subtle, but no less interesting, is the professor's worry over occupying a double-bedded room, an anxiety that invokes, in a curiously inverted form, the famous knightly emblem of the Templars of two riders on a single horse. It does seem true that Parkins is on a rather backward quest or pilgrimage to overcome his painfully acute lack of social prowess: when he reports that "my friends have been making me take up golf this term," we wonder where these absent friends are at the feast, why they do not accompany him to the seaside, and whether social acceptance will finally come with improvement of his game.[69] James's ghost stories, by contrast, were famously first read aloud to male friends of mixed generation at Christmas, while as a younger man, he himself had enjoyed in Felixstowe "delightful parties" at "The Lodge" (possibly the near-anagrammatic inspiration for the Globe?). He received invitations to stay there, he says, only after having "attained years of discretion."[70]

If the impulse here, then, is "to retreat to connect," perhaps it makes a kind of queer sense that James has exported the architecture of Cambridge to the coast? For indeed I would argue that this is just what James has done with the creation of his ruined Templar preceptory, which likely found its inspiration in Cambridge itself—in the early twelfth-century Church of the Holy Sepulchre, affectionately known today as the Round Church, the oldest and most architecturally complete of the handful of specimens of its unusual shape in Great Britain.[71] While there is no evidence that the Order had any involvement in its construction, the structure clearly owes its inspiration to the same model as round Templar churches: the Church of the Holy Sepulchre in Jerusalem. Moreover, the Round Church at Cambridge is even closer to home in James's original draft of the story, in which the opening "hospitable hall" scene takes place not in a fictional St. James's College but in the actual St. John's College, located directly across Bridge Street from the Round Church, with which it once shared intimate associations. In the early days of St. John's, the Round Church was used as its college chapel.[72] Moreover, in the ground-level baptismal window, to the right of the main door on the southern "side" of the church, are four golden swastika emblems framing the two large Chi Rho monograms above and below the central baptismal image.[73] The whistle Parkins discovers among the ruins of the round church in Burnstow is inscribed with swastikas, and so, given the total absence of any historical association between Templars and that symbol, it seems very likely that the Round Church of Cambridge at least partially inspired what Parkins finds. At the very least, the appearance of such unusual symbols in such a striking building located in the heart of James's own Cambridge could hardly fail to attract the attention of a scholar with such keen interests in church architecture and fabric.

Professor Parkins, though, has no such interest, so it seems worth noting that James has him examine the preceptory specifically in order "to oblige Mr. Disney," whose name is another allusion close to home, this time to the Disney Chair of Archaeology at Cambridge. In fact, the detail casts a phantom line directly into the author's own vita, for James had himself applied for and failed to secure the Disney chair early in his career; his biographer Richard William Pfaff refers to "his somewhat audacious hope of being elected to the Disney Professorship of Archaeology at the age of thirty," despite his decided lack of experience in the emergent field.[74] As a young man, he had accompanied D. G. Hogarth on an expedition to Cyprus, but Pfaff reports that the young scholar's contributions to the excavations were poorly executed: "it may be suspected that for all his enthusiasm, MRJ's heart was in archaeology only on a part time and rather eccentric basis."[75] It is curious, to say the least, that James evokes both the Disney chair and charges of amateurism precisely at the moment when "Our Professor" (capitalized in the original) enters the ruins of the round church: "Few people can resist the temptation to try a little amateur research in a department quite outside their own, if only for the satisfaction of showing how successful they would have been had they only taken it up seriously. Our Professor, however, if he felt something of this mean desire, was also truly anxious to oblige Mr. Disney."[76] If we wish to distance James from his protagonist, the operative phrase would be "a department quite outside their own," but the implication cannot be easily avoided that the hyperprofessionalized Parkins is to be punished for wandering, as an utter novice who can barely translate basic Latin, into a field in which he has no business.[77] Such a reading, if anything, seems further confirmed by one interpretation of the enigmatic syllables that show up on the famous whistle: "O thief," the translated inscription accuses, "you will blow, you will weep." The scholar must keep that which is committed to him; anything more (or less) is disciplinary transgression and professional theft.

WHISTLING IN THE DARK

It may be premature, however, to settle on any translation of the whistle's warning without a more detailed examination of its inscription, a source of much speculation. In particular, critics have targeted the cross of Latinate syllables found on one side of the whistle:

FLA
FUR   BIS
FLE

Simplicity has not been the goal of all solvers of this puzzle. One acrobatic attempt, for example, involves considerable cunning and studious attention to medieval morphology, with three separate uses of *fur* (twice as a verb, once as a vocative) and with *bis* functioning both as a marker of the future tense (*-bis*) and as an adverb in itself (*bis*, "twice"). The resulting message reads, "O thief, you will polish it, you will blow it twice, you will regret this, you will go mad."[78] However, the two most common interpretations are much simpler. The first (already mentioned) uses *bis* twice as a future tense ending, interpreting *fur* as a vocative noun:

Fur, flabis, flebis (O thief, you will blow, you will weep)

The second, perhaps more tempting approach, uses *bis* as the ending for all of the three other syllables, which seem grouped by their linguistic similarity (*f* plus a vowel and liquid): *Flabis, flebis, furbis* (You will blow, you will weep, you will go mad), as it is usually rendered. This second option seems to necessitate, however, a fairly counterintuitive, spatially awkward reading of the syllables, so that they are taken in the following numbered order:

FLA[1]
FUR[3]   BIS
FLE[2]

Nothing seems to justify this odd rearrangement except the elements' perceived reflection of the plot; though Parkins never actually goes mad, we are told that he would have "lost his wits" had the colonel not intervened, and this of course echoes the allusive implication of the title that "a' should gae mad" if the call of the whistle were to be answered. In fact, in the latest and most fully annotated edition of James's fiction to date, we are told that "Furbis Flabis Flebis" can be translated as "You will blow, you will weep, you will go mad."[79] But, if all else were valid, this *ordering* would translate, "You will go mad (*furbis), you will blow (*flabis*), you will weep (*flebis*)."[80] The trivial error is telling in that it shows the strain of two impulses in conflict: one to find the most elegant answer, and the other to confirm our expectations of what the tale seems to be about.

Nevertheless, I would suggest that such potential "errant readings" are not necessarily unmeaningful, given that they are rather encouraged by the alluring symmetry of applying *bis* thrice. But before discussing the significance of the "wrong" reading, I would like to offer evidence for what I think is the "right" one—though I apply these scare quotes advisedly. The "correct" solution, I think, is in fact one that has often already been proposed (though never confirmed), namely, the interpretation mentioned above that uses *bis* only twice. I base this on a reading of an oddly neglected aspect of the riddle, the swastikas that surround the famous line:

卐QUIS EST ISTE QUI VENIT卐

Scholars have tended to keep the two inscriptions of the whistle separate, often concluding in desperation that the *fur-fla-fle-bis* puzzle is insoluble and even deliberately open-ended.[81] But James, a lover of puzzles both antiquarian and jigsaw, is unlikely to have passed up his chance to fabricate something more coherent. In fact, I suggest that the swastikas (though likely first inspired by the windows of the Round Church in Cambridge) offer an additional clue. Their arms point, quite literally, to the solution. But before we can see this, we need to return to the original 1904 edition of *Ghost Stories of an Antiquary* (see fig. 1), for it turns out that all subsequent editions, up to the present day, have changed the shape of the swastikas to a generic form. Presumably, the initial switch was made to economize on printing costs, but even carefully annotated editions like the lavish *Pleasing Terror*, as well as the authoritative recent edition from Oxford University Press, make the change silently, so that the original form of one of horror fiction's most famous objects seems to have lain forgotten for nearly a hundred years.[82] In 1904, though, James's swastikas looked very much different (fig. 2).

卐QUIS EST ISTE QUI UENIT卐

Notice that each right arm is curiously bracketed, forming a unique variation on the swastika or "fylfot-cross"—one that without a doubt James invented.[83] The story manuscript provides several additional points to observe (fig. 3).

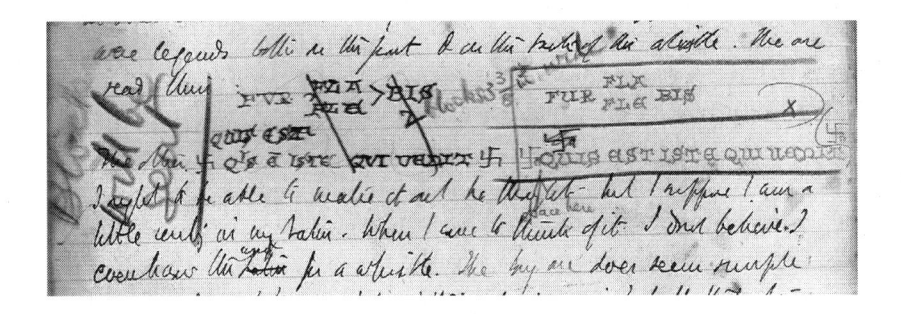

The preferred material is at the right of the page, marked with a circled X and boxed by editorial blue pencil. But James's discarded designs on the left reveal a process of revising the puzzle. Not only did he consider and reject the Roman V for U and the medieval abbreviations for *quis* and *est*, but he also quite unmistakably changed the "normal" swastikas to ones with brackets.

What could this addition of brackets signify? The answer begins to emerge when we realize that the swastikas correspond to the spatial layout of the riddle on the other side of the whistle:

FLA

FUR   BIS

FLE

The cross shape of the swastika matches the layout of the puzzle exactly, down to the detail of the right "arm" of each being notably different. *BIS* stands out from its peers, just as the bracketed arm stands out from the others. The bracketed swastika, then, *maps onto the puzzle,* telling the solver to take *bis* twice, along a bracketed route: *Fur, fla-bis, fle-bis* (O thief, you will blow, you will weep). It is worth remembering that as an expert in medieval manuscripts, James was very attuned to the potential significance of the spatial layout of texts; indeed, a great many of his publications on the decorative programs of manuscripts and church buildings "read" his visual subjects in a narrative sequence (for instance, his *Notes of Glass in Ashridge Chapel*).

The clue of the brackets is frightfully subtle, but the manuscript of the story furnishes us with strong evidence that this is their intended function. In the first discarded version of the riddle (crossed out by James), whereas the swastikas are conventional, the FUR-FLA-FLE-BIS layout includes an element that never makes it to the final draft: a V-shaped angle bracket (>) transparently joining FLA and FLE to BIS. The clear implication (perhaps too clear for James's taste) is that BIS is to be used twice, with FLA and FLE: *Fur, flabis, flebis* (O thief, you will blow, you will weep).[84] In the authorized version there is no V-bracket linking FLA and FLE to BIS—but with its removal a new element has been added to the flip side of the whistle, so that the bracket has found a new home on each swastika flanking QUIS EST ISTE QUI VENIT. It is not difficult to infer a motivation behind this change: feeling the V-bracket too obvious a giveaway, James hits upon the idea of encoding, obliquely, the same clue in the swastikas (the original presence of which, as I have argued, had a separate antiquarian inspiration). By replacing the direct V-bracket with the indirect key of the swastika brackets, James increases both the riddlesome ambiguity of the whistle's Latin and also its potential for "errant" readings. But when the eccentricity of the swastikas was steamrolled away in later editions, the puzzle was impoverished.

If we now feel ourselves reasonably assured of providing the "right" reading of the riddle, we might then conclude that we have the key to interpret the rest of the narrative: *Fur, fla-bis, fle-bis* (O thief, you will blow, you will weep). Parkins, we might quite correctly conclude, is punished for his transgression, which (as I have discussed) may be interpreted as having thievishly appropriated the academic discipline of the professional archaeologist. But as my discussion in the introduction concerning the generally liminal position of the antiquary's position on the amateur-professional divide suggests, such a conclusion involves knotty contradictions of its own. Indeed, there is a long-standing tendency in Jamesian criticism to take the author's academic status as self-evidently impeccable, ever-gray, and self-assured, so that whatever haunts his protagonists comes not from within but from "the Great Outside" to wrinkle the smooth surface of a complacent professional existence.[85] Thus, though "You will blow, you will weep, you will go mad" has often found its champions, the more spatially logical version of this approach is never raised, for it implies that there comes something from *within* to precede the summoning up of the specter: **furbis flabis flebis* (you will go mad, you will blow, you will weep). But **furbis*, if it were derived from *furĕre* (to go mad, to rave), could potentially imply not only madness but also desire, a mad fervency: "You will have a mad passion, you will blow, you will weep." In the future tense, however, the expected second-person singular form of the third-conjugation *furĕre* is *fures* (you will go mad).

The form *furbis* must thus remain an "incorrect" reading, both sexually and grammatically, and the brackets offer a subtle indication against that solution. Yet James also leads his reader into temptation with this elegant if errant alternative path. That route, too, would quite "wrongly" imply that it is the internal passions of Parkins that lend this narrative its undeniable thrill—rather than the blandly correct "finders weepers" logic of a haunted whistle and its accidental theft.

The errant reading of the enigma offers not so much condemnation ("O thief!") but a progress toward purification in which the mad passion (**furbis*) is followed by an errant act (*flabis*) and its terrifying correction and repentance (*flebis*). Parkins will weep, and we are reminded that James invokes *Pilgrim's Progress* (specifically, Apollyon's confrontation of Christian in the Valley of Humiliation) as the professor makes his halting way back to the worldly round of the Globe Inn along the liminal zone of the haunted strand, shadowed by a "belated wanderer." The scene is repeated in a kind of waking dream—truly one of the most frightening passages in ghostly literature.[86] Here, however, is only one fulfillment of the title's beckoning promise: Oh, whistle, and I'll come to you, my lad. The sheeted menace eventually arrives, but other men also come answering the call, including "rude Mr. Rogers" from the prologue, who had earlier offered to serve as Parkins's companion, occupying the empty bed "to keep the ghosts off."[87] Now he comes to comfort Parkins, who is to be haunted no longer by the dark society of the Templars but rather by the clean, chivalric embrace of the original "hospitable hall of St. James's College." Folded into the chilling threat of the title, then, is a message of convivial, mentoring reassurance for the scholarly lad gone astray, and indeed it is the colonel and not the ghost who assures Parkins: "You know where I am if you want me during the night."[88] It is the colonel, too, who answers Parkins's whistling "cry upon cry at the utmost pitch of his voice"; he rides to the rescue, holds vigil, disposes of the whistle, and burns the bedsheets: "Later on the smoke of *a burning* ascended from the back premises of the Globe" (emphasis added).[89] The language suggests an almost ceremonial kind of cleansing in that "place of burning," *Burnstow*,[90] and we might infer that Parkins, pulled back from the brink, has found a purified relationship with at least two male companions whose discretion and support he can now call upon. In a sense, we might say, he has learned to whistle.

Mostly, however, the tale fails to follow through on these implications, falling back on a generically "correct" conclusion. Like a stock Gothic monk or a plain sheeted ghost, the last paragraph seems veiled in the most empty of conventions. Reported aftershocks for Parkins's night of fright include shaky nerves, chastened humility, and a tendency to be spooked by "the spectacle of a scarecrow in a field late on a winter afternoon."[91] Here we end with the flimsiest man of straw, but readers of the story do not soon forget its "terrible weight."[92] The tempestuous sense of longing and struggle in the tale— so evocatively conjured by the image of the haunted runner on the shore, clambering endlessly over sea barriers—calls distantly but insistently for the correction of an errant academic self that is at once painfully disconnected from homosocial collegiality and professionally detached from disciplines of studious devotion. Antiquarianism, even as it was growing anachronistic, seems to have represented a category of queerness that commanded real admiration in the hospitable halls of King's College, Cambridge, where James worked to find a home and an institutional usefulness despite the errancy of his many attachments. In this incorrect reading, then, Parkins's moonlighting moment as an antiquary is not a mistake to be corrected so much as something like a wandering way home.

2

RECASTING THE ANTIQUARY

In the last year of his life, the *London Mercury* asked James to "recapture the mood in which he wrote *Ghost Stories of an Antiquary*."[1] The result was his final published story, "A Vignette," which recalls the author's childhood home, the hall of Great Livermere rectory, Suffolk, its garden, and surrounding parkland. As an eerie mood piece, the tale is quite successful, though we never do "glean any kind of story" behind the tale's haunting, a cloaked figure sighted through a gate separating the garden from "a belt of trees of some age which we knew as the Plantation."[2] Misgivings for this Plantation gate become the focal point of dread as the narrator recalls himself as a boy peering through its square aperture. The malevolent face he spies there, and the "draped form shambling away among the trees," provide a fair facsimile of the affectively powerful images of James's earliest tales: the winding-sheet-like writhings in "Oh, Whistle," for example, or, more ominous still, the motionless figures at the crossroads in "Count Magnus"—the latter representing an even less tolerable encounter.[3] After all, while Professor Parkins escapes the whistle ghost relatively unscathed, the same cannot be said for the victim of "Count Magnus," though Mr. Wraxall receives plenty of fair warning: "And I tell you this about Anders Bjornsen, that he was once a beautiful man, but now his face was not there, because the flesh of it was sucked away off the bones. You understand that? My grandfather did not forget that."[4] Yet readers remember such passages in James not for their ruthlessness alone but for the screened glimpses of it we receive through various distancing devices—in this case, the spare and wooden, saga-like narration of a native Swede.

As I noted in the introduction, the brutality of this tale is not traceable to anything so fraught as a ruined Templar preceptory. The count himself is a puzzling original for a villain, unrecognizably redrawn as he is from the much milder life of Count Magnus Gabriel De la Gardie (1622–1686). James, though, almost certainly would have understood the significance of Count Magnus in terms of his importance to medieval studies, for De la Gardie was directly responsible for the present residence in Stockholm of one of the world's most precious manuscripts, the Codex Argenteus, or "Silver Book," a copy of the Gospels translated into Gothic and written with shimmering silvery ink upon fine purple parchment, making it a rather gaudy primary witness to that dead language. Count Magnus bought the book in 1662 for the equivalent of thirty pounds sterling and, before donating it to his homeland, rebound it in a lavish silver cover (to match the ink), on which he had engraved an emblem of Time releasing Truth along with an account of his donation and his coat of arms.[5] In James's story, though, De la Gardie's "wealth of armorial ornament" is found on a padlocked mausoleum rather than on a deluxe manuscript, and in fact (as Rosemary Pardoe has detailed),[6] there is virtually nothing in the original Count Magnus's life history to justify James's portrait of almost demonic domination and feudal cruelty: "If his tenants came late to their work on the days which they owed to him as Lord of the Manor, they were set on the wooden horse, or flogged and branded in the manor-house yard. One or two cases there were of men who had occupied lands which encroached on the lord's domain, and whose houses had been mysteriously burnt on a winter's night, with the whole family inside."[7] Nor is there much in Mr. Wraxall's character (aside from "over-inquisitiveness") that seems to merit one of the grimmest fates in all of James's fiction. Like Count Magnus, though, Wraxall is modeled on a historical figure, Sir Nathaniel William Wraxall (1751–1831), a notoriously gossipy and careless writer of travel books (with a particular interest, like James's Wraxall, in northern antiquities).[8] The historical Wraxall seems to have died more peacefully than his fictional counterpart, but not before earning a degree of infamy, as we read in the *Edinburgh Review*:

> Men, measures, scenes, and facts all
> Misquoting, misstating,
> Misplacing, misdating,
> Here lies Sir Nathaniel Wraxall![9]

The epitaph is a reminder that error is not the birthright of antiquaries alone, but infects also the debased commercial instinct.[10] Count Magnus pleases to put his immortal seal on the past, but the bloodcurdling quality of the tale is generated largely through the dread differential charge of the chattily abject Wraxall in contact with such magisterial command.

If the stakes of Jamesian terror are poised precariously between such extremes, it may speak to the way in which scholarly standing in this era is a "composite product" of unreconciled elements.[11] In the nineteenth century, much past-oriented research still took place among wealthy amateurs working within closed networks of antiquarian learning, circles restricted to those with sufficient social connections and leisure to pursue such hobbies. Class status and connections, rather than academic training and credentials, unlocked access to archives, libraries, even academic positions. But the rise of a "new academic caste" within Britain's reformed medieval universities marked a shift toward an occupational academic professionalism remodeled in line with the higher professions of law, the church, medicine, and the military.[12] It was a slow, shambling shift, however, and one full of contractions and half starts, especially at a place like King's, where a cloistered sense of equality among privileged peers would be threatened by the kind of institutional hierarchies the new professionalism entailed. Parkins leans much too heavily on his professorial position, to the resentment of his colleagues. And although, in retrospect, the process may seem to have elevated the status of these fields, from hobby to specialist career, the vocational aspect of the new professionalism would have struck many of the older school as potentially degrading.[13] An anomalous figure like Lord Acton (1834–1902) "uniquely combined social, political, and intellectual eminence," so as to embody multiple claims to academic stature, yet it was "patrician poverty rather than scholarly ambition that had impelled [Acton] to take up university employment" as Regius Professor of Modern History at Cambridge in 1895.[14] His call for a new "sacred band of university workers" was born of cold necessity as well as high ideals.[15]

The uncomfortable source of James's own patrician poverty has not commonly been stressed, though the history is well documented. His family was the pinched remnant of a well-known dynasty of slave owners, "one of the oldest if not the oldest" colonizing families that ran sugar plantations in Jamaica. And they were not "mere absentee proprietors," as Hugh Paget reports approvingly in the inaugural volume of the *Jamaican Historical Review*—in an article that celebrates the James family for possessing the clearest historical claim to authentic Jamaican identity and for boasting a crowning jewel in the career of "the late Provost of Eton."[16] Prior to "the catastrophic blow which the abolition of the slave trade struck the planter class in 1807," the James family lived and flourished in Jamaica for nearly three centuries, though they were careful to ensure (as James's ancestor William Rhodes James—the first of many of that name—stipulated in his will) that each of their sons "by the first convenient opportunity" was to be educated in "Old England."[17] The long line of James boys educated at Eton (several were sent there in the eighteenth century) thus begins as a colonial imperative to maintain contact with English soil, tradition, and identity. But by 1818 fortunes on the plantations had drastically declined, and James's grandfather chose to reestablish his family in England, where James's father, Herbert, was born in 1822. Settling eventually in Aldeburgh, the family lived modestly, and (although their charity work evinced "the full aristocratic instinct for service") they were well aware of how reduced they were in the world, having "suffered financially from the emancipation of the slaves."[18]

Nor had this family memory receded by Monty's day. A notebook surviving among James's papers in the Fitzwilliam details the contraction of the family's holdings in Jamaica in the years 1806–20. James has filled the unused pages of this ledger with notes on the medieval manuscripts of the library at Lambeth Palace and other antiquarian matters, but he evidently took a keen interest in his own family's history.[19] In a letter of 1887, he notes that his brother Sydney had shown him family papers, which revealed "that at one time we possessed 3,160 slaves."[20] Sydney himself opens his own personal memoir with this family lore: "My paternal grandfather, William Rhodes James, was the last slave-owner of the family, and the last of four successive William Rhodes Jameses who carry back the line to the beginning of the eighteenth century. He was the proprietor of two large estates in Jamaica, where his ancestors had been since Cromwellian days. I have various papers recording sales and purchases of slaves by him."[21] The correspondence of this William Rhodes is just possibly connected to the opening of one of James's late stories, "An Evening's Entertainment":

> Nothing is more common form in old-fashioned books than the description of the winter fireside, where the aged grandam narrates to the circle of children that hangs on her lips story after story of ghosts and fairies, and inspires her audience with a pleasing terror. But we are never allowed to know what the stories were. We hear, indeed, of sheeted spectres with saucer eyes, and—still more intriguing—of "Rawhead and Bloody Bones" (an expression which the Oxford Dictionary traces back to 1550), but the context of these striking images eludes us.[22]

For this intriguing phrase, one of James's sources of curiosity may well have been an 1837 letter to grandfather William Rhodes, in which is related a gruesome anecdote of a drunken woman allegedly suffering spontaneous combustion: "But I should not frighten you with any of my Rawhead & Bloodybone stories so will not for the future."[23] As I have preserved in this quotation, the phrase "Rawhead & Bloodybone stories" is underlined in the original document, a cross-written letter that James inherited among his grandmother's surviving papers. Whether or not this underlining is the later work of James himself, he certainly would have been interested in the phrase as he perused his grandam's correspondence. It is surely the case, too, that many readers of James today would find these Jamaican roots surprising.

My purpose in acknowledging this history is not to visit upon James the sins of his ancestors or—despite my invocation of "Count Magnus"—to suggest that we read his fictions as allegorizing family history. But if in James's generation the practitioners of a newly occupational medieval studies joined in the process of inaugurating an "intellectual aristocracy" within the universities, in which cultural capital compensated for economic, it is important not to romanticize the ashes out of which it arose. Certainly any idealization of James's homegrown Englishness—any nostalgic sense of untroubled continuity and heritage drawing him to an insular antiquarian past—must reckon with this history. But we must also contextualize James's reputation for mastering clashing scholarly identities, for marrying the productivity of the specialist to the leisurely lifestyle of the "gentleman antiquary." Lord Acton himself reportedly marveled at this capacity:

> When Monty James was in his early thirties, Lord Acton came here with his older and wider fame and his insatiable curiosity about

people. "You know Montague James?" he asked a King's man. "Yes, I know him." "Is it true that he is ready to spend every evening playing games or talking with undergraduates?" "Yes, the evenings and more." "And do you know that in knowledge of MSS. he is already third or fourth in Europe?" "I am interested to hear you say so, Sir." "Then how does he manage it?" "We have not yet found out."[24]

In anecdote after anecdote we find Monty conducting research while socializing at a railway terminal, Monty pranking friends as he skims the *Anglo-Saxon Chronicle,* Monty simultaneously entertaining guests and books: "Manuscripts and priceless texts often strewed the table amid pipes and siphons, but the humorous yarn and thrilling ghost story filled the longer pauses."[25] Even his clutter, amid which he would "work in the shade, with steep banks of stratified papers on either hand," shelters a symbol of his casual, studiously luxuriant approach to scholarship.[26] James cultivated this impression, as he remarks in his study of the library of Bury St. Edmunds: "the instinct of the chase of my favorite game, namely, manuscripts, is soon excited by such a search as this. So that even though the search might have been utterly unproductive and useless, it is probable that it would have been prosecuted."[27] James's considerable gifts—above all, his legendary memory—allowed him gamely to perform a seemingly miraculous feat of what Pierre Bourdieu calls "unintentional learning," expertise freed from the indignity of practical urgency and the debasing economics of the knowledge industry.[28] Yet such a performance was also made possible only by the rarified positions he held at elite institutions and the free access they granted to the gated past.

In this chapter, though, I propose to examine how James's fictions reflect a less sanguine view of the academic landscape than is often recorded in memoir and tribute. James reached his prime during decades in which the conditions of academic labor in Britain were very much in flux. Turbulence was felt in a number of ways, but the stories I examine here reflect intimate corners of scholarly experience not always considered in works of disciplinary history. They do so through figures of frighteningly mixed (a)vocational elements: Karswell of "Casting the Runes" and Baxter of "A View from a Hill" are compelling villains precisely because their scholarly transgressions defy easy categorization, their monstrosity comprising an admixture of antiquarian excess and occupational degradation. Each in the end must be cast out, but even in their banishment these figures remain fascinating for the way in which they direct attention to the dark sacrifices that medieval studies makes in remaking its scholarly culture. In "Casting the Runes," the shifting character of academic communities and scholarly networks is the story's dominant concern, but the full implications are not evident until we explore the tale's central medievalism and the way in which James "recasts" the runological tradition. The dark pleasures of vicious reviews are only the beginning, James suggests in this strange parable of academic publishing, and we find something even stranger in "A View from a Hill," where an initially clear-cut pastoral premise is prismatically refracted through the horror and attraction of Baxter's magicked field glasses, an instrument allowing for indefensible encounters with the past. Here is another antiquary whose time has come, but James allows no great satisfaction for his passing.

THREE MONTHS WERE ALLOWED

> I don't care much for your thin ghost, nor do I think it good. Perhaps I am not clever enough to understand it—but you have a charming style.
> —Oscar Browning, in a letter to M. R. James

"Casting the Runes" is among James's most-anthologized tales, and it was adapted in Jacques Tourneur's classic 1957 film, *Night of the Demon*, which in turn inspired major elements of the 2009 thriller *Drag Me to Hell*.[29] Some have gone so far as to suggest it as an inspiration for the 1998 Japanese blockbuster horror movie *Ringu*[30] (and its various remakes and sequels), as James's plot similarly turns on the haunted exchange of cursed objects—slips of paper inscribed with runes, in this case, rather than a videotape. The story opens with an increasingly exasperated series of rejection letters from the secretary of an academic association to a certain Mr. Karswell, a rebuffed would-be authority on the history of alchemy who demands to be allowed to present his research at an upcoming meeting. Mr. Secretary is eager to suppress the name of the expert reviewer, Mr. Dunning, who has rejected Karswell's submission. Ultimately, however, the scorned author acquires knowledge of his identity and seeks revenge by slipping Dunning deadly magical runes as he examines manuscripts in the British Museum, a research space that, being "accessible to amateur as well as well as professional scholars, provided an apt site for the exploration of disciplinary boundaries," as Ruth Hoberman has argued.[31] It is here that Karswell "casts the runes," but he does so only after first sending Dunning a series of threatening messages, the most notable of which comes in the form of a quasi-alchemical advertisement/obituary embedded in the glass of a railway carriage, and indicates cryptically that "three months were allowed" to one of Karswell's former victims, John Harrington.[32] Harrington had viciously reviewed one of Karswell's books and, after receiving his own runic curse, suffered a mysterious fate, tumbling out of a tree to his death. In the end, though, Harrington's brother teams up with Dunning to return the runes to Karswell, who becomes a victim of his own curse. The runic magic is thus a direct and suggestively symmetrical response to professional academic review, and indeed the story scans easily, in semi-allegorical fashion, as a reflection on these practices and institutions, the dark marks of scholarly invective rounding back for their revenge.

A few critics have begun to consider the implications of these curses. Shane McCorristine notably describes Karswell as "an adversary who stood, in James's milieu, for scholarly imposture and diabolical autodidactism—a situation of blatant and unacceptable avocation."[33] McCorristine's characterization, though, does not address this complication: that Karswell's own chief adversary, Dunning, is also described as a man of leisure, who himself pursues medieval studies as something of a serious hobby. What, then, makes Dunning's avocation acceptable and Karswell's not? One answer would be simply that Karswell lacks Dunning's aristocratic status and educational training, and indeed Mike Pincombe has detected in the tale "a hidden narrative of class-war, in which the wealthy ex-tradesman Karswell has to pay the price for his attempt to intrude upon the precincts of the gentry."[34] Much of Pincombe's reading is persuasive, and I would not cast aside this insight, or those of McCorristine. But the dynamics of class and professionalism in the tale may be clarified with more detailed and focused attention to the issue its runes most readily seem to suggest—scholarly vitriol, the dark marks of specialists savaging each other in print. For indeed the quarter century or so prior to the publication of "Casting the Runes" was marked by the recasting of scholarly exchange and peer review in the context of an emergent academic publishing industry, with new specialist venues to be established in caustic opposition to professed work of a more popular and commercial orientation. James's creative runologies in the tale point up the unsettling stakes of this shift, for Karswell's curses are calibrated with cruel precision, and they whisper of a needful and lasting malice in all branches of "antiquarian science."

Before we turn to runes, though, I would like to offer an alternative to the commonplace of Jamesian annotation associating Karswell with the occultist Aleister Crowley, who was a student at Cambridge in the 1890s and went on to become an infamous public figure (though not by the time this tale was written).[35] I would propose that a possibly more plausible (and potentially illuminating) source of inspiration for Karswell is Oscar Browning (1837–1923), a resident fellow at King's and the college's most prominent and colorful figure from his arrival in 1877 until his involuntary retirement in 1909. The notorious personality of "the O. B." (as he was often called, with or without the definite article) loomed tremendously large at Eton and King's, and by all accounts Browning was "one of the few people [James] consistently and thoroughly disliked."[36]

James's dealings with the older man naturally evolved over the years, beginning with undergraduate days, when he was in the habit of entertaining friends with O. B. impersonations and once had to ask forgiveness for—accidentally?—slipping Browning an unflattering caricature drawn by another student ("so that the fault is mine for having thoughtlessly stuck it into the frame of a picture").[37] As James aged and advanced in his career, the two men came to stand on a more equal footing as colleagues whose administrative business and shared scholarly interests brought them into frequent contact (Browning wrote history; James's surviving letters to him discuss authors and texts ranging from Bede and Aldhelm to *Njál's Saga*).[38] Both were hospitable dons, the two most prominent figures at King's in their day. They came in time to be regarded as linked opposites; the memoirs of alumni often contrast their characters, values, and Sunday-evening gatherings in nearby suites of the Gibbs Building. After soaking in James's august company ("keeping Montem," as it was called),[39] undergraduates would cross the hall to the O. B.'s "at-home" salons in order to "mingle with inferior mortals," in the words of E. F. Benson.[40]

The O. B.'s reputed character lines up so well with Karswell that it is surprising that the case has not been made before. Browning, for instance, was widely perceived to be an extraordinarily flamboyant self-promoter ("self-interest and self-advertisement were, at bottom, his real motives"),[41] so that "his immense egotism made him something of a *bête noir* to Monty."[42] It is easy to see this distilled darkly in the figure of Karswell, who urgently "wants to tell us [i.e., the members of an academic association] all about" his research.[43] Karswell's insistent need to pontificate before Dunning's colleagues forms the basis for the opening sequence of James's tale, but even in physical appearance and interests, the O. B. is a striking match for Karswell, who is described as a "fat," "stout, clean-shaven man" with a "dreadful face."[44] The O. B.'s obesity was a widely remarked and lampooned attribute, and James himself records in his memoir that Cambridge undergraduates had awarded the beardless Browning "a prize for [being] the ugliest man."[45] Karswell is portrayed as a connoisseur of music, passing the runes to Harrington in an analytical program of a musical performance in London; Browning was well known for going out of his way to attend such events and for hosting gatherings with much musical entertainment, including performances on an "Obeophone" (a chapter of his first biography is titled "Music and Controversy").[46]

Of course, Karswell's central and driving attribute as an antagonist is that he is "very easily offended, and never forgave anybody."[47] Such words suit almost no one so perfectly as Browning, whose career at King's was a chronicle of controversy, grudge, and high dudgeon, leading James early to conclude, "That man, believe me, is the worst I know."[48] Few who read the opening of "Casting the Runes" could fail to be struck by this description from Ian Anstruther's biography of Browning: "whenever a meeting had broken up, letters asking for explanations or demanding outright, abject apologies from all those who had dared oppose him flew from one staircase to another, across the shadowy college courts, like whirling leaves in a winter storm. The files concerning King's are crammed with them."[49] A. C. Benson recalled that "he was combative and quarrelsome, and an unscrupulous adversary. He scarified his opponents in public and in private." As a dinner guest, he would drag along "bags and bundles of papers—the ashes of extinct controversies."[50]

But the greatest offense came at the close of the O. B.'s career, and this time James found himself in the thick of it. In 1905 Augustus Austen Leigh, the provost of King's, died, and Browning "seriously hoped to succeed him."[51] Instead, James was elected:

> One of the first duties that fell to the new Provost, Dr. M. R. James, who tried to make things as easy as he could for O. B., was to tell him that the Council had only reappointed him to his post of History Tutor for three years—the usual term being seven—and that at the end of that period, since he would then be over seventy, an age

at which the Council considered it was time to give way to younger men, he would probably be superannuated. O. B. was deeply shocked at this news, which he regarded as an intrigue of his enemies to get rid of him.[52]

And so it was that only three more years of Cambridge life were allowed; as Browning notes, James personally informed him of this news as they were leaving morning chapel.[53] An appeal was made, but again it was James's role to convey the ruling of the Stipends Committee, this time in writing: "On the other hand I must tell you that it is clear to me that the Council are not at all likely to change their view on the question of a renewal of your appointment."[54] James might have gone on: "No personal question (it can hardly be necessary for me to add) can have had the slightest influence on the decision of the Council." But this latter assurance was not written for the sake of the O. B.; these are rather the words of Mr. Secretary to the disgruntled Mr. Karswell of Lufford Abbey.

The first reading of "Casting the Runes" most probably took place during Christmas at King's, just as the wave of this great controversy was cresting.[55] It is not difficult to imagine James's first audience spotting a local resonance in Karswell (accustomed as they already were to relentless spoofs of the O. B.).[56] That is not to say that James was Browning's public adversary; by all accounts, he was a calming influence on the college during the affair.[57] Nevertheless, in Shane Leslie's view, the "Dons hated [Browning] with the same futility with which they indulged most human emotions, and in the end they cast him forth unkindly."[58] Browning departed "angry and resentful" and "number[ing] the Provost amongst his enemies. 'Monty James,' he wrote airily some years later, 'for whom I have little respect, was as bad as any of them.'"[59]

But Browning's departure was not simply a matter of King's breaking ties with one of its more fractious sons. It also marked an important moment of university professionalization, to the extent that the O. B.'s ouster was a signal of shifting academic culture and standards as much as it was an enforcement of age restrictions.[60] In fact, in 1904 Browning was denied his application for a doctorate by the Cambridge Special Board for History and Archaeology, which had assessed his published work—though prolific—as not up to standard. More broadly, the O. B.'s reputation for being a "hack historian and a mere journalist" must be understood in the context of a contemporary sense of urgency to differentiate between serious academic work and historical writing pitched for a commercial audience. The new, university-based scholarly publication was to be defined not so much against the work of "gentlemen antiquaries" in the Oldbuckian amateur mold as against professed but populist historians who catered to the demands of the general literary marketplace, selling their writings directly to the public, rather than gaining compensation for them indirectly through academic position. In the context of a greatly expanding readership in history, it was often these commercially oriented writers who threatened (and helped define in opposition) academic specialist identity and authority; discrediting their work in print became an Oxbridge imperative in the late nineteenth and early twentieth centuries.[61] As Mike Pincombe has convincingly detailed, Karswell is strongly associated in James's tale with a disreputable commercialism, from his employment of menacing advertisements to the dark warnings he sends, "addressed in a commercial hand."[62] Surely, this taint applies also to Karswell's research, which is sensationalist and undisciplined, possibly calculated to thrill a popular audience.

The O. B., too, was not above crass market considerations when it came to his scholarly productions; he is said to have warned undergraduate students at King's not to read his own book, for it was written only for "grocers and cheesemongers, and it would be no good for them."[63] In one of the first sustained studies of early academic publishing in the humanities, Leslie Howsam has in fact recently argued that "Browning is a prime example for this period of the historian with a foot in both literary camps, writing one day for the university presses and the new scholarly journal, and the next for a publisher more interested in commerce than in correctness."[64] And yet, while Browning's own work was often viewed by the university professionals as suspect, Howsam credits Browning with having made important contributions, behind the scenes, to a collaborative Oxbridge effort to found the *English Historical Review,* the appearance of which in 1886 is considered a landmark in professional academic publishing in England.[65] The initial obstacle to its viability, however, was predictably a question of audience and economics: how could a specialist journal hope to support itself? In the early years of the *EHR,* a real attempt was made to avoid its becoming "merely the organ of specialists," lest it alienate generally educated readers.[66] By the early 1890s, however, it had become clear that the journal would perforce be limited to a narrow academic audience, and steps were taken to economize, including reducing the number of copies printed and ending the practice of compensating authors.[67] The latter measure also had the side effect of discouraging contributions from working historians who wrote for a living outside the financial support of universities.[68] Browning and James both published work in the *EHR*; it became one of James's most frequent venues, along with the *Journal of Theological Studies* (*JTS*), founded in 1899.

Caution and restraint were hallmarks of the *JTS*, *EHR*, and other historically focused academic journals inaugurated in this era. In his 1903 inaugural speech at Cambridge for the Regius Professorship in History (another position to which the O. B. aspired in vain), J. B. Bury vigorously asserted the status of history as "a science, no less and no more."[69] Bury's speech caused a quite stir at Cambridge, but it was really the culmination of several decades of the widespread promulgation of the ideal that professional historiography would acquire scientific status only by banishing the "allurements of style" and the "spell of drowsy narrative" that characterized literary treatments of history.[70] As its first issue notes, the *JTS* was meant to be "a regular organ of communication between students whose lives are spent, at the Universities and elsewhere, in the pursuit of scientific Theology."[71] Here, scientific theology meant historical research into religion, including both doctrinal issues and more strictly textual, philological, and bibliographical concerns (James's research fell into the latter camp, making the *JTS* "an ideal vehicle for [his] biblical work").[72] Although it is impossible to establish a neat division between popular and professional histories and historians of this era (as Browning's career illustrates), the rhetoric of "the historical sciences" was a powerful touchstone of scholarly discourse, one in line with James's own detail-accumulating, antispeculative academic style. His well-known aversion to theoretical speculation is not easily separated from this strain of professional culture (the oft-cited quip "James hates thought" is attributed to Oscar Browning).[73] When James let fly the most acrimonious words of his career ("flaying" an essay by the Cambridge academic Jane Harrison), his stated motivation was to suppress "crude and inconsequent speculations of this kind, which go far to justify those who deny to Comparative Mythology the name and dignity of a science."[74]

James's ideal of scientific dignity perhaps also includes a sense of what Peter Novick has termed "transpersonal replicability."[75] If the natural sciences aimed to arrive at results that could be reproduced across different laboratories, objectivity in the historical sciences would be measured by the extent to which well-trained historians examining the same primary sources came to the same conclusions. The new academic publishing venues of the era reflected this ideal, as Howsam argues: "The quarterly academic periodical . . . was a medium well suited for promoting the ideology of objectivity and transpersonal replicability, the notion that professionalization meant that one trained scholar's interpretation was essentially the same as another's."[76] The multiauthored *Cambridge Histories,* initiated in 1902 by Lord Acton, reflect confidence that the conclusions of professional academics could neatly align to form a coherent whole (James contributed a chapter to the first volume, as well as one to the *Cambridge History of English Literature,* published in 1907).[77] Theoretically, too, both the specialist journal and the collaborative history obviated much undignified (and ungenteel) room for debate. Speculative scholarship meant divisive scholarship, and, though the expectation may seem naïve from the vantage point of the present, the new professionalism could seem to promise a "prophylactic" against much bitter academic controversy.[78] As the prefatory note to the first issue of the *EHR* explains, "The object of history is to discover and set forth facts, and he who confines himself to this object, forbearing acrimonious language, can usually escape the risk of giving offense."[79] And yet such comity among university professionals could arrive only after roundly demolishing the reputations of commercialist scholars and "drumming the amateurs out," as Rosemary Jann puts it.[80] Note that Harrington's review of Karswell's book aims not so much to correct the author's views (and his split infinitives) as to simply remove him from the conversation: "I must say if I'd been the author it [the scathing review] would have quenched my literary ambition for good. I should never have held up my head again."[81]

And yet James's own publications are scattered over multiple, and not always overlapping, domains. Prior to 1901, James published his research most frequently in the *Proceedings of the Cambridge Antiquarian Society* and the Anglican newspaper the *Guardian.*[82] The pattern takes something of a turn after the founding in 1899 of the *Journal of Theological Studies,* however, when James more and more submitted articles principally to specialist journals. In the last thirty-five years of his career, James contributed more than sixty articles and reviews to either the *JTS* or the *EHR,* as well as to many other scholarly journals.[83] He never, however, abandoned publishing work in other venues. In 1909 James was elected to the Roxburghe Club, for which organization he went on to edit and/or introduce more than a dozen volumes. Founded in 1812 (at a dinner commemorating the Duke of

Roxburghe's acquisition of a rare edition of Boccaccio), the organization is by tradition severely restricted both in membership and in terms of the accessibility of the books it produces. In addition to aristocrats enthusiastically devoted to the aesthetics of print and the pleasures of "bibliomania," the club commonly admits a few more academically minded members (James was in this category), whose contributions help raise the general quality of club scholarship.[84] But the focus from the beginning was notoriously exclusionary, so that nonmembers found it extraordinarily difficult to consult Roxburghe editions, which were printed in limited numbers and refused sale to outsiders, including even research libraries. Partly this served to preserve these editions as rare collector's items, but it also shielded members from exposure to criticism and their books from bad reviews: "Club insiders needed never fear much scrutiny from the outside world," as David Matthews points out.[85]

The Roxburghe Club represents an extreme case, but it could be considered emblematic of the insularity of many antiquarian institutions and networks. On the other hand, the advent of academic specialist journals offered occupational scholars a very different brand of exclusivity and, although his approach at times risked "verging on connoisseurship," James was able to find shelter in that world, too.[86] The implications of these observations for "Casting the Runes" are not clear-cut, but it would seem at least that "unacceptable avocation" may not fully capture what disturbs us about the "Abbot of Lufford" and his academic bad blood. There are many unacceptable *vocational* elements here, too, held in unstable suspension in the strange portrait, but the necessity of pulverizing Karswell's scholarship is only the tale's starting point. The runes to follow hold the real interest, so that the effects of the hex can be read as a symptom of Dunning's own sense of scholarly purity, as well as an indictment of the specialist forms of publishing and constricted academic culture adopted by university professionals. Nor are transpersonal replicability and the elimination of scholarly invective slated to arrive anytime soon. Those pleasures remain, remade into something more insidious—or at least that is the implication of James's engagement with his dark materials.

RECASTING THE RUNES

Although annotators of "Casting the Runes" have found no exact parallel for Karswell's runic curses, James is clearly drawing on a well-established body of popular and academic runology. For instance, at the very moment that Dunning receives his runic curse, he hears "his own name whispered behind him," in what is probably an understated etymological reference. The medievalist John M. Kemble, in an early and influential article on runes, explains:

> [The word *rune*'s] original meaning is strictly that of *mysterium, a secret:* hence the privy counsellor of a prince is called his rûn-wita, *e secretis,* his secretary, the person who knows his secrets (Beôwulf, l. 2650). And so the verb rynan, which is derived directly from it, means, *to whisper, to tell secrets,* a sense which we still retain under the corrupt form to *round* in one's ear. So also Rûna denotes a whisperer; but in its far earlier and truer sense, a magician, one who knows or practises secret arts, in which sense it is found in the compound word hel-rûna.[87]

A similar discussion is found in Anna C. Paus's chapter "Runes and Manuscripts" in the 1907 *Cambridge History of English Literature,* which (as I've noted) includes a contribution by James.[88] We can be confident, then, that the author of "Casting the Runes" is playing off a set of associations well known to him. When Mr. Secretary is unable to protect the secret of the single-blind review, vengeance is inevitable. The whispering noise distracts Dunning, and Karswell slips him the curse.

The "casting" of these runes itself is also not purely a Jamesian invention, though the story effects a significant twist on the tradition. In much nineteenth-century scholarship it was largely taken for granted that tales of pagan lot casting (as, for example, to determine sacrificial victims) implied rune-inscribed objects. The story of Radbod, king of the Frisians, was commonly cited. In Alcuin's *Life of Willibrord,* the pagan king is shown casting lots to determine who should die to appease the wrath of a god whose sacred cattle and spring had been defiled.[89] In a review of the first two volumes of George Stephen's foundational though eccentric *Old-Northern Runic Monuments of Scandinavia and England* (1866–68), R. J. King explains that Radbod's lots were "distinct auguries or divinations; and the 'casting' [of] them consisted in throwing a number of Runes—cut probably on the bark of trees—on a broad outspread cloth, and then marking the manner in which they lay disposed."[90] Of course, this type of "casting the runes" is quite distinct from what Karswell does, and Jacqueline Simpson notes that "there is nothing in archaeology or in medieval texts which corresponds at all closely to the way the evil Mr. Karswell uses runes in this story."[91] Perhaps not, but in translations of medieval texts, at least, we can find the idea of "casting the runes" in a sense other than casting lots. In a section of the *Poetic Edda* known as "Helgakviða Hundingsbana" (The Lay of Helgi the Hunding-Slayer), Dag, the son of a man Helgi has murdered, avenges his father with a spear lent to him by Odin. As Helgi's widow curses Dag for this act, he attempts to exculpate himself in these words (translated as an appendix to an 1870 translation of the *Völsunga Saga* by Eiríkr Magnússon and William Morris):

Odin alone
Let all this bale loose,
Casting the strife-runes
'Twixt friends and kindred.

In 1873 James's schoolmaster at Temple Grove, O. C. Waterfield, presented him with a copy of this book, which he eventually bequeathed to Eton.[92] Was the passage an inspiration for the tale's title, if not exactly for the magic practiced by Karswell?

It seems plausible, but James probably also had the aleatory sense of "casting runes" very much in mind. At the very end of the tale, Karswell's casting finally caroms back when Dunning is able to return the runes to their sender. James details the curser's comeuppance: "an English traveller [Karswell], examining the front of St. Wulfram's Church at Abbeville, then under extensive repair, was struck on the head and instantly killed by a stone falling from the scaffold erected round the south-western tower."[93] Karswell's slightly slapstick death is particularly appropriate in its locale, for Saint Wulfram was another missionary to Radbod's realm who contested the king's practice of casting lots for ritual sacrifice: the ninth-century anonymous *Vita Vulframni* (strongly associated with Alcuin's *Life of Willibrord*)[94] details how Wulfram saves through prayer the boy Ovon from being killed in that very way in honor of Odin.[95] Karswell's death takes the action of "casting" in a more direct sense, as the curse is thrown back in the form of a physical projectile. At the same time, the sense of impersonal judgment is restored: Karswell's fate is delivered with divine sanction from on high. Of course, even Odin's "strife-runes" in the translation of Helgi's lay are directed (according to Dag) in scattershot fashion, cast into the midst of human affairs in a general incendiary spirit.

The most striking thing, then, may be the variations James has fashioned from his sources, "recasting" the action of *to cast* so that judgments from on high are mingled with the darkly personal. In the context of the story's obvious interest in the dynamics of scholarly acumen, academic grudge, and blind review, there is potentially great significance in the tension between these various senses of the verb. We might feel this strain even in the story's opening series of rejection letters from Mr. Secretary (suggestively, we are allowed to see only one side of the correspondence). His increasingly terse dismissals are thick with bureaucratic, impersonal, passive, and otherwise roundabout constructions, even as Karswell is assured that "no personal question" had played a role in the society's decision. Nor is there room for appeal: "our laws [do not] allow of your discussing the matter with a Committee of our Council, as you suggest."[96] In the wake of this rejection, Karswell's curse will be calculated to send up such language, casting it back as he advertises the interval between Harrington's receiving the runes and his sudden death: "Three months *were allowed*" (emphasis added).[97]

The fearful symmetry of Karswell's curses is evident too in the odd manner of Harrington's death, which is a "mysterious business," as Mr. Secretary explains: he "shins up a tree—quite a difficult tree—growing in the hedgerow: a dead branch gives way, and he comes down."[98] The peculiar doom executed by the curse is evidently on some level meant to parallel the castigation of his reviewer, who had criticized Karswell for pursuing a dead branch of knowledge—witchcraft—with an absurdly loose comparative methodology (perhaps comparable, in James's view, to the kind of scholarship for which he would later flay Harrison in the *Classical Review*). Moreover, the connection between this deadly "Tree of Knowledge" and James's engagement with runology may lead us back (if we, too, dare to compare) to possible Old Norse sources of inspiration that attributed the invention/discovery of runes to Odin.[99] As described in an oft-quoted section of the thirteenth-century "Odin's Rune Song," Odin wins original knowledge of the runes by mounting and sacrificing himself on a mighty tree. The mysterious episode concludes with Odin "receiving" runes and then tumbling down from the tree:

nýsta ec niðr
nam ec up rúnar

opandi nam
fęll ec aptr þaðan

(I spied adown / I caught up runes, / crying I caught / fell I thence again)[100]

The tree from which Odin falls has routinely been identified with Yggdrasil, the immense sacred ash of Norse mythology, and it is easy to see why the nineteenth-century historian and comparative mythographer George William Cox would note of Yggdrasil, "This mighty tree . . . in Odin's Rune Song becomes a veritable tree of knowledge."[101] Like Helgi's lay, "Odin's Rune Song" is found in the *Poetic Edda,* at the end of a section known as the Hávamál (The Sayings of Hár), where Hár (or Hárr) translates as "the high one," i.e., Odin. Immediately following his account of receiving the runes, Hár enumerates various aspects of his acquired runic knowledge, including powers analogous to Karswell's: "if a man declares hatred to me, harm shall consume them sooner than me."[102] Paus notes that "Odin is represented in the *Edda* as sacrificing himself in order to learn their use and hidden wisdom" and, citing Saxo Grammaticus, explains that "the god sometimes stooped to use them for purposes of personal revenge."[103] Harrington, however, is not as skilled in casting back as Hár is, and the secret knowledge he gains on his runic tree comes in the form of a broken neck. Thus the parallels here seem quite suggestive, though we may be compelled to employ Karswell's own loose comparative methods if we are to work through the possible implications.

Perhaps one further suggestion will be allowed, though I offer it here with some uncertainty and hesitation. Harrington's fate is sealed when "a gust—a warm gust it was"—catches the slip of paper and blows it into the fire, reducing the runes to "a single ash."[104] It is the moment of no return for the victim, yet this "ash" might give us pause. The "ash" (or *æsc*) is a common Anglo-Saxon rune, ᚫ, descended from *ansuz**, the *a*-rune of the elder *fuþarc* (that is, the runic alphabet, named for its first six letters). In a story that explicitly (and, for James, uncharacteristically) withholds the haunted inscription from the reader, reference in this context to "a single ash" is at least suspicious.[105] And there may be more. In the later Anglo-Saxon *fuþorc,* a vowel shift (a > o) had transmuted the *a*-rune into an *o*-rune, ᚩ, renamed *os* or "mouth." The new ᚩ-rune now occupied ᚫ's former fourth position in the runic alphabet (hence the *fuþarc* becomes the *fuþorc*), while ᚠ (now called the "ash") was relegated to near the back of the runic pack, representing a fronted [æ] sound. Thus the "ash" and "mouth" runes are tightly entangled: in more than one sense, they share a single character.[106] It may seem antiquarian to spell out this history, but it is striking to note that just as a "warm gust" reduces Harrington's runes to "a single ash," Dunning experiences the same "gust of warm, or even hot air" right before coming into contact with his own runic horror: "What he touched was, according to his account, a mouth, with teeth, and with hair about it, and, he declares, not the mouth of a human being."[107] Are Harrington's deadly ash (ᚠ) and Dunning's dreadful mouth (ᚠ) two manifestations of a very similar runic curse?

Whether or not this pattern was James's intention, the image of a monstrous mouth invading one's most private inner sanctum—Dunning feels the mouth in "the well-known nook under [his] pillow"—returns us to the question of the thematic upshot of Karswell's curses.[108] As we have seen, these spells have a hellish quality of a Dantean kind. The miseries meted out are calculated to suit the offense (James's work on biblical apocrypha, we should note, had clarified the pedigree of such symmetrical punishments in medieval literature).[109] Karswell has been rejected by the academic establishment, and he casts back in a way that calls into question the ideology and expectations of the new professionalism. In particular, the production and circulation of knowledge seems most immediately evoked by his runic instrument of revenge: if the specialists have their secrets and secretaries, Karwell responds with his own mysterious runes, his own whispering mouths in hidden spaces. With professional scholarship, as Anthony Grafton points out, comes not only long-form peer review but an increasingly understated, shorthand set of codes and conventions, such as the "subtle but deadly 'cf.'" These are marks that confer silent opprobrium—the "scholarly version of assassination."[110] Moreover, the asymmetrical structure of single-blind review (the power dynamic Dunning enjoys as a member of the——— Association)[111] is reflected in the anonymity of Karswell's casting: Dunning must sleuth out for himself who slipped him the damning script.[112] The same goes for Harrington's offense, for book reviews in professional journals are notoriously unaccountable, not being themselves subject to peer review or restraints observed in other kinds of academic writing.[113] In both cases, the transformation of the usual sense of "casting the runes"—from divination to malevolent assault—can be read as an implied challenge to the professional fiction that reviewers' judgments arrive blindly, dispassionately, and impersonally from on high. On the contrary, Karswell's critics had "made a game of" dismantling his book, while a manuscript draft of the story reveals that Harrington had taken a "peculiar pleasure" in writing the review.[114]

The same manuscript passage reveals that Karswell's work displays "flagrant examples of nearly all the offenses which an ill-trained and self-sufficient researcher can commit."[115] The slur of "self-sufficiency" reminds us that one of the high promises of professional specialist publishing was the establishment of systematic comity, expert consensus, and collaboration. But the effect of Karswell's curse is to close round on him an "intangible barrier," an intense sense of isolation: "It seemed to him that something ill-defined and impalpable had stepped in between him and his fellow-men."[116] If James conceived the new professionalism to be—at its best—a reorganized return to a tight-knit "sacred band" of elite specialists (antiquarianism recast), Karswell's curse is to reveal a darker side of that promise. For the exchange of runes anonymously from one hostile stranger to another seems uncannily well suited as a metaphor for the innovation of a narrow scholarly public that is at once more select and specialized to one's very particular personal interests (besides Karswell, Dunning is "the only one in the country" who studies alchemical manuscripts)[117] and yet insidiously impersonal (each instance of casting the runes is specifically made possible only because the victim has no more than a vague inkling of his rival's appearance).[118] Antiquarian networks give way to a faceless profession, where peers are known by their byline alone, and Dunning is dragged into a new and claustrophobic kind of hell.

And the sense of dread drags, too, in a tale that is exquisitely timed to the tortuous rhythms and rituals of modern academic life. It seems somewhat paradoxical that although he is by professional reputation England's top expert on the history of alchemy, Dunning "hasn't published anything on the same subject yet."[119] Pincombe interprets this as evidence that Dunning is a mere "amateur pursuing his own interests."[120] But James's emphasis is on how Dunning's leisure affords him a disciplined restraint in delaying publication on any particular subject until he has completed a well-rounded investigation. In that sense, it is his very "antiquarian" lifestyle, with its open-ended schedule, that allows him to pursue his research with such strict professionalism. Lord Acton himself, despite his depth of expertise, was known for extreme reluctance to publish anything prematurely, out of an "acute, almost overwhelming sense of the gravity, the sanctity of history," in the words of the medievalist F. W. Maitland.[121] Like Dunning, he therefore published little.

Such professional pains are perhaps quietly signaled just before Karswell casts the runes: "It was in a somewhat pensive frame of mind that Mr. Dunning passed on the following day into the Select Manuscript Room of the British Museum, and filled up tickets for Harley 3586, and some other volumes."[122] Critics have been at a loss to explain the significance of Harley MS 3586, a volume of two fourteenth-century cartularies, documents detailing the legal rights and foundation of Wormsley Priory and St. Martin's at Battle. These texts lack any apparent relationship to the black runic magic that Dunning is about to experience, and commentators have puzzled over the detail, which nevertheless appears to have been quite deliberately chosen.[123] I would propose that we are to understand that Dunning, a scholar of the history of medieval magic, is researching the background of Walter Map (ca. 1140–ca. 1210), a probable relative of whom ("Walter Map son of Walter Map of Wormsley") personally granted lands to what became Wormsley Abbey, donations documented in folios 68–75 of Harley 3586. If James himself had been examining this otherwise unexceptionable manuscript, Map would likely have been the reason, for indeed the medieval writer was for James a particular and long-standing preoccupation. As early as March 1892 he was reading a paper on Map to the Chitchat Society; decades later he was to publish both an edition (1914) and a translation (1923) of Map's major work, *De nugis curialium,* a compendium of "courtiers' trifles," including most notably a number of entertaining supernatural stories (of medieval ghosts, demons, and magic) in which James found "great satisfaction."[124] In the 1983 revised joint edition of James's two books on Map, Harley 3586 is discussed in detail on the introduction's second page in an effort to establish the author's background. It is dry stuff; someone like Karswell probably would have skipped ahead to the good parts, such as Map's lurid tale of the punishment of a wicked cleric: "thou shalt on the third day after this be caught up alive by devils into the air at the third hour." Fair warning, but Dunning—unlike his wicked amateur adversary—is a serious scholar who grounds his studies in the meticulous examination of unsensational sources, such as this unassuming Harleian cartulary.

Such painstaking pleasures of professional scholarship take time, of course. Karswell's curse, however, disrupts this temporality, driving Dunning into the academic doldrums, "a brooding blackness" replacing his measured and restrained productivity, "and he seemed robbed of all initiative."[125] James is almost certainly mapping his fiction here according to both medieval and modern patterns of terror. Sheridan Le Fanu's "The Familiar" (featuring a similar plot of revenge) seems particularly relevant as a model, given the tale's pacing: "the victim's dim forebodings of what is to happen gradually growing clearer; these are the processes which generally increase the strain of excitement," as James once wrote of this tale of drawn-out dread.[126] What is distinct in "Casting the Runes," however, is the union of these techniques with James's scholarly themes. The lacunae in the victims' lives are precisely calibrated to the inexorable calendar of academic publishing, and all its intimately anonymous cycles of bad blood: "I instantly took a pen and dipped it in gall and flayed her," James reported of his attack on Jane Harrison, "to appear in our next":[127] Harrison was instantly flayed weeks before she felt it, and "Casting the Runes" captures brilliantly that sense of delayed effect, of impulsive submission and forestalled publication, spiteful review and injured response—all the deadly intervals between one round of runes and the next. In 1909, the O. B. may have seemed like a corrosive element to be purged once and for all from Cambridge life, but Karswell's curses suggest that the new professionalism is marked by impurities all its own. After all, in both Harrington's and Dunning's cases, "three months were allowed," a span that would seem arbitrary and meaningless without reference to the emerging standard of academic periodicals—the eviscerating immediacy of scholarly controversy drawn out at a *quarterly* pace. Academic rancor was not an innovation of James's generation, but it did grow new teeth as professionals felt the imperative not to perish in print. Cast back, the story seems to warn, and acknowledge those things of darkness thine.

A VIEW FROM A HILL

> Now farewel, Shepherd, sith this Hill
> Thou hast such doubt to clime

Many of James's tales feature university men on holiday, and an argument could be made that his fiction is generally pastoral in the sense of its tendency to project the *negotium* of professional life onto a rustic, antiquarian landscape.[128] Few of the stories, however, so openly invite allegorical interpretation as "A View from a Hill," the very title of which seems to promise perspective. The hilly prospect, in fact, is a fairly well trodden bucolic symbol; Edmund Spenser, in the seventh (July) eclogue of his "Shepheardes Calender," grounds a meditation on worldly and intellectual ambition in the metaphor of climbing rustic slopes:

> And they that con of Muses skill,
> sayne most what, that they dwell
> (As goteheards wont) vpon a hill,
> beside a learned well.[129]

Spenser's dialogue gravitates toward the position that such climbing ultimately is dangerous (whereas "In humble dales is footing fast, / the trode is not so tickle"),[130] and we might say the same of James's story. The tale is related from the vantage point of "a man of academic pursuits," Mr. Fanshawe, who visits a new friend, Squire Richards, at that man's estate in the "depths of the country" of southwestern England, just at the start of a summer holiday. While Fanshawe is seeking "a quiet resting-place after days of sitting on committees and college meetings," Richards is a landed gentleman antiquary, and the visit begins with a leisurely lunch under the squire's lime tree by the side of a stream. Afterward, the gruff but amiable host lends his guest a pair of uncommonly heavy field glasses, which Fanshawe uses to scan the surrounding countryside from a hill.[131] The squire, though, is puzzled when Fanshawe describes what he sees. Through the glasses he spies the stately tower of a fine medieval church on a distant knoll and, on another, the spectacle of men gathered around a gibbet. This is not a present scene but a vision of the past made possible by the magic instrument. Through Patten, Richards's wary servant, the men come to understand that these binoculars are the handiwork of an amateur antiquary named Baxter who fabricated liquid filters for them by boiling the excavated bones of medieval men. With this strange instrument, Baxter could see "through a dead man's eyes" directly into the past, allowing him to indulge in darkly mundane antiquarian pleasures, including the publication of an accurate sketch of a long-destroyed priory church (of "Fulnaker") in the transactions of the local County Archaeological Society.[132] Baxter pays for these deeds when wrathful ghosts lead him to an ancient place of execution, where they leave him with a broken neck. Fanshawe, though, does not learn of this backstory until a bicycle and binoculars expedition culminates in a terrifyingly ticklish experience of his own on Gallows Hill.

The evident pastoral-horror qualities of the story are underscored by the names Richards and Fanshawe, likely inspired by Sir Richard Fanshawe (1608–1666), a noted English author and translator of pastoral poetry whose 1664 translation of *Il pastor fido* remained in James's day the standard English edition of Giovanni Battista Guarini's immensely popular play. Fanshawe also translated into Latin John Fletcher's *Faithful Shepherdess,* and produced as well his own famous pastoral ode exhorting noblemen to abandon London for their country estates, where they might "rowle themselves in envy'd leasure" (and be less politically bothersome to the king in times of war).[133] The names suggest that James is quite aware of the notes he is striking throughout the story, from the friends' relaxation in the "shade and scent of a vast lime-tree" (a possible allusion to Coleridgean pastoral) to the arcadian "word-painting" that James displays in describing the view from the hill, perhaps even to the emphasis that James places on Fanshawe's walking stick, the shepherd's staff or *virga* being a classic bucolic prop.[134]

One other link to pastoral tradition is worth noting. In the preface to his *Collected Ghost Stories* (1931), James noted that Herefordshire was the imagined scene of "A View from a Hill," and Jamesians have made more than one attempt to identify the original of Fulnaker Priory and other landmarks in the story. Results have been inconclusive, but I would point out that the most prominent hills in Herefordshire are the Malvern Hills, one of the most scenic spots in all of Britain.[135] For seventeen years (1897–1914), James's brother Sydney was headmaster of Malvern College, which, as Sydney himself writes, "is backed on the west by the noble range of the Malvern Hills. . . . They provide excellent opportunities for walks and runs, and the air of Malvern seems to me, among many other people, to be exceptionally invigorating."[136] It would probably be an unproductive exercise to attempt to map James's fictional topography onto the environs of Malvern (though the range does in fact include a "Hangman's Hill," and though Great Malvern Priory church, like Fulnaker, does have a prominent square, central tower with corner pinnacles).[137] What I would rather stress is that James's "View from a Hill" in Herefordshire has a very strong literary resonance, for the Malvern Hills are the imagined site of the most famous pastoral-allegorical poem of the English Middle Ages, *The Vision of Piers Plowman* (a "work of real genius," in James's opinion).[138] The poem opens:

> In a somer seson · whan soft was the sonne,
> I shope me in shroudes · as I a shepe were,
> In habite as an heremite · vnholy of workes,
> Went wyde in þis · world wondres to here.
> Ac on a May mornynge · on Maluerne hulles
> Me byfel a ferly · of fairy me thou3te;
> I was wery forwandred · and wente me to reste
> Vnder a brode banke · bi a bornes side,
> And as I lay and lened · and loked on þe wateres,
> I slombred in a slepyng · it sweyued so merye.
> Thanne gan I meten · a merueilouse sweuene,
> That I was in a wildernesse, · wist I neuer where,
> As I bihelde in-to þe est · an hiegh to þe sonne,
> I seigh a toure on a toft · trielich ymaked
> A depe dale binethe · a dongeon þere-Inne,
> With depe dyches & derke · and dredful of sight.[139]

For James to have his rusticating Fanshawe wander into these same hills in the summer season—there to reflect on the professional study of the past—seems like no accident.

But what are the stakes of James's pastoral tale of terror? As the tale's opening passage notes, the friendship between Richards and Fanshawe was formed during an "official inquiry in town," business that seems to have a bearing on the question. As several of James's editors have remarked, there is considerable reason to identify the Pembrokeshire antiquary Henry Owen as the likely model for Squire Richards, for the gruffly affable portrait James paints recalls him in many respects.[140] From June 1913, and continuing "almost every year until [Owen's] death in 1919," James had vacationed at his new friend's country estate near Haverfordwest in Wales. The friendship had grown out of their work together on the Royal Commission on Public Records, an examination of the state and organization of public archives in England and Wales (no doubt the "official inquiry" alluded to). This commission was the first such official investigation since the original Public Record Office Act of 1838, legislation intended to centralize and rationalize the custody of documents "still scattered about in repositories, of which none were very suitable, and many dangerous and inconvenient and under no general direction."[141] This and subsequent legislation led to the establishment of the Public Record Office in 1838, but by the time of the Royal Commission (beginning in 1910), there remained much to be done to ensure the protection, preservation, and accessibility of the nation's historical records.

As the commission's reports detail, the process of rationalizing and centralizing Britain's public records raised complex and potentially contentious questions. Philippa Levine notes that the Public Record Office's policy of remitting fees for literary research (as opposed to, for example, legal inquiries) suggested an unstated "moral hierarchy," with amateur gentlemen's hobbies privileged over vocational and materially motivated investigations. And yet the need to restrict archival access to qualified persons implied a need for institutionalized scholarly accreditation, so as to prevent those "with very slender literature" from accessing materials responsibly handled only by experts "who have devoted themselves to these enquiries and obtained reputation."[142] Professional archivists sufficiently proficient in historical languages, paleography, and research methods were also clearly required, though the commission's first report (1910) noted that a clerk of the Record Office typically "learns his work by doing it" and recommended in the future at least one year of additional specialized training for all staff.[143] Still, Levine credits early specialists in the Public Record Office—and not in the university system—as representing the earliest English professionals in the historical fields. They were trained experts who regarded their labor as an important national service.[144]

The second commission report was delivered by 18 June 1914. However, production of the third report, which focused on local archives and provincial records, was delayed until after the war, but for the disruptions of which (James regrets), "a great deal of good might have resulted."[145] The third report notes that some local authorities, in fact, had used the war as a "convenient pretext" for refusing the commissioners access to records neglected under their care.[146] As one reviewer of the report noted, "resistance by Beadledom is to be expected" as a matter of course, but the stakes of allowing open access to public records had arguably risen considerably by 1919.[147] Since the time of the 1838 Public Record Office Act, reforms leading to expanded access to government documents had raised concerns of national security and diplomatic sensitivity, but as a special section added to the third report notes, many of the commission's initial findings were only complicated by the events of 1914–18. Not only would provisions for storage and administration need to be reconsidered in light of the suddenly accelerated "immense mass" of records produced during the war (as if history had literally acquired greater weight); there was a sober sense of these documents' potential to "expose the neglect of duty or errors of judgment that have been responsible for national inefficiency or disaster."[148]

On the heels of this final report, James began serving on a second Royal Commission, this time to consider the position of the universities following wartime upheaval. Cambridge and Oxford had previously been completely self-financing institutions, but severe inflation during and after the war compelled both to request emergency government funds. In response, the Asquith Commission was formed in late 1919 to report on the mission and organization of the ancient universities. By 1922 the commission had submitted its recommendations, which in general tended to centralize power within the university system and weaken the traditional autonomy of the individual colleges. They included measures to reform university government, to emphasize graduate-level training, to reorganize faculty work assignments to "secure sufficient leisure" for research, and to open the institutions to a broader spectrum of undergraduate diversity.[149] This last recommendation was imperfectly enacted. The abolition of compulsory Greek (strongly opposed by James) removed a social barrier, but, as Thomas Heyck remarks, on the question of women's access, the commission "had a golden opportunity to act, but did not."[150] The exact contributions James made to this commission are unknown, though his general attitude can be guessed. He refers to the time spent on the committee as "dreary days," which he escaped only when "a severe cold caught from some reformer came to deliver me."[151] This is a perspective shared by Fanshawe, of course, who gratefully escapes to the country after the grind of committee drudgery.

By the time "A View from a Hill" was published, then, the implied scope of Fanshawe's "official inquiry in town" encompassed long-standing tensions—of amateur access and local authority, of centralization and professionalism—now weighted with a certain postwar urgency. At the same time, the Royal Commission on Public Records was also a subject of personal nostalgia for James, as his memoir makes plain: Owen passed away in 1919, just after signing its third report. There is a clear sense in "A View" that Squire Richards represents a vanishing ideal of the local amateur scholar of the kind exemplified (and gently satirized) in the figure of Jonathan Oldbuck in Walter Scott's exceptionally popular 1816 novel *The Antiquary*. As Fanshawe and Richards stroll through the latter's estate, "the Squire, who was great on earthworks, pointed out various spots where he detected or imagined traces of war-ditches and the like."[152] This gentle gibe distinctly recalls a memorable scene in *The Antiquary* where Oldbuck lectures his young acquaintance Mr. Lovel on the landscape from the top of "a gentle eminence" that "commands a fine view." After Lovel admits to seeing before him "something like a ditch, indistinctly marked," Oldbuck remonstrates: "Indistinctly!—pardon me, sir, but the indistinctness must be in your powers of vision—nothing can be more plainly traced—a proper *agger* or *uallum*, with its corresponding ditch or *fossa*. Indistinctly, why, Heaven help you, the lassie, my niece, as lightheaded a goose as womankind affords, saw the traces of the ditch at once."[153] Oldbuck then launches into an imaginative vision of the war ditch as seen in Roman days, concluding with lines adapted from Beaumont and Fletcher's *Bonduca*:

> —See, then, Lovel—See—
> See that huge battle moving from the mountains,
> Their gilt coats shine like dragon scales;—their march
> Like a rough tumbling storm—see them, and view them,
> And then see Rome no more!—[154]

But Oldbuck's imagined detection of the ditch, as well as his rapturous time-traveling view from the hill, is swiftly deflated as Edie Ochiltree (a mendicant wanderer) appears and announces that he had been present to witness the construction of the earthwork only twenty years earlier. Oldbuck's embarrassment (and anxiety lest Edie should publicize his gaffe) dogs the antiquary for the rest of the novel, but even Edie idealizes Oldbuck's general wisdom and judgment: "for a' the nonsense maggots that ye whiles take into your head, ye are the maist wise and discreet o' a' our country gentles."[155] Such is the category James makes of Owen in the person of Richards: the rustic amateur antiquary as prone to local error but blessed with the leisure to develop wisdom as well as a vivid sense of many fields ("you'd better take a general look round first," he advises Fanshawe on the hill's summit).[156] James's own wide-ranging scholarship has been praised for the very same virtue—his commentary in Roxburghe publications described as "a landscape garden . . . carefully planted to reveal vistas that link it with every other aspect of the surrounding country."[157]

But there are many other ways we might view this hill; the only very certain thing seems to be James's awareness of it as a potent pastoral symbol.

On a quite literal level it represents a provincial point of view associated with resident antiquaries like both Baxter and Squire Richards, scholars who defined their intellectual fields according to the local places—the actual fields—in which they "grubbed about," to borrow the squire's phrase.[158] But the hill might also promise a more expansive view: "a vision of history which we cannot win, standing on our lower slope," to quote once more J. B. Bury's plea for scientific history, promising "a true knowledge of the past and to see it in a dry light."[159] The rusticating university man mounting a hill might well view its ascent as reflecting, in a way quite analogous to the logic of Spenser's eclogue, professional standing, academic aspiration, and the "dry light" of transpersonal replicability (at least before the introduction of Baxter's liquid filters). After all, Fanshawe on holiday would be "going down" to visit Richards, in the common phrase for taking leave of Cambridge or Oxford, centers of academic life to which one "goes up" regardless of physical topography. As Paul R. Deslandes has noted, these expressions disclose a "somewhat skewed symbolic and geographical interpretation of the world (especially among those who departed the university for northern locations)."[160]

But the skewed view on the hill is also complicated—to say the least—by the haunted field glasses, an instrument now in the possession of Richards but belonging more properly to the perspective of Baxter.[161] In fact, the moment at which Fanshawe raises these glasses to his eyes represents the point in the story where we decisively shift from pastoral nostalgia to a creeping antiquarian unease. In 1913, Cambridge professor Arthur Quiller-Couch felt that the university had largely escaped "the more calculating malignity of Royal Commissions," so that "a hundred daily reminders connect us with the Middle Ages, or, if you prefer Arnold's phrase, whisper its lost enchantments."[162] Fanshawe, fleeing the postwar university, clearly longs to reconnect with an enchanting "medieval" mode of existence, as if Squire Richards himself is residing within his favorite subject of study. The glasses provide a vision of past reality in its architectural texture—the fine look of Fulnaker's tower, most obviously—but they may also suggest access to what Hans Robert Jauss calls a past "horizon of expectations."[163] Absurdly simplified, the horizon of that medieval past would be defined by a clear binary of salvation (church) and damnation (gallows hill), so that the field glasses provide not only a material vision of the past but a spiritual one as well. The view is reminiscent in this respect of that afforded Piers Plowman in the passage cited above: there, the divide is represented by hellish *depe dyches &*

derke and a heavenly *toure on a toft* (tower on a hill). Of course, the *fair felde of folke* in the middle cannot see these levels, but the medieval mind felt their presence—just as Fanshawe will come to detect something more sinister in the pristine English countryside. Yet the initial fantasy of the field glasses, on first glance, seems of a piece with an Oldbuckian capacity for a kind of temporal stereoscopy, the eye of the squire's leisured present merging with the perspective of the presecularized, preindustrial, preprofessional past in one seamless outlook. In fact, this latter observation provides one explanation for the odd detail that Richards himself cannot see anything through the magic binoculars. Like someone peering through a telescope at his own feet, the squire's perspective is already too close to what the glasses display. He cannot grasp the focal plane.[164]

But it is Baxter's vision, not Richards's, that comes to disturb. James's narrative device seems calibrated to perform a kind of antiquarian optometry—clarifying the distinction between one kind of amateur vision and another. It is easy enough to spot the ethical problem with Baxter's unorthodox methods, the gruesomeness of his orbital brew of stewed bones. But this is only one approach he takes; he also fashions for himself a mask made from a human skull, a simpler if apparently less effective way to "look through a dead man's eyes."[165] That perspective seems to be the real point and pleasure of his activities, and the metaphor lives on in medieval studies: "Although seeing with medieval eyes is impossible for us," writes Laura Kendrick in her recent essay "Games Medievalists Play," "we can try to use ekphrastic passages like the one above as 'medieval spectacles' to correct the distortions of our modern vision."[166] Yet it is nevertheless telling that the "corrected" visual data Baxter's glasses provide are not inherently lost, forbidden, or irrecoverable: by toponym alone we know that Gallows Hill was once a place of execution and that the tower of Fulnaker could have easily survived to the present (like that of Great Malvern Priory). As a reward for black magic, these visions seem utterly pedestrian, indeed revealing nothing fundamentally inaccessible. Nor would James necessarily conceive of the medieval era strictly in terms of unbridgeable alterity. In a lecture on humor in the Middle Ages he stresses that, although rare, "[t]here were men of mediaeval times who looked upon life with the same eyes as ourselves" (his prime example is Walter Map).[167] But if the magic here is not to erase difference or to achieve reconstruction, what is it?

Christopher Cherry (in an article in the journal *Philosophy* not otherwise interested either in James or in medieval studies) has argued that "A View from a Hill" illustrates not a question of epistemology but rather a longing for the experience of "sheer pastness," the "past as radically disconnected from the present." Cherry calls this "distinctively weird" desire for the past "aesthetic" ("for want of a better word").[168] In recent years the complex pleasures of engaging the past have been explored by a number of medievalists, including, among others, Nicholas Watson, Thomas Prendergast, Stephanie Trigg, Carolyn Dinshaw, and of course Jauss, who like Cherry discusses medieval difference in terms of distance and aesthetic experience.[169] But Cherry also emphasizes the crossing of that distance, the "unimpeded vision from the present to the past" that Baxter's binoculars allow. What is crucial, he says, is "temporal bi-location," though what he describes is very distinct from (even opposed to) a stereoscopic merging of present and past of the kind we see in Squire Richards's antiquarian outlook. Instead, "the subject belongs to, and is aware of belonging to, the present but 'returns' episodically to a past which he is able to spectate." Here, then, is the crucial aspect of James's optics: "Fanshawe, on the receiving end of the binoculars, is firmly planted in the—that is, his—present, and knows it (which is why he finds the business so disturbing). So the all-important feature of self-conscious retro-perception is assured. He has an eye in both the past and present, and yet his present eye remains dominant." The fantasy here, Cherry emphasizes, must remain a fantasy, simply because this desire to experience the past in the present cannot logically be fulfilled without appeal to supernatural metaphor. If we could time travel, the past would become present and thus "flat and insipid," losing its atmospheric quality of pastness.[170] Something else is wanted, and this alternative brand of temporal "binocularity," we come to recognize, is the story's main concern: its central fantasy and a source of unrest.

Cherry's discussion is invaluable for understanding James's "View," but his interest in the story is casual and limited to its value for illustrating his own philosophical concerns. In fact, he misreads the tale badly on a point that is central to James's pastoral-horror, referring to Fanshawe as "a man of leisure and antiquarian interests."[171] Fanshawe, of course, is pointedly not a man of leisure, and the pastoral longing provoked by professional academic life is the story's point of departure. Its conclusion, however, is the casting out of Baxter, whose sacrifice, like that of Karswell, purifies the profession. In fact, Baxter is frog-marched off to his death by ghosts who conduct themselves less like medieval revenants than like agents of a shadowy central authority:

"'Tis best you mind your own business. Put in your head," the ghosts tell a startled neighbor who is unlucky enough to witness the moonlit abduction. Louise Fradenburg, analyzing desire for the Middle Ages from a Lacanian point of view, argues that medieval studies has attempted to sacrifice pleasure and the enjoyment of pastness for the sake of an asceticized professionalism: "What I mean to emphasize is our need to continue examining the powerful consequences of our relations with the dead, and the modes of enjoyment at stake therein. To be a medievalist entails for many of us a way of loving and enjoying what is gone, often *because* it is gone; and 'love' and 'enjoyment' here are understood as potentially entailing the ambivalence, the rage, the avidity of incorporation of which psychoanalysis speaks when it speaks of love."[172] Fradenburg emphasizes that professional ascetic piety involves its own particular pleasurable sacrifices, and, arguably, James's work as a whole registers in many ways how desire for discipline and rigor can, counterintuitively, come to feed an "antiquarian" set of impulses. After all, Fanshawe's situation is actually closer to Baxter's than to that of the squire, at least in the need that both men have to sell their time professionally (Baxter works as a watchmaker in town). And Baxter's portrait is not all that unusual—boiled bones aside. In fact, it rather uncannily adumbrates the career of Basil Brown (1888–1977), an antiquary who—along with being an accomplished telescope enthusiast—is credited with the most significant archaeological discovery in the annals of Anglo-Saxon studies, the ship burial at Sutton Hoo.[173] According to one contemporary, Brown accomplished his fieldwork by "bicycling around the lanes and using binoculars (when access was not permitted) to study exposed sections of sand and crag." Brown had "a quite remarkable flair for smelling out antiquities. . . . His method was to locate a feature and then pursue wherever it led. . . . The sad thing is that with training he might have been a brilliant archaeologist."[174] Yet the sense of regret in "A View from a Hill" is not so much for talent left unprofessionalized as for the pleasures of amateurism itself, a mode of enjoyment no longer possible in the present.

Our first hint of this comes in a dream Fanshawe has the night after his view from the hill. He finds himself strolling through a kind of prelapsarian antiquarian garden with "a rockery made of old wrought stones, pieces of window tracery from a church, and even bits of figures." Feeling a strong impulse to pull out and examine a sculptured capital, he removes it only to find—to his great anxiety—a tin label with the injunction "On no account move this stone." But out of the dark gap left by his curiosity emerges a quite peculiar terror, analogous in some ways to the disembodied runic mouth that menaces Dunning:

> Something stirred in the blackness, and then, to his intense horror, a hand emerged—a clean right hand in a neat cuff and coat-sleeve, just in the attitude of a hand that means to shake yours. He wondered whether it would not be rude to let it alone. But, as he looked at it, it began to grow hairy and dirty and thin, and also to change its pose and stretch out as if to take hold of his leg. At that he dropped all thought of politeness, decided to run, screamed and woke himself up.[175]

The cuffed hand beckons with an invitation to join a sacred band of university workers, those who will legitimate the labor of this garden, but it swiftly shrivels to reveal a deficiency, a thinness at the root of the enterprise.

What makes James shrink from the hard bargain of the new professionalism? It is not only the leisure, privacy, and privilege of the gentleman scholar, though James certainly registers these losses with regret (and makes it clear that he does not at all enjoy the drudgery of committee work). There is something more, hinted at enigmatically in the ending, where, as the field glasses are laid to their final rest, we seem to be invited to consider what, if anything, was the value of Baxter's bizarre and erratic encounters with the past:

> As they smoothed the turf over it, the Squire, handing the spade to Patten, who had been a reverential spectator, remarked to Fanshawe: "It's almost a pity you took that thing into the church: you might have seen more than you did. Baxter had them for a week, I make out, but I don't see that he did much in the time."
>
> "I'm not sure," said Fanshawe, "there is that picture of Fulnaker Priory Church."[176]

What is it about Baxter's encounter with Fulnaker Abbey that is worthy of this wistfulness? After Fanshawe wakes from his dream, he strains to recapture its impression: "He lay awake for some little time, fixing the details of the last dream in his mind, and wondering in particular what the figures had been which he had seen or half seen on the carved capital. Something quite incongruous, he felt sure; but that was the most he could recall."[177] I would argue that the elusive incongruity of these figures on the capital is related to the temporality Fanshawe experiences on the hill—a vision that uniquely allows him "to grasp the past," in Cherry's words.

In his conclusion, in fact, Cherry offers a "palliative" for those "reluctant irretrievalists" who feel this impossible desire to experience a sense of present pastness. As a surrogate for the supernatural metaphor of haunted binoculars, Cherry recommends the experience of excavating an ancient object untouched since its original deposit, so that "no developmental history intervenes."[178] The telescoping of time afforded by such excavation allows the past to touch the present, so to speak, to collapse temporal distance while paradoxically maintaining it. Cherry does not mention, of course, that pursuing such a palliative would be—for an unskilled amateur in this day and age—ethically questionable. And this may be, oddly, the very thing that makes Baxter's instrument so compelling. At any rate, Fanshawe seems to raise a very similar metaphor when he attempts to open the wooden case containing the binoculars: "Why, your disgusting Borgia box has scratched me, drat it," he complains.[179] The reference here is probably to "the notoriety of the Borgias as poisoners," as noted by Jones, who sees here foreshadowing of the poisonous contents of the field glasses' liquid filters.[180] But the particular allusion may be sharper, for the notion of a "Borgia box" in this context probably recalls the Borgias' practice of wearing rings with secret compartments, or "boxes," of poison, which they supposedly might apply to enemies by way of a fatal handshake (the device is explicitly mentioned in "The Ash-Tree").[181] A delicious anecdote (probably spurious) circulated in James's time recounting how, as it happened one day, a modern gentleman was examining an authentic Borgia poison ring in a Paris shop when he inadvertently scratched his finger and nearly lost his life.[182] The force and novelty of this urban legend derive from its temporal strangeness: the distance of bygone malice matched by the intimacy of the insidious cut. Here, then, would be a poisonous analogue to Cherry's palliative: the past pricking the present across a gulf of time. A "Borgia box," we might say, is a very fitting case for Baxter's glasses, as this is exactly the experience the instrument allows.

S. T. Joshi understands that the blood of Fanshawe's cut finger "triggers the supernatural effect," but what have really been sacrificed in the story are the incongruous pleasures of amateur encounters with the past:

medievalisms unmediated by context, method, or defensible, professional purpose.[183] It is not just that amateur triumphs like those of Basil Brown have been regulated out of existence; it is that medieval studies itself has purified its disciplines, distancing itself (as Dinshaw might say) from the affective thrills of the past's "touching" the present.[184] Baxter indulges as well in other delectations, including some (his "certain love of opposition and controversy") aligned with those of Karswell.[185] James would be pleased to see the end of such gratifications, no doubt, if that were in fact to be the transpersonal windfall of specialist publishing. But the atmosphere we feel most strongly at the conclusion of these two tales is not one of relief or release from the enchantments of amateurism. We are left only with apprehension, dreadful misgivings for the hard bargains of future professional life. The relish of the past, we fear, has turned to ashes in the mouth.

3

EX CATHEDRA

It is something of a mystery to his biographers why M. R. James was never ordained in the Church of England, despite the strength of his faith and the suitability of his talents.[1] But if James long identified as a scholar and researcher, the better question may be how his chosen line of work came to be conceived as a profession largely separate from the church. Certainly, many in the late nineteenth century sensed that a movement was under way toward the secularization of scholarly culture, with the clergy's devotion to other duties increasingly edging out time for academic work. In his 1878 book *The Cathedral: Its Necessary Place in the Life and Work of the Church*, E. W. Benson (father of A. C. and E. F.) expressed concern over this trend, noting the "ominous kindly silence" that would now fall when clergymen made attempts to engage in serious intellectual conversation.[2] Such impressions were supported by measurable indications of institutional change. A steep decline in ordination rates for Oxbridge graduates in the late nineteenth century coincided with a growing divide between clerical vocations and academic and educational professions, part of a larger trend in which many of the church's other traditional functions—pastoral support, relief for the poor, administration of institutions such as marriage—were being at least partially adopted as new responsibilities of the state.[3] The abolition of religious tests and compulsory chapel—and of the celibacy requirement—meant that English educational life was less and less explicitly tied to a particular religious discipline, practice, or viewpoint, although some institutions, especially those heavily attended by the upper classes (epitomized by James's own Eton and King's), continued to be closely affiliated with the Anglican Church.[4] Such a shift—howsoever we wish to account for or conceptualize it—brought inevitable friction: it was common knowledge that James was aligned with the "godly" party at King's, and when elected provost was urged to accept by Luxmoore, lest the college "fall into the hands of the philistine & agnostic."[5]

Though these institutional shifts were no doubt evident enough, the exact meaning of a "secularized" profession was probably as unsettled in James's day as it is in our own. The term itself first arose in English to describe the transfer of church buildings and property to an ownership outside original religious foundations, although etymologically the word can be traced back further to the Latin *saeculum* (a generation, an age), or (later, in medieval use) "the world," the latter sense informed by a Christian distinction between a mortal temporality and a spiritual reality outside worldly time.[6] The division between secular and sacred realms, we might say, has always also demanded temporal splits, a pattern repeated historiographically in the enduring conceptual break between the modern and medieval periods. And yet many professed medievalists of the present day have come to view the concept of secularization as a troublesome foundation stone of their discipline, one that precariously establishes the Middle Ages both as an identifiable period and as a sacred object of professional study. In this area, for example, the recent work of Kathleen Davis is particularly noteworthy for arguing that modern concepts of sovereignty are founded in a colonial periodization that defines both the European past and non-Western cultures as "religious, static, and ahistorical."[7] Davis's arguments are connected to a larger critique of temporal schemes that, in Johannes Fabian's famous phrase, "deny coeval" status to peoples thereby defined outside Western secular modernity.[8] Thus the establishment of the Middle Ages as a category is fundamental to the creation of a "sacred" modern scholarly discipline cleansed of such impurities as personal whim, imaginative speculation, or religious belief—or at least the illusion of such an achievement. For Bruno Latour, though, such apparent purification only serves to abet the proliferation of an unacknowledged network of impurities that operate, as it were, below the surface. In actuality, he insists, "we have never been modern."[9]

For these and other reasons, the coherence and legitimacy of these intersecting categories have often been called into question. And even among those who claim for the Western present a distinctly secular era, the shift is often conceived not so much as a clean break from Christianity but as a mutated reiteration of the time that secularization succeeds. Reinhart Koselleck, for example, has argued that modern faith in limitless progress functions "to satisfy soteriological demands" previously discharged by an eschatology that allowed for an indefinitely deferred end of time (and, in the indeterminate and emptily ahistorical meantime, for an institutionally stable church).[10] In this temporal scheme, the End remains in the vaguely remote offing through the working of an unspecified *katechon,* the mysterious "restrainer" named by Paul in his Second Epistle to the Thessalonians, in which he assures the faithful that, although the end times were imminent, they had not yet arrived. Whatever this *katechon* is—the Holy Roman Empire, some thought, or some other temporal force—it works to restrain and delay the coming of the Antichrist whose arrival heralds the beginning of the End. However, in the modern era (Koselleck argues), a principle of progress substitutes for this function, producing in its stead not an elastically uneventful gap in salvation history but rather an accelerated sense of change along with a rich, full sense of the difference between one time and another.

Again, though, it is difficult to keep these middle times from blending together. On the one hand, we might imagine, there is the ahistorically minded Middle Ages itself, a past world that viewed its present in terms of a community of faithful living in the hallowed interval between Christ's Resurrection and the Second Coming. On the other, there is an emptier time as conceived through the secular lens of periodization, a Middle Ages we come to recognize retrospectively, whether as a more or less real and isolable epoch dividing ancient from modern or as a powerful if illusory "period concept" inextricably entangled with the history of imperial rule. Either way, the muddle highlights the complexity involved in keeping present temporal needs separate from those of the past—a division that in academic circles would also map onto the elusive distinction between mere medievalism and a medieval studies that aspires to a disinterested recovery of the past. And this project of modernizing the profession—one in which James, as we have seen, was heavily if not unambivalently invested—breeds a particularly fascinating set of paradoxes also because the objects of study are so closely associated with his personal faith. Ultimately, massy questions of modern secularization—whether it truly may be said to exist, whether it defines a new era—are more than I can attempt to address here directly. But it may be possible to achieve something more local, confining myself to the particularities of James's fiction. My primary care in this chapter, therefore, will be for perceptions and tensions, and in particular for those that James may have had and felt in relation to his own work as a professional student of the Christian Middle Ages.

A secularization of modern academic culture might indeed produce ambivalence, particularly for those whose investments in the past are multiple and diverse: for those who find, among other things, both scholarly interest and religious significance in antiquarian objects—or some conflicted mix of the two. For instance, James spent a good deal of his academic life gathering and analyzing biblical apocrypha, materials that would have been regarded by a man of orthodox belief as delusional (if fascinating) complications to the true scriptural record.[11] James's earliest academic publications are his most blunt, but his basic attitude remained consistent: "To me there is real pathos in the crude attempts of these ignorant or perverted souls to tell their friends or their disciples what—to be feared or hoped for—lies in the unseen future or on the other side of the grave."[12] As early as 1883—in an essay delivered to the Chitchat Society—we find James agonizing over the slim possible value of studying such materials: here, New Testament apocrypha are identified as the perfect nadir of "useless knowledge," the object of an unhealthy and perverse scholarly attention. And yet James is drawn to the subject, and concludes by noting that if his audience can provide justifications that "afford any loophole toward the gratification of those instincts within me which I have been steadily snubbing during the whole of this paper, I shall be thoroughly satisfied."[13] As Roger Luckhurst points out, James's professional efforts to systematize the study of apocryphal texts could function as a way to contain the inherent challenge such writings posed to the textual foundations of his faith.[14] Here is one form of satisfaction. Inevitably, though, the main loophole through which James must slip is cut in the name of historical completeness:

> But if the pathos is obscured to many readers by the crude fancy or the barbarous language, not many will deny that these books possess considerable historical value. The high-road will serve us well enough if we want to visit our cathedral cities: but in order to get an idea of

the popular architecture of the district we must often digress into obscure and devious by-paths. The apocryphal books stand in the relation of by-paths—not always clean or pleasant—to the broad and well-trodden high-roads of orthodox patristic literature.[15]

Thirty years later, we find the loophole largely unaltered, James citing the value of apocryphal texts to "the lover and student of mediaeval literature and art" but warning against their originary misconception: "The truth is that they must *not be regarded only from the point of view which they claim for themselves*. In almost every other aspect they have a great and enduring interest" (emphasis added).[16] This maxim applies comfortably enough to errant and patently eccentric apocrypha. But such a paradox of disinterested study—that a text's misguided "sense of itself" is *alone* to be excluded from serious professional consideration—arguably grows more troubling as we turn to antiquarian objects closer to home.

It is a tension we feel in James's first ghost story, "Canon Alberic's Scrap-Book," a tale centered around the medieval cathedral of Saint-Bertrand-de-Comminges. As I have touched upon in the introduction, the inaugural horror of the Jamesian canon manifests itself through an image redrawn "from the life" but ultimately derived from the Testament of Solomon, an early apocryphal text in which the biblical king struggles to command demons. In James's intense version, their potential for shocking violence—not held fully at bay—is associated with Alberic's dismantling of medieval books, savagery that Dennistoun finds "unprincipled" (to say the least) but that seems actually to have been performed with some semblance of order—one informed in particular by the traditional stages of Christian salvation history, so that the reconstituted book begins at the beginning with despoiled illuminations from Genesis, followed by scraps from King David's Psalms, followed by a precious excision from a patristic commentary on the words of Christ. Dennistoun, by contrast, would impose on the codex his own—postmedieval—sense of order, for even as he leafs through the book, he begins assigning preliminary dates and provenances, first steps in the process of inflicting on the broken book a professional's sense of bibliographic regularity. Alberic's biblioclastic activities displace local manuscript contexts in a way repulsive to the professional, and this sense of scholarly ruination is perhaps why Dennistoun alludes later to the demon-infested wastelands of Isaiah 34 (a text crucial to another tale of cathedral devilry, discussed further on in this chapter). And yet that Dennistoun, the systematizing scholar, comes to recognize a sympathetic affinity with the abject Alberic is evident in the tale's striking change in attitude toward the canon, whose wicked ghost, at the outset, terrorizes the verger: "He was laughing in the church," the frightened man reports to his distressed daughter.[17] By the tale's epilogue, though, Dennistoun and the narrator are making a special pilgrimage to visit the tomb of Alberic, for whom Dennistoun is now sponsoring requiem masses: "I hope it isn't wrong: you know I am a Presbyterian."[18] Inevitably, the scrapbook is taken off to Cambridge (minus the troublesome drawing, which is photographed and destroyed). But there remains an almost penitential sense—traceable in so many of James's stories—that outside expertise should never quite take precedence over local beliefs and structures of meaning.

A cathedral destination, particularly one as remote as Saint-Bertrand-de-Comminges, is an apt point of departure for this theme. Such places are not after all the natural home of professionals. On the contrary, they are sites in which local, amateur, communal, and daily engagements with the past come first, where the pretense of academic distance collapses. Stephanie Trigg has meditated on the elastic fashion in which cathedrals—in contrast to exclusive specialist preserves such as the manuscript reading room—must accommodate a diversity of visitors, from worshipper to tourist, from pilgrim to scholar. Professed medievalists, she stresses, often undergo a "mixed experience" walking through such spaces, one informed by the multiple (and sometimes irreconcilable) investments a single person can make in the past.[19] James's own case offers a striking example. For him, we can be sure, cathedrals were liminal locations in which work and leisure, critical distance and personal belonging, mingled. For thirty years, between his undergraduate years until the outbreak of the Great War, he regularly spent his holidays with friends on cycling expeditions abroad, eventually visiting nearly every cathedral in France. Saint-Bertrand was only a drop in his bucket list, and nearer to home he was equally assiduous in the pleasures of church architecture.[20] In the early 1890s, James was considering adopting this avocation as his primary specialty as a scholar, with a particular interdisciplinary ambition to employ literary evidence in the explication of what he called "Christian archaeology," including church glass, wall painting, and sculpture.[21] Ultimately, however, James's interest in medieval art was to remain largely a pet interest, at least in comparison with his contributions to textual and bibliographic fields, his enjoyment of cathedrals a sanctuary from the regular routines of the university calendar.

Cathedrals—particularly English cathedrals—do, however, hold an important place in his ghost stories. Chronotopes for historical and cultural continuity, in which present meanings are nested within ancient stone, cathedrals function in James's fiction as sites for interrogating fears built into the very fabric of medieval studies. As this chapter will detail, two of James's stories in particular—"The Stalls of Barchester Cathedral" and "An Episode of Cathedral History"—are especially constructed around "cathedraly" settings, but they share in addition a very similar literary architecture. In each tale a carefully worked medievalism serves as a kind of narrative keystone, joining together the affective thrills of the tale to its thematic thrust. In Barchester, the crucial piece is James's frightening refashioning of an Old English poem, a remaking that upends the text's Christian vision even as the arch-villain archdeacon Haynes sacrifices all for the sake of bureaucratic order and system. His zeal, James implies, is of a piece with the "restorative" work that that will sweep away the local furnishings of Barchester's choir, leaving behind in its place a bare ruin. But the Gothic Revival of the nineteenth century is confronted even more squarely in Southminster, where James again shows his distaste for arrogant outsiders intent on leveling the untidy particularity of local antiquities for the sake of an ersatz abstraction. As we will see, restoration becomes a monstrous attempt to resurrect a fabricated past.

But is there anything at stake here beyond contempt for the architectural absurdities of the previous midcentury, a pernicious period in James's estimation, but one that by his day was itself already receding well into the past? There may in fact be a case to be made that James's antirestoration narratives are best understood within the sight line of his own time and position as a reluctant member of a rising first generation of university professionals, whose engagements with the past also entailed tensions of local expertise, scholarly synthesis, and the secularization of English heritage. As the center of medieval studies shifted away from parochial antiquarianism, university scholars were faced with new stress points in a profession counterweighted by the authority of experts at home in their fields. Local attachments and isolated meanings, the observances and convictions of resident enthusiasts, must give way to the national project of colonizing a backward past. Enthroned within the Oxbridge establishment, James was clearly a part of this program, but he also seems to have struggled with its implications. A new equilibrium was required, but few blueprints were available apart from those patterns established by the very reformers James had most reason to revile. Quite apart from local outrages visited upon the stones and institutions James loved, here is much of the weight holding these tales together.

NIGHTMARE OF THE ROOD

"The Stalls of Barchester Cathedral" (1910) was first published in the *Contemporary Review* with a subtitle that reflects its framing device: "Materials for a Ghost Story."[22] The tale opens with the narrator beginning to make sense of a sequence of events pieced together from a published obituary along with a box of unpublished letters and journals discovered in a college library. The Jamesian narrator has been cataloguing manuscripts in this institution and in this way has come across the documents, out of which he is permitted by the librarian "to make a story . . . provided I disguise the identity of the people concerned."[23] The disguise he chooses is the fictional cathedral of Barchester, borrowed from Trollope's famous Barsetshire novels, a choice that reflects an obvious parallel with the best known of these, *Barchester Towers* (1857), the first chapter of which describes the anxiety of Archdeacon Grantly as he attends the deathbed of his father, the current bishop.[24] Grantly genuinely loves his elderly father but knows that his own chances to succeed him to the bishopric depend upon a swift death before political winds shift. In the event, the bishop dies too late and his mourning son is disappointed in his ambition, though Trollope portrays with sympathy the good man's conflicted position.[25] James's version of this plot is altogether darker, with the ambitious Dr. Haynes not only longing for the death of Archdeacon Pulteney, who "refused to depart until he had attained the age of ninety-two,"[26] but indeed actively arranging for the nonagenarian to break his neck at the bottom of a staircase.

Once Pulteney is out of the way, the newly installed Haynes sets about a reforming effort to clean up and systematize his predecessor's neglected post. All goes well until Haynes happens to place his hand on some curious wooden carvings in the cathedral stalls, touching off a series of supernatural horrors that end with his own death on the staircase, "the object," apparently, "of a brutal and murderous attack."[27] In an epilogue to the narrative of Haynes's downfall, the narrator visits Barchester and learns more about the later history of the wooden statuettes. He finds that one of the carved figures ended up eventually being salvaged from a wood yard—before finally being burned to ashes by a father whose children found it frightening. Before its destruction, though, the figure had broken apart, yielding a scrap of paper with an enigmatic description of words heard in a dream:

> "When I grew in the Wood
> I was water'd wth Blood
> Now in the Church I stand
> Who that touches me with his Hand
> If a Bloody hand he bear
> I councell him to be ware
> Lest he be fetch away
> Whether by night or day,
> But chiefly when the wind blows high
> In a night of February."
> "This I drempt, 26 Febr. A° 1699. John Austin."[28]

It is surprising that past discussions of this tale have not raised the issue of the clear source of John Austin's dream. But there can be no real doubt that James is deliberately echoing the Old English *Dream of the Rood*, a renowned early medieval poem describing a vision of the Holy Cross (or "rood"; OE *rōd*).[29] One of the most outstanding and distinctive features of the poem is its use of prosopopoeia, first-person narration from the perspective of the cross itself, which relates for the dreamer its singular life history as a tree harvested from the forest and transformed first into a *fraco[ð]es gealga* (gallows for the criminal) before being glorified as the sacred cross of Christianity.[30] The resemblances between this text and the inscription found in the Barchester statuette are striking, to say the least. Compare James's text with the beginning of the cross's speech in *The Dream of the Rood*:

> "Þæt wæs geara iu—ic þæt gyta geman—
> þæt ic wæs aheawen   holtes on ende,
> astyred of stefne minum.   Genaman me ðær strange feondas,
> geworhton him þær to wæfersyne,   heton me heora wergas hebban;
> bæron me ðær beornas on eaxlum,   oððæt hie me on beorg asetton,
> gefæstnodon me þær feondas genoge."

(That was a long time ago—I can still remember it—that I was hewn down from the edge of the woods, separated from my stump. Strange enemies carried me off and made of me a spectacle; they commanded me to lift up their criminals, men who bore me there on their shoulders, until they set me on the hill, where many enemies made me fast.)[31]

A bit further on, narrating the crucifixion, the cross remarks: *Eall ic wæs mid blode bestemed* (I was all wetted with blood), a detail that survives as well on the eighth-century Northumbrian Ruthwell Cross, which contains a partial text of the poem carved into its stone.[32] The other major analogue for *The Dream of the Rood* is an inscription found on the Brussels reliquary, which was believed to hold fragments of the True Cross:

Rood is my name. Once long ago I bore
Trembling, bedewed with blood, the mighty King.[33]

Needless to say, these parallels—with what we well might call James's "Nightmare of the Rood"—cannot be considered coincidental. In fact, the first three lines might be thought of as a kind of riddle that misleads the solver into guessing "Holy Cross" as its implied false answer: "When I grew in the Wood / I was water'd wth Blood / Now in the Church I stand." From there, of course, the description grows darker, and, knowing the backstory, we recognize that the speaker is not a sacred object so much as a cursed, heathen one, a wooden relic of the Hanging Oak that once stood in "Holywood," the name of which hints at a pre-Christian meaning of *halig* and calls attention to the process of pagan conversion embodied, in multiple ways, by the Old English poem.[34]

Here, then, we again see evidence of James's interest in enigmatic texts. But the choice to refigure *The Dream of the Rood* as a kind of visionary riddle was not conjured in a vacuum, considering the long-standing tendency for scholars to compare the *Rood* poem to a range of medieval textual categories. Albert S. Cook, in his edition of 1905, remarks on the generic oddity of *The Dream of the Rood* ("The second part, the address of the cross, is unique in its composition")[35] and likens the rood's speech to Greek and Latin epigrams, epitaphs, and ekphrasis, as well as to the inscription on the

Alfred Jewel (the handle of a pointer used to aid the reading of texts): *Ælfred mec heht gewyrcean* (Alfred commanded me to be made).[36] The formula *X me fecit* (So-and-so made me) is a common one for ancient and medieval engraved objects, and in James's deliciously titled story "The Malice of Inanimate Objects," similar words adorn the victim of a malicious razorblade: *GEO. W. FECI* (which could be translated as "I George W. did [this]" or "I George W. *made* [this]").[37] It is a cutthroat inscription that renders the marked man a lifeless object.

The genre of James's Barchester text likewise dumbfounds its readers: "'I suppose it is a charm or a spell: wouldn't you call it something of that kind?' said the curator. 'Yes,' I said, 'I suppose one might.'"[38] Here, quite likely, is an allusion to the medieval source's reputation for standing alone, *sui generis*. James's text is indeed difficult to classify: is it, in fact, a charm or spell? A demonic dream vision, a prophetic revelation? More than anything, the Barchester "Nightmare of the Rood" assumes the character of a riddle of the first-person kind, a form particularly favored in Anglo-Saxon England. This makes some sense, for the lion's share of Cook's analogues for *The Dream of the Rood* are drawn from medieval riddle collections: the Latin enigmas of Symphosius (fourth–sixth century), Aldhelm (ca. 639–709), Tatwine (d. 734), and Eusebius (eighth century), and especially the famous vernacular riddle collection found in the tenth-century "Exeter Book" anthology of Old English poetry. Yet Cook's survey concludes that such comparisons are limited: "As a matter of fact, it can hardly be maintained that the narrative of the cross contains anything enigmatic, but only that the mode of description, involving quasi-personification and an account in the first person, resembles that of the riddles."[39]

James, however, seems to emphasize and to augment this base resemblance with borrowings from the conventions of Old English riddling. For instance, the next three lines, "Who that touches me with his Hand / If a Bloody hand he bear / I councell him to be ware," echo a common detail of first-person riddles in the Exeter Book: onions, cups, and other objects telling of being touched, gripped, and handled by men and women.[40] Moreover, James's restrictive *who*-clause readily recalls the paratactic style of these verse riddles: *feleþ sona / mines gemotes seo þe mec nearwað, / wif wundenlocc* (Soon enough she will feel that contact with me, the one who confines me, the woman with braided hair).[41] This reaches beyond sexual metaphor (in this last example) to physical violence in Exeter Riddle 24 (to be solved *boga* [bow]), which warns of irreversible harm to anyone, *gif hine hrineð þæt me of hrife fleogeð* (if that which flies from my insides touches him).⁴²

The Dream of the Rood also resembles many Old English riddles in its focus on the transformation of raw materials or living creatures—ore, oxen, sheep—into manufactured objects: iron swords, leather shoes, parchment manuscripts. The most common version of this riddling pattern in the Exeter Book involves living trees remade as wooden objects: oaken ships, drinking cups, the beam of a battering ram, among others. Exeter Riddle 92 has been commonly solved since James's day as "beech tree" (fashioned into various items, including a wooden shield):

> Ic wæs brunra beot,   beam on holte,
> freolic feorhbora   ond foldan wæstm . . .
>   . . . Nu eom guðwigan
> hyhtlic hildewæpen. . . .
>
> (I was the joy of brown creatures [i.e., beech mast], a tree in the forest,
> a beautiful living creature and a plant of the earth. . . . *Now I am a joyful battle-weapon of the warrior*)⁴³

Here, and in many Old English transformation riddles of this type, the shift in description of the speaker's former life to that of its greatly altered present is signaled by a clause with *nu* (now) in the stressed position. It is a very common and distinctive feature of these texts, and numerous examples might be cited. An initial *Nu* marks the truncated split from one state to another in just the same way as we find in James's speaking oak statuette: "Now in the Church I stand." In one final example, Exeter Riddle 73 speaks from the perspective of a spear carved from the wood of an ash tree:

> Ic on wonge aweox,   wunode þær mec feddon
> hruse ond heofonwolcn,   oþþæt me onhwyrfdon me
> gearum frodne,   þa me grome wurdon,
> of þære gecynde   þe ic ær cwic beheold,
> onwendan mine wisan,   wegedon mec of earde,
> gedydon þæt ic sceolde   wiþ gesceape minum
> on bonan willan   bugan hwilum.
> Nu eom frean mines   folme bysigo[d]

(I grew up in the field, dwelled where the earth and sky fed me, until in my elder days they changed me—when they became hostile to me—from the condition I previously held in life. They altered my essence, carried me from the earth, carried it out so that I must—against my nature—bow at times to the will of a killer. *Now I am active in the hand of my lord*.) (Emphasis added.)[44]

Needless to say, it is not my purpose here to propose new analogues for *The Dream of the Rood*; these connections have in fact long been noticed—and that is part of the point. James's borrowing is not a vague reference but, as we would expect, shows a detailed familiarity with and subtle understanding of the medieval poem and the comparative and scholarly traditions surrounding it. And the effect is a "Nightmare of the Rood" that selectively mirrors the darkly enigmatic potential of its source text, while transforming it into something altogether darker.[45]

There is strong evidence that the *Rood* poem is not simply borrowed at tale's end as a resonant antiquarian touch but is in fact the essential seed from which the narrative grows. Murder and its supernatural punishment are the obvious focal points here, and these two elements are represented in the text, respectively, by the oaken staircase on which Pulteney and Haynes die and the statuettes carved from the roodlike Hanging Oak. The poetic justice is plain. The particular way in which Haynes sacrifices Pulteney in the name of managerial efficiency is very suggestive as well: "Why, as far as I can make out, there was a stair-rod missing, and [the maid] never mentioned it, and the poor archdeacon set his foot quite on the edge of the step—you know how slippery that oak is—and it seems he must have fallen almost the whole flight and broken his neck."[46] This death is no mere mischance, but neither, perhaps, is it an accident that a "stair-rod" brings about Pulteney's downfall. The word, which refers to metal pins used to hold staircase carpets in place, is also a perfectly apt compound to describe the tale's "stair-rood" structure. As the Anglo-Saxon cross declares, *Rod wæs ic aræred* (I was raised up as a *rōd*).[47] Such wordplay might come naturally to a master of dead languages.[48]

At any rate, it is clear that James has grafted a theme of murder onto the *Rood* poem, a rather surprising transformation indeed. It is possible, though, that James's choice is influenced by medieval precedent and the legend of the "Tree of Cain," in which it was imagined that widespread homicidal enmity sprouted up more or less literally as wicked vegetation watered by the blood of Abel.[49] The roots of this tradition include apocryphal texts such as the Acts of Thomas, where the blood brings forth thorns and thistles, and Aldhelm's *Carmen de uirginitate:*

> Inde prava seges glitibus densescet acerbis,
> Sanguine purpureo dum scaevus rura cruentat

> (Thence an evil harvest of rough brambles grew up thickly, when the recreant sprinkled the fields with purple blood.)[50]

In several Old English texts and biblical illustrations (the latter a particular specialty for James, of course), these thorny growths branch out into full-blown trees, as Charles D. Wright has shown: "the illustration of the slaying of Abel in the Old English Hexateuch, which shows bright streams of Abel's blood watering a tree-like growth, is as graphic a representation as one could wish."[51] Such a wicked crop may seem inappropriate, given that Abel's innocent blood was typologically linked to Christ's, but as Wright notes, Aldhelm seems to have been "undisturbed by (or unconscious of) the incongruity."[52] For James (a published authority on Aldhelm), such incongruity appears also to be acceptable—and perhaps even part of the point.

A clear case can be made, after all, that the Cain-like Haynes is not so much bloodthirsty as simply driven by a false ideal, a perverse idolatry of professional order.[53] The murder of the archdeacon seems largely motivated by Haynes's wish to put the archdeaconry "upon a proper footing," in James's darkly playful phrase.[54] Haynes accordingly sets about reforming and organizing the affairs of his new office with zeal, and even once the haunting begins he protests in his diary that he has "acted for the best."[55] And this brings us to one of the most curious uses James makes of his Anglo-Saxon source. A prominent aspect of *The Dream of the Rood* is the cross's determination to serve his lord (Christ) in the painful process of crucifixion: *Þær ic þa ne dorste ofer Dryhtnes word / bugan oððe berstan* (I did not there dare, against the word of the Lord, to bend or to break).[56] The poet's conceit is that it would have been possible for the speaking cross, disobediently, to save his lord, *ac ic sceolde fæste standan* (nevertheless I had to stand firm).[57] This resolution is repeated six separate times within thirteen lines, so that Cook marvels, "Over and over is repeated—'I dared not bow,' 'I must needs stand fast.'"[58] Compare this to James's account of Haynes's diary entry, recorded as his terror escalates:

> *Jan. 11.*—Allen left me to-day. I must be firm.
>
> These words, *I must be firm,* occur again and again on subsequent days; sometimes they are the only entry. In these cases they are in an unusually large hand, and dug into the paper in a way which must have broken the pen that wrote them.[59]

Haynes's resolve to stand fast must be read as an ironic reversal of the cross's fidelity, but it is a commitment to executing efficiently the duties of his office, rather than Christian faith, that obsesses him: "Not long after this it is evident to me that the archdeacon's firmness began to give way under the pressure of these phenomena. . . . Throughout this time, however, he is obstinate in clinging to his post."[60] Haynes has made an idol of his office; it is a post upon which he sacrifices everything, including himself.

But the enigmatic wooden statuettes themselves do not survive, either. They, along with the rest of the choir's furnishings, are eventually swept away by the Gothic Revival:

> When you enter the choir of Barchester Cathedral now, you pass through a screen of metal and coloured marbles, designed by Sir Gilbert Scott, and find yourself in what I must call a very bare and odiously furnished place. The stalls are modern; without canopies. The places of the dignitaries and the names of the prebends have fortunately been allowed to survive, and are inscribed on small brass plates affixed to the stalls. The organ is in the triforium, and what is seen of the case is Gothic. The reredos and its surroundings are like every other.[61]

Various Gothic revivals and survivals have characterized every century of English architecture, secular and sacred, since the end of the Middle Ages.[62] In his final volume of fiction, James was literally to belittle the excesses of this history with his tale of a haunted doll's house in "Strawberry Hill Gothic."[63] But the Gothic Revival that figures in James's cathedral tales focuses on a very specific historical episode of nineteenth-century church architecture, in which a synthetic "skin" of Gothic ornament was applied to the fabric of hundreds of churches throughout England.[64] As we have seen, James's Barchester is said to have been renovated by Sir Gilbert Scott (1811–1878), a key figure in a movement that James viewed with regret and contempt. Scott was a central proponent and practitioner of this midcentury boom in the Gothic "restoration" of church architecture inspired by the ideals of A. W. N. Pugin (1812–1852) and promoted by the Cambridge Camden Society, an (originally) undergraduate group dedicated to the "holy science" of ecclesiology. Ecclesiologists of this school sought to restore the character of Anglican churches to what Pugin and others considered the culmination of medieval architecture, the (curiously named) "Early Late Middle Pointed" style, a supposed pinnacle reached in the first decade of the fourteenth century. Much of the terminology introduced by this movement ("decorated," "perpendicular," etc.) has become standard among professionals.[65] But although these abstractions were often grounded in rigorous and careful research, they also reflected a highly platonic understanding of the authentic past: "Real Antiquity . . . as an amalgam of observations that have been collected together, regimented, and analysed by historians in much the same way as artists since the Renaissance had studied ancient sculpture and human anatomy to derive an ideal image of the human form."[66] To "restore" a church, then, did not necessarily mean returning it to its particular former, local state so much as bringing it into conformity with a general medievalizing ideal, a predigested architectural past that Pugin, Scott, and many others thought reflected the lost communal values of preindustrial and precapitalist "Gothic" society. To make way for this revival, much older material would have to be swept away. An early revivalist, James Wyatt (1746–1813), was nicknamed "Wyatt the Destroyer" for his restoration of cathedrals such as Salisbury and Hereford, two of the three churches James acknowledged as inspiring both his Barchester and his Southminster in "An Episode of Cathedral History."[67]

Although we might expect it, the damage to Barchester does not appear the direct work of Haynes. James does, however, strongly hint that Haynes was on the path to initiating destructive cathedral renovations in the months leading up to his death:

> For just three years he is occupied in reforms; but I look in vain at the end of that time for the promised *Nunc dimittis*. He has now found a new sphere of activity. Hitherto his duties have precluded him from

more than an occasional attendance at the Cathedral services. Now he begins to take an interest in the fabric and the music. Upon his struggles with the organist, an old gentleman who had been in office since 1786, I have no time to dwell; they were not attended with any marked success. More to the purpose is his sudden growth of enthusiasm for the Cathedral itself and its furniture.[68]

This enthusiasm is limited to some amateur "archæological investigations" (allowing the narrator to cite ominous descriptions of the statuettes), but the clear implication is that Haynes's reforming spirit is headed in the same general direction as the forces that will produce the Gothic Revival's desecration of Barchester's choir.[69] In a sense, Haynes's death represents the cathedral's striking back.

And so the tale's central, generative medievalism—its "germ," so to speak—may be deemed particularly appropriate, given the Old English *Rood* poem's notorious resistance to literary generic classification as well as its place within the history of English Christianity. The enigmatic *Dream* represents the stubborn particularity of the medieval artifact, whether textual or material—that which cannot be reduced to a reproducible pattern. But it is also a figure of conversion, and a reminder that holy things can suffer transformation. James's frame, meanwhile, links Haynes's martyrdom to the narrator's work as a systematizing academic who discovers his "materials for a ghost story" as he wearily wades among manuscripts "of a kind with which I am only too familiar."[70] But the librarian also trusts James not to betray the institution's faith: "I think I can trust you not to publish anything undesirable in *our* catalogue" (emphasis added). Certainly the nature of James's vocation demanded deep sensitivity to local contexts, whether textual or in terms of the communities whose books he catalogued. But if James's "Nightmare of the Rood" amplifies its source's focus on enigmatic transformation, we may suspect also a connection to the transformations professionals make when they sacrifice the sacred past.

RESURRECTING A MYSTERY

Much of a cathedral's meaning is acquired in the accumulation of its local history as it moves forward through time. So too, perhaps, a ghost story, or at least one with as complex roots as James's "An Episode of Cathedral History," which features another enigmatic Jamesian creature emerging from an equally mysterious tomb. As we turn to this tale, however, we must be aware of more than one kind of mystery. The first of these, Dickens's *Mystery of Edwin Drood,* is not medieval, but it leads us to the architectural history of a medieval cathedral. The second is the genre of the "mystery play," a form that in James's day was understood to have evolved out of church rituals built into the fabric of the cathedral. I will return to the latter in time, but both are related, most concretely by James's curious creation of a plain, empty altar tomb to house his horror, an object that stands at the center of medieval drama, local cathedral history, and, of course, this ghost story itself, as we shall see. A long history of reform, restoration, and revival, eternally disrupting the symbiotic balance struck between a cathedral's past and its present needs, is the most obvious villain at the intersection of these mysteries, but it is equally important that we understand how James blends these separate scholarly interests into a single meditation on how we inhabit the past. To clarify the pattern, we must recognize that James's background as a medievalist and a bibliographer led him to tell stories in which very precise architectural, literary, and liturgical references appear in plain sight as a kind of creative analogue to scholarly footnotes—that he entombs his horrors in layers of allusion that we may well miss if we are too quick to put monster over all other matters, as most previous readings of the tale have done.

More on this critical tendency in a moment, but first a very brief summary of the story may be useful. "An Episode of Cathedral History" is, at least on the surface, of the jack-in-the-box variety of ghost stories not uncommon in James's fiction, in which a supernatural being lurks in a sealed-off location (a chamber at the bottom of a well, a disused room in a country inn, and so on) until it is unintentionally liberated through accident or curiosity.[71] This iteration is more of a "jack-in-the-pulpit" story, for here the malignant supernatural agent is released when a Gothic Revival restoration party, against the admonitions of local citizens, removes the wooden choir pulpit of "Southminster Cathedral" and discovers an unknown tomb encased beneath it. Following weeks of unease, during which a number of persons in the cathedral environs fall ill and even die, a representative assembly meets in the choir to open the tomb—only to have the cause of the unhealthy effects flee, leaving them, or some of them, in the dark. Our guide to these events is the cathedral's principal verger, Mr. Worby, who witnessed them as a boy (watching the memorable climax from a perch high up in the triforium) and who relates them some fifty years later to a visiting scholar, Mr. Lake.

Perhaps more than any other James story, this tale has attracted attempts to classify the species of its supernatural antagonist.[72] James's particular background would seem to invite such efforts of taxonomy: his academic work on pseudepigrapha and biblical apocrypha included, after all, bodies of lore so remote and rhizomatic that they fascinate us into speculating on how they might be transfigured in fiction by an academic expert. In the case of "An Episode," the question of classification is at once both raised and confounded by speculations on the part of members of James's own fictional cathedral community, as when one canon remarks that the previous night's uneasy sleep held "rather too much of Isaiah 34.14 for me."[73] Here again is the passage that Dennistoun alludes to in connection with the haunting of Saint-Bertrand-de-Comminges. A reader who follows Canon Lyall's suggestion to look it up will read in the Vulgate of Jerome: "et occurrent dæmonia onocentauris et pilosus clamabit alter ad alterum ibi cubavit lamia et invenit sibi requiem" (The wild beasts of the desert shall also meet with the wild beasts of the island, and the satyr shall cry to his fellow; the screech owl also shall rest there, and find for herself a place of rest).[74] Translation quickly fails us, for even between the Latin and the English we can see the competition of natural and supernatural agencies—wild beasts and screech owls jostle for the reader's attention with *dæmoniae, onocentauri,* satyrs, and *pilosi* (literally, "hairy ones"). Then there is the enigmatic lamia, which is also featured in the last words of the story as terminal epigraph[75] and epitaph: Lyall affixes the inscription *ibi cubavit lamia* (There the lamia has dwelled) to the empty tomb's northern face. The lamia of Isaiah has been variously translated as "screech-owl," "Lilith," "she-demon," "night-creature," "night-bird," "night-monster," "night-spirit," "night-raven," and "night-hag."[76] As James supplies no translation of that particular word, readers and critics have selected freely among these choices and others of their own invention, while varying a good deal even in ignoring the perfect tense of *cubavit* as they have glossed the inscription in the past ("There lay a sorceress"), present ("Here lies a vampire"), and future ("There shall be the lair of the night monster," or witch, or vampire).[77] As these examples also suggest, many have assumed the feminine nature of the creature in question (despite the fact that it is described as "a thing like a man" by our only eyewitness) and its possible status as some kind of vampire, albeit a rather unconventional one—nothing, for instance, like what we find in *Carmilla* by James's favorite author, Sheridan Le Fanu.[78] Still, the tale has enjoyed a dubious afterlife as a staple of vampire fiction anthologies, a generic affiliation apparently grounded largely, if not solely, in the ambiguity of this single word.

What can be lost in all this speculation is the simple observation that "lamia" appears merely as a scriptural allusion produced by one of the story's characters—Canon Lyall—and is not necessarily to be taken as an authoritative or defining label for what has emerged from the tomb. In fact, it would be just as legitimate to posit an association with the other creatures mentioned in Isaiah 34:14 (those demons, satyrs, and hairy ones who cry out to one another), as indeed some critics have done. By contrast, I would argue that the nature of the haunting in "An Episode of Cathedral History" is not so much a matter of teratological lore as it is a function of the larger narrative context from which the monstrous thing arises. Such an argument is in line with the responses of the first recorded audiences of the tale. In January 1912, Maisie Fletcher tells us, "Then we all went into the billiard room and Monty read his ghost story to the entire joy of the company. It's one of the very best and had all the best characters, a perfect verger, and dean and chapter."[79] Arthur Benson, in a diary entry for 18 May 1913, similarly recorded that "Monty read us a very good ghost story, with an admirable verger very humorously portrayed—the ghost part weak."[80] What these first listeners may have sensed about this ghost story, with its "perfect verger" but "weak" ghost, is that its primary concern lies not so much with the undead but with the living community that breathes life into the ancient structure of the cathedral. I would argue, in fact, that the most useful approach to understanding this haunting is to investigate the background materials not of the monster but rather of its lair.

"An Episode of Cathedral History" is predictably preoccupied with architecture, its narrative shaped by church layout and ornamented with the technical vocabulary of cathedrals. We might expect nothing less from a scholar who produced numerous reviews, articles, and guidebooks on the subject, and we might well assume that the cathedral of this tale simply merges in its fictional fabric various cathedral features culled from James's wide experience in the field—as James himself asserts in noting that his Southminster, like his Barchester, was a "blend of Canterbury, Salisbury, and Hereford."[81] James would surely know best, yet here I plan to foreground the importance of quite a different cathedral, Rochester, as much for its physical structure as for its very particular history. It is the literary history of Rochester with which we must begin—specifically with *The Mystery of Edwin Drood*, that legendary tale of obsession and intrigue set in the Rochester-based cathedral town of Cloisterham. As readers of the novel will recall, John Jasper, the chief villain of the work and the cathedral's choirmaster, schemes to murder his nephew Edwin Drood because he (Jasper) has become infatuated with Edwin's fiancée, Rosa Bud. And as even those who have not read it know, Dickens had reached the point in his serialization where clues to Drood's disappearance were beginning to accumulate and interlace when the author suffered a sudden stroke and died. Only half the novel was written; Dickens left behind no plot sketch, no indication of the functions of several recently introduced characters, and not even any proof that young Drood actually had been successfully murdered by the opium-clouded Jasper.

The lack of closure launched numerous acrobatic feats of literary sleuthing, with dozens of solutions and sequels published in the following decades. James himself in 1905 penned a lighthearted report on an imaginary "Edwin Drood Syndicate" for the *Cambridge Review* in which he engaged some of the central questions left by the unfinished novel.[82] In July 1909, James and five others formed a real-life Drood syndicate and visited Rochester in order "to examine the possibilities of various theories on the spot—*e.g.* What access was there to the crypt? Was there anything answering to the Sapsea monument? What were the relative positions of the Vineyard, Durdles's yard, Minor Canon Corner? etc.—and a very memorable week-end we spent there."[83] Unfortunately, James admits that the party "did not hit on any illuminating facts"; he seems particularly disappointed to have found no exemplar of the tomb of Mrs. Sapsea, where, in his own solution to the plot, he was convinced that Drood's still-living body had been secreted by John Jasper.[84] In his review of his friend Henry Jackson's 1911 book *About Edwin Drood*, he provides an interpretation of the frontispiece of the *Edwin Drood* serial, which he reads as if it were a historiated miniature—using the same kind of attention to grouped imagery that we find in his manuscript descriptions—and concludes that Dickens intended Drood to survive Jasper's attempt at strangulation, to return to Cloisterham disguised as Dick Datchery, and ultimately to confront his uncle in the very tomb where he had been left for dead: "Central picture, end, the pale person cannot be a phantom as the figure casts a shadow on the wall behind him."[85]

All of this Droodish activity coincides with James's composition of "An Episode of Cathedral History" and, if only we listen for them, we can hear the bells of Cloisterham tolling quietly throughout James's Southminster. Both stories are set in quiet English cathedral towns south of London in the middle of the nineteenth century; both contain important characters who are head vergers; both contain arrogant, aloof chapter deans whose comeuppance readers eagerly anticipate. James imports Dickens's lovely coinage of "cathedraly" for "cathedral-adjacent," and in both works watchful visitors stay in the cathedraly home of the verger. Mr. Worby, James's verger, inherits both the native insights and the wall-tapping mannerism of "Stony" Durdles (as James wrote in his Drood syndicate essay, "This person, it will be remembered, possessed an extraordinary faculty of detecting, by means of tapping, the presence and even, to some extent, the nature of foreign (or other) bodies lying behind masonry").[86] The preoccupation announces itself explicitly in the story's opening scene, when Lake and Worby approach Southminster Cathedral at night with a lantern: "'Anyone might think we were Jasper and Durdles, over again, mightn't they?' said Lake, as they crossed the close, for he had ascertained that the Verger had read *Edwin Drood*." Once inside, Worby leaves Lake to fetch some papers:

> Not many minutes had passed before Worby reappeared at the door of the choir and by waving his lantern signalled to Lake to rejoin him.
> "I suppose it is Worby, and not a substitute," thought Lake to himself, as he walked up the nave. There was, in fact, nothing untoward.[87]

The suspicion that the figure in the distance may be a "substitute," coupled with Worby's act of signaling Lake with a lantern, strongly evokes one of Dickens's most famous ghost stories, "The Signal-Man," which opens with the narrator and the tale's protagonist mistaking each other for ghosts ("The monstrous thought came into my mind . . . that this was a spirit, not a man") and ends with the signalman perishing when he mistakes the warning of an engineer for the voice of a ghostly substitute.[88]

But the main reason for pursuing these comparisons is to direct us back to Dickens's Rochester, where James's syndicate went searching for architectural clues and where we may find some of our own. The nineteenth-century renovation of this church was less encompassing than that of other diocesan seats, but in one respect it stands alone: the striking alterations to the Rochester choir and to the eastern end of the cathedral generally. Between them, Lewis Cottingham (who brought the Gothic Revival with him during twenty years of projects beginning in 1825) and Gilbert Scott (who in the 1870s deliberately reworked or negated much of what his predecessor had done) dilated the choir from a restricted and claustrophobic space to the open, airy, accessible minor transept it is today. Their overall vision was to refashion the "monastic" eastern end of the small cathedral for a new generation's use.[89] While much of what they accomplished was surely necessary and valuable for the stabilization of the structure, James, like his colleague Sir William Hope, could not but have despaired at a number of attempts to remove old materials and medievalize new ones into existence.[90] For his part, Cottingham "swept away" much of the older woodwork in the choir (including paneling, cornice work, and the choir pulpit itself) and replaced it with newly made medieval fittings. But his work resulted in two quite astonishing discoveries: a remarkable fourteenth-century painting of the Wheel of Fortune on the wall behind the destroyed pulpit, and the largely intact tomb of Bishop John de Sheppey, complete with painted figural effigy, walled up behind a thick layer of chalk and plaster between two arches leading from the choir to the presbytery, where it had been secreted, invisible and unsuspected in the midst of constant traffic, for at least two hundred years. In his exultation over the latter discovery, Cottingham took the extraordinary step of privately printing a sort of promotional "press kit"—a multipage pamphlet with custom engravings depicting his discovery of the tomb, the foremost of which shows the architect himself describing de Sheppey's monument to a group of visitors.[91] So similar is the triumphant response that James provides for his vindicated restorers that one feels he could almost have written it from Cottingham's engraving: "The removal of the base [of the pulpit]—not effected without considerable trouble—disclosed to view, greatly to the exultation of the restoring party, an altar-tomb—the tomb, of course, to which Worby had attracted Lake's attention that same evening."[92]

Fifty years after Cottingham, Gilbert Scott removed the eastern extension of the choir stalls, which had cut up the minor transept since the Middle Ages; in so doing he reduced the size of the choir but opened up the entire eastern transept. In an act of passive aggression or aesthetic integrity (take your pick), he moved the new choir pulpit that Cottingham had designed out into the nave and built his own new one for the choir; this he chose to place in its current position, against the pillar across the northeast transept, moving it from its traditional location across from the bishop's throne and next to the de Sheppey tomb that Cottingham had discovered.[93] The single disruption to the complete openness of the minor transept was now the monument of Bishop John Lowe: a plain rectangular fifteenth-century altar tomb that had been built lengthwise against the outside of the altar screen behind the former pulpit, but now sprouted like a mushroom from the floor of the wide open north–south transept. Because of the chain reaction of other restoration decisions—the removal of the choir pulpit, the removal of the eastern choir stalls—Gilbert Scott may have felt that he had no other option than to dismantle and move the tomb of Bishop Lowe some thirty feet away, adding it to a sort of ghetto of seventeenth-century monuments in the onetime Chapel of St. William. But Lowe had specifically directed in his will that his tomb be placed *ex opposito sedis episcopalis* (across from the bishop's seat), and its position had been used by several generations of architectural historians to localize monuments and altars that were subsequently destroyed. Unmoved by Scott's defense that the reorganization was made necessary by the other alterations and the close quarters of the small cathedral, Sir William Hope did not disguise his contempt: he maintained that Lowe's tomb was "an ancient landmark in the topography of the church, and its removal is therefore the more unjustifiable."[94]

By the time James and his Drood syndicate visited Rochester in July 1909, a trail of restoration, tomb discovery (de Sheppey), and tomb movement (Lowe) was not just available in print resources like Hope's *Architectural History* but was still within the living memory of the cathedral community. The tomb discovered in James's Southminster Cathedral has undeniable similarities to the discovery circumstances of the de Sheppey tomb and the former location of the Lowe tomb; it also resembles the Lowe tomb strongly, though only a researcher or a visitor to Rochester would know this—strangely, no image of it has appeared in print before or since Thorpe's edition of *Custumale Roffense* in 1788.[95] Thus while James's assertions that his cathedrals are compilations of certain known structures seem plain enough, we in fact find ourselves at the all too familiar critical loggerheads between intention and reception. No, Southminster is *not* Rochester (or the Cloisterham of *Edwin Drood*), but neither is it any of the three other sites he names.

The blending of mysteries does not end here, either, if we pause to consider closely several key points found in James's very careful descriptions of that rather inexplicable object at the center of the tale, a hidden altar tomb "rather awkwardly placed" on the north side of the choir, with no name attached to it, and, even more strangely, completely empty.[96] We must try for a moment to consider this object as a very literal tabula rasa, for the expectations of horror fiction may easily lead us astray: many readers since James's day have no doubt assumed that the tomb's corpse has been removed or reanimated in supernatural fashion, or that the tomb has been constructed or adopted to cage the horror that emerges from it. Either way, we might easily imagine that the wooden panels boxing in the tomb were first put there to help imprison a rogue supernatural creature. Yet that assumption makes very little sense in terms of the precise details James supplies. If anything, the tomb's former covering suggests careful efforts to protect its surface from damage, much more than it implies panicked fear of what lies within: "The structure had been most carefully boxed in under the pulpit-base, so that such slight ornament as it possessed was not defaced."[97] Upon closer inspection, the original object of this careful encasement mysteriously seems to have been to *preserve* the tomb rather than to bottle up its contents.

It is also unclear why the creature no longer runs amok in the narrative present, though we do know that by the time of Worby and Lake's night expedition the haunting is long over: Worby has no fear of entering the cathedral alone at night.[98] We also know when it left: Worby as a boy is a witness, if not exactly an eyewitness, to its departure as it emerges from the tomb and, knocking over Dean Burscough, flees the cathedral. Worby and most of the others at the scene fail to actually see the creature because they are distracted by a baffling commotion on the other side of the choir, which is heard—inexplicably—just *before* the creature emerges from the tomb: "there come a most fearful crash down at the west end of the choir, as if a whole stack of big timber had fallen down a flight of stairs."[99] Later inspection reveals no sign of anything having fallen, leading some critics, rather unconvincingly, to posit the presence of two separate entities acting in cahoots: "one in the tomb and one wandering the countryside seeking to free its mate from its imprisonment."[100] The idea receives some slight support from the allusion to Isaiah 34:14, where we read that "the satyr shall cry to his fellow," a reference that has led James's most recent editor to seek the satyr's fellow in another Jamesian tale altogether.[101] This rather tangled line of interpretation seems to suggest that we can only parse the story's climactic moment of horror by again looking to the mythology of the lamia—and even then the moment is deeply unsatisfying because it is not even consciously experienced by the arrogant Dean Burscough, the obvious target of James's contempt. In any other Jamesian tale of supernatural comeuppance, we would expect to relish a moment where the monster embraces or presses upon his victim with terrifyingly proximity, "the linen face . . . thrust close into his own."[102] In this story, though, the linens are left harmlessly on the floor of the tomb, while the dean remains blissfully unaware of what hit him. It is indeed a very strange scene.

But it is also oddly familiar. The simple key to clarification, I would suggest, is to consider the many ways in which this final supernatural event appears crafted to echo the Resurrection narrative of the New Testament. In this light, the empty tomb fairly gapes with scriptural significance, even were it not for the discovery inside of two scraps (a bit of paper and the torn piece of a dress), eerily similar to the *linteamina posita et sudarium quod fuerat super caput eius* (the linen cloths lying and the napkin which had been upon his head) that Peter saw in the sepulcher.[103] Recall, too, how the dean orders the tomb sealed and professes worry about the superstitious "arrant nonsense" easily accepted by "Southminster people" (*et dicant plebi surrexit a mortuis et erit novissimus error peior priore* [and they will say to the people that he has risen from the dead and the last error will be worse than the first]).[104] The opening of the Southminster tomb produces consternation consonant with that of the soldiers scattered by Christ's rising, but—even more strikingly—the inexplicable commotion at the other end of the choir now makes perfect sense, not through the explanation of a hypothetical "second satyr" but in terms of biblical precedent and what happens at the moment when the sepulcher is opened and the rising is revealed: *et ecce terraemotus factus est magnus* (and behold there was a great earthquake).[105]

The opening of the Southminster tomb is one of the most theatrical moments in James's fiction, and in more than one sense. The thunderous "fearful crash" at the tomb's opening erupts like a sound effect in a staged reenactment of the Resurrection, and there is much evidence to link the mystery of this moment to the medieval genre of mystery plays, popular performances that retold biblical events in the vernacular.[106] Often performed in cycles, with individual episodes produced by craft guilds or "mysteries" (Latin *ministeria*), such plays focused on key moments of salvation history, such as the Resurrection—an event that made for a moment of high drama indeed, the slumber of soldiers shattered by a supernatural din:

> Awake! awake!
> Hillis gyn quake,
> And tres ben shake
> > Ful nere a too.
> Stonys clevyd,
> Wyttys ben revid [deprived],
> Erys ben devid [made deaf]—
> > I am servid soo.[107]

In at least one early dramatization of the Resurrection, this clamor was produced by knocking sticks together: "the which one bare the Parte of a wakinge Watcheman who (espiinge Christ to arise) made a continual noyce like to the sound that is caused by the Metinge of two Styckes."[108] Such stagecraft closely recalls the clattering disturbance in "An Episode," so that there is no need to account for it with a posited second creature clumsily raising a ruckus offstage. Rather, emphasizing the affinities of the story's climax with the mystery play tradition allows us to make sense of a haunting that is distinctively theatrical.

In setting the scene, James has Worby recall the exact placement of the principal players with a director's eye for the dramatic, pinpointing their positions with reference to liturgical east, west, south, and north: "we heard the verger that was then, first shutting the iron porch-gates and locking the south-west door, and then the transept door. . . . Next thing was, the Dean and the Canon come in by their door on the north, and then I see my father, and old Palmer, and a couple of their best men, and Palmer stood a talking for a bit with the Dean in the middle of the choir."[109] Worby and his boyhood friends in the triforium, of course, can see all this because they have balcony seats for a very staged fright. The spectacle is so carefully blocked out that Worby is overwhelmed trying to explain the movements of all the principal actors: "Well, you can't expect me to tell you everything that happened all in a minute."[110] He does not catch sight of the creature itself, but he is able to re-create a visual memory of the investigators, who are—like the traditional four guards of the tomb—thrown into stylized confusion, something like a painted or carved tableau of the Resurrection, with each figure variously "tumbled over," "making off down the choir," or "sitting on the altar step with his face in his hands."[111] In the York Resurrection, the soldiers fall into similar disarray, startled as they are in the traditional upheaval:

II. MIL. What tyme he rose good tente I toke;
The erthe that tyme tremylled and quoke.
All kyndely force than me for-soke,
Till he was gone.
III. MIL. I was a-ferde, I durste not loke,
Ne myght had none;
I myght not stande, so was I starke.[112]

Similarly, in James's story, the one figure we never see is the "resurrected" creature itself, though we understand that it must have hurried west up the choir before departing "out through the north door."[113] (Exit monster, stage right.)

There are other strong clues that these dramatic elements of the tale are quite specific, closely tied to James's familiarity both with liturgical history and with the conventions of mystery plays. One of the clearest indications of this comes prior to the climax, when, like Pilate and the Pharisees securing the tomb against a false resurrection, the dean and chapter order workmen to set about, as it were, *signantes lapidem* (sealing the stone).[114] The efforts of James's craftsmen are no more successful than what would be expected in mystery play slapstick:

"It appears Palmer'd told this man to stop up the chink in that old tomb. Well, there was this man keeping on saying he'd done it the best he could, and there was Palmer carrying on like all possessed about it. 'Call that making a job of it?' he says. 'If you had your rights you'd get the sack for this. What do you suppose I pay you your wages for? What do you suppose I'm going to say to the Dean and Chapter when they come round, as come they may do any time, and see where you've been bungling about covering the 'ole place with mess and plaster and Lord knows what?' 'Well, master, I done the best I could,' says the man; 'I don't know no more than what you do 'ow it come to fall out this way. I tamped it right in the 'ole,' he says, 'and now it's fell out,' he says, 'I never see.'"[115]

The confusion of these craftsmen—inseparable from the fallen language of their comic eye dialect—recalls countless such scenes in the mystery play cycles, perhaps none more poignantly ironic than the York Crucifixion, in which bickering soldiers strain to fix Christ's body onto a recalcitrant rood: "I hope [think] þat marke a-misse be bored," one complains, while his companion rejoins, "Why carpe ʒe so? faste on a corde, / And tugge hym to, by toppe and taile."[116] Mystery plays of Christ's burial and Resurrection feature similarly clueless attempts to resist the supernatural, as when Annas and Pilate set about sealing the tomb:

> *Annas.* Loo! here is wax fful redy dyght,
> Sett on ʒour sele anon ful ryght,
> Than be ʒe sekyr [secure], I ʒow plyght—
>   He xal [shall] not rysyn ageyn.
> *Pilatus.* On this corner my seal xal sytt,
> And with this wax I sele this pytt;
> Now dare I ley he xal nevyr flytt
>   Out of this grave, serteayn.[117]

But when the seal inevitably fails, Pilate's underling soldiers receive the blame in a tongue lashing that recalls Palmer's frustrated repetitions: ("What do you suppose I pay you your wages for? What do you suppose I'm going to say to the Dean . . ."):

> *Pilatus.* What! what! what! what!
> Out upon the [thee], why seyst thou that?
> ffy [fie] upon the, harlat,
>   How darst thou so say?
> Thou dost myn herte ryght grett greff!
> Thou lyest upon him, fals theff;
> How xulde [should] he rysyn ageyn to lyff,
>   That lay deed in clay?[118]

Mystery plays are known for this same style of comedy—and Dean Burscough's cluelessness fits the standard role admirably, whether he is ordering the tomb sealed like a second Pilate, out-Heroding Herod as he storms from the cathedral, or tumbling down like the astonished soldier over whom Christ clambers in the Chester Resurrection.[119] The typical villain of the mystery plays is, in David Bevington's words, a "self-blinded worldling" who fails to recognize the grand narrative of which he is a part.[120] The dean, in like fashion, never even realizes he is in a ghost story.

Readers would be forgiven, though, if they failed to notice that the tale's narrative drifts into the generic territory of mystery plays. This is another very reticent medievalism in James's fiction, though one with a good deal of significance—in particular when we see how thoroughly joined this pattern is with the larger architecture of the story, both figuratively and literally, for the staging of a Resurrection drama specifically within a cathedral is not a mere freak of James's antiquarian imagination. In fact, in James's day, it was understood that all medieval mystery plays originated directly as an evolved form of liturgical drama, which in turn had proliferated specifically from an originary "germ" or seed in nothing other than "primitive" Easter plays of the Resurrection. Church ceremonies known as the *Visitatio sepulchri* or *Quem quaeritis* (short for the query, *Quem quaeritis in sepulchro, o Christicolae?* [Whom do you seek in the tomb, O Christians?]) were performed during the Easter services in which clergy played the roles of the women discovering the tomb empty of Christ's body; the body was often represented by a large metal cross that, on Good Friday during the rite of the *Depositio crucis*, had been wrapped in cloth and "entombed" amid great ceremony and chanting, along with the lighting of a "Sepulcre-candell" (a whiff of these rites can perhaps be caught when "a bit of a candle" is lit to inspect James's haunted tomb).[121] The dean's startled exclamation "Good God!" may serve too as an ironic variation on the traditional words of praise shouted at the moment when the Resurrection is revealed: "Alleluia! Resurrexit Dominus!"[122] In this key scene, then, James is in effect staging not simply an adapted version of the Resurrection but a haunting reenactment of the liturgical dramatization of that event. The cathedral's ritual past has come back to life.

We can further anchor these associations to the architectural elements of the story when we revisit the significance of the strangely plain and unmarked altar tomb, which, Worby notes, is curiously unoccupied: "we don't own any record whatsoever of who it was put up to."[123] As a blank tomb with a missing occupant, this object makes very little sense, but in relation to both the *Quem quaeritis* ceremony and English architectural history its significance is plain. James's tomb must surely be taken as the structural core of what is called an Easter sepulcher: an elaborate liturgical prop used in the *Quem quaeritis* rite to represent Christ's tomb. The typical features and position of such sepulchers match James's description of the haunted tomb with the kind of precision with which we are by now familiar. Here is Alfred Heales's description of Easter sepulchers in an article from 1868: "There can be little or no doubt that it [the typical Easter sepulcher] was a temporary wooden structure, framed so as to be easily put up when required, and afterwards removed, and that it stood on the north side of the choir or chancel. There are, however, numerous high or altar tombs set in a recess in the like position, which were probably inclosed within the framework, and served as the 'sepulchre' itself."[124] Compare the description of James's tomb, which is a "plain altar-tomb" that stands "on the north side of the choir" (a location emphasized more than once in the tale).[125] Except in extraordinary circumstances such as those specified in the will of Bishop Lowe of Rochester, this is the precise location where we would expect to find an empty tomb that is not really the tomb "of anybody noted in 'istory," but rather the architectural remains of the ceremony of the sepulcher. As we read in the *Rites of Durham* for Good Friday: "two Monkes did carrye [the cross] to the Sepulchre with great reverence, which Sepulchre was sett up in the morninge, on the north side of the Quire, nigh to the High Altar."[126] Worby and Lake agree that the tomb dates to the fifteenth century, and it so happens that just such a sepulcher-tomb was erected in 1485 at Stanwell, Middlesex, under the direction of Thomas Windsor's will: "My body to be buried on the north side of the quire . . . before the image of Our Lady, where the Sepulchre of Our Lord standeth, whereupon I will that there be made a plain tomb of marble of competent height, to the intent that it may bear the blessed body of Our Lord, and the Sepulchre at Easter to stand on the same."[127] So James's "plain altar-tomb," like the "plain tomb of marble" Windsor orders placed over his grave, is likely not an "Easter Sepulchre" proper but rather the base for one. Francis Bond notes that "hundreds of such tombs remain . . . it must, however, be borne in mind that many are only pedestals on which the temporary wooden framework of an Easter sepulchre was placed."[128] So it would seem that the peculiar and empty altar tomb, "on the north side of the choir, and rather awkwardly placed," makes perfect sense both architecturally and in the context of the haunted mystery play revival that James stages around it.

James is also quite reticent in revealing the nature of the tomb's encasement, which as I have noted was done "most carefully . . . so that such slight ornament as it possessed was not defaced." The Easter sepulcher, along with the *Quem quaeritis* ceremony itself, was a notable casualty of the Reformation, so that the wooden structures were either destroyed ("given to the poor for firewood") or repurposed ("of others were made cupboards, biers, hencoops, steps, and necessities").[129] It is an irony, then, that the pulpit's sounding board is itself repurposed by the Gothic Revivalists "as a table in a summer-house in the palace garden."[130] The shadow of de Sheppey in Rochester Cathedral looms large here, for that painted tomb, as I have noted, is a striking example of a tomb preserved from defacement by being walled up during the Reformation, only to be triumphantly rediscovered by the forces of the Gothic Revival. In James's tale, though, the painted effigy of de Sheppey has been replaced with something much less dramatic—much more like the shifted Lowe altar tomb—yet still harboring great historical (and supernatural) significance. The dean's zealous demolition crew betray no knowledge of this history when they "disclosed to view, greatly to the exultation of the restoring party," an Easter sepulcher, which itself had been preserved only by concealment from the notice of earlier reformers.

WHOM DO YOU SEEK IN THE TOMB?

James's tomb, I have argued, is just as important as, and perhaps more significant than, the particular species of "lamia" that dwells therein. Or rather, "has dwelled," for the episode concludes with the resurrected beast having escaped the cathedral, presumably to remain permanently on the lam, as it were, in the world. But now, with its lair carefully explored, let us return to the monster, which is characterized by features common to several other ghosts in James's canon: "hellish night-abomination(s) midway betwixt beast and man," in the words of H. P. Lovecraft.[131] Even for a Jamesian haunt, however, the creature or demon of "An Episode of Cathedral History" seems particularly drawn to resemble a kind of Darwinian "missing link": "A thing like a man, all over hair," with "two legs, and the light caught on its eyes."[132] These features seem only accentuated by the names of the canons who first discuss "the crying" of the creature: "it was Mr. Henslow that one, and Mr. Lyall was the other." Michael Cox notes that the first of these is likely a tribute to Cambridge graduate John Stevens Henslow (1796–1861), a "botanist and naturalist on the *Beagle*, who presided over the celebrated debate on Darwin's *Origin of the Species* at the British Association in 1861."[133] In that light, a "Lyall" would be a quite natural pairing for a "Henslow," since Charles Lyell (1797–1875), one of the foremost scientists of the nineteenth century, was also an influential mentor to Darwin and played a key role in the development and publication of his work on evolutionary theory.

What, though, has Darwinism to do with medieval drama? Quite a bit, as it happens, in the widespread opinion of academic medievalists of James's era. In fact, the apparent development of later dramatic forms from the original "germ" of the *Quem quaeritis* ceremony was generally considered an exemplifying case for the application of evolutionary theory to literary history—its "type specimen," so to speak. The decade or so immediately preceding James's writing of "An Episode" was a high-water mark for scholarship pursuing this approach.[134] John Matthews Manly, in his 1907 essay "Literary Forms and the New Theory of the Origin of Species," expressed "a high degree of confidence that in studying the origin of the Visit to the Sepulcher—i.e., of the Easter trope, 'Quem quaeritis in sepulchro?'—we are studying the origin of the drama in mediaeval Europe."[135] Or rather its rebirth, for the idea was often that, as E. K. Chambers details in his influential *Mediaeval Stage* (1903), the Easter sepulcher was the site of the resurrection of a dormant "dramatic instinct," a spark of the human imagination otherwise smothered by the Dark Ages. From this origin, Chambers and others sought to map out how all medieval and postmedieval drama—of ever-increasing complexity—proceeded, passing along identifiable "step[s] in the dramatic evolution" as it broke free of "the liturgy, out of which it *arose*" (emphasis added). Note the double significance of the verb and the implied parallels between Christ arising from the tomb and the reawakening of Drama from its grave. Figurative and literal resurrections overlap. One of the first "steps" of this literary evolution, in fact, comes when "dramatic action" rises out of mere ritual, "through the introduction of the figure of Christ stepping . . . out of the sepulchre, in place of a mere symbolical indication of the mystery." Thus it is that Drama arises again and steps forth from the Christian sepulcher, a rich irony in which Chambers rejoices: "an inevitable and ironical recoil of a barred human instinct within the hearts of its gaolers themselves."[136]

As Chambers makes explicit, then, the evolutionary narrative that he and others advanced was specifically a secularizing one. As he puts it, the formerly pagan dramatic instinct, resurrected in liturgical drama, eventually "broke the bonds of ecclesiastical control," adapting to a secular (and superior) dramatic habitat within the Renaissance playhouse.[137] The metaphor is strikingly reminiscent of the events narrated in James's "Episode," where a creature born of the Easter sepulcher rises up, "evolves," and effects its own dramatic cathedral jailbreak, roaming thereafter at large in the world. It is unlikely, however, that James's narrative is simply recapitulating, without irony, this surmised phylogeny of English drama. Yet it is probable that James at least partially recognizes the professional legitimacy of applying evolutionary theory to such subjects: his own work with manuscripts, after all, found profound inspiration in the methodologies of biological science.[138] But regardless of any shared sympathy for applying such principles to antiquarian subjects, James would surely recoil at the idea of substituting an "outmoded providential" view of history with a narrative of evolved and ascendant secular culture. One key irony in that regard would be the centrality of salvation history to the genre of the mystery play cycles, whose essential function—through intricate typological buttressing and an exuberant zest for anachronism—was to dramatize the selfsame version of history that the evolutionary model seeks to displace and replace. Here, in fact, may be the keystone that locks together the story's two main medievalizing anxieties: the place where the Gothic Revival and the evolutionary theorizing of mystery plays meet. James's story suggests that both of these are false attempts to reconstitute the past, sham resurrections whose very analytical and evidential rigor distorts the local medieval meanings they purport to restore.

As an antidote, James offers us Worby, an amateur cheerfully willing to cycle freely among practical, aesthetic, quasi-scientific/chronological ("fifteenth century, we say it is"),[139] and religious responses to the cathedral, along with a kind of felt institutional instinct (akin to the stone tapping of Stony Durdles). Like the church itself, Worby is able to accept the conglomerate of the cathedral's episodic history and its many heterogeneous reimaginings—absorbing them into its sprawling fabric. Lake, we sense, respects this capacity, yet he himself tends to maintain a polite professional reserve, audible in the gaps of dialogue as the comically wordy Worby joins together incompatible elements: "Now of course I should be glad enough to take that view but—mind the step, sir—but, I put it to you—does the lay of the stone 'ere in this position of the wall (which he tapped with his key), does it to your eye carry the flavour of what you might call Saxon masonry? No, I thought not, no more it does to me."[140] The synesthesia of Worby's feeling for stone (a mixture of sight, sound, touch, and even taste) resounds with a broader sense that the cathedral's fabric cannot be reduced to a single pattern or meaning.

Here, then, is a less literal way to find significance in the lamia quotation, if we choose to read it in its larger context of Isaiah 34, which warns of coming desolation:

From generation to generation it shall lie waste; none shall pass through it for ever and ever. But the cormorant and the bittern shall possess it; the owl also and the raven shall dwell in it: and he shall stretch out upon it the line of confusion, and the stones of emptiness. They shall call the nobles thereof to the kingdom, but none shall be there, and all her princes shall be nothing. And thorns shall come up in her palaces, nettles and brambles in the fortresses thereof: and it shall be an habitation of dragons, and a court for owls. The wild beasts of the desert shall also meet with the wild beasts of the island, and the satyr shall cry to his fellow; the screech owl also shall rest there, and find for herself a place of rest.[141]

Franz Delitzsch, a contemporary of James's, called the prophecy of God laying waste to Edom "the negative reverse of building,"[142] an apt description for what those forces of reform and restoration, crying out to each other across cathedral history, have carried out. But what Chambers and other modern scholars have also done—in the eyes of James, I would argue—is to reduce an accumulated local, communal, and lived religious significance to a singular evolutionary "fact." This alone they seek in the tomb, and it is indeed a very bare and empty object they uncover.

The medievalisms of "The Stalls of Barchester Cathedral" follow a very similar arc, with the false sacrifice of Pulteney linked to the Gothic Revival that will sweep away the comfortable furnishings of the church, leaving behind quite literal bare and ruined choirs. The haunted carvings of the stalls are among the sacrificed items, effectively undoing the process of sacralization—the *halig* becoming holy—enigmatized as a transformation riddle in James's version of the *Rood* poem: "I grew in the Wood. . . . Now in the Church I stand." *The Dream of the Rood* is a poem interlaced with overlapping forms of conversion—conversion of forest tree to holy relic, of terrifying bloodshed to gemlike perfection, of Anglo-Saxon heroic convention to the metaphorics of Christian sacrifice. Haynes's Cain-like crimes perversely invert this pattern, linking secularization of the sacred to the murderer's desire for a new age of purified professional order and organization: "'ὁ κατέχων,'" a sympathetic correspondent exults with Haynes, "(in rather cruel allusion to the Second Epistle to the Thessalonians), 'is removed at last.'"[143]

This allusion hints that the stakes of the story are not limited to the vicious ambitions of one wicked archdeacon (or even, as Helen Conrad

O'Briain wittily suggests, an answer to the medieval question whether *possit archidiaconus salvus esse*?)[144] but touch on larger questions to which the professional study of the sacred past gives rise. The κατέχων of Paul's letter, discussed at the beginning of this chapter, enigmatically refers to an unspecified "restrainer" whose function it is to delay the coming of what is usually understood to be the Antichrist (whose time of tribulations the Thessalonians suspected had already arrived). Following this reference, an implicit comparison between Haynes and the Antichrist is inevitable, and indeed the "Nightmare of the Rood" concludes with darkly apocalyptic overtones.[145] But we might also emphasize the periodizing significance of the allusion, for the clear implication is the arrival of a new era (one linked uneasily to the Jamesian narrator, who is charged with cataloguing manuscripts along with narrative facts), and removing the κατέχων signals a clean break from a period in which all manner of things have been allowed to run together in undisciplined confusion. The clear business of the modern medievalist, by contrast, is to separate out matters of a purely academic interest, though James's medievalizing stories leave reason to doubt whether such a project is wise or even possible. Certainly the cathedral tales do not demand a single solution, nor do they ask that we stand fast in our ever-shifting relation to the past.

In the next chapter, I will turn to broader questions of scholarly time and how the chronic contradictions of James's academic medievalism may find expression in his fiction. Particularly in his later stories, we may detect a painful awareness of other temporal dynamics, not limited to periodizing divisions of sacred and secular times. Much of the best scholarship on James's "cathedraly" tales has rightly stressed how the villains of Southminster and Barchester have stripped their institutions of an original spiritual meaning, the way a revivalist sweeps away inconvenient furnishings.[146] While I hope that the observations of this chapter add something to this view, the tales examined here—especially "An Episode of Cathedral History"—seem to me also potentially congenial to the promise of a more eclectically disunified relationship to the past, one open to multiple styles and modes of engagement. These would include local, amateur, affective, and aesthetic responses as well as religious ones, alongside the "scientific," and even perhaps exuberantly creative impulses such as that which led James to build his own haunted cathedrals from found materials. If the Gothic Revival sought an ideal distillation of the past, James's own blend (of Canterbury, Salisbury, and

Hereford, along with Dickens's Rochester and the other medieval materials and texts discussed here) suggests the capacity of the living past to accommodate multiple occupants. The medieval cathedral itself points the way, a contradictory product of clashing times with room enough for all.

4

A DESIDERATUM OF WINGS

The most ambitious academic project M. R. James ever undertook was never published. Between 1926 and 1930, James wrote catalogue descriptions for about a thousand medieval manuscripts housed in Cambridge University Library, receiving large batches of priceless books at his rooms in Eton in a traveling lockbox to which only he and the CUL librarian had keys. For such a titanic task efficiency was essential, and an assistant would prepare in advance a form with each manuscript's basic information, so that James could "proceed to business straight" with each item.[1] As he wrote a friend in 1927, he kept the CUL's "staff running to and fro very busily" as he made haste to complete the work in a little over four years.[2] Richard W. Pfaff has noted with regret that despite this heroic effort, it was not possible for James to put sufficient care into every description, and that the project was undertaken, unfortunately, "at a time in his life [James was in his mid- to late sixties], in physical circumstances, and at a stage in the development of manuscript cataloguing, at which such a casual approach was no longer very useful."[3] Indeed, James himself did not feel qualified to evaluate every manuscript in the collection, and in October 1930, having amassed copy filling "six cases of the folio size," he announced to the university librarian A. F. Scholfield that his contribution to the task was finished and offered recommendations for what further work would be required "for the completion of a proper catalogue."[4] His recommendations went unheeded. Two years later, in October 1932, James entreated university syndics not to let the project drop, but by July 1933, when he accepted £500 as belated compensation, James had resigned himself to an indefinite delay: "I can't suppose that I shall survive to see the row of tomes." He never did, and to this day the catalogue remains unpublished.[5]

One small bit of James's CUL catalogue did, however, find its way into print: a necromantic "experiment" found on folio 144r of a fifteenth-century medical miscellany, Cambridge University Library Manuscript Dd.11.45, which he borrowed for the core of a ghost story. The line between James's work as a manuscript cataloguer and his imaginative fiction is nowhere so clearly crossed as in his appropriation of this odd little text:

> An experimēt most ofte proued true to find out
> tresure hiddē in ye ground, theft, manslaughter
> or anie other thynge /
>
> Go to ye graue of a ded man & three tymes call hȳ by his nā at ye hed of ye graue, & say y^u N. N. N. I coniure y^e, I require y^e, and I charge ye bi y^i christendome, y^{tt} y^u hast taken & receyued, at ye font stone, & by ye power & might of ye father, & of ye sonne, & of ye hollie ghost, y^t y^u takest leaue of ye Lord Raffaell, and Nares and thou askest leaue, this night to come & tell me trewlie, of ye tresure y^t lyeth hid in such a place, or in what place it is, or in what place it lyeth, hou I may best com therby, or by what manner of meanes & wayes. Then take of ye earth of the graue at the dead bodyes hed, & knitt it in a lynnen cloth, & put it under ye right eare, and sleape ther uppō, and whersoeuer y^u lyest or slepest, y^t night he will com & tell y^u trewlie in wakyng or sleping, so y^t y^u shalt haue a verie iust knowledg of y^i desyre, what so euer y^u shall aske hyme.

On the last day of December 1931, James resurrected this curious text for one of his final tales (too late for inclusion in his canon-establishing *Collected Ghost Stories*, published earlier that year). "The Experiment" (subtitled "A New Year's Eve Ghost Story" and bearing the cryptic epigraphic promise that "Full Directions will be found at the End") tells the story of a wicked wife and stepson who attempt to use the necromantic text to locate the missing property of Squire Bowles, whom they have murdered.[6] Their plot, no surprise, goes terrifyingly awry, and James reveals as a coda the "directions" borrowed directly from his CUL catalogue, albeit in a reduced and edited form, omitting the words I have underlined above and regularizing many of the archaic and abbreviated forms.[7] The cuts make sound sense from a reticent storyteller's point of view, and the tale concludes with the open-ended menace of the dead's promised return "in waking or sleeping."[8]

But the source of these edits grows murky when we note that the *very same* abridged words in James's story were *also* omitted from the draft of the manuscript catalogue he made for Cambridge University Library. From surviving records we know that sometime between 27 November and 20 December 1926, James had access (via the traveling lockbox) to CUL MS Dd.11.45.[9] We might assume that the ghost-story writer, as he worked to meet his deadline in late 1931, used his cataloguer's notes from this period as the exemplar for his fictionalized version. We know, however, that by this time his official descriptions had long since been sent on to Cambridge, never to see the light of print. So, although other scenarios are possible, it seems fairly reasonable to assume that James made a second and identically abridged copy of the text (with the intent of exploiting it someday in a ghost story) back in late 1926 as he worked on the catalogue. At least this seems as likely a chronology as any (even if we could open James's mouth from beyond the grave, could we trust his account?). But the curious effect of tracing this source back is that we never arrive at a moment when the academic editing of James the cataloguer can be separated in sequence from the manipulative skill of the tale-teller. The fact that one abridgment serves two such different purposes throws off all expectations of priority or original intention. As it stands, multiple motivations behind the singular act seem forever entangled: was it thus cut down to include only core information for a scholarly catalogue—or was this particular abridgment instead governed by the artful instincts of a master of reticent fiction? The best answer, oddly, seems to be *both at once*.

That authors make choices for more than one reason is no revelation, but the moment fascinates for the way it so thoroughly blends James's scholarly and creative instincts. And indeed, the untying of knotty sequences of ambiguous traces in order to reveal both the early history of manuscripts and their later "wanderings and homes" was a central purpose of James's own work as a cataloguer. "This work, which may not unfairly be called superficial, or at least preliminary, has been a great solace," James wrote in his memoir. "It has resulted in the accumulation of a heap of scraps of odd miscellaneous information, scraps which often enough are found to be really threads connecting one book with another, and perhaps in the end helping to link up a whole group, and reveal a whole chapter in the history of a library."[10] The poignant tension of this passage lies in the temporal valence of the "great solace" James's lifework has generated, and in whether that pleasure looks forward to a distant future "in the end"—when one might finally escape the gravity of preliminary study—or whether the cataloguer is fated ever to wallow away in a pottering present. And we might note how well the odd promise prefacing James's 1931 tale ("Full Directions will be found at the End") echoes the wistful self-assessment of his cataloguing career, the sense that—as he wrote elsewhere—"time as it passes continually brings new elucidations, and the cataloguer, when he nears the end of his task, is sure to have raised his standard, and to see the defects in his earlier descriptions, which by that time have got into print."[11] At the close of one's labor, will full directions arrive too late? For the cataloguer, the fated answer is always yes, but by the final day of 1931, the outdated culmination of James's preliminary career was well on its way to remaining in draft for good.

It is possible to argue that "The Experiment" not only reflects the particular case of the CUL catalogue but in fact gives voice to something more generally harrowing in the cataloguer's temporal position. As Pfaff has noted, the failure of James's final project could well be taken as emblematic of a broader anxiety of academic life: "That [the CUL catalogue] has never been published is not only an indication of the curious, and unsatisfactory, kind of undertaking that project was, but also a reminder that finality in catalogues of MSS, as in all other scholarly enterprises, is a relative matter."[12] Finality (and its frustration) is rather loudly announced at the opening of "The Experiment," as we read of a conscientious country rector in the "last days of December," making a fair vellum copy of his parish's registry from the foul paper draft he has been compiling over the course of the previous year. His careful work, however, requires a hasty addition when the death of Squire Bowles is suddenly announced. Thus the occasion of the story's publication on the last day of the dying year, with time running out, is directly reflected in the plot, and in fact an intense sense of haste pervades the tale from beginning to end. The wicked Madame Bowles is eager for "the burial very quick," the rector and his servant bustle about for no obvious reason, and indeed the narrative itself careens to its conclusion after several precipitous missteps by the murderous widow and son. Some of this hurry is explained by events, and some seems to be there simply to keep pace with the tale's tempo: "We could have waited," the son complains, while his mother protests, "You know how hurried I was that day." Every conversation is supercharged with urgency: "And tell me, tell me quick!" the mother demands when her son returns from conducting his dark "experiment."[13] It is almost as if James's own pressure to finish—he had missed his Christmas deadline—becomes the text's ambient theme.

Perhaps all this inexplicable posthaste is one reason why Rosemary Pardoe feels that "The Experiment" is a "difficult tale" with an "unsatisfactory nature."[14] But while this assessment might be justified, her annotations do not address the tale's central difficulty: what is either a careless glitch in the plotline or, as I would argue, a deafeningly reticent touch from a manuscript expert. It may also be a nod to the contents of CUL MS Dd.11.45 itself. I refer to the pivotal scene in which Madame Bowles and her son puzzle over where the dead squire may have hidden his fortune:

> "You have been at his books and papers, Joseph, again today, haven't you?"
> "Yes, mother, and no forwarder."
> "What was it he would be writing at, and why was he always sending letters to Mr. Fowler at Gloucester?"
> "Why, you know he had a maggot about the Middle State of the Soul [i.e., purgatory]. 'Twas over that he and that other were always busy. The last thing he wrote would be a letter that he never finished. I'll fetch it. . . . Yes, the same song over again.
> "'Honoured friend,—I make some slow advance in our studies, but I know not well how far to trust our authors. Here is one lately come my way who will have it that for a time after death the soul is under control of certain spirits as Raphael, and another whom I doubtfully read as Nares, but still so near to this state of life that on prayer to them he may be free to come and disclose matters to the living. Come, indeed, he must, if he be rightly called, the manner of which is set forth in an experiment. But having come, and once opened his mouth, it may chance that his summoner shall see and hear more than of the hid treasure which it is likely he bargained for; since the experiment puts this in the forefront of things to be enquired. But the eftest way is to send you the whole, which herewith I do; copied from a book of recipes which I had of good Bishop Moore.'"

Here Joseph stopped, and made no comment, gazing on the paper. For more than a minute nothing was said, then Madame Bowles, drawing her needle through her work and looking at it, coughed and said, "There was no more written?"

"No, nothing, mother."[15]

After pondering this, Madame Bowles elects to write Mr. Fowler to announce her husband's death and to return the "letter that [the squire] never finished," as Joseph characterizes it. In return, they receive a package of papers from Mr. Fowler, including, we are led to understand, the text of "the experiment," which they of course quickly come to grief attempting to use. But therein lies the glitch: if the letter accompanying the text was never finished and thus was never sent to Mr. Fowler, how can Mr. Fowler now possess "the experiment" in order to send it back? James puts a good deal of indirect pressure on this paradox, pausing the breakneck plot long enough to allow the wicked conspirators to gape over the letter's incompleteness. Otherwise, he allows the contradiction to stand unglossed.

An antidote to this apparent anachronism may lie in the contents of CUL Dd.11.45 itself. The text of "an experimēt most ofte proved true" is found on the recto side of folio 144. Just two folios earlier, on 142r, however, is perhaps the most important item to be found in the manuscript, the text of a letter that—like that of Squire Bowles to Mr. Fowler—is meant to announce and accompany a copy of a newly discovered text lent from one enthusiastic scholar to another. Instead of a spell offering insight into the "Middle State of the Soul," however, this text tempts us with the potential insight it may hold into the literary culture of the Middle Ages. As the letter writer informs his friend, "Praying ȝow yat ȝe will resayfe and kepe to we speke samyn of Syr William Cuke preste of Byllesbe ane Inglische buke es cald Mort Arthur, as ȝe may se wrytten of my hand in ye last end of ye buke" (I request that you will receive and keep, until we speak together, from Sir William Cuke, priest of Byllesbe, an English book which is called the *Morte Arthure*, as you can see written in my hand at the end of the book). Like Fowler, the letter's recipient is to keep the book "styll ȝour selfe to we speke samyn" (secretly yourself until we speke together), unless "tristy frendis" (trusty friends) can be found to return it to the writer's care. Scholars are still evaluating the significance of this letter for Arthurian studies, but James of course could not have failed to recognize its potential importance, and his catalogue entry (in which he copies out the full, unedited text) would have been the letter's first appearance in print—had the project been published.[16] The parallel occasion, purpose, and tone of this letter (accompanying a scholarly discovery lent from one enthusiast to another) are very suggestive, and herein may lie the key to James's apparent narrative glitch—for the "*Morte Arthure* epistle" is not a *finished* letter, but at the same time neither is it "a letter that he never finished," as Joseph characterizes his stepfather's text. Instead, it is simply the rough version of a letter that was presumably later rewritten in clean copy. So too, we come to realize, was Squire Bowles's letter not so much "unfinished" as merely a *draft*. One might in fact argue that the draft letter of CUL Dd.11.45 is just as thoroughly embedded in the fabric of "The Experiment" as its eponymous neighbor on folio 144. Not only does the distinction between "unfinished" and "draft" explain the tale's chronology; it also links up with the opening sentence of the story, where we read of the rector's "custom to note baptisms, weddings and burials in a paper book as they occurred, and in the last days of December to write them out fairly in the vellum book that was kept in the parish chest."[17]

Foul copy and fair, then, seems to be James's reticent theme, built into the temporal logic of the tale itself, stealthily warping its surface chronology. At the same time, if we consider together the convergence of this peculiar narrative strategy with the tale's anxious tempo and the occasion and timing of its publication, it is hard not to see broader significance in the fate of Bowles and his misunderstood letter. At the very least we are invited to feel outrage at the dullard Joseph's rifling the scholar's orphaned papers, failing to comprehend or scrutinize them with the sensitive eye of the specialist, even if that specialist was obsessed with a "Middle State of the Soul." James defined his own life's work as preliminary, even somewhat purgatorial, but built into that definition is the all-important distinction between an unfinished, cut-off ambition and the first draft of work actually on track to completion. The latter is the optimistic reading, of course: the hope that the sequence can be solved, the timeline untangled, and all the amassed materials "found to be really threads connecting one book with another," as James hoped. But much of the unsettling eeriness of James's fiction is associated with worry that this teleologically ambitious work might never add up, that it might in fact run against the grain of scholarly advancement or become lost among its own perverse and scrappy obsessions. The temporal illogic of "The Experiment" might be considered a perfect example of James's conviction that the reader of ghost stories should be left "just a little in the dark as to the working of their machinery."[18] But it is also telling that James breeds the unsettling temporal deformations of this tale specifically by engaging with his own work as cataloguer and ardent student of medieval manuscript textuality.

In fact, in this chapter I will argue that the unsettling and affectively powerful sense of time fueling the thrills of James's fiction may be characterized as a "medievalized" temporality.[19] To begin to analyze the contradictory dimensions of such time, it is first important to stress that I speak here of the medieval as a mobile temporal category, largely detached from strict chronologies or stable timelines.[20] The medieval, as many scholars of medievalism have stressed, is not so much a clear-cut, identifiable time period as it is a flexible temporal trope, one that is in turn as beckoning and threatening to the present as it is applicable to the past.[21] That is not to deny that a sense of historical periodization is what produces the idea of the Middle Ages in the first place, an ongoing process that dates back at least to Petrarch's perception of an era of *tenebrae* (darkness) following Roman antiquity.[22] If it was not until the early nineteenth century that the terms "medieval" and "the Middle Ages" were actually coined in English, we know that the knot of associations binding those "dercke and vnlearned times" began forming far earlier: phrases such as *media tempestas* (middle time) are attested as early as the fifteenth century.[23] There is obviously a long track record of viewing this era in romantic and utopian, as well as dystopian, terms (the latter emphasizing ignorance, violence, and "Gothic" irrationality). We can safely assume that James's academic background would make him skeptically immune to the more imbalanced fantasies, though his fiction may at times parody or wryly reproduce them (the Templars come to mind).[24] What is perhaps more powerful in both James's academic and creative work, however, is the underlying paradigm of the medieval as a temporality "in the middle," an open-ended gap or pause in the march of time. The medieval, Nicholas Watson writes, "is assumed to have had purposes of its own, an identity not connected in any linear way with the present."[25] Or if there is a connection, it is characterized by chaotic survival and distortive transmission, so that we tend to view the Middle Ages "through typologies that define it as interval, as void of a meaning of its own," in the words of Dagenais and Greer, yet glutted with sterile detail, scribal intrusion, and triviality.[26] Medieval time is time best forgotten, existing only to be corrected, superseded, or repurposed as raw material.

In some respects my argument here, that James's fictions rely on a "medievalized" sense of time, follows the lead of recent scholarship that examines, in the words of Carolyn Dinshaw, the effects that "representations of medieval temporal worlds [have] on their postmedieval readers."[27] Particular temporal systems of the past—for example, the premodern apprehensions of time embodied in *Mandeville's Travels* or in the writings of the medieval mystics Margery Kempe and Julian of Norwich—can be seen as offering the promise of expanding the ways in which we experience the present.[28] For these ghost stories, though, I see as more central the modern concept of the medieval itself, a temporal category that for James is particularly complicated by clashing narratives of professional advance and institutional retreat. And any discussion of the subject must begin by underscoring just how profoundly James's own life was shaped by "medieval" institutions, enclaves in which school loyalty could take precedence over all else. In the world of public schools, even the historically accurate pronunciation of Latin could be resisted as a threat to institutional autonomy, an encroachment of "the foreignness of scientific scholarship."[29] The dark conditional sentences of "A School Story" would have been pronounced in a way that reflected dedication to the anachronistic Latin of an earlier age.

It would be hard to overestimate James's own intense sense of devotion to the two institutions established by King Henry VI, foundations after which he named his own memoir *Eton and King's*. In that book, as well as in countless other writings and speeches, he expresses pious as well as deeply personal appreciation: "I allow myself to dwell on the thought of the real greatness, the augustness, of the ancient institutions in which I have lived: to which I have owed the means of gaining knowledge, the noble environment that can exalt the spirit, the supplying of temporal needs, and almost every single one of the friendships that give light to life: have owed all this and more for nigh on fifty years."[30] I would stress that the "temporal needs" that Eton and King's supplied James went well beyond food, shelter, and finances. The augustness of medieval stone and pedigree provided James a sense of institutional prestige and purpose that sheltered an otherwise desultory "antiquarian" existence. This was James's own sense of his life:

> The truth is I am a very immature creature, with not much clearer vision of life than I had when I left school. It is a constant puzzle or if not puzzle, surprise, to me that I have never shared the ambitions or

speculations about a career which ordinary people have, and ought to have, choice of profession, home of one's own, and all such. I believe there never was a time when I have had more of a programme than to find out all I could about various matters and to make friends. Positions and objectives have been the same. It has not been the case of amiable modesty but something more like indolence or, if a long word is better, opportunism.[31]

This antiquarian program of living, which James finds so enigmatically inadequate, is reflected throughout his fiction in various anxious guises. One example, discussed in greater detail below, concerns the bibliophile Mr. Humphreys and his inheritance, a property dominated by a librarylike labyrinth and its neighboring "Temple of Friendship." But if James confesses to being as "immature [a] creature" as when he left school, it would be fair to point out that he never actually did leave, a failure that many have linked to the impression that he remained all his life locked in institutionally arrested development.

Time after time James's friends and intimates, as well as his enemies, level the charge. A. C. Benson considered him "a kind of child," while Lytton Strachey, as I noted in the introduction, reproached him for living "a life without a jolt" as an eternal teenager.[32] A much more sympathetic voice, that of James's old Eton tutor Luxmoore, feared that "with his amazing knowledge & power of absorbing learning without seeming to work, with his boyish & untidy humour & his unruffled goodness [James] is a dangerous model for young men who have to make their way in the world."[33] Readers of his ghost stories have long had access to such portraits. A reviewer of Pfaff's biography lingers over a photograph of James, recalling the terror he felt as an adolescent for the preternatural "sleekness" of James's "neat self-contained face."[34] It is a baby-faced horror we find in the stories themselves: a "large, smooth, and pink" visage peeking out of the bushes ("the mouth was open and a single tooth appeared below the upper lip"), or a monstrous chrysalis unearthed in a dream: "So with many groans, and knowing only too well what to expect, he parted these folds of stuff, or, as it sometimes seemed to be, membrane, and disclosed a head covered with a smooth pink skin, which breaking as the creature stirred, showed him his own face in a state of death."[35] I would venture to connect such images to the author's scholarly self-image, for even James's choice of research areas seems perilously vulnerable to charges of childishness. Pfaff registers such associations in defending James: "This was not because of an immature fascination with the obscure or the trivial, but because what really interested MRJ was not so much what chiefly interests biblical scholars as what interests medievalists."[36] Even within the fledgling field of medieval studies, though, there were patches considered especially marginal, and to these James of course was often drawn. As Elizabeth Scala documents, women medievalists have often found themselves relegated to marginalized areas within the field, encouraged to pursue texts considered minor or otherwise appropriate for female scholars.[37] James's choice of subjects was his own, but the areas he studied were marked by a gendered antiquarian immaturity.

On the other hand, the encyclopedic quality of his descriptive catalogues could be said to redeem their position in time. In this era, the mapping of even the remotest byways of the past was reimagined as part of a teleologically ambitious project, as James's colleague, J. B. Bury (1861–1927), laid out the agenda for a packed Cambridge audience in 1904:

> The gathering of materials bearing upon minute local events, the collation of MSS. and the registry of their small variations, the patient drudgery in archives of states and municipalities, all the microscopic research that is carried on by armies of toiling students [is to be done] . . . in the faith that a complete assemblage of the smallest facts of human history will tell in the end. The labour is performed for posterity—for remote posterity; and when, with intelligible scepticism, someone asks the use of the accumulation of statistics, the publication of trivial records, the labour expended on minute criticism, the true answer is: "That is not so much our business as the business of future generations. We are heaping up material and arranging it, according to the best methods we know."[38]

As readers will note, Bury's vision coincides quite closely with statements James made concerning his own scrap-accumulating, preliminary work of recovering the medieval library. Of course, such ideals were not without precedent. Winged Time prizing open the tomb of Naked Truth was chosen by Count Magnus De la Gardie for his silver casing of the Codex Argenteus, an emblem echoed in James's tale at the fatal moment for the fly-by-night Wraxall: "'Heaven is my witness that I am writing only the bare truth—before I had raised myself there was a sound of metal hinges creaking, and I distinctly saw the lid shifting upwards.'"[39] After re-encasing the codex, however, De la Gardie had the book's original medieval binding discarded—to the horror of modern professionals.[40]

Yet again, the "microscopic" scrutiny James applied in his manuscript catalogues is infected also by temporal commitments quite apart from Bury's sense of an abstracted, scientific, and future-oriented profession. James's manuscript work, in fact, tended to begin and end with institutional commitments, proceeding library by library and college by college, each catalogue designed to honor individual foundations (the first was for Eton). It is probably significant, in fact, that the only negative review his catalogues received actually focused on the author's status as an outsider who failed to accord sufficient respect for a revered figure in one college's history.[41] Yet the alpha and omega of James's ambitions, to chart the "wanderings and homes of manuscripts," were always to remain locally defined and therefore potentially provincial in scope—if elevated by Oxbridge privilege. As Lynda Dennison has remarked with a note of regret, "James never ventured out of the field of collection-cataloguing into that of class-cataloguing," an apparent failure of professional development that coincides with the perception of his dangerously immature and institutionalized life.[42]

Thus even James's comfortable standing as university don, college provost, and pioneering cataloguer of manuscripts might be perceived as temporally perilous, though his medieval homes arguably provided bedrock to which wandering scholarship might be anchored—to institutional tradition, college rites and routines, and venerable dates of foundation. It is certainly suggestive that so many of James's hauntings are encountered outside the university setting, often by vacationing scholars, as if to leave institutional time is to venture into dangerously untethered temporal states. Yet James's choice to spend his life in home institutions would have been perceived by many contemporaries as a failure to enter the full ranks of adult responsibility, as James himself worried. Such a reading of donnish existence resonates with the recent writings of scholars who have, in expansive and inspiring ways, prospected alternative and nonnormative (queer) modes of experiencing time. Heteronormativity, they argue, has a strong temporal dimension, demanding a particular script of expected stages and events.[43] The passing of childhood into maturation and marriage; childrearing, old age, and the empty nest; death and the bestowal of inheritances to successive generations:

these could all be considered routine stages of "repronormative time."[44] Such times tend to be in sync with broader temporal frameworks that render chronologies visible and meaningful: the times of nation, empire, public institutions, and standardized history, for example, are closely tied to ideologies of progress, productivity, and the promise of a future represented by the protection and education of children. But in understanding James's own orientation in time, national and educational institutions present something of a paradox—for it seems evident that medieval foundations both redeemed and shunted awry the track of his antiquarian life.

The cultivation of such an existence and program of living might be viewed as a kind of temporal luxury that James could afford primarily through the unique position he held in "medieval" Cambridge and Eton. But embracing this place also entailed the taint of scholarly anachronism, so that a figure like James could easily be seen as pursuing advanced research in a field or mode behind the times. His celibate academic lifestyle linked him with a traditional view of the college don as, in the words of Leslie Stephen, a "strange monastic being who ought to be sent back to live in the middle ages."[45] Yet even within James's cloistered Oxbridge, often viewed as straggling behind other universities in its uneven commitment to up-to-date research, there was a sense that a new era was arriving. As a rhetoric of professionalism came to dominate the "historical sciences," an amateur or "antiquarian stage" (to borrow a phrase from James's own mentor, the Cambridge-based Henry Bradshaw) emerged as an unofficial middle period on the timeline of scholarly progress.[46] As James's colleague and sometime collaborator D. G. Hogarth noted in 1899, "there is [now] a tendency to insist on experimental and almost mechanical methods of examination which, compared to those of the dilettante period, denote a great advance in system."[47]

The dilettante or antiquarian period of medieval studies is defined not only by erratic methods but, more fundamentally, by a failure to cordon off the past as scholarly object from the contamination of what is contemporary. The study of medievalism involves critically examining postmedieval appropriations of the period, yet as Britton J. Harwood has noted, "Surely there is no form of study that is not also a medievalism; and of course there is no medievalism that is not also a form of study."[48] Though traditionally many in the profession have endeavored to shore up the distinction between creatively anachronistic "presentist" medievalism and rigorously "pastist" medieval studies, David Matthews has highlighted the tendency of this imagined boundary to drift, so that the antiquarian stage remains at least a generation removed from the present day: "good medieval studies, disinterested medieval studies, is always what we are doing *now*."[49] If at present that way of thinking is being challenged, acknowledgment of the inevitability—even desirability—of mixing present with past has been a long time coming. Many medievalists increasingly welcome what Jeffrey J. Cohen calls "temporal interlacement," in which alterity and continuity are at once emphasized. Cohen in fact advocates a metaphor of the medieval itself for this reconceptualization of time as "unbounded middle," repurposing the concept of the Middle Ages and its temporal associations.[50] For James and his generation, however, the presentism of amateurs would also be inseparable from the concept of the medieval, but in a much less promising guise—the dilettante period a dubious continuation of the age it irresponsibly engages.[51] Medievalized time of this kind is often felt in James's fiction, if not eagerly embraced. In "A School Story," for instance, Samson's body at the bottom of the well is identified only by a Byzantine coin onto which he has "rather barbarously" scratched his own initials.[52] Such marks seem to imply that amateur engagements reproduce premodern temporalities, queasily (and medievally) dragging them into the present.

In fact, the barbarous era of the dilettante or antiquary—an inevitable by-product of the impulse to periodize the profession—is analogous to the medieval in many respects. Like the medieval, such antiquarian time seems retrograde and turbulent, disconnected in a fundamental way from time conceived as proceeding in a steady, laminar flow of simple and stable chains of causality.[53] "Nothing seems to have come harder to the medieval intelligence," James once fumed, "than the simple consecutive numbering of the leaves of a volume."[54] Like the medieval, too, the antiquarian era is never quite done and dusted. In fact, the relationship between antiquarianism and the medieval is often conceived of as the former's not allowing the latter to rest decently in oblivion. The antiquarian document, as Ina Ferris notes, "insistently returning to dust-covered old manuscripts, represents regressive energies in a progressive world."[55] So many of James's stories are electrified by moments in which such stray antiquities trouble the otherwise stable relationship of past to present: a prayer book printed in an uncommon year; a "neatly-folded vellum document" under the shifting floorboards of Number 13; the state trial papers of "Martin's Close," in which ghastly vernacular cruelties walk hand in hand with the sordid history of everyday English.[56] Even when such antiquities are not of the period, strictly defined, they nevertheless evoke a medievalized sense of time, dredged up through intermediary enthusiasts.

A classic formulation of this antiquarian failure is a pair of satiric lines directed against Thomas Hearne (1678–1735), an early medievalist of "black-letter memory" and of tattered reputation well before James's day:

Pox on't quoth Time to Thomas Hearne
Whatever I forget you learn.

As I will discuss in greater detail toward the end of this chapter, Hearne's own scholarly diaries become a central source for one of James's antiquarian terrors, a beastie embodied by a disgusting excess of hair—sprouting from a scrap of cloth inadvisedly reproduced in facsimile. Again, this story evokes a sense of medievalized time quite separate from the conventional period dates of the Western Middle Ages. The haunted cloth is eighteenth century but is characterized as "reelly lovely medeevial stuff" in the suggestive eye dialect of James's tradesmen, who, though attracted to the material, also "scented something almost Hevil in the design" (hairlike lines that do not, quite, converge together). The Hevil-medeevial here represents a kind of irredeemably stranded time that can serve no purpose in the present (even as curtains). Yet James actually admired Hearne's scholarly work—the main inspiration for all this antiquarian terror—for being ahead of its time in terms of scholarly rigor and accuracy. James in fact relies on Hearne's own text (transcribed "as faithfully as possible") for his edition of Blacman's memoir of Henry VI (published in 1919, the same year as the ghost story in question). As one might expect, this edition is presented as a "memorial of our Founder," though James feels bound to acknowledge the failings of a reign troubled by deep civil discord and the king's own mental illness. Nevertheless, "[t]he evils which his weak rule brought upon England have faded out of being: the good which in his boyhood he devised for coming generations lived after him."[57] An evil time and an antiquarian impulse: these are unlikely foundations for the future.

I will return to Thomas Hearne in time. What interests me more broadly in this chapter are the peculiar dimensions of antiquarian time in James's fiction and their relation to other temporal commitments: of institution, of profession, of the many acts of academic and creative medievalism that came to absorb so much of his attention. But of all the scholarly projects James undertook in a long life, his catalogues of medieval manuscripts are perhaps most fascinating for their temporal multivalence. Preprofessional in more than one sense, they link timelines of individual colleges and collections to broader disciplinary horizons. They trace medieval homes and wanderings, as if the past were a mazy tangle to set straight. They aim at comprehension but remain finally in draft. Above all, they fully occupy the time of a scholar who experienced his own extraordinary industry as a kind of puzzling indolence: "I do not know how far these remarks will go towards convincing anyone that researches of this kind are worth the time spent on them; if they fail to do so, I shall have to do as best I can without the sympathy of my critics. I am afraid, in any case, that I must plead guilty to having spent a great deal of time over this particular research and also to an intention of continuing such pursuits in the future."[58] The preemptive defensiveness against hostile critics is rather curious, given how overwhelmingly positive were the published reviews of James's catalogues (with the exception noted above). Yet his catalogue prefaces are studies in temporal anxiety, the "onslaughts of every future specialist" menacing the delayed and yet premature cataloguer, although "so far the experts have treated me with great kindness" (these words written in his early forties).[59] Here James's humility shines through, of course, but so does a genuine preoccupation with the transitional, "middle" quality of his scholarship, as well as its doubtful trajectory in time, as if cataloguing work might medievalize its practitioners. In this way James's lifelong project—as well as its figuration in his imaginative fiction—is uneasily in sync with antiquarian times.

GHOST OF THE OAK GALL

It is safe to say that the endangered temporality of the manuscript cataloguer is the reticent theme of "Mr. Humphreys and His Inheritance," though the story's many eerie extras (including an ominously mobile Irish yew) may tempt us away from the library-labyrinth metaphor standing at its center. Quite a lot of ink has been spilled in tracing the tale's derivations from "the early literature of evil" in order to reveal its "Satanic symbolism" and the "maze of secrets" that are thought to reveal the convolutions of James's dark intent.[60] Certainly, at least a patina of esoterica lends the tale atmosphere, yet poring over the constellation of diabolical references too intently could lead to readings that neglect more basic elements, and in particular the story's central metaphor comparing the cultivation of garden mazes to the particular angle of Humphreys's scholarly inclinations in his inherited library, the site of the thing "creeping up as it were out of unknown depths and emerging at the appropriate spot—the center of the plan of the maze," as James once summarized for a befuddled reader.[61] In an early draft now housed in the King's College archive, in fact, the creeper does not crawl from a map of the maze at all, but rather appears within "a volume of the projected Catalogue of the library."[62] In both versions, though, the real prize of Humphreys's inheritance is bibliographic, so that desire for the "long, interesting, tranquil process" of cataloguing the library overshadows the rest of the estate and manor, a building that seems "to desiderate wings."[63] The droll phrase conjures academic and book-collecting culture, the obscure desires of bibliophiles, as James once wryly remarked: "I might go on to make a list of *desiderata* . . . but it is probable that a good many of the items would only be desired by myself."[64]

The tale begins with the arrival of Mr. Humphreys at his newly inherited country estate, which he tours in the company of a comic caretaker, Mr. Cooper, an affable, semi-educated man susceptible to unintentionally meaningful errors of speech. Humphreys's new residence has a few very notable features: a fine library in the mansion and, on the grounds outside, an overgrown garden maze. There is also a "Temple of Friendship," which along with the labyrinth was constructed by his grandfather, inherited by his uncle, and is now handed down to Humphreys. The garden maze had been kept closed during his uncle's life, but now Humphreys obliges Cooper's curious daughter by unlocking the labyrinth and allowing her access to its secrets. The maze, however, confounds Miss Cooper and all others, with the exception of Humphreys himself and one other person: Lady Wardrop, a researcher of garden mazes who is finishing up a book on the subject. Both Wardrop and Humphreys are able to find their way easily to the center of the maze, where they find a metal sphere somewhat like a "celestial globe" but inscribed with darkly inverted asterisms of Cain, Chore, Absolom, and other sinister figures. Two Latin inscriptions offer additional clues: *Secretum meum mihi et filiis domus meae* (My secret is for me and for the sons of my house) (set as a motto at the maze's entrance) and *penetrans ad interiora mortis* (penetrating to the interior of death) (originally laid out one letter per stepping-stone in a path within the maze). Still further secrets are penetrated when Humphreys discovers in the library a mutilated seventeenth-century book with a marginal text, "*A Parable of this Unhappy Condition,*" telling of a young man who, "like *Theseus*, in the *Attick Tale*," ventures inside a terrifying maze. But matters finally do come to a head when, at the request of Lady Wardrop, Humphreys draws up a map of the maze and sets out one evening to trace a fair copy for the benefit of her project. As he sits in the library poring over this work, he notices a dark spot at the center of the maze map, a mark that gradually assumes the depth and horrific fascination of an infernal hole—through which a wasplike creature emerges. Humphreys lurches back, blacks out, and, later, after learning that the globe at the center of the actual maze holds the ashes of his abominable ancestor, orders the labyrinth destroyed. A coda from Mr. Cooper sums up all: "these many solemn events have a meaning for us, if our limited intelligence permitted of our disintegrating it."[65]

What does this have to do with manuscript cataloguing? Let us attempt to disentangle a few clues leading up to the story's "Jamesian wallop," for, as James noted in the preface to a 1908 descriptive catalogue, "no medieval manuscript can be justly called quite uninteresting, and the blame lies with the cataloguer if he has failed to penetrate the secret."[66] But Humphreys has inherited his deadly secrets to penetrate from an uncle described by Cooper—that malapropism machine—as a "valentudinarian" [*sic*] who suffers a "general absence of vitality," like a "flash flickering slowly away in the pan" (note how the intrusive *n* of vale[n]tudinarian allows for an implied near rhyme with "antiquarian"—as if amateur scholarship were a wasting condition). It is Cooper's disintegrated meanings, too, that prime the appearance of the ghost with a series of references to medieval ink. Offering a clumsy benediction upon Humphreys's arrival, Cooper declares, "May your residence among us be marked as a red-letter day, sir." Pleased with his sentiment, he later echoes it in front of Mrs. Cooper, who attempts to shore up her husband's polite intentions, adding to it a wish of longevity: "and many, many of them." Humphreys notices the temporal incongruities of both statements and offers an extension of the metaphor much too textual for present company, a group not readily familiar with manuscript rubrication: "[He] attempted a pleasantry about painting the whole calendar red, which, though greeted with shrill laughter, was evidently not fully understood."

Humphreys is badly out of sync, socially, and is eager to retreat to the library, where he plans to enjoy his inheritance: "The drawing up of a *catalogue raisonné* would be a delicious occupation for winter. There were probably treasures to be found, too: even manuscripts." Indeed there are, as Cooper marvels: one of the books was "all done by hand, with the ink as fresh as if it had been laid on yesterday, and yet, he told me, it was the work of some old monk hundreds of years back."[67]

This second metaphor of medieval ink ushers in what is to befall Humphreys in the library, where he attempts to trace a plan of the labyrinth to oblige Mrs. Wardrop, making a "careful collation of it with the original."[68] The moment serves to tease readers with the essential flavor of Jamesian terror on the dust jacket of the recent Oxford University Press edition:

> Before correcting the copy he followed out carefully the last turnings of the path on the original. These, at least, were right; they led without a hitch to the middle space. Here was a feature which need not be repeated on the copy—an ugly black spot about the size of a shilling. Ink? No. It resembled a hole, but how should a hole be there? He stared at it with tired eyes: the work of tracing had been very labourious, and he was drowsy and oppressed. . . . But surely this was a very odd hole. It seemed to go not only through the paper, but through the table on which it lay. Yes, and through the floor below that, down, and still down, even into infinite depths. He craned over it, utterly bewildered. Just as, when you were a child, you may have pored over a square inch of counterpane until it became a landscape with wooded hills, and perhaps even churches and houses, and you lost all thought of the true size, of yourself and it, so this hole seemed to Humphreys for the moment the only thing in the world. For some reason it was hateful to him from the first, but he had gazed at it for some moments before any feeling of anxiety came upon him; and then it did come, stronger and stronger—a horror lest something might emerge from it, and a really agonizing conviction that a terror was on its way, from the sight of which he would not be able to escape. Oh yes, far, far down there was a movement, and the movement was upwards—towards the surface. Nearer and nearer it came, and it was of a blackish-grey colour with more than one dark hole. It took shape as a face—a human face—a burnt human face: and with the odious

writhings of a wasp creeping out of a rotten apple there clambered forth an appearance of a form, waving black arms prepared to clasp the head that was bending over them.[69]

It is a dizzying passage of heightened horror, both in its hallucinogenic spatial distortion and in the figure of its insectoid specter. The basic supernatural implication is clear, though. The ancestor's "pore mortal coils" (in Cooper's words), charred and interred in the center of the labyrinth, emerge from a supernatural hole in the center of the map of the maze as Humphreys pores over his tracing.[70] The inverted celestial globe thus lets loose a burned bogey blackened by cremation as well as (we infer) infernal fire. Humphreys has penetrated to the porous interior of death—or he would have done, had his studious head not snapped back.

But we must not overlook the most striking aspect of this image: the way it emerges from what Humphreys takes at first to be an ink spot ("an ugly black spot about the size of a shilling. Ink? No."), linking the tale's climax to its rich catalogue of ink metaphors. The English word *ink* traces back to the Latin *encaustum* from the Greek ἐγκαίειν (to burn in), but I would argue that the image James produces has greater depth than that of a simple visual metaphor. The diabolic creature assumes a very specific shape, one stemming from the material grounds of manuscript studies, so that the creeping, clambering creature with its "odious writhings of a wasp" seems to have the "appearance of a form" of nothing other than a *gall wasp*. As James knew as well as anyone else alive, medieval ink was manufactured from oak galls, commonly referred to as "oak apples," excrescences formed on oaks and other trees when a parasitic gall wasp (of the genus *Cynips*) lays its eggs within the growing buds of the tree. When the larvae develop, the wasps burrow out, leaving behind the oak apples. Rich in tannins, these spherical galls were ground up and infused with liquid to form the core substance of most ink of the Middle Ages. James more than once elsewhere makes metaphoric use of this medieval recipe, for instance when assuring the readers of his memoir that "I have not often used a pen with gall in it,"[71] or (to note the exception) on the occasion of "flaying" Jane Harrison ("I instantly took a pen and dipped it in gall").[72] In a lighter moment, he wrote to Gwendolen McBryde, "For my own part I am not sure whether the pig's bristle or the oak gall is the better badge for me."[73] Given how James frames Humphreys's horror with a series of playful references to medieval ink, then, it seems a reasonable enough Rorschach to class this writhing, wasplike thing among those creatures who brought forth the dark substance of medieval writing. At the very least, they seem close kin.

How, though, to interpret this ghost of the oak gall? It seems to live in the crosshairs of James's larger library-labyrinth metaphor, which in this context leads us back to the cataloguer's relationship to time. Manuscript research, especially the work that chiefly defined James's own academic legacy, is not primarily about spatial mazes so much as temporal ones: from the study of scribal *ductus*—the sequence of angled strokes a quill makes on parchment—to all of the cataloguer's puzzles of provenance and blind passages of transmission. But there is also the temporality of the project itself, the "scientific"-antiquarian faith that, in the words of Bury, "a complete assemblage of the smallest facts of human history will tell in the end." Such a project could revert to a dubious endpoint, as the story seems anxiously aware: trace the ink back far enough and you might find nothing more than a parasitic insect—a desideratum of wings? The future seems likewise empty for a profession that threatens to breed, if not medievalism, then at best a medievalized relationship to time, an endlessly expanding middle period of transmission, the ink of the monks forever fresh. But how to avoid, in the words of James's bravura pastiche, "put[ting] one more to the *Catalogue* of those unfortunates" lost in the labyrinth of the library?[74] In the next section, I propose to examine the ways in which James figured the reclamation of antiquarian time within other temporal frameworks. After all, as he cautioned a youthful audience a few years after writing this tale, "there are a good many ways of living which are to the Empire what the maggot is to the apple."[75]

TIME AND THE TEMPLE

By academic calendar and school clock tower, James's life was timed to the foundational rhythms of education and research.[76] His academic homes were, emphatically, all-male institutions, and James certainly wished to keep it that way. He was consistently an opponent of women earning degrees at Cambridge, and his career spanned decades of debate and controversy on the issue. Matters came to a head in May 1897 when a proposal to grant women titular degrees was voted down by members of the university amid a dramatic public display of opposition in Cambridge, undergraduates in straw boaters packing every open window and crowding the pavement below. Effigies of women scholars were strung up in the streets, along with banners bearing misogynist slogans. When the vote was announced, the triumphant mob marched on Newnham Hall to exult in their victory. The men disbanded only after cooler college heads made an appeal to their sense of chivalry.[77] As Darryl Jones notes, a photo of the spectacle outside the Senate House is to be found among James's papers, apparently a memento of the triumph.[78] Even in 1897, though, Cambridge's refusal to grant degrees to women was recognized by many outside the institution as retrograde and even anachronistic. A scathing piece in the *Daily Graphic* referred to "Medieval Cambridge" and decried the "mental isolation" of a culture out of step with widespread institutional reform (between 1878 and 1895, most English universities outside Oxbridge had opened their doors to women).[79]

The refusal to grant women even the *titles* of degrees was particularly indefensible given that women from Girton and Newnham had been allowed to display their mastery of the tested subjects both in the Previous ("Little-Go") and Tripos examinations since the 1870s. Even when a stellar scholar like Agnata Frances Ramsay (1867–1931) achieved the only first-class ranking awarded in the 1887 classical Tripos exam (James received his own firsts in 1885), she was granted neither an official degree nor membership in the university, the right of even the most mediocre male graduate.[80] Ramsay was to remain in Cambridge only as the wife of the master of Trinity College—married to him "on the strength of her examination papers," in the condescending words of Shane Leslie, writing in praise of James's choice to reject, in stated contrast to Ramsay's husband, "the academical form of matrimony which had begun to destroy the calm character of the celibate colleges." That a woman's participation in the university examinations served little purpose beyond marriageability is the undisguised theme of "Lubrietta," one of E. G. Swain's *Stoneground Ghost Tales* (1912), a collection dedicated to James (its "indulgent parent"). In the tale, a sentimental evaluator of Cambridge exams is nudged by paranormal events to raise the marks of a female candidate whose marriage prospects hinge on passing. Indeed, there were few opportunities for women to pursue further education or academic careers after these exams, so that even a truly superb performance like Ramsay's often marked the practical boundary of a woman's academic achievement.

Such limitations do not seem to have troubled James very much, or many of his associates, who feared in particular giving alumnae a role or a voice in university government. William Ridgeway, to whose 1913 festschrift James contributed an article, was a particularly vocal proponent of the view that women generally harbored "a deliberate desire to control and dominate" the affairs of men, and arguably James's fictional portrayals of women (the bulldozing personality of Mrs. Anstruther in "The Rose Garden," just for example) reflect similar suspicions.[81] In 1896 a syndicate at Cambridge put forward a compromise position that accordingly separated the question of the *titles* of degrees from university membership or privileges such as use of the University Library (under this plan, women were to be granted the first but none of the others). As a member of this committee, James strongly opposed even this concession and along with three others refused to sign the report.[82] This was the proposal eventually defeated in May 1897, sparking the triumphant mob. On that occasion James read on the floor of the Senate House a speech in which he argued that degree titles would eventually lead to full university membership for women: "it is abundantly clear that in a very few years a mixed university we shall be—I suppose until the men leave us, and we become Pure again."[83] As it happened, James got his wish and Cambridge held out against full university membership for women for fifty more years, shamefully outlasting even Oxford (1919) by more than a quarter century.

This institutional purity for which James advocated in such uncharacteristically unreticent fashion was widely defended in terms of Cambridge's educational mission. Paul R. Deslandes has detailed how the male undergraduate's time in Oxbridge came to be seen as a crucial interval of masculine isolation and competition in his passage to elite manhood, and how coeducation was seen as a basic threat to that core function of the colleges. Although James did very little formal teaching or lecturing, his influence was often perceived as crucial to the undergraduate experience. A. C. Benson saw this very plainly as a unique role that would be spoiled by the presence of women: "indeed I do not want [James] interfered with in this matter: he fills a very peculiar niche, he is a lodestar to enthusiastic undergraduates; he is the joy of sober common-rooms. I wish with all my heart that the *convenances* of life permitted Egeria herself to stray into those book-lined rooms, dim with tobacco-smoke, . . . to take her place among the casual company. But as Egeria cannot go to [James], and as [James] will not go to Egeria, they must respect each other from a distance, and do their best alone."[84] Egeria, an unnamed "academical lady," is named for the rejected counsel and company she would offer James, but the pseudonym also brings to mind the early medieval pilgrim to Jerusalem (as well as those sacred spaces into which the modern Egeria is forbidden to stray). Yet James's "peculiar niche" might be considered all the more surprising given the incomplete course of his own passage beyond King's. As Deslandes finds, the "tendency [of college fellows] to delay or permanently eschew the natural course of masculine development by remaining in the college environment rendered them, in the minds of many undergraduates, no longer men but merely dons, a separate category of existence altogether."[85] As we have seen, even his own tutor considered the boyishly antiquarian James "a dangerous model for young men who have to make their way in the world." Nevertheless, James remained a lodestar for their lives, and they, in turn, provided an institutional justification for his own perilous place in time.

The temporal ramifications of this dynamic, I would argue, are the primary concern of one of James's most disturbing fictions. "The Tractate Middoth" features a plot, in fact, that turns precisely on the exclusion of women from Cambridge and its priceless libraries. As many contemporaries noted, women at Cambridge were not only denied their rightful degrees; they were also excluded from university resources, lectures, laboratory equipment, and, of course, books. It was particularly galling that even the faculty of the women's colleges "could only use one of the world's finest libraries on the same conditions as members of the public." Granting degrees or university membership for women would have addressed this issue, and indeed access to Cambridge University Library was a major bone of contention in the larger debate over "the woman question."[86] The renowned medievalist W. W. Skeat (1835–1912), a close associate of James's mentor Henry Bradshaw through their work together at the University Library, remarked that "even the BA degree would enable them to take 5 books at a time out of the University Library on a ticket countersigned by 'their tutor.' I am entirely opposed to the admission of women to 'privileges' of this character. And I honestly believe they are better off as they are."[87] Doubtless James would have concurred, and so it is perhaps more than a little perplexing to observe—as we shall see—that he constructs the plot of one of his more famous ghost stories precisely around the denial of this privilege to a woman, presented as a gleefully mean-spirited act.

The gender politics of the research library are evoked early on in "Tractate," when we get an offhand glimpse of "one of the prefessers with a couple o' novels" at the circulation counter, a detail probably connected with "the convenient fiction" (as David McKitterick explains) "that resident senior members taking books away from [the University Library's 'Novel Room'] did so on behalf of their lady friends."[88] But even more bluntly, in the story's opening paragraph, the conniving John Eldred announces that he "believed he was entitled to use" the library, and as we learn he is indeed "on the list of those to whom that privilege was given"—presumably a list of the names of men with degrees from Cambridge and therefore lifelong members of the university. We soon learn that Eldred's motive in visiting the University Library is to retrieve and destroy a damaging will written by his uncle and inserted into an obscure book—an edition of the title's *Tractate Middoth*—donated to the institution. The will is potentially harmful to Eldred, for it supersedes an earlier document written by his uncle just before his death, bequeathing him the entirety of his estate. The uncle, appropriately named Dr. Rant, has pitted his niece Mary against Eldred for no reason other than simply the sadistic fun of watching—from beyond the grave—the two struggle to locate the hidden document, Mary to gain the inheritance and Eldred to block her claim by destroying the will. On his deathbed, Rant tells both about the existence of the will but informs Mary with relish that it is hidden "in a place where John can go and find it any day, if only he knew, and you can't." This place, it transpires, is the University Library, a fact that Eldred can determine only through years of work: "But all [Rant's] books were very carefully catalogued: and John has the catalogue: and John was most particular that no books whatever should be sold out of the house. And I'm told that he is always journeying about to booksellers and libraries; so I fancy that he must have found out just which books are missing from my uncle's library of those which are entered in the catalogue, and must be hunting for them."[89] Eldred has privileges, but Mary (and her grown daughter) will need a university man, the young librarian Mr. Garrett, to penetrate the secret for them and ultimately track down the missing tractate before Eldred can fulfill his dark design. The women, though, disappear from the narrative once Garrett steps in, appropriating the mystery without their knowledge (in fact, he actively conceals from them his efforts) and eventually securing the future of the inheritance for himself after Eldred meets a grisly end. The perfunctory coda is crowded in a crabbed hand at the bottom of the last page of James's holograph manuscript of the story, now housed in the archive at King's College: "There is no great difficulty in imagining the steps by which William Garrett, from being an assistant in a great library, attained to his present position of prospective owner of Bretfield Manor, now in the occupation of his mother-in-law, Mrs. Mary Simpson."[90]

If James's plot device edges Mary out of the narrative, Rant's wicked scheme equally hinges on library privileges denied to women. For an author so strongly in favor of just such restrictions, though, the choice seems quite puzzling. After all, Rant is clearly a figure of temporal perversity. When his shade, with its desiccated pate ("it looked to me dry, and it looked to me dusty"), returns from a bizarre grave to watch over the tractate, his ghost is strongly reminiscent of this contemporary satire on Cambridge irrelevance: "The sour man graduate [drawing] his fluttering gown closer round his lean legs as he flits, shadow like, among historic shades mumbling brazen shibboleths and nodding a wooden head. Well the women will survive and these men are only a survival."[91] Rant's peculiar methods of torture, moreover, are designed to arrest the timelines of its victims, locking them into a bibliographical "hunt that might waste a lifetime," as Mrs. Simpson fears.[92] Eldred, too, is put "on the stretch" by Rant's scheming and spends twenty years reverse-cataloguing a library to track down the tractate. Wasting lifetimes in this way seems to be Rant's main antiquarian intent, and the image of him buried sitting upright at a table, in eternal lucubration, is perfectly emblematic of the temporality he embodies.

The impression that James has figured all-male Cambridge as a nest of ingrown timelines is only confirmed by close attention to the central artifact of the story. The *Tractate Middoth* is a very real book, constituting a section of the Talmud dealing mainly with minute details of the rebuilt Temple in Jerusalem, its literal measurements and other details of ritual and restriction associated with its architecture.[93] (This particular edition, with commentary by the celebrated medieval scholar Nachmanides, seems to be fictitious.) Along with much counting of cubits, there is, for example, the description of a chamber in which logs are examined for worms (lest they pollute sacred fires) and discussion of the way priests must avoid touching altar stones with iron trowels, "for iron was created to shorten man's days, while the Altar was created to lengthen man's days."[94] This last bit of sympathetic magic is perhaps in a way analogous to the *Tractate*'s thematic fit within the tale, for just as Rant has deposited his twisted will within this book, he has also secreted the *Tractate* itself away within the sacred walls of Cambridge University Library, a temple with its own priests, arcane rules, and exclusive privileges. Like houses like. Indeed, just as James's tale opens with a discussion of who has access to the library's inner vaults, the *Tractate Middoth* itself constitutes one of our two major sources of knowledge of the Temple's outer "court of the women," so named not because "it was exclusively devoted to that sex, but [because] no women were allowed to advance beyond it."[95] But the *Tractate* also resonates beyond the court of the women, as a metaphor for the cataloguic measuring that Eldred must undertake in order to locate the book. As we have seen, measuring the temple of the medieval library was the chief ambition of James's academic career, a project that perennially threatened to "waste a lifetime" in its mazy chambers.

Again, then, it is the temporal valence of this work that signifies most strongly. Before going any further, however, we should pause to recognize that James's story, in which a Hebrew text plays such an important role, is deeply invested in a phobic Judaic metaphor. It is not, unfortunately, the only place in James's fiction where he employs recognizably anti-Semitic images in implicit opposition to a sense of normative Englishness. In "The Uncommon Prayer-Book," the biblioklept Mr. Poschwitz ("black-haired and pale-faced, with a little pointed beard and gold pince-nez") is adjudged not "a reel Englishman at all" and suffers a grim fate for his avarice.[96] In a real-world analogue to this fictional Jewish threat, James composed a heated letter dated 3 September 1918 attempting to convince (unsuccessfully, in the event) the connoisseur Henry Yates Thompson to preserve his manuscript collection "safe for England" rather than allowing it "to be dispersed again among Boches Jews & Transatlantics." Avoiding such a thing, he wrote, would be a "permanent service to the nation & the race."[97] It may be considered ungenerous to single out an isolated statement such as this from private correspondence, and it is true that we could also point to instances where James's scholarship serves—on the whole—to debunk virulent and dangerous historical myths. His discovery and detailed analysis of Thomas of Monmouth's vita of Saint William of Norwich, for example, helped expose the delusional grounds of a central case in the medieval development of the venomous blood libel (the accusation that Jews engaged in the ritual murder of Christian children and the consumption of their blood).[98]

I would also argue that the text of "The Tractate Middoth" is focused less on religious or ethnic identities per se than on using old-dispensation spirituality as a metaphor for unregenerate scholarly time. Nevertheless, the chilling overtones of this metaphor require careful and explicit acknowledgment, for the line (if it exists) between supersessionary metaphor and anti-Semitic rhetoric is painfully easy to cross. James himself crosses it in an undated sermon to a student assembly at Eton:

> I think it needs to be emphatically said that the Law as it came to the Jews after the captivity was beautiful to them and was the seed of admirable qualities and values: because we know very well that what they made of it in succeeding centuries was far from admirable. The verdict is: Ye have made the commandment of God of none effect through your tradition. The multitudinous refinings upon the Law were many of them quite harmless—some of them were devised in order to get round the commandment and others to close up all the loopholes by which ordinary people might evade their obligations: all were extraordinary feats of oriental subtlety. Now in the end, as the Apostles said, they put a yoke on the necks of those who wanted to enter into the Kingdom of God, such as neither we nor our fathers were able to bear. And the ingenuity and the untiring persistency which devised these masses of rules are the qualities which—when they are applied to the affairs of life—are responsible for all that ~~we dislike~~ makes us dislike the Jews now. The quibble by which Shylock was cheated of his pound of flesh and a great deal besides was just the sort of thing that he would have been delighted to invent himself.
>
> So there is a danger in tradition as well as a safeguard. If it welded the Jews together and made it possible for them to preserve their nationality it also made them develop some very unamiable qualities—blinded their eyes and hardened their hearts—and was to no slight extent responsible for the dreadful treatment they met with from other nations. Not that I mean to excuse these other nations for the way in which they treated the Jews: only I do say that the Jews made themselves most difficult to deal with.
>
> Now Eton is a place where we live very much on tradition. You have guessed that I was coming to that.[99]

There is no way to excuse the ugliness or irresponsibility of these words—delivered to an audience of Eton boys over whom James had enormous influence. But as a reflection on the potential sterility of institutional rules and traditions, the passage offers insight into the strained supersessionary logic of "The Tractate Middoth."

That logic is fairly clear when we take a step back. Rant devises a bizarre mechanism of temporal stagnation associated with the Talmud, the Temple, and the cataloguic measuring of its dimensions. The temporal sterility that this plot produces in Eldred is displayed in the old-fashioned dundreary whiskers ("Piccadilly weepers") he wears, a feature easily mistaken for the *payot*, or sidelocks, dictated by Talmudic law. Eldred is not to be taken as literally Jewish, however, but rather as a representation of an unredeemed antiquarian temporality (of one lost in the cataloguic task of "measuring the temple" of the library). As in his speech at Eton, James is tapping into a Christian tradition, dating back to the Middle Ages, of associating Jews with the *sterilitatis obprobrium* (shame of sterility) (in the words of the Venerable Bede) considered inherent in a Jewish approach to divine law, rules, and traditions.[100] As Edward Wheatley has noted, such medieval metaphors are closely linked to the topos of the purported spiritual blindness of Jews, a notion that James alludes to in his sermon.[101] "Let their eyes be darkened," Paul writes of Israel, "that they may not see."[102] A related blindness haunts both Eldred and Rant, the ghost of the latter terrifying Garrett in the stacks: "the eyes were very deep-sunk; and over them, from the eyebrows to the cheek-bones, there were *cobwebs*—thick. Now that closed me up, as they say." The fate of Eldred, on the other hand, is sealed by an inky apparition that in some respects recalls Mr. Humphreys's inheritance: "First, something black seemed to drop upon the white leaf and run down it, and then as Eldred started and was turning to look behind him, a little dark form appeared to rise out of the shadow behind the tree-trunk and from it two arms enclosing a mass of blackness came before Eldred's face and covered his head and neck."[103]

That Eldred's face is blotted out as he struggles to suppress his uncle's will is no accident, nor is the fact that his death is officially attributed to a "weak heart."[104] In *De civitate Dei*, Augustine notes of the Jews, "When they do not believe in our Scriptures, their own Scriptures, to which they are blind when they read, are fulfilled in them."[105] The Old exists to be fulfilled and superseded by the New: this is the temporal logic that understands "Jewish law, Jewish understanding, Jewish being as the past"—not only as defunct but as representing, as Steven F. Kruger argues, a "spectral" pastness that obstinately refuses the futurity of a Christian present.[106] As a postincarnational document, Kruger notes, the Talmud in itself represents a threat to a temporal order that finds the very notion of a "Jewish present" in some respects unthinkable. Layering on commentary by Nachmanides (1194–1270)—a celebrated Jewish scholar who famously defended Talmudic learning against Christian disputants at Barcelona in 1263—only intensifies this sense of disjointed time. After publically claiming victory (and gaining the grudging respect of Jaime I of Aragon), Nachmanides was forced into exile, embodying "a Jewish temporality violently removed from the present."[107] In James's tale, the supersessionary reckoning is capped by a visual illusion: Rant's last will and testament at first glance seems to be Hebrew but is subsequently revealed to be English disguised in a kind of Hebraized script (in an analogue to Eldred's anglicized faux *payot*). The discovery is made at the inquest: "'it is not Hebrew at all. It is English, and it is a will.'"[108] Eldred (whose name might be interpreted as "old *ræd*," i.e., ancient "counsel, wisdom, or ordinance") is overcome, the literal testament is regenerated, and Garrett finds bride and future prospects both in a single stroke. It is a tidy, if disturbing, narrative trick.

At the center of the device, though, remains Mary's exclusion from the library. Antony Oldknow has argued that "The Tractate Middoth" would cause James's "influential listeners to reflect on the status of women" and that James himself might have "hoped [that his tale might] sensitize audience members with impulses for change."[109] The story's supersessionary logic, however, cuts in a quite different direction. In building a plot around Mary's plight, James does indeed loudly raise the issue for anxious consideration, but he does so only in an attempt to correct what he sees as its distorted orientation in time. The narrative is calculated to show that women's educational exclusion is not the actual problem: the impulse to blindly enforce such a tradition for the wrong reasons—to delight in the rule itself in an "unamiable" spirit—that is the bogey that Rant represents. We are meant to be repelled by his evident delight in the cruel ordinance for its own sake. Garrett's narrative arc—in which a young man enters the sacred, all-male university space on the lady's behalf—closely mirrors the ideological understanding of Oxbridge as a vital retreat set aside for intense homosocial interaction and competition preparatory to elite manhood. Along the way, the exclusionary tradition that Rant has exploited is redeemed in spirit—just as the will is recognized as being really English after all.

In this troubling ghost story, then, we can see James at pains to affirm the temporal bearings of his university, or at least one of its more contentious regulations. To recognize James's ingenious escape clause, however, is not to find it convincing. Few readers today, I trust, would.[110] In fact, the plot mechanisms that James devises—the unlikely chance meeting on the train, the perceptual trick of Englishing the will, the perfunctory marriage—are disconcertingly analogous to Rant's machinations. It becomes quite difficult to separate Rant's "extraordinary feats of oriental subtlety" from James's own narrative contrivances, so that we recognize the tale's own supersessionary logic as "just the sort of thing that [Rant] would have been delighted to invent himself" (to appropriate twice the words of the Eton speech). As an institutional apology, then, "The Tractate Middoth" raises more temporal unrest than it dispels, and at the center of that unsettled sense of time is the work of book cataloguing itself. The metaphors that James's story generates have more than one dimension, but the image of measuring out days in the temple of the library draws our attention to the manuscript scholar's own "peculiar niche" (to recall Benson's phrase) within his institutions.[111] James's stories were first read to an audience of largely unmarried, cloistered fellows who lingered in Cambridge at Christmas break, the university emptied of the undergraduate life that lent its Gothic halls a vicarious vitality. If James was a lodestar to such men, he in turn was living, as it were, on borrowed time. Such relationships, James strained to believe, redeemed an otherwise hopelessly antiquarian temporality—or at least incorporated its swerving lines within an institutional architecture.

TIME TO THOMAS HEARNE

The Cambridge hauntings of "The Tractate Middoth" are an exception to a general Jamesian rule. Quite unlike such contemporary emulators as Arthur Gray (the master of Jesus College, who, writing under the ironically medievalized pseudonym "Ingulphus," published a book of his own antiquarian ghost stories in 1919), James rarely used university settings for supernatural tales.[112] Even the story draft "The Fenstanton Witch," featuring a pair of misguided fellows of King's, restricts its horrors off campus. In *Eton and King's* James explicitly notes the incompatibility of ghosts and colleges:

> Ghosts and ghostly phenomena are rare in Colleges, and highly suspect when they do occur. Yet, on the staircase next to mine was a ghostly cry in the bedroom. I never heard it—never, indeed, heard

of it until a visitor of mine staying in those rooms one Christmas described it at breakfast. Then certain seniors, Fred Whitting and Felix Cobbold, showed no surprise: *they* knew about it, and knew whose voice it was believed to be—that of a man who died in 1878. They had kept it to themselves, and I shall not put it into print.[113]

If we are to believe the marginalia in Shane Leslie's copy of this memoir, James in fact understood the unprintable cause of this haunting to be sexual scandal. The man is identified as "the bursar—by suicide, after a supposed intrigue with a chorister. [A]cc[ording] to AF Scholfield there was a Mr King who said it is a very lamentable thing to be turned out of the College at 70 and above all to be turned out for fornication!"[114] On one of his visits, Luxmoore himself was said to have heard the spirit lamenting in the stairwell. Whether the former tutor was hearing things (and whether James had all his facts straight in this case), it is fascinating to reflect that such ghosts of sexual victimization, silenced scandal, and institutional shame were rumored to howl just outside the very rooms of the Gibbs Building in which James regaled guests with horrors of his own.

As this chapter's final section will detail, the scandalous background of a very similar haunting has long stood unnoticed in plain sight since its appearance in James's 1919 volume, *A Thin Ghost and Others*. I have argued so far that manuscript cataloguing figures in James's fiction as a source of much temporal uneasiness, an emblem of unsettled time tenuously anchored to the integrity of medieval institutions. The horror of "The Diary of Mr. Poynter" is centered around the disturbing failure of such foundations, embodied in the strange and debauched death of an eighteenth-century Oxford undergraduate. What is telling, though, is how this horror is filtered through the scholarly remains of Thomas Hearne, a dubious forerunner of James. Annotators of the tale have identified James's inspiration as Hearne's 1715 edition of John Leland's *Collectanea*, an antiquarian anthology of notes, biographical sketches, and manuscript catalogues that was, as Michael Cox notes, "a bibliographical event of great importance and formed part of the historical substructure of MRJ's own work."[115] But, as I will show, the pattern is set not by the *Collectanea* but rather by Hearne's own "antiquarian diary," a work that interleaves scraps of past malice and excess with timelines of the present.

Thomas Hearne (1678–1735) was indeed a curious and rather controversial figure in the history of James's profession. His surviving diaries, along with serving as a rich repository of antiquarian learning, colorfully record the man's many feuds, academic and otherwise, which were often fueled by the charged religious and political atmosphere of the eighteenth century (Hearne's Jacobitism famously cost him the chief librarianship of the Bodleian). While James seems genuinely to have admired Hearne's contributions to early medieval studies, he would nevertheless have been well aware of the abuse the irascible Hearne suffered at the hands of his critics, the most famous example of which I have already cited. These are the oft-reprinted lines by an epigrammist whose identity has been lost to history:

Pox on't quoth Time to Thomas Hearne
Whatever I forget you learn.[116]

Hearne was the target of very similar satire in Pope's *Dunciad,* where he appeared as "Wormius," a dry-as-dust antiquary "on parchment scraps y-fed":

To future ages may thy dulness last,
As thou preserv'st the dulness of the past![117]

Both couplets are relatively benign versions of this idea, but the notion of Hearne's work as a drain on the productive flow of time is widely expressed elsewhere with considerable bile. A censorious, book-length evaluation of his career appeared the year after his death, accusing him of "*wasting* not employing, a Life of Fifty odd Years," while a 1788 letter to the *Gentleman's Magazine* praised and decried Hearne's work in a single breath—for having both arrested and advanced the progress of national history through the "mental sickness" of antiquarianism: "Instead of manly erudition . . . his prefaces shew the most trifling and abject pursuits. . . . We are forced to despise the man to whose labours we are obliged."[118] Certainly, James himself was massively obliged: his work of tracing and cataloguing manuscripts relied heavily on information and texts surviving uniquely in Hearne's published and unpublished writings. In fact, by James's day, Hearne's reputation had been partially rehabilitated by many who likewise valued his uncommon faithfulness to original documents (perversely preserving them "purely corrupt," as contemporaries complained).[119] Nevertheless, an intertwined sense of personal and professional abjection lingered. Foundational, yet a pox upon futurity: it was a legacy of academic medievalism that might eerily resonate with James's own.

Small wonder, then, that for James, Hearne's diaries suggested possibilities for a ghost story. The tale is focused around a discovery that "Mr. James Denton, M.A., F.S.A., etc. etc., sometime of Trinity Hall" makes in a very similar antiquarian journal after purchasing its manuscript, sight unseen, from a London book auctioneer. Inside the book he finds pinned a scrap of fabric imprinted with a pattern that "reminds one of hair," and that immediately appeals to the tastes of his overbearing aunt. Denton and she live alone together and are in the process of decorating a new country manor; they decide to have the pattern reproduced as curtains. The realization that something is wrong comes gradually. "No doubt," Denton observes, "it was suitable enough for a curtain pattern: it ran in vertical bands, and there was some indication that these were intended to converge at the top."[120] We later learn that, in the reproduction for curtains, the vertical bands are made to come together, a decision that Denton comes to regret (one should not allow strands to cross: a timeless safety tip). Whatever the supernatural logic at play, though, the chintzes give rise to something horrible, which Denton at first mistakes for his pet spaniel:

> Then he thought he was mistaken: for happening to move his hand which hung down over the arm of the chair within a few inches of the floor, he felt on the back of it just the slightest touch of a surface of hair, and stretching it out in that direction he stroked and patted a rounded something. But the feel of it, and still more the fact that instead of a responsive movement, absolute stillness greeted his touch, made him look over the arm. What he had been touching rose to meet him.[121]

Fleeing the room and, the next day, the manor itself, Denton searches the diary, only to find two or three pages of it pasted together. Steaming these pages open, he reads Mr. Poynter's account of the origin of the patterned fabric he has had reproduced: we learn from the diary that a certain "personable young gent" named Everard Charlett had the reputation of being a "loose atheistical companion, and a great Lifter, as they then call'd the hard drinkers." Guilty of many unnamed "extravangancies" and "debaucheries," Everard was eventually "found in the town ditch, the hair as was said pluck'd clean off his head." Years later, his coffin is opened by accident and is found to be full of hair. This hairy fate seems fitting, for Everard had been nicknamed "Absalom" on account of his great beauty and his notably long hair, which before his death he had memorialized in a rather strange way: he had the image of his locks reproduced in the form of a printed fabric, which he hung as a kind of tapestry in his lodgings.[122] (The biblical Absalom, of course, had been "hung by his hair to a snaky tree," as also mentioned in "Mr. Humphreys and His Inheritance.")[123] Poynter had collected a scrap of this fabric in his diary, and now a disgusted Denton finds reason to burn it along with the reproductions.

To begin to make sense of this odd tale, we need to appreciate how closely Poynter's diary is modeled on Hearne's writings. We know that James had Hearne in mind when dreaming up Poynter's diary, simply because he tells us so: "It was then that he made certain of the fact, which he had before only suspected, that he had indeed acquired the diary of Mr. William Poynter, Squire of Acrington (about four miles from his own parish)—that same Poynter who was for a time a member of the circle of Oxford antiquaries, the centre of which was Thomas Hearne, and with whom Hearne seems ultimately to have quarrelled—a not uncommon episode in the career of that excellent man."[124] The reference here, as I have noted, is to Hearne's own antiquarian diaries, running to 145 handwritten octavos in manuscript and published in eleven printed volumes under the title *Remarks and Collections* by the Oxford Historical Society between 1885 and 1918 or 1921.[125] Hearne's diaries are just as James describes Poynter's: "As is the case with Hearne's own collections, the diary of Poynter contained a good many notes from printed books, descriptions of coins and other antiquities that had been brought to his notice, and drafts of letters on these subjects, besides the chronicle of everyday events."[126]

Hearne's *Remarks and Collections* is unquestionably James's dominant source and inspiration for his eighteenth-century pastiche. For instance, Poynter's characterization of Everard as, among other things, "a personable young gent., but a loose atheistical companion, and a great Lifter, as they then call'd the hard drinkers," echoes the language Hearne uses to describe scores of other "debauched" young undergraduates in early eighteenth-century Oxford. Such youths are often under the accusation of atheism, and are frequently in danger of death or expulsion from the university. We find in Hearne the tale of an "Atheistical Fellow" and a "merry Companion" who, before he is executed for manslaughter, requests that a friend "put now and then a Bottle of Ale by his Grave." Another, like Everard, is "a beautifull, handsome Person, but most miserably debauch'd." These "topping Gentlemen's Sons" often "wear their own hair" rather than wigs, and are occasionally found dead in ditches. We even hear of "a very great Lifter" who expires with glass in hand.[127]

The portrait of Everard Charlett, then, seems to be a blend of such debauched young men in Hearne, but James's borrowings extend beyond simply echoing the language of eighteenth-century scandal. For instance, Poynter reports that Everard is "of the same Family as Dr. Arthur Charlett, now master of ye Coll.,"[128] and that Everard "no doubt would have been expell'd ye Coll., supposing that no interest had been imploy'd on his behalf, of which Mr. Casbury had some suspicion."[129] We may infer that this "interest" is employed by Arthur Charlett, who is accused in Hearne's diary of doing the same for a certain Mr. George Ward ("commonly called for his loose way of Living Jolly Ward"): "Ward being a Favourite of the Master's, nothing is done against him, tho' he ought to be expelled both the College & University."[130] The historical Arthur Charlett (1655–1722) in fact plays a large role in *Remarks and Collections,* where it is clear (in Hearne's mind at least) that Charlett is the antiquary's chief enemy at the university.[131] Charlett is often "lashed" by Hearne, who mocks him as "Dr. Varlett" and characterizes him as an ambitious, petty, "malicious, busy Man."[132] Hearne's most common charge is that Charlett has "a strange, unaccountable Vanity," and so the fictional Everard Charlett's own self-involved personality (epitomized in his erecting a "memoriall" to his own hair) accords well with the intellectual and professional vanity of his historical kinsman.

But the most striking detail we find in Hearne's diaries is that Mr. Poynter himself is also no Jamesian invention but was in fact another of Hearne's real-life professional enemies. In the *Remarks and Collections,* John Poynter (1668–1754) (he is rechristened William in James's tale) receives the lash of Hearne's pen nearly as often as Charlett. To say that Hearne "seems ultimately to have quarrelled" with Poynter is a wry understatement, for from his very first mention of him, on 27 October 1713, Hearne is at odds with this rival antiquary over their differing interpretations of a newly discovered Roman pavement at Oxford. Throughout the rest of the diaries, Hearne abuses Poynter in both Latin and English: he is "ineruditus," "insipiens," "silly," a "Dull Simpleton," a "Cockbrain'd Fellow," and, most frequently, "that Block-head."[133] In aggregate, Hearne's serial abuse of Poynter is quite comical and would no doubt have caught the eye of James, a careful reader of the *Collections*. At any rate, James seems to go out of his way to hint at the identification of these Poynters. For instance, Poynter is described as the "Squire of Acrington," a town that does not exist, at least not where James locates it in the tale. The historical Poynter, however, was from Alkerton, a town in Oxfordshire on the very border with Warwickshire. This fact accounts for a small, offhand exchange between Denton and his friend at the book auctioneers' salesroom: "'Why, I thought there might be some Warwickshire collections, but I don't see anything under Warwick in the catalogue.' 'No, apparently not,' said the friend. 'All the same, I believe I noticed something like a Warwickshire diary. What was the name again? Drayton? Potter? Painter—either a P or a D, I feel sure.' He turned over the leaves quickly. 'Yes, here it is. Poynter. Lot 486. That might interest you.'"[134] The passage makes little sense until we understand that "something like a Warwickshire diary" means a diary written by a man living in Acrington/Alkerton, a town just on the border of Warwickshire.[135] James is not simply borrowing a name; he is writing with the most minute details of Poynter's biography in mind.

This fact turns out to be significant, for there is more to Poynter's history in Hearne than antiquarian invective. In fact, Poynter's career came to an abrupt and scandalous end in 1732:

> On Wednesday night Nov. 29 last Mr. John Pointer, Chaplain of Merton College, was examined before the Warden of that College, Dr. John Holland, on the point of sodomy, he having been accused of sodomitical practises. Two persons of the College, Postmasters, I hear, of a good reputation, were ready to make their oath, and there were not wanting many other proofs, but their oaths were foreborn, and for quietness Pointer was advised to go off from the College, and forbid reading Prayers as Chaplain there any more. Accordingly he went off on Monday Morning Dec. 4, 'tis supposed into Northamptonshire, where he hath a vicarage. He hath withall a little Estate near Witney in Oxfordshire. He hath been guilty of this abominable vice many years. *This is the same Pointer* [emphasis added], who hath been mentioned by me more than once formerly, as a Pretender to Antiquities, which he knows little of. He hath been with the foresaid Dr. Holland, as he hath also with Dr. Potter Bishop of Oxford, to whose son of Christ Church he was a kind of Subtutor.

But this and other Vices are become so common in England, being spread from beyond sea and from a most loose Court at London where there is no Religion, that they are not by many looked upon as sins.[136]

Hearne's glee at his enemy's disgrace is barely suppressed as he puns on the "point of sodomy" brought against Poynter. As I have italicized in the passage, Hearne explains that "this is *the same Pointer*, who hath been mentioned by me more than once formerly, as a Pretender to Antiquities, which he knows little of." Recall that James introduces his antiquary by explaining that he is "*that same Poynter* who was for a time a member of the circle of Oxford antiquaries, the centre of which was Thomas Hearne, and with whom Hearne seems ultimately to have quarrelled." It is difficult to doubt that James knew about Poynter's fall or that James's fictional Poynter is—in some sense of identification, at least—"the same Pointer" sent away for "sodomitical practises" in Hearne's diary.

Nor is there only one reference to Poynter's possible sexual transgressions in Hearne. Four years earlier, in 1728, Hearne observes:

The B^p of Oxford, D^r. Potter, hath a son of X^t C^h., a young lad, whom he hath made student. His tutor is M^r. Bateman of that College and that heavy blockhead John Poynter of Merton College is to inspect him & is with him (I hear) all day, if not anights too, and is for that reason by several styled young Potter's nourse. This (were there nothing else, as there are several things besides) shews the B^p to be a man of a shallow understanding, otherwise surely he would never have pitched upon such a dunce as John Poynter. Sometimes another of Merton College performs the same office in Pointer's absence. The lad lyes in the Lodgings of his father at X^t C^h, the father himself living altogether at Cudsdon.[137]

The implication of Poynter's serving as "young Potter's nourse" every day, "if not anights too," is pretty clear, and this notorious corruption of the tutor's role is recorded also in the diaries of Thomas Wilson (1703–1784): "This evening I hear that Mr Pointer Chaplain of Merton 40 years standing was called upon a complaint made by one of the Commoners of the House whom he had got into his chamber, and after urging him to drink, would have offered some very indecent things to him. He has been long suspected of Sodomitical Practices, but could never be fairly convicted of them. They say he behaved with the utmost boldness and confidence."[138] A careful reader of antiquarian diaries (as James most certainly was) would find such incidents at least as memorable as the fact that Poynter's hometown was Alkerton, on the border of Warwickshire.

No surprise, then, that James redacts his tale's fictional diary, supplying the following note in brackets: "[Several lines describing his unpleasant habits and reputed delinquencies are omitted]."[139] This touch is yet another echo of Hearne's diaries, or rather of the diaries as edited by the Oxford Historical Society, which employs the same format and punctuation to note omissions. But while the OHS tends to signal extraneous material ("[Notes of a printed book omitted]"),[140] James brackets what is unprintably central for both Poynter's fictional diary and the historical record, leaving us with many questions and a bundle of narrative threads that do not converge into coherence. Most obviously, the title of the story might lead us to suppose that the haunting has something to do with Poynter's own life, a suspicion reinforced by the secrets we find in Hearne's *Remarks and Collections*. Is Poynter, then, to be taken as Everard's lover? Could the scrap of cloth be understood as a memento of their relationship? That conclusion seems ruled out chronologically (the fictional Poynter belonging to a later generation than Everard) and by the impassive tone of the diary entry itself, which tends to suggest that its author's interest is merely a matter of local curiosity. And yet we might also pause to observe that the pages of this entry are deliberately pasted together, a detail that tends to suggest that the diarist has recorded and concealed his information for private reasons, whether of sympathy or shame—or some other sense of association with what has been omitted.

The converging lines—the "scraps which often enough are found to be really threads"—never do quite come together, which may be appropriate for a tale of queer antiquarian time. Hearne's diary provided James with a model text for such a temporality, one in which strands of everyday life are unnervingly interleaved with a dangerously unfinished past. Like a corpse of hair, Everard's "lovely medeevial stuff" seems to warn of an extravagantly infertile past whose relationship to the present never passes out of draft or ceases to proliferate. And although some medievalists today seek to rethink an entangled, temporally rich present as "unbounded middle," I have argued in this chapter that many of James's later fictions find such medievalized time—and its relationship to a recrudescence of transitional scholarship—an abundant source of disquiet. James once remarked that his own view of university life was "sadly monastic," but he remained ardently grateful for the solace and relief that college homes offered his unusual temporal needs, a debt he paid in part with manuscript catalogues that came to define a preliminary life. This work, superficial or not, was a tribute to institutions he guarded with reticent intensity, though he was well aware of deficits charged to their account. By the time "Poynter" was published in 1919, of course, we must add the disaster of war to any list. In the final chapter of this book, I will accordingly turn to James's most famous postwar ghost story, and its curious relationship with the role he played in the design of Great War monuments and their official words of remembrance. James's status as a kind of institution of academic medievalism made it practically inevitable that he would lead the way in memorializing loss. In his haunting fictions, however, we may also sense the antiquary's perennial failure to forget.

5

TO THE CURIOUS

"I commend to you the virtue of curiosity, inquisitiveness." Here is James's core message for the young assembly of Shrewsbury School in November 1918, delivered mere days after he found himself, as he says in the opening of the same address,

> standing in the dark and the rain on the steps of the church of Eton, the sister of this in which we are met, and I was looking down upon a mass of nearly 1100 boys, each of whom held a lighted torch. From the roof of one of the ancient buildings that surrounds us the Last Post was sounded and again it was sounded from a more distant place in the midst of a deep stillness. And the boys passed out. It was the end of our celebration of the signing of Peace.[1]

That James chooses the importance of being inquisitive as a theme for this occasion is perhaps not as surprising as it seems. Curiosity is a constant watchword in his sermons and addresses, especially when offering counsel to young audiences, though James's take on the virtue has a rather distinctive inflection.[2] "It is a vast advantage to be curious," he would explain, "by which I do not mean addicted to asking questions, but rather being ready to allow that what our friends take trouble to inquire into is probably worth our own attention."[3]

For James, curiosity is not to be considered purely a drive to inquire or to serve abstract academic fields. It is much more often expressed as a mode of honoring and augmenting relationships—specifically male, intergenerational ones produced within close-knit educational institutions. As I have discussed at several points throughout this book, James's lifetime saw the emergence of new career paths for university men, professionals whose work it was to rethink the way both research and teaching were conducted. In prewar Cambridge, these reforms had specifically involved a shift away from reliance on for-hire intercollegiate coaches and toward a model of instruction carried out by permanent fellows within individual colleges. These "new dons" were not aloof scholars who ignored undergraduates (as had been, notoriously, the case in the past) but saw themselves as dedicated mentors. In the Eton-King's ambit, this tradition encompassed figures such as William Cory, H. E. Luxmoore, Oscar Browning, and of course James himself, who made it his particular business to cultivate close relationships with undergraduates even when serving in the college's higher offices.[4] These "pastoral" responsibilities were considered paramount. In this climate, indeed, undue emphasis on rigorous and disinterested inquiry (an "addiction to asking questions") could be seen as undermining deeper collegiate values—even if such an attitude limited the academic prestige of one of England's flagship universities. In the years prior to the Great War, a good deal of rhetoric denounced the scholarly failings of a cozy and insulated Cambridge, especially in comparison to the research productivity of German universities. The response of the dons was often defiant: their real business was to make "not books but men."[5]

James's emphasis on curiosity is something to keep in mind as we attempt to make sense of his late masterpiece, "A Warning to the Curious," the title of which has often been taken as a key both to this particular story and to the author's thematic concerns more generally. The narrative in fact bears considerable similarity to "Oh, Whistle, and I'll Come to You, My Lad" (1904), as if James were recombining elements culled from his own most famous piece of fiction. Both stories, for example, stage terrifying (and now iconic) pursuits along very similar shorelines, dwindling strips of land clinging to wooden sea barriers with Martello towers looming in the distance. In each case, a haunted young man receives aid and advice from an older mentor encountered in an East Anglian seaside inn, though the sickening fate of Paxton in "A Warning" contrasts with that of Parkins from "Oh, Whistle," who escapes relatively unscathed. But a capacity for self-referential reflection, for manipulating the conventions of a genre he himself helped shape, should not be mistaken for James's running out of ideas. If "A Warning to the Curious" is to be read as a late-career return to old imaginative stomping grounds, it has achieved acclaim nearly equal to that of "Oh, Whistle," its medievalizing complexity as compelling and difficult to reduce to a single message, moral, or "warning."

The story is also, crucially, a postwar return. Were there space here for a full sketch of James's later life, the central importance of the Great War could scarcely be overemphasized, in terms of both personal loss and professional duty. His two-year tenure as vice-chancellor of Cambridge began in 1913, so that the peak of James's administrative responsibilities arrived just as the university faced an unprecedented crisis, including the quite credible threat of invasion.[6] In *Eton and King's,* James writes movingly of a Cambridge rapidly emptied of undergraduates, including scores of young men he had befriended and guided in their early careers.[7] During the war, he personally comforted and corresponded with many soldiers at the front: "I am no hand at expressing what I have at heart—but I do not think that matters as between you and me," he wrote in 1916 to Gordon Carey on his departure for France.[8] The memory of such devotion had a long afterlife; in 1970, A. G. A. Hodges wrote a letter to the King's archives in which he recalls James's inviting him personally to view Codex D (Cambridge's priceless ancient manuscript of New Testament writings): "the great man lovingly explained to [me the] mysteries of abbreviation, and we worshipped the splendid uncials." Later, in 1916, Hodges was set to depart for the front and "felt exactly like a man going to the guillotine." After evensong services one night before his deployment, his old mentor caught up with him:

> There stood James waiting in the rain. He put his arm round my shoulder and led me off to the old Lodge, as if I had been his son, or grandson. I can see him now, in the study in his great armchair, in the light of a big fire, tall, dignified, gentle, sad.
>
> Perhaps he was aware of what I was thinking. Perhaps he was thinking the same thing. Apart from other dangers and tribulations, about six months later I took the full blast of a 9.45" shell, at a distance of about 3 feet. There were no blood-banks or blood transfusions in those days. My thoughts had very nearly found fulfillment.
>
> I never came back to Codex D.[9]

For James, memories of war were not a personal matter alone but were intimately connected with institutional duties. As vice-chancellor and as provost of both King's and Eton, he had frequent occasion to eulogize the dead—his particular eloquence on the subject was frequently noted.[10] And even before hostilities ended, James found himself at the center of efforts to plan permanent war memorials. As a prominent member of the Eton War Memorial Council from its inception in early 1917, he played an influential role in the form such monuments took. Thorny local, historical, aesthetic, religious, architectural, and political issues faced James and his colleagues (including several men who formed the core audience of his annual ghost-story sessions), and the council and its various subcommittees met dozens of times in the years during and immediately following the war.[11] The first project completed at Eton was a bronze frieze along the colonnade under Upper School, featuring memorial inscriptions by James and a long list of the fallen—each name listed with the soldier's year of graduation and the initials of his housemaster (the latter touch an addition that James supported in committee).[12] In a memo to the council dated "St George's Day, 1917," James laid out the advantages and drawbacks of this and a number of other proposed projects, most of which ultimately also found fruition: a vellum "Libro d'Oro," also inscribed with names of casualties; stained glass depicting medieval and modern soldiers; a monument in the mold of a thirteenth-century Eleanor Cross; a scheme to replace the stall canopies of College Chapel with new woodwork that would both serve as a surface for memorials and, "by hinge panels or otherwise," allow access to long-concealed fifteenth-century wall paintings (a side benefit that was, as James admits, "very attractive to me").[13] As this list suggests, many of the proposed memorials had a medievalizing theme that the council considered suitable.[14] The memorial tapestries that James helped design for Lower Chapel, to cite another example, featured the story of the dragon slain by Saint George—a knight in silver armor with an embroidered face modeled on a contemporary Eton schoolboy.[15]

One function of these war memorials that James had such a hand in creating was to serve as "symbolic foci of bereavement" to compensate for a painful lack of physical remains, as the bodies of fallen soldiers in the Great War were generally not repatriated.[16] This was a theme to which James often returned in his memorial speeches: the "nameless graves by the thousands," the fact that "some lie in foreign earth and some in the deep waters: and if they have helped to keep homes for others, they have none themselves."[17]

James's intense focus on memorial activity in this period raises the question of how such themes are reflected in his fiction. A disturbing if ambiguous instance may be the strange fate of Everard Charlett in "The Diary of Mr. Poynter" (1919), a story in which (as I have discussed in the previous chapter) antiquarian temporalities are ominously intertwined with implications of "sodomitical practises." But hints of sedition are also implicated, if only through the Oxford undergraduate Everard's being compared to the biblical rebel Absalom, who *erexerat sibi cum adhuc viveret titulum qui est in valle Regis dixerat enim non habeo filium et hoc erit monumentum nominis mei* (erected for himself, while he lived, a pillar that is in the Valley of the Kings, for he said, "I have no son and this will be a memorial [*monumentum*] of my name"). By contrast, Everard's "memoriall" to his hair takes a quite different and altogether eerier form, one of curtainlike "lovely medeevial" hangings that match the vanishing contents of his coffin: "breaking by mischance, [it] proved quite full of Hair."[18] What, we might ask, is the relation between Everard's perverse, self-erected memorial tapestries and the ones James was just at that time commissioning for Eton?[19] Does the connection lie in some kind of warning, as the etymology of *monument* (from the Latin *monere*, to admonish, to warn) might suggest?[20] Certainly, these memorials present the link between medievalism and commemoration in very different ways.

Outside his fiction, however, James's status as a renowned medieval scholar probably contributed to a strong sense that his words had the power "to accommodate the human toll of the war in a vision of historical continuity," as Stefan Goebel characterizes the medievalizing emphasis so often seen in Great War memorials.[21] Perhaps that is one reason why James was personally invited to ghostwrite the inscription for the official commemorative scrolls—numbering more than a million—that George V sent to soldiers' next of kin, along with bronze plaques honoring their sacrifice, in the immediate wake of the war.[22] Here, James was speaking not only for the nation but for the Crown; a recent article on war memorials even refers to James's text as "the King's words."[23]

I would like to begin a discussion of "A Warning to the Curious," then, by first registering a remarkable fact: that the same commemorating words from James's scroll can be found inscribed on a stone public war memorial that is situated in the very path along which the fictional Paxton hurries off to his supernatural death. Paxton is lured away from an inn called The Bear and down along a stretch of sand and shingle, where he meets his death near the foot of a Martello tower, just out of sight of the friends who rush to save him. In the introduction to his 1931 *Collected Ghost Stories*, James himself confirmed that the inspiration for "Seaburgh," the fictional setting of the tale, was the shoreline at Aldeburgh, with The Bear an obvious alias for The White Lion, a seaside hotel where James took rooms on several occasions from 1921 up through the publication of "A Warning" in 1925.[24] Paxton's doomed path—from the inn's seaward door and down along the shore to the Martello tower—was one that James was himself in the habit of taking,[25] and this route passes directly by the prominent memorial, unveiled in 1921 and still standing today.[26] James's authorship of the scroll inscription, however, was not publicly revealed until the week after his death in 1936.[27] In the early 1920s, then, James alone could have known, as he took his long walks to the Martello tower, that his own words were inscribed at the base of the towering stone cross, facing the sea and the battlefields of France beyond:

THEY

WHOM THIS

MONUMENT COMMEMORATES

WERE NUMBERED AMONG THOSE

WHO AT THE CALL OF

KING AND COUNTRY

LEFT ALL THAT WAS

DEAR TO THEM

ENDURED HARDSHIP

FACED DANGER AND FINALLY

PASSED OUT OF THE SIGHT

OF MEN BY THE PATH OF DUTY

AND SELF-SACRIFICE

GIVING UP THEIR OWN LIVES

THAT OTHERS MIGHT LIVE IN

FREEDOM

Let them who come after see to it
that their names be not forgotten[28]

It is striking to discover that James's own words commemorating the war dead have stood so long unnoticed in plain view at the site of one of his most famous fictional hauntings.

James's authorship of the text on this memorial is especially worth noting because memories of the Great War so clearly shadow this tale of a curious young man who stumbles onto an antiquarian discovery while touring a seaside town. As Paxton comes to learn, a recently defunct family, the Agers, had been guarding for generations an Anglo-Saxon crown buried near the coast as a kind of national amulet against invasion, to "keep off the Danes or the French or the Germans," in the words of the local rector.[29] The implications are ominous if not entirely clear, and James's handling of his theme is accomplished—characteristically—with a light touch. There is, for instance, no indication, implicit or otherwise, that duty might lead the able-bodied Paxton to be anywhere other than on vacation in East Anglia. Yet in draft (though not in the published version), James actually identified 1917 as the year in which a curious and carefree Paxton begins meddling around the site of the buried crown.[30] Is Paxton to be taken literally as a rank shirker of duty, as some have concluded? The tone of the story hardly bears out such an interpretation, and (given James's revisions) it might be more accurate to say that the youth, whose name suggests peace, occupies at the tale's beginning something like a temporally alternate world—a peaceful and pleasantly trivial "1917" untouched by industrialized war. Yet Paxton's experiences leading up to his violent death seem to parallel, if darkly, those of his decimated generation, as for instance when he considers how best to "trench across the mound" in search of archaeological treasure. Paxton suffers for his transgression like no other sympathetic figure in James's canon, despite his efforts to reinter the crown with the aid of two older men (one an obvious stand-in for James), who offer the youth their best advice and aid. Yet upon their departure, they glimpse what they mistake as a "long dark overcoat lying where the tunnel had been": surely both the shade of William Ager, last surviving guardian of the hoard, and a haunting reminder of trench-coated figures in tunnels elsewhere.[31]

James's first readers, in fact, had similar impressions. The year after *A Warning to the Curious and Other Ghost Stories* was published, Charles Mackintosh, an admirer of James's fiction and a recent resident of Aldeburgh (at Wyndham House, "the house just below the church"), wrote James with his local observations on the story and its setting:

> We should have been saved some sleepless nights in the earlier years of the war had we known of the "3 crowns," as that legend with the

exercise of a little imagination would have comforted us much when in residence, when we daily heard that the beach at Aldeburgh was regarded as one of the best spots for a German landing.

The knoll in which (in your story) the silver crown was found is well known to us, and when I last saw it it was partly surrounded by a deep trench, part of the efforts at fortification of the regiment in occupation of the town.[32]

Much of the disquieting power of "A Warning to the Curious" would seem, then, to flow from the way in which it channels dense memories of war into the traditional form of the ghost story.[33] A reading through this lens, however, has yet to find full, satisfying expression among critical responses to the tale, and in fact discussions of "A Warning" commonly (if surprisingly) make no mention of its Great War context at all.[34] Perhaps this is partly because the legend of the crown seems so bafflingly to depict one of James's otherwise more likable protagonists as a form of traitor—a potential underminer of national security. At any rate, Paxton's death has invariably been interpreted as a ghastly means of underscoring the "warning" the story purports to offer. Indeed, the memorable title of the tale often serves as critical shorthand in the evaluation of James's fiction more generally, so that "a warning to the curious" is said to be "the paradigmatic motto" of his ghost stories, the "climactic statement" of their themes, and "as clear a crystallising of James's intent as you will find."[35] Certainly, the phrase chimes easily with generic expectations of curious antiquaries succumbing to "the dangerous seductions of knowing" and "the dreadful itch of pure curiosity, morbid, perverse and inexplicable," to quote two representative formulations of what imperils Paxton.[36] Other engagements with the story, those very few that have given serious consideration to its war context, have found the warning clearly directed against Paxton's petty (or treasonous) indulgence in antiquarian curiosity at the expense of wartime security.[37]

Here, however, I propose to examine anew this "problem of Paxton" in the light of James's intricate handling of his medieval sources, especially Anglo-Saxon literature and archaeology. I wish in particular to unearth the tale's relationship to *Beowulf* and that poem's reception history, as well as the legend of Saint Edmund and the now largely forgotten Anglo-Saxon burial mounds at Snape, a stone's throw from James's fictional haunted barrow in "Seaburgh." The effect of studying these points of contact is to complicate what the tale's famous title purports to offer, to wit, "a warning." In fact, I would argue that the story is not so much a cautionary tale as it is a bereaved mentor's rumination on war and its memory, both collective and personal, commemorative and corrosive. The story is no admonition against curiosity, as has often been assumed, but is rather a restless *requiescat in pace* for those who, like Paxton, fell well outside the reach of sound advice, sufficient warning, or the capacity of the present to make decent and lasting sense of the past.

LEGENDS OF THE CROWN

In the tale's atmospheric opening, the landmarks of Aldeburgh/Seaburgh evoke recollections that are vivid but of undefined import, as if the narrator were employing a medieval "method of loci" without being able to fully retrieve what has been stored away. "[B]ut why do I encumber you with these commonplace details?" he asks, and we never return to an answer. In keeping with the ghostly genre's penchant for distancing techniques, James employs in this story a subtly complex frame, with the opening narrator soon replaced by the voice of a "man whom I had been able to oblige," who makes the narrator his confidant in telling the tale. First, though, the narrator records a drifting set of childhood impressions that "come crowding to the point of the pencil when it begins to write of Seaburgh."[38] In these disconnected, apparently aimless opening passages (a "pocket memoir," as one critic puts it),[39] far-off childhood memories seem invaded by more recent events, as when James describes the "flat clacking" sound of bells he recalls hearing "on a hot Sunday in August, as our party went slowly up the white, dusty slope of road" to an Aldeburgh church.[40] This stray, detached memory, especially in the context of the tale it prefaces, is uncannily redolent of a passage in *Eton and King's*, published just a year after "A Warning to the Curious":

> ... and then came August 4th, 1914.
> On the Sunday I was in a country church in Kent, praying for peace. On the Monday I went back to Cambridge, and then began the long succession of consultations in which emergency legislation was devised, the resources of the University placed at the disposal of authority, measures settled with the Town as to action in case of hostile landings.[41]

But in August 1914 James was in Kent—not in East Anglia—and there is no indication that the story's studiously offhand "word-painting business" might have any meaning beyond childhood nostalgia. These linked, drifting images of Aldeburgh past and present finally do, though, lead up to a description of a landmark with concrete narrative significance: the haunted barrow of the tale, a monument that will in fact prove the repository of medieval memory, in the stead of dense personal recollection: "there is a ridge that goes that way; and the ridge ends in a rather well-defined mound commanding the level fields of rough grass, and a little knot of fir trees crowns it. And here you may sit on a hot spring day, very well content to look at blue sea." This, we come to learn, is the very mound of the Anglo-Saxon crown set there "to keep the Germans from landing," a sobering imperative quite familiar to James.[42]

As a medievalist, James would also be aware of his haunted mound's resemblance to the dragon's barrow in *Beowulf*:

> Beorh eallgearo
> wunode on wonge   wæteryðum neah,
> niwe be næsse,   nearocræftum fæst

> (The mound stood ready in the field, near the sea waves, newly constructed on the headland, secured with cunning craft)[43]

This mound in turn might lead us to recall many other sites of mourning in *Beowulf*, from Scyld's funeral ship of the poem's opening to *Biowulfes beorh* itself, built high on the sea's edge in the poem's memorable conclusion. But James's legend, a fabrication that has at times been taken for authentic Suffolk lore, draws on other medieval sources as well.[44] Likely inspirations for the three protective crowns include a medieval Welsh tale, East Anglian heraldry, and an apparently very real episode of antiquarian folly in which an Anglo-Saxon crown was discovered at Rendlesham and immediately melted down for its metal.[45] Even more important, though, is the association of the crowns with Saint Edmund, the Anglo-Saxon king executed in 869 by Viking invaders, who in Ælfric's account dispose of their victim's decollated head in a thicket, lest it be recovered and buried as the foundation of a church in the martyr's memory. The head, however, miraculously calls out, allowing it to be located. James was fond of relating how he once localized a former Bury St. Edmunds manuscript by noticing the distinctive words scribbled above a crowned head drawn on a slip of parchment: "Here, here," the head calls, signaling to nearby Christians its location (and, to James, the book's provenance).[46] But the particular connection of Edmund's legend to the heraldic crowns was notably developed later by John Lydgate (ca. 1370–ca. 1451) in his "Banners of St. Edmund," which explicates the three crowns of East Anglia in terms of Edmund's "Royal dignyte," "virgynyte," and "martirdam the thrydde."[47] A most striking manuscript illustration of Lydgate's three crowns of Edmund can be found in Harley 2278, a presentation copy produced for Henry VI (the founder of Eton and of King's) to commemorate his visit in 1433 to Bury St. Edmunds—a foundation just next door to James's boyhood home of Great Livermere and a longtime subject of his scholarly attentions.[48] Eton, King's, Bury St. Edmunds: for James, the crowns lay close to home.

In "A Warning," however, local claims on the medieval past are betrayed by the curiosity of an outsider. Paxton must cautiously sniff out the crown: knowledge of its location is restricted to the tight-lipped memory of Seaburgh's citizens, who "say" among themselves where it is buried, "but they don't tell."[49] The history of Aldeburgh is of a piece with such protectiveness, for it had been the home of very real Anglo-Saxon burial mounds raided by curious amateurs. The mounds themselves, at Snape just outside Aldeburgh, were leveled in the 1940s and '50s and the land is now occupied in part by a hog farm. Long before they were destroyed, they yielded stunning discoveries,[50] including burial urns, a glass claw beaker, the remains of a clinker-built ship, and a gold finger ring set with a Roman intaglio, which last rather unusual item very likely influenced James's presentation of the crown as being "set with some gems, mostly antique intaglios," a detail some critics have regretted as "anachronistic" but might better be described as firmly embedded in the specifics of Snape archaeology.[51] These artifacts were found in 1862, but other grave goods are thought to have been looted in 1827, when "seven or eight gentlemen," reported to be Londoners, opened several barrows and found "quantities of gold rings, brooches, chains, etc."[52] Like Rendlesham's crown, these treasures were probably melted down.

But by recasting the crowns of Saint Edmund as a supernatural bulwark against invasion on his home turf of Aldeburgh, James is also shadowing a larger national effort to remember the Great War as a struggle of pure defense, a project often inflected by memories of the medieval. Goebel points out that the "messiness of the Western Front" and the lack of historical precedent of conflict with Germany "hindered the process of medievalisation," but that "some local memorial projects overcame both obstacles by re-locating the front from the Continent to the British North-Sea coast where Viking and Norman invaders had landed in the past." This narrative of the war's nature "had no better embodiment than St Edmund," and Goebel lists several war memorials that draw upon the imagery of "the Suffolk martyr."[53] James's legend of the haunted crowns clearly evokes this medievalized national memory but, as I will argue, the linking of the legend to *Beowulf* complicates the script considerably.

LAY OF A LAST SURVIVOR

Given the attention and annotation that "A Warning to the Curious" has received, it is surprising indeed that *Beowulf* has not figured in the discussion. A thief removes a cursed Anglo-Saxon treasure from an ancient barrow, an act that imperils a nation and raises the wrath of a monstrous guardian: in summary form, the debt seems unmistakable. Indeed, as I was readying an article version of this chapter for publication, A. S. G. Edwards observed in *Notes & Queries* the broad narrative similarity between the two texts.[54] Prior to that note, critics were more likely to linger over the implications of James's passing reference to *Great Expectations* than its medieval analogues.[55] The reason for this, again, may be the reticent touch of James's style; perhaps the most outright reference comes when The White Lion is rechristened The Bear, an understated reference to Beowulf's well-known ursine associations.[56]

In the hospitable hall of The Bear, the elders offer a warm, avuncular reception to a wayfaring youth: "it was obvious that he wanted company; and as he was a reasonable kind of person—not the sort to bestow his whole family history on you—we urged him to make himself at home."[57] The bone-dry reference to Beowulfian patronymics hints at the extent to which the anonymous, connectionless Paxton differs from Hygelac's nephew, the son of Ecgtheow, or from any young Anglo-Saxon warrior whose traditional calling card is patrilineal descent. In a heroic context, too, we expect words exchanged between men of two generations to reinscribe ancient codes of masculine virtue and action, but the resigned sense of fate that Paxton describes so frequently in his narrative seems more aligned with the aleatory dangers of the Great War than with an Anglo-Saxon sense of *wyrd* (which *oft nereð / unfægne eorl, þonne his ellen deah!* [often saves an undoomed man, when his courage is strong!]).[58] Still, the older men are most earnest in their desire to advise the companionless Paxton—to guide and to mentor him, to warn him and to ward off danger: "He was very submissive and *piano* about it all: ready to do just what we thought best, but clearly quite certain in his own mind that what was coming could not be averted or palliated." There is indeed a creeping sense that what he faces is beyond the mentors' formulaic resources, or even their comprehension: Paxton "dropped into a chair," the narrator reports, with a note of baffled if sympathetic embarrassment, "and I believe he began to cry."[59]

Paxton's problem, that he has "suffered something of a shock" and doesn't "know how to put it back," is never to be solved, and the best the mentors can do is to follow Paxton as he retraces a path of trauma through the phobic landscape. The threesome decline to go "along the front," but still their chosen route evokes nothing so much as trench warfare: "a narrow path with close high hedges, through which we hurried as Christian did through that Valley."[60] Here James again echoes a memorable scene in "Oh, Whistle"— in which the ghost who pursues Parkins is compared with the "foul fiend" approaching Christian in *Pilgrim's Progress*.[61] But the Valley of Humiliation (so apt for puffed-up young Parkins) has been replaced for Paxton with the Valley of the Shadow of Death, and the narrator suspects that "one who was on their side, so to say, had us under surveillance."[62] The curse cannot be walked back, and the dread is wrapped up in retrospective futility, recalling Beowulf's barrow-side ruminations on a father who suffers the senseless loss of a son: *ond he him helpe ne mæg, eald ond infrod, ænige gefremman* (And, old and wise, he cannot do anything at all to help him).[63]

Frederick Klaeber (in 1922) considered this "Lament of the Father" one of two exceptional digressions in the second section of *Beowulf*, the other being the "Elegy of the Last Survivor" (or "Lay of the Last Survivor," as it is often called), in which the last member of an ancient race keens a song of loss as he buries the wrought heritage of a vanished nation.[64] The lament begins with an image of war's destructive power, even before the industrial era:

Heald þu nu, hruse,   nu hæleð ne mostan,
eorla æhte!   Hwæt, hyt ær on ðe

gode begeaton;   guðdeað fornam,
feorhbealo frecne   fyra gehwylcne
leoda minra   þara ðe þis [lif] ofgeaf,
secga seledream.

(Now hold, O Earth, now that men cannot, the possessions of nobles! Lo, good ones previously obtained it from thee; death in war, a terrible deadly evil, carried away each of the men, each of my people, each of those who gave up this life, the hall-joy of men.)[65]

Such a lamentation is painfully appropriate, it hardly needs remarking, to the *feorhbealo frecne* (terrible loss of life) of the Great War, and James emphasizes that the narrator, too, is the tale's last survivor: "Oh, of course, it's only my word you've got to take for all this: Long's dead."[66]

In James's ghost story, however, the narrator is not the only last survivor; there is also William Ager, spectral guardian of the crown. It is in fact in the crucial matter of the Agers that the Beowulfian substratum becomes at once most central to the narrative and most philologically exact. The men of the Ager family, we learn, have traditionally held nightly vigil over the Saxon mound during times of war, in protection of the crown that protects the nation. The last of the branch, William, dies from "exposure and night watching" just prior to Paxton's arrival in Seaburgh: "And he was the last of the branch. It was a dreadful grief to him to think that he was the last, but he could do nothing. . . . So the last of the holy crowns, if it's there, has no guardian now."[67] The passage might almost translate an imagined lacuna in the "Lay of the Last Survivor": *Swa giomormod giohðo mænde,* we read of the last survivor, *an æfter eallum* (so the sad-minded one grieved aloud, one alone after all the rest).[68] But Paxton will, in fact, discover that the barrow retains its guardian—for the ghost of Ager lingers and, in the end, destroys the young man for his transgression.[69] James makes it perfectly clear, moreover, that Paxton's fate is sealed precisely because he has *touched* the crown; we are told more than once that this is why Paxton's mentors escape retribution: "We had not ourselves touched that bit of metal, and I have thought since that it was just as well," remarks the narrator in a moment of donnish understatement consonant with Beowulfian litotes.[70] Presumably, too, the Saxon crown of the martyr's memory is *galdre bewunden* (enwrapped in a spell), so that *hrinan ne moste / gumena ænig* (no man might be allowed to touch [it]), as is the famously cursed Beowulfian hoard, gold that damns anyone who touches it—unless they are accorded divine permission.[71]

Whether Beowulf himself receives such permission (and so escapes mortal guilt and punishment for troubling the hoard) is left somewhat ambiguous, a situation that has prompted long-standing scholarly debate.[72] In particular, the key passage in *Beowulf* concludes with a notoriously cryptic pair of lines, 3074–75, a "locus desperatus," as countless critics have concurred—a much-contested crux that has received truly voluminous commentary both before and after James's day.[73] To attempt to summarize these matters would be to plunge into depths well beyond my purpose, but the lines in question read:

Næs he goldhwæte   gearwor hæfde
agendes est   ær gesceawod.

(By no means had Beowulf with gold-greedy eyes before [his death] surveyed the owner's [i.e., the dragon's] inheritance more accurately.)[74]

The translation provided here (including the bracketed clarifications) was accepted as making "at least passable sense" by Klaeber, who explains that "in its general intent the statement is evidently a declaration of Beowulf's virtual innocence."[75] Among the many uncertainties in this crux of the curse is the identity of the *āgend* in the phrase *āgendes ēst* (inheritance of the *āgend*). Regardless of much later and ongoing debate, the relevant point from our perspective is that Klaeber in 1922 favored an interpretation in which the *āgend* is the dragon—the monstrous guardian of the hoard.[76] Old English *āgan* means "to own," so that the etymologically appropriate gloss that Klaeber provides for *āgend* is "o w-ner" ("spaced small capital letters indicate direct modern representatives") and the favored translation of *āgendes ēst* is "the owner's [i.e., the dragon's] inheritance."[77] The suffix of *āgend* has an agentival (no pun intended) function roughly equivalent to the modern suffix *-er*, so once again James is very subtle in his allusions when he bestows "a very old name" on the guardian *Ag*-ers in what amounts to a very reticent *figura etymologica*: "'To be sure,' he said, 'now that's another curious story. These Agers—it's a very old name in these parts, but I can't find that they were ever people of quality or big owners—these Agers say, or said, that their branch of the family were the guardians of the last crown.'"[78] The precise narrative and philological fit, along with the highly marked, peculiar phrasing ("big owners—these Agers"), strongly argues that James, a medievalist known for his love of detail, is embedding the East Anglian owner-Agers in the linguistic bedrock of *Beowulf.*

As examples throughout this book illustrate, the meanings that James invests in his frightening fictions are quite often ensnarled with multiple associations. They are rarely reducible to a simple or single reference, and, if only for that reason, we cannot ignore the more obvious etymology for *Ager*, from the Latin *ager* (field, land). The Agers, after all, are the guardians of a crown said to protect the land from invasion, so that multiple etymological threads are likely implicated in the web of associations James is weaving.[79] As William's ancestor memorializes himself on the flyleaf of his prayer book, "Nathaniel Ager is my name and England is my nation."[80] Nor can we fail to notice that "Agar's Plough" is the name of one of Eton's playing fields—fields on which, according to the banal old saw, vigorous English youth supposedly once secured a predetermined victory.[81] However we choose to etymologize, though, a fierce sense of national memory clearly motivates the Agers, while Paxton plays the role of the abject and anonymous thief, whose actions in *Beowulf* are also the *orleges or* (cause of calamity) on a national scale.[82] The logic seems inescapable: "Paxton [is punished] because he is unpatriotic," as Mike Pincombe has squarely put it.[83]

In fact, the very choice of reenacting *Beowulf* in East Anglia, of inscribing the poem in native English soil, might easily be interpreted as an act of literary and philological nationalism—and one with particularly fraught precedents. On the one hand, the connection seems natural, for more than one scholar has found reason to locate the composition of *Beowulf* on "Anglian soil."[84] But the way in which the story implies a relationship of cultural heritage between the environs of Snape and the events of *Beowulf* is reminiscent of how, as Alfred Hiatt remarks, "early students of the poem, often motivated by nationalist impulses, attempted to pin down the location of *Beowulf* in parts of modern-day north Germany, Denmark, Sweden, and in more than one instance, England."[85] Speculation included an imagined historical Beowulf who "dwelled in East-Anglia" and whose beloved uncle supposedly lived on "the coast of Suffolk, Hygelac's territory."[86] But it has been much more common to locate the historicity of the poem's events abroad, and it is now well documented that early study of *Beowulf* was dominated by attempts to annex the poem, often by German scholars who considered it "dasz älteste *deutsche* . . . Heldengedicht."[87] Moreover, although the situation was changing in the 1920s, *Beowulf* scholarship was rather a source of national embarrassment for English academics in the decades prior to the war, advanced German methodology producing "in England something like an inferiority complex."[88] In this light, James's choice to recast an episode of *Beowulf* in terms of the threat of German wartime invasion might well suggest that *ownership*—national, literary, philological—is potentially at stake.

The combined force of these observations might seem to confirm Pincombe's view, that Paxton receives a condign sentence of death for his lack of patriotism.[89] And yet what the *Beowulf* substratum most clearly highlights is that Ager's zeal to protect the crown is monstrously obsessive and destructive. Indeed, when at tale's end the elder men elect to let sleeping dragons lie, it is quite unclear whether their motivation is to protect England from invasion or to shield other curious souls from Paxton's fate: "What were we to say at the inquest? It was a duty, we felt, not to give up, there and then, the secret of the crown, to be published in every paper."[90] And it is very suggestive that the Beowulfian crux of which James makes most precise use is one that, if Klaeber was correct, appears to parse favorably the spiritual implications of Beowulf's having troubled the owner's arrogated inheritance (*agendes est*). Ager's unregenerate rage is all his own and simply does not scan as an authorially sanctioned curse against curiosity, a quality that James vigorously sought to foster in the young men he mentored, before the war and after.

We are left, then, with a profound disconnect between the uncompromising logic of the plot (a young man pays with his life for meddling with a national memorial) and the mournful tone and resonant contexts of a story that presents itself much more like a bereaved mentor's restless elegy than a monstrously crude fable. A useful analogy here may be to contemporary English scholarship on *Beowulf* that regretted the poem's emphasis on monsters, "a disproportion that puts the irrelevances in the centre and the serious things on the outer edges," in the words of W. P. Ker in 1911.[91] In a famous essay, Tolkien was to topple this view once and for all.[92] Yet although Ker felt that "there is nothing commoner, except dragons," he was also impressed by the way in which the poem transcended its "cheap" plot: "it is impossible to mistake the poem for one of the ordinary tales of terror and wonder."[93] I suspect that James, as a pre-Tolkien medievalist and as the aging author of the young, bloody century's most celebrated tales of terror, may have been drawn to emulate the achievement of *Beowulf*: to transcend the generic cheapness of monster stories in this literary memorial of the dead.

From this perspective, we might see the brutal logic of the plot as established precisely for the sake of allowing it to erode away in the telling. By all accounts, James nursed a bitter political grudge in the wake of the war: "*Qui a voulu cette guerre*? I want to go on saying that to a German till he is sick in my presence. We who have not been out to fight or do anything have no right to be noble or forgiving: it is a miserable state, troublesome and corrosive. Let us not think about it."[94] Ager's cadaverous guardianship is likewise a miserable way to remember the dead, and there is an uncanny relationship between the martyr's buried crown and Paxton's terrifying fate: "His mouth was full of sand and stones, and his teeth and jaws were broken to bits. I only glanced once at his face."[95] The degeneration of living youth into half-excavated artifact suggests that the corrosive memorializing of Ager lays waste and lithifies the identity of the dead—transforming their living remembrance into something damaged and strange.

But there is no good way to remember this loss. The averted glimpse of Paxton's broken face must also be an image of the violence that memorials strive to forget, so that his wounds open up, as well, the horror of what we might call *un-memorialized* memory. Paxton's disfigurement is no stock image selected to deliver a "pleasing terror" in the cozy ghost-story tradition. Facial mutilation, endemic for obvious reasons in trench warfare, was a very particular anxiety associated with the Great War, and Suzannah Biernoff has recently detailed how this "worst loss of all" (as contemporary press accounts characterized soldiers' shattered faces) was an anxious subject both of public discourse and of a widespread "culture of aversion." Part of this "collective looking-away" involved the fashioning of prosthetic masks. Great skill was needed, and famed sculptors such as Robert Tait McKenzie pioneered the art, often relying on prewar photographs.[96] During the same period, McKenzie was also called upon to sculpt the central Cambridge Great War Memorial (unveiled in 1922), which took the form of a bronze soldier striding home with a German helmet in his rucksack as a souvenir of victory.[97] This memorial, one of the more nakedly nationalistic examples of the genre, was commissioned by Arthur Shipley, James's colleague and a companion on the 1892 trip to Saint-Bertrand-de-Comminges associated with the writing of "Canon Alberic's Scrap-Book" (originally titled "A Curious Book").[98] Shipley had succeeded James's successor to the vice-chancellorship in 1917.[99]

If the art of war memorials and facial restoration were closely related, the reading of wounds was also a form of memory that James knew well.

In a speech at the unveiling of the memorial Roll of Honor of the Cambridge Tipperary Club in 1916, James took as his text what at first seems an uncomfortably inappropriate passage from *Macbeth* in which Siward asks after his fallen son "whether the boy had his wounds in front. 'Ay, on the front' is the answer. *'Why then, God's soldier be he.'*" To raise the issue of soldiers' potential cowardice in this context seems at first incongruous, even grossly offensive. But, in a masterly move, James goes on to upend Siward's brutal sentiment by declaring that every soldier who died at the front died with "wounds in front," concluding that *all* the war dead are now "God's soldiers, as they were the King's. They are training for the front."[100] Here is wordplay that shores up the collective memory of the dead, even as it raises the painful insecurity of individual action and honor in a war whose wounds were not always easily or safely legible: "Of course you feel that you were nonplussed at the liquid fire," he wrote in 1915 to a soldier wracked with guilt, "and I love you all the better for saying so: and I should like to know who would not have felt as you do, or done any better."[101]

How, then, to remember Paxton's wounds? He receives them in front, yes, but he is no Saint George setting forth to meet the monster along "the path of duty and self-sacrifice," in the words of the commemorative scroll. Lured from The Bear out along the strand, he rushes forward in the belief that he is following the two mentors who at every turn have attempted to guide him in his difficulty. The unrelenting spirit has cast a glamour over his eyes, and the older men realize with impotent horror that he is racing unknowingly straight into the face of Ager, who will turn, as Paxton rounds the corner of the battery wall, with sudden ferocity to destroy him: *duguþ eal gecrong, / wlonc bi wealle* (the troop all fell, glorious by the wall), keens the Wanderer in a moment of Old English elegy as famous as the "Lay of the Last Survivor."[102] But Paxton's death by the battery wall is by no means glorious, and the tale's final sequence is focused intensely on the agonizing inability of the well-intentioned mentors to alert the curious youth to the danger he faces—in other words, to deliver a desperate "warning to the curious." That the content of this warning, the particular advice that might have been delivered, is impossible to formulate even in retrospect, is perhaps precisely where the tale locates its most indelible horror.

The meanings invested in Great War memorials have received considerable scholarly attention in recent years, and no single perspective prevails. Some have seen monuments like the one at Aldeburgh as expressions of personal and collective bereavement, while others stress their potential to refortify embattled nationalist narratives or, conversely, to provide a warning against future conflict.[103] Reinhart Koselleck has noted how the political investments of war memorials inevitably fall away, despite their promise to safeguard such meanings along a "temporal vanishing line."[104] James's own reticent intentions are often difficult to pin down, but we should not underestimate his dedication to both artful misdirection and scholarly precision. Paxton's final fictional path draws a line between two very real monuments that even today remain standing: one inscribed with James's own ghostwritten words and the other, the Martello tower, an enduring symbol of national defense. The tale's haunting conclusion, however—with Paxton heading down the dwindling strip of shingle to an anonymous death—also implies a crumbling away of geographical convictions, the sea sweeping away the battery wall, reminding us of James's many investments as an Englishman, medievalist, and mentor. The story never returns to its opening fiction, that this is a tale confided to James by a lone, last survivor. The frames collapse and the exiled voice of the author seems to reassert itself in withdrawal: "And I have never been at Seaburgh, or even near it, since."[105]

AFTERWORD:
PROFESSIONS OF RETICENCE

An attempt has been made in this book to understand the ghost stories of M. R. James in conversation with his scholarly work, both in the intricate particulars and in the more general pressures shaping academic professions over the course of his singular career. I hope to have brought out aspects of this interrelation that prove compelling, or at least worth further consideration. Still, I fear that some may feel I have missed the mark in laying insufficient emphasis on James's sole purpose as he often stated it: to inspire "a pleasing terror in the reader."[1] There may be truth in the charge. Still, the quality that readers continue to value most in these tales—their dread capacity to deliver jolts—is not easily separated from James's medieval studies.

Certainly, the credentialed persona of the medievalist has an effect on the reader, whom James famously aimed to put into "the position of saying to himself, 'If I'm not very careful, something of this kind may happen to me!'"[2] Part of that necessary caution, I have argued, is to avoid wandering afield academically, and James often mines anxieties of amateurism in priming the reader's reaction. Razor-thin, though, could be the line separating emerging standards of rigor from a retrogressive excess. Professional judgment makes all the difference, in both weighing evidence and apportioning horror: "a modicum of blood, shed with deliberation," was his considered prescription.[3] Reticence was a doctrine he would eternally preach, but professional restraint also implies learned reserves that are fundamentally inaccessible to the nonspecialist. Even the legends of James's illegible handwriting—not always quite so bad, in my experience—seem less a slur on penmanship and more a paleographical metaphor for the impenetrable stores of antiquarian knowledge underpinning his thrills. Yet it pleases readers to make themselves vulnerable to James, in the dark and alone with his expertise.

That sense of command allows for medievalisms of a livelier sort. James saw the postmedieval associations of the Middle Ages as providing the wrong atmosphere for a ghost story: "Anything, we feel, might have happened in the fifteenth century."[4] An accumulated Gothic overlay, however, becomes a convenient screen for suggesting an even nastier revival, so that James often conjures naïve or indulgent appropriations of the past only to strip them down to something more raw. The tastes of Miss Oldys come to mind: the "mingling of modern elegance and hoary antiquity" she finds in her residence at Whitminster, her initial romantic delight in a talisman that will eventually fill the hall with sawflies and their dry, outsized feelers.[5] "Some degree of actuality is the charm of the best ghost stories," James understood, and his tales manipulate degrees of medievalism to great effect.[6] He therefore relentlessly returns us to archival sources, pseudo or otherwise, as if the gross materiality of the medieval text—its physical description, its feel as former skin, its alterations of "hair and flesh" (the two sides of each parchment sheet, the remnant of a book's animal origin)—stood in opposition to more diplomatic approximations of the historical record. No wonder that James's ghosts of scholarly transgression tend toward the fleshly, for this was the spirit of much of his own research.

"We do not want to see the bones of their theory," James says of ghost-story writers, and he follows his own advice with care.[7] But he also leads us to read like an antiquary. I am not the first to be led down this path, but the present study may represent one of the more immoderate attempts to rearticulate those "fragments of ostensible erudition" we find so abundantly suggestive in his stories.[8] These scraps often enough appear to be really threads linking the experience of medieval studies to other matters of considerable weight. That weight, in turn, is not to be discounted as a source of the tales' affective power if what interests us most remains the mechanism of their frights, the way in which James disturbs the surface of his stories with "gradual stirrings diffusing an atmosphere of uneasiness before the final flash or stab of horror."[9] The readings of this study trace the tensional stress behind such effects to a number of associated themes. James would have us know that his ghost stories are not "possessed by [an] austere sense" of authorial responsibility, but they nevertheless continue to resonate with their sense of carnal and institutional longing, of antiquarian and professional pleasure.[10] They convey the irreducibly provincial character of the past, as well as temporal binds of the medieval present. They share sacred territory with loss, malice, memory, and failure. "Reticence conduces to effect," and few tales draw us in with such disquieting appeal.

NOTES

INTRODUCTION

1. Lane, "Fright Nights," 105.
2. Cox, *Informal Portrait*, 79; Pfaff, *Montague Rhodes James*, 141.
3. For a bibliography of James's extensive academic writing, see Pfaff, *Montague Rhodes James*, 427-38. James was awarded the Order of Merit in 1930.
4. James, *Ghost Stories of an Antiquary* (1904) (hereafter *GSA*), 3. Unless otherwise indicated, citations to James's stories are taken from this and his other original editions: *More Ghost Stories of an Antiquary* (1911) (hereafter *MGSA*); *A Thin Ghost and Others* (1919) (hereafter *TG*); *A Warning to the Curious and Other Ghost Stories* (1925) (hereafter *WTC*); *Collected Ghost Stories of M. R. James* (1931) (hereafter *CGS*).
5. Cox, *Informal Portrait*, 106-7.
6. *GSA*, 6.
7. *GSA*, 15.
8. *GSA*, 19.
9. To borrow an apt phrase from the excellent *A Podcast to the Curious* by Will Ross and Mike Taylor, http://www.mrjamespodcast.com (accessed 10 June 2014).
10. *GSA*, 24.
11. Mark Gatiss, "The Dead of Night," *New Statesman*, 21 December 2012-3 January 2013, 77; H. P. Lovecraft, "Supernatural Horror in Literature," *Recluse*, no. 1 (1927): 56.
12. Cox, *Informal Portrait*, 149; Richard W. Pfaff, "James, Montague Rhodes (1862-1936)," in *Oxford Dictionary of National Biography* (Oxford: Oxford University Press, 2004).
13. Cavaliero, "Limitations of the Ghost Story," 133-42.
14. *GSA*, viii.
15. See, for instance, Smith, *Ghost Story, 1840-1920*, 168-85.
16. James, "Some Remarks on Ghost Stories."
17. *GSA*, 188.
18. See the journal *Ghosts & Scholars* (1979-2001) and the *Ghosts & Scholars M. R. James Newsletter* (2001-present), available in print and also online at http://www.users.globalnet.co.uk/~pardos/Biblio.html.
19. See Cox's edition of *Casting the Runes and Other Stories*; Joshi's editions of *Count Magnus and Other Ghost Stories* and *The Haunted Dolls' House and Other Ghost Stories*; the Rodens' edition *A Pleasing Terror: The Complete Supernatural Writings*; and Jones's edition of the *Collected Ghost Stories*.
20. Dennison, "Introduction," *Legacy of M. R. James*.
21. James was fascinated by this "futile, but exceedingly curious, work," writing both an 1899 article on the subject (in which he appeals to "some leisured person" to edit it) and a retelling of the story for children (!) in his *Old Testament Legends* (London: Longman's,

Green, 1913), 107–19. Rosemary Pardoe's useful summary and reprints of James's article and retelling are found in "M. R. James and *The Testament of Solomon*," *Ghosts & Scholars* 28 (1999): 46–57 (phrases quoted here at 54).

22. For more on this book, see Michael Gullick, "The Codex Gigas: A Revised Version of the George Svensson Lecture Delivered at the National Library of Sweden, Stockholm, November 2006," *Biblis* 28 (2007): 5–19.

23. "Sweden also profited at this time, and got its lovely *Codex Aureus* (once at Canterbury), its *Codex Argenteus* (the Gothic Gospels at Upsala), and its *Gigas*, or Devil's Bible, which came from Prague." M. R. James, *The Wanderings and Homes of Manuscripts* (New York: Macmillan, 1919), 55.

24. For more on De la Gardie and the Codex Argenteus, see chapters 2 and 4. The opening of "Count Magnus" cites a travel writer, Horace Marryat, whose guides include extensive discussion of both the De la Gardie family and the Devil's Bible, including a variation of the legend in which the demon image is captured on the page as he completes his work. Horace Marryat, *One Year in Sweden; Including a Visit to the Isle of Götland* (London: John Murray, 1862), 393.

25. A. S. G. Edwards, "M. R. James, 'Canon Alberic's Scrap-Book' and 'Dennistoun,'" *Notes & Queries*, new ser., 58 (March 2011): 105.

26. The connection was previously noted in Colin Pink, "The Real Dennistoun," *Ghosts & Scholars* 19 (1995): 32.

27. *GSA*, 14–15.

28. Richard Utz, "Coming to Terms with Medievalism," *European Journal of English Studies* 15, no. 2 (2011): 107.

29. Sullivan, *Elegant Nightmares*, 73, remarks of James, "in the context of his life, the writing of ghost stories seemed eccentric and unorthodox, almost a blemish on an otherwise spotless career." The most obvious analogues to James in this respect, of course, are C. S. Lewis and J. R. R. Tolkien of Oxford, eminent medievalists well known outside the academy for their imaginative fiction (in contrast to James's work, the medievalizing aspect of their fiction has received considerable critical attention in the past thirty years or so).

30. This passage concludes an undated lecture in James's hand written for delivery to an unnamed society (described in the paper catalogue as a "lecture on demonology"). CUL, MS Add. 7484/box 2/32. The lecture consists largely of summaries of three texts: the so-called magic book of the medieval scholar Michael Scot (d. ca. 1235), Johann Weyer's *De praestigiis daemonum* (1563), and the Testament of Solomon (a source for "Canon Alberic's Scrap-Book"; see note 21. Canon Alberic's tale (1895), however, cannot be the story James offers to read here, for his lecture refers to John Rylands Library, Latin MS 105, which the Rylands Library did not acquire until 1901 (James may have had access to the book as early as 1900, when it was in the possession of the Earl of Crawford: see Pfaff, *Montague Rhodes James*, 276–77). At any rate, most of James's work on the Crawford-Rylands manuscripts was conducted in the period 1905–1910 (Pfaff, 276), and indeed the summary found in "On Demonology" follows closely the structure of the entry in James's catalogue, the publication of which was delayed by the Great War. See James, *A Descriptive Catalogue of the Latin Manuscripts in the John Rylands Library at Manchester*, vol. 1 (Manchester: Manchester University Press, 1921), 187–88. It seems certain, then, that this lecture was delivered no earlier than 1901, and probably sometime after 1904, so that the story in question is likely from *MGSA* or possibly even a later collection.

31. Leslie Workman, editorial, *Studies in Medievalism* 7 (1995): 2. Along with the more recently established journal *Postmedieval*, *Studies in Medievalism* is considered the premier venue for research in this area. For a more recent volume dedicated to defining the field, see Karl Fugelso, ed., "Defining Medievalism(s)," special issue, *Studies in Medievalism* 17 (2009). For useful recent surveys, see also Elizabeth Emery and Richard Utz, eds., *Medievalism: Key Critical Terms* (Cambridge: D. S. Brewer, 2014); David Matthews, *Medievalism: A Critical History* (Cambridge: D. S. Brewer, 2015); and Louise D'Arcens, ed., *The Cambridge Companion to Medievalism* (Cambridge: Cambridge University Press, 2016).

32. Pfaff, "James on the Cataloguing of Manuscripts," 107.

33. Dennison, "Introduction," *Legacy of M. R. James*, 9.

34. Pfaff, *Montague Rhodes James*, 42.

35. Christopher N. L. Brooke, *A History of the University of Cambridge*, vol. 4, *1870–1990* (Cambridge: Cambridge University Press, 1993), 342.

36. McCorristine, "Academia, Avocation, and Ludicity," 60.

37. Hughes, "Murder of the Cathedral," 91, 73.

38. Dinshaw, *How Soon Is Now*, 96.

39. Lovecraft, "Supernatural Horror in Literature," 50.

40. *GSA*, 18–19.

41. Cox's note in James, *Casting the Runes*, 302n8; Cox, *Informal Portrait*, 106; *DNB*, s.v. "Shipley, Arthur." The likely reference to Shipley warns against seeking a single moment of genesis for James's stories. If we assume that "Canon Alberic's Scrap-Book" is one of two tales read at the Chitchat Society (the minute book only mentions "two ghost stories"), a version must have existed by 28 October 1893. Shipley, however, was not appointed a lecturer of morphology until 1894. The generally accepted *terminus post quem*, on the other hand, is James's first trip to Saint-Bertrand-de-Comminges in the spring of 1892, documented in a letter to his parents on 1 April of that year (CUL, MS Add. 7480/D6/338). But in an earlier letter, written when James was still at King's preparing the itinerary for this trip (including the planned visit to Comminges) and informing his parents about his traveling companions (Shipley is described as "a don a teacher of biology but a very nice little man"), James writes, "By the way if Gracey [James's sister] can find my story about Comminges I shd rather like it" (CUL, MS Add. 7480/D6/337). Assuming that this "story about Comminges" is an early version of "Canon Alberic's Scrap-Book," it is clear James did not write the tale's first iteration on the basis of personal experience of that place, as is usually supposed, but probably relied instead on written descriptions from sources such as travel guides (we know from correspondence as early as 1887 that James had long wished to visit Comminges: see CUL, MS Add. 7480/D6/275–76). Moreover, it seems likely from this that James had already shared a version of the story with his family, since he assumes that they will recognize the document. Was it actually James's intention to read the story to his companions on the way to Comminges, or even to redraw some of its details "from the life"? At any rate, the story continued to be reworked even after its first publication in the *National Review* in 1895, with James changing the protagonist's name from Anderson to Dennistoun for its appearance in *Ghost Stories of an Antiquary* (1904).

42. Arthur E. Shipley, *Zoology of the Invertebrata* (London: Adam and Charles Black, 1893), 415.

43. Christopher Stray, *Classics Transformed: Schools, Universities, and Society in England, 1830–1960* (Oxford: Clarendon Press, 1998), 124–25. Waldstein's student, the

future archaeologist R. C. Bosanquet (1871–1935), was another member of the audience with academic ambitions.

44. *GSA*, 18.

45. On the "biological" approach James took to medieval studies ("just as though he were listing insects he had caught"), see Pfaff, *Montague Rhodes James*, 57–58.

46. Jon H. Roberts and James Turner, *The Sacred and the Secular University* (Princeton: Princeton University Press, 2000), 87.

47. *MGSA*, 121.

48. For this aspect of manuscript study, see especially Jonathan Wilcox, ed., *Scraped, Stroked, and Bound: Materially Engaged Readings of Medieval Manuscripts* (Turnhout: Brepols, 2013).

49. *GSA*, 183–84.

50. *GSA*, 199.

51. *MGSA*, 13.

52. James later returned to the well, so to speak, for a rather more didactic and broadly humorous take on the public school experience; he first read "Wailing Well" for Eton Boy Scouts in July 1927.

53. *MGSA*, 6.

54. Tim Card, *Eton Renewed* (London: John Murray, 1994), 148.

55. Quoted in Jones's introduction to *CGS*, xiv.

56. CUL, MS Add. 7480/D6/14.

57. Ibid., D4/66, dated 20 December ("c. 1879").

58. King's/PP/MRJ/F/4 (dated 8 August 1918).

59. Sheldon Rothblatt, *The Revolution of the Dons: Cambridge and Society in Victorian England* (New York: Basic Books, 1968), 190.

60. Paul R. Deslandes, *Oxbridge Men: British Masculinity and the Undergraduate Experience, 1850–1920* (Bloomington: Indiana University Press, 2005), 59.

61. Jones's introduction to the *Collected Ghost Stories*, xii.

62. See Cox, *Informal Portrait*, 127–29.

63. *GSA*, vii.

64. King's/PP/MRJ/E/2 (dated 1899). A second letter from James to McBryde survives (CUL, MS Add. 7481, M120b), in which James lists the stories that McBryde would need to illustrate.

65. The language James uses with McBryde resembles the passionate tone adopted by his own beloved tutor, Henry Elford Luxmoore ("what I shall do without you I don't know," Luxmoore wrote James shortly after his pupil's graduation. "I hope the time will not come when we shall fail to clasp hands through the post. . . . I cannot spare you at all"), whose pedagogical ideals were heavily influenced by the example of William Johnson (Cory) (1823–1892). Johnson had inspired many Eton masters of this era to pursue intensely close, sympathetic relationships with pupils ("a sort of romance," in the words of David Newsome, *On the Edge of Paradise: A. C. Benson, the Diarist* [London: John Murray, 1980], 2). In 1872, Johnson was forced to resign his post at Eton under a cloud of suspected sexual impropriety: "he was dangerously fond of a number of boys. Although he probably did not allow his affections to take any physical form, he permitted intimacies between the boys" (Tim Card, *DNB*, s.v. "Cory, William Johnson"). A. C. Benson's diaries make it clear that Etonians of James's generation were well aware of these possible transgressions

(for example, writing that Johnson's beautiful soul was "pulled off its pedestal by the foul cur which he could not control": see Newsome, *Edge of Paradise*, 80–82). Of Luxmoore's letters to James (co-edited by James himself for publication in 1929), Pfaff warns, "How a modern reader reacts to this sort of language is scarcely relevant" (*Montague Rhodes James*, 23), and yet it is probably worth noting that the pedagogical tradition embraced so warmly by James and his tutor was instituted amid whispers of sexual misconduct.

66. The sixty-seven surviving letters from McBryde to James (CUL, MS Add. 7481, M57–M123) do not suggest a romantic attachment or sexual interest, at least on McBryde's part.

67. Newsome, *Edge of Paradise*, 260–61. Newsome's book draws on the many unpublished volumes of Benson's diaries, censored excerpts of which were previously edited by Percy Lubbock himself, after Benson's death, in *The Diary of Arthur C. Benson* (New York: Longmans, Green, 1926). Lubbock also edited the letters of Henry James in 1920, carefully removing language deemed uncomfortably homoerotic. For this edition and Lubbock's own sexuality, see Michael Anesko, "The Queer Case of Percy Lubbock," in *Monopolizing the Master: Henry James and the Politics of Modern Literary Scholarship* (Stanford: Stanford University Press, 2012), 73–108.

68. Benson, of course, was a very close companion. His diary entry for 28 May 1910 gives a sense of the bonds of familiarity between these men: "I had arranged to go out with M. R. J., but P[ercy].L[ubbock]. and Oliffe Richmond ousted me, and they arranged to start early and return late. I was rather vexed; they don't see how rude it is, nor does Monty." *Diary of Arthur C. Benson*, 193. These friendships had their start when Lubbock and Richmond were still undergraduates, and in 1903 James had traveled with Richmond to Wolfenbüttel in Germany to help settle the date of a manuscript important to the younger man's fellowship dissertation. Howard Sturgis was not a close companion, but James certainly socialized with him on occasion (he was a good friend of his brother Sydney's). See Sydney Rhodes James, *Seventy Years* (London: Williams & Norgate, 1926), 15–16.

69. King's/PP/MRJ/X/1/3 (dated 2 August 1964).

70. Newsome, *Edge of Paradise*, 333.

71. Cyril Alington, *Lionel Ford* (London: Society for Promoting Christian Knowledge, 1934), 16.

72. Newsome, *Edge of Paradise*, 132, 30.

73. On the purchase of the "Oh, Whistle" manuscript, see Rosemary Pardoe, "Bain," *Ghosts & Scholars M. R. James Newsletter* 3 (January 2003): 37–38. Benson became Walpole's confidant in 1905, when the younger man made to him "one of the most *intime* confessions I have ever heard, which I must not speak of here. The boy is evidently in very deep waters. . . . But the thing is really very ghastly. . . . The horror of it is that the voice of God, of conscience, of association is on one side; and on the other the strong, silent, force of nature, pulling blindly, heavily, constantly. How *is* one to believe in a God who sets these two forces at work against each other, to tear a soul in pieces?" In the summer of 1906, Benson was much shaken when Walpole openly declared his love. Benson recovered only after Walpole departed and three new visitors (Howard Sturgis, A. C. Ainger, and Percy Lubbock) arrived in his stead. See Newsome, *Edge of Paradise*, 176–77, 207–8.

74. *TG*, 11.

75. *WTC*, 182–83.

76. In a guidebook published the same year as this story, James discusses the "wicked old giant," which he considers "surely of very great antiquity" and "perhaps the most striking monument of the early paganism of the country." M. R. James, *Abbeys* (London: Great Western Railway, 1925), 149.

77. See Philippa Levine, *The Amateur and the Professional: Antiquarians, Historians, and Archaeologists in Victorian England, 1838–1886* (Cambridge: Cambridge University Press, 1986).

78. Quoted in ibid., 13.

79. As Susan A. Crane writes in "Story, History, and the Passionate Collector," in *Producing the Past: Aspects of Antiquarian Culture and Practice, 1700–1850*, ed. Martin Myrone and Lucy Peltz (Aldershot: Ashgate, 1999), "the passions of historical collecting had shifted from personal, idiosyncratic, and élite networks to nationalist, collective and representative ones. The transition from one form of passionate historical collecting to another can be described as a shift from stories to histories, from fragments to totalities, from cabinets to museums. The displacement of the antiquarian, the devaluation of one form of passionate interest in artefacts, and the subsequent burial of a personalized expression of historical consciousness, then came to characterize the museums, historical profession, and historiography of the nineteenth century.... The antiquarian thus represents a pivotal figure, both actor and artefact, in the story of the shifting desires for history in modern Europe" (11–12).

80. In 1903, in the same month that "Oh, Whistle" was first read to friends, these words of Leslie Stephen appeared in print: "The old-fashioned antiquary was what used to be called a 'humourist'; a man with a quaint and perfectly unreasonable hobby; loving to collect obsolete knowledge the more because it was utterly uninteresting to anybody else.... In the same way [that Darwin studied earthworms] Dryasdust, by preserving records, mainly because they were antiquated, has provided materials from which the modern historian undertakes to reconstruct a picture of the past, and to lay the foundations of social science." Stephen, "Some Early Impressions—Editing," *Atlantic Monthly*, December 1903, 750.

81. See Kelly Eileen Battles, "The Antiquarian Impulse: History, Affect, and Material Culture in Eighteenth- and Nineteenth-Century British Literature" (PhD diss., Michigan State University, 2008).

82. *Edwardian Excursions: From the Diaries of A. C. Benson, 1898–1904*, ed. David Newsome (London: John Murray, 1981), 29.

83. *WTC*, 14.

84. *GSA*, 79.

85. To borrow an observation from *A Podcast to the Curious*, episode 3, 20 October 2011.

86. J. B. Bury, *An Inaugural Lecture* (Cambridge: Cambridge University Press, 1903), 42.

87. Rosemary Jann, *The Art and Science of Victorian History* (Columbus: Ohio State University Press, 1985), 222.

88. To borrow a phrase from the resonant title of Battles's dissertation (see n. 81 above). As an observer remarked in 1888, "English editors have paid comparatively little attention to spelling, to the scholia, to MSS, and to emendations. An opinion apparently prevails in Germany, and is becoming increasingly prevalent in England, that these things constitute the most important portion of the study of classical literature [so that it] can

only be properly understood by one . . . who has groped for treasure among the antiquarian dustheaps." Quoted in Stray, *Classics Transformed*, 209-10.

89. *The Letters of Dorothy L. Sayers, 1899-1936*, ed. Barbara Reynolds (New York: St. Martin's Press, 1996), 71 (26 January 1913).

90. The advertisement appears, among other places, in the endpapers of Terrot Reaveley Glover, *Studies in Virgil* (London: Edward Arnold, 1904).

91. Stray, *Classics Transformed*, 144.

92. Pfaff, *Montague Rhodes James*, 127-28.

93. J. H. Clapham, "The Provost of Eton," *Cambridge Review* (9 October 1936), reprinted in *James: Praepositus necnon amicus*, 20.

94. Anthony C. Deane, *Time Remembered* (London: Faber and Faber, 1945), 132.

95. James, *Eton and King's*, 240.

96. R. E. Balfour to James, 6 December 1930, King's/PP/MRJ/D.

97. From James's introduction to Collins, *Ghosts and Marvels*; Lubbock, *Memoir of Montague Rhodes James*, 40.

98. King's/MRJ/X/1/3 (pp. 8-9).

99. Jones's introduction to the *Collected Ghost Stories*, ix.

100. The phrase is E. F. Benson's (one of those present at James's famous 1893 reading), in a thinly fictionalized account of the Chitchat Society in his novel *David Blaize of King's* (New York: George H. Doran, 1924), 75. Benson describes the club as meeting "every Saturday evening in the rooms of its members in rotation, the host reading a paper on some subject connected with Literature or Art, or something equally improving. The members consisted partly of dons, partly of undergraduates who consorted together on terms of sociable equality, and discussed each other's papers with engaging frankness" (75-76). James's choice to read ghost stories in October 1893 seems to have been an unusual one; on other occasions he read essays on church portals, the medieval writer Walter Map, and "useless knowledge." CUL, GBR/0265/SOC. 65, "Minutes of the Chitchat Society."

101. James to his parents, dated 1878, CUL, MS Add. 7480/D6/110.

102. A. C. Benson (b. 1862) and E. G. Swain (b. 1861) are two notable exceptions.

103. Luxmoore to A. T. Loyd, Christmas Eve 1902, in *The Letters of H. E. Luxmoore*, ed. M. R. James and A. B. Ramsay (Cambridge: Cambridge University Press, 1929), 110.

104. In "The Story of a Disappearance and an Appearance," James wryly has his protagonist remark, "I thought I could be sure of keeping awake over this [an installment of Dickens's *Pickwick Papers*], but I turned out as bad as our friend Smith." I take this as a playful jab at Owen Hugh Smith, who was present at the Christmas gathering in 1912 (see James's "Greek New Testament Diary," CUL, MS Add. 7517, which records guests for each year), the winter before the story was published in the *Cambridge Review* (June 1913). In his memoir *Eton and King's*, James notes someone falling asleep during a reading.

105. The readings are usually said to have typically taken place on Christmas Eve, and many may have, but it is curious that of the known dates of readings, none falls exactly on that day (28 October 1893, 25 December 1899, 23 December 1902, 21 or 22 December 1903, 28 December 1906, January 1912, 18 May 1913).

106. According to a notation in James's hand (manuscripts are to be found in CUL, MS Add. 7482/box 1), there was only one performance of *Alex Barber*, which took place "perhaps on 23 December 1896." James played the lead, while S. G. Lubbock, E. G. Swain, W. M. Hemingway, W. J. Stone, and L. F. Giblin played supporting roles. All of these men

(with the exception of Hemingway) are known to have attended the readings of James's supernatural tales. It was Stone himself, according to Lubbock's memoir of James (p. 32), who suggested to James the idea of "Number 13," while it was Giblin's suggestion in 1903 that led to the publication of James's first collection. In CUL, MS Add. 7484/box 2/65, James describes the audience that witnessed the plays, which he notes was overwhelmingly young, male, and "exceedingly select." For *Blew Beard*, see CUL, MS Add. 7484/box 2/60. See also James's parody of the Faustus story, *Auditor and Impresario*, performed in 1907 and published in the *Cambridge Review* (June 1927): 489–94.

107. Among those known to have been present at James's readings, several had their own collections of ghost stories published, including E. G. Swain (*Stoneground Ghost Tales*, 1912), H. W. F. Tatham (*Footprints in the Snow*, 1910), and Arthur C. Benson (*The Hill of Trouble*, 1903; *The Isles of Sunset*, 1904). Arthur Gray, master of Jesus College, who served with James on the council of the Cambridge Antiquarian Society, published *Tedious Brief Tales of Granta and Gramarye* in 1919. R. H. Malden, who first encountered James at King's as an undergraduate, was inspired to begin writing his own stories in 1909 (collected as *Nine Ghosts* in 1943). R. H. Benson, Arthur's brother, published more than one book of supernatural fiction. Apart from James, however, the most celebrated of this circle was to be another Benson brother, E. F., who went on to publish three separate collections of "spook stories" and who wrote in his 1920 memoir, "Intellectually (or perhaps aesthetically) I, like many others, made an unconditional surrender to [James's] tastes." *Our Family Affairs* (London: Cassell, 1920), 233.

108. The manuscript of this story (King's/MRJ/A/7) is dated 1911 in James's hand, and it seems likely enough that the story was composed for Christmastime at King's. If so, Ramsay was among James's guests that year who would have been present for the first reading, according to his "Greek New Testament Diary" (CUL, MS Add. 7517, fol. 28v). The tale was read on other occasions as well (see chapter 3).

109. Peter Ackroyd, *Albion: The Origins of the English Imagination* (London: Doubleday, 2003), 392.

110. James, "Some Remarks on Ghost Stories," 172.

111. Ibid., 171.

112. *CGS*, viii.

113. Simpson, "'Rules of Folklore.'" James's statement is drawn from the preface of *CGS*, viii.

114. *MGSA*, 32.

115. See Simpson, "'Rules of Folklore,'" 13; Evald Tang Kristensen, *Jyske Folkeminder*, vol. 4 (Copenhagen: Karl Schonbergs Forlage, 1880), 217.

116. *WTC*, 75.

117. Simpson, "'Rules of Folklore,'" 13.

118. *WTC*, 81.

119. M. R. James, "Twelve Medieval Ghost-Stories," *English Historical Review* 37 (1922): 419.

120. *WTC*, 75.

121. "Dr. M. R. James, O.M.," *Times* (London), 13 June 1936.

122. James, "Twelve Medieval Ghost-Stories," 413–14.

123. Ibid., 414, 418, 417.

124. See Jean-Claude Schmitt, *Ghosts in the Middle Ages*, trans. Teresa Lavender Fagan (Chicago: University of Chicago Press, 1998), 12–13, 25–27, and 142–47; Jacqueline

Simpson, "Repentant Soul or Walking Corpse? Debatable Apparitions in Medieval England," *Folklore* 114 (2003): 389–402.

125. James, "Twelve Medieval Ghost-Stories," 418–19. The translation is that of Simpson, "Repentant Soul or Walking Corpse," 397.

126. Walter Map, *De nugis curialium (Courtiers' Trifles)*, ed. and trans. M. R. James, rev. Christopher N. L. Brooke and R. A. B. Mynors (Oxford: Clarendon Press, 1983) (original text and translation published in 1914 and 1923, respectively), 203, 205, 207, 345, and passim.

127. *GSA*, 143.

CHAPTER 1

1. Lee Patterson, "On the Margin: Postmodernism, Ironic History, and Medieval Studies," *Speculum* 65, no. 1 (1990): 102.

2. Quoted in Philippa Levine, *The Amateur and the Professional: Antiquarians, Historians, and Archaeologists in Victorian England, 1838–1886* (Cambridge: Cambridge University Press, 1986), 45; Margaret F. Stieg, "The Emergence of the *English Historical Review*," *Library Quarterly* 46, no. 2 (1976): 126.

3. See James Turner, *Philology: The Forgotten Origins of the Modern Humanities* (Princeton: Princeton University Press, 2014), 43. Medievalists in recent decades, however, have often questioned the usefulness of viewing textual variation in terms of error. As R. Howard Bloch writes in his "Introduction: The New Philology Comes of Age," in *Rethinking the New Medievalism*, ed. R. Howard Bloch, Alison Calhoun, Jacqueline Cerquiglini-Toulet, Joachim Küpper, and Jeanette Patterson (Baltimore: Johns Hopkins University Press, 2014), "Rather than seeing scribal literary transmission over time as adulterating the works they addressed, we perceived the existence of multiple versions as betokening an active milieu of reproduction that could only be called interventionist" (15). Influential in this shift have been the writings of Paul Zumthor (esp. his *Essai de poétique médiévale* [Paris: Éditions du Seuil, 1972]). See also Bernard Cerquiglini, *In Praise of the Variant: A Critical History of Philology*, trans. Betsy Wing (Baltimore: Johns Hopkins University Press, 1999) (original French edition 1989).

4. For an illuminating discussion of errancy in these extended senses, see Seth Lerer, *Error and the Academic Self: The Scholarly Imagination, Medieval to Modern* (New York: Columbia University Press, 2002).

5. Jon H. Roberts and James Turner, *The Sacred and the Secular University* (Princeton: Princeton University Press, 2000), 85–87.

6. See, for example, *Scrapeana: Fugitive Miscellany* (London, 1792), 123.

7. For this process in context, see Turner, *Philology*.

8. Pfaff, *Montague Rhodes James*, 42.

9. James uses the phrase as the title and as a governing metaphor for his introductory guide *The Wanderings and Homes of Manuscripts* (New York: Macmillan, 1919).

10. M. R. James, *The Western Manuscripts in the Library of Trinity College, Cambridge*, vol. 4 (Cambridge: Cambridge University Press, 1904), v.

11. Gaselee, "Montague Rhodes James," 432.

12. Erving Goffman, *The Presentation of Self in Everyday Life* (Woodstock, N.Y.: Overlook Press, 1973), 43.

13. Dennison, "Introduction," *Legacy of M. R. James*, 6, notes "James's lack of interest in certain texts; he had more of an eye for the 'unusual' or 'particular,' and certainly the illuminated!"

14. Pfaff, *Montague Rhodes James*, 183.

15. Dinshaw, *How Soon Is Now*, 31.

16. Lane, "Fright Nights," 108.

17. Pfaff, *Montague Rhodes James*, 121.

18. In the fictional version, the line of discovery is reversed, so that the antiquary's purpose is "tracing the whereabouts of the painted windows of the Abbey Church of Steinfeld," and he is led by deduction to travel to "a private chapel—no matter where." *GSA*, 231–32.

19. The wicked Gothic monk, like so much else in James's fiction, is a very self-aware medievalism. As James says in a lecture at Downing College dated "before 1900," "If you were to read some of the novels patronised by your grandfathers & great-grandfathers, you might be inclined to suppose that monks were a strange race of men muffled in dark robes who generally had only one hand & carried a large knife in the other, & who wandered about, concealing themselves behind the corner, appearing at unexpected moments and saying in sepulchral tones 'Beware.' This would not be a correct idea." CUL, MS Add. 7484/box 1/79, fol. 4v.

20. *GSA*, 270.

21. *GSA*, 231. The translation is James's own and is supplied in a footnote in his text. The biblical text itself is adapted from Job 28:1, with *absconditur* (it is hidden) replacing the original *conflatur* (it is melted/refined).

22. *GSA*, 235.

23. *GSA*, 235.

24. The key publication on this text in James's day was Henry Morley, *English Writers II: From Caedmon to the Conquest* (London, 1888), 224–25. For a summary of the considerable scholarship since then, see Dieter Bitterli, *Say What I Am Called: The Old English Riddles of the Exeter Book and the Anglo-Latin Riddle Tradition* (Toronto: University of Toronto Press, 2009), 74–79. James's familiarity with medieval riddling is not to be doubted. His chapter in the first volume of the *Cambridge History of English Literature* (1907) includes an authoritative discussion of Aldhelm's *enigmata*.

25. *GSA*, 250.

26. *GSA*, 262.

27. See the illustrated bookmark by Dallas Goffin, available for purchase online at the *Ghosts & Scholars* website. Image available at http://www.users.globalnet.co.uk/~pardos/Cards20.html (accessed 29 July 2016). See also Cox's note in James, *Casting the Runes*, 316n93.

28. *GSA*, 266.

29. For instance, one might cite Symphosius's Enigma 94, the solution of which is the preposterously specific "one-eyed seller of garlic." The enigma plays on different kinds of "heads": the vendor has one human eye but thousands of heads of garlic. Folk riddles often similarly play with the difference between creaturely eyes and those of needles, potatoes, etc.

30. The abbot has left an additional mocking clue in the south aisle of Steinfeld Abbey: "In the tracery lights of that I was startled to see some fragments and coats-of-arms

remaining—Abbot Thomas's shield was there, and a small figure with a scroll inscribed 'Oculos habent, et non videbunt' (They have eyes, and shall not see), which, I take it, was a hit of the Abbot at his Canons." *GSA*, 255–56.

31. See Cox's note in James, *Casting the Runes*, 316n93.

32. *GSA*, 233. Again the translation is James's. Darryl Jones notes that this text is a conflation of two lines from Revelation. *Collected Ghost Stories*, 437.

33. *GSA*, 252–54. The translation is once again James's own, as is the decision to leave the French text untranslated. As Jones notes in *Collected Ghost Stories*, 438, the abbot seems here to have adopted the words of a Lombard coronation ceremony (a warning not to touch the king's rightful crown).

34. *GSA*, 254.

35. The third-declension Latin noun *custos* can be either feminine or masculine in grammatical gender.

36. Also note Somerton's assurances to Gregory: "it's *perfectly* safe in the daytime. You know what I mean. It lies on the step, you know, where—where we put it." *GSA*, 231, 243.

37. *GSA*, 263–64.

38. See Jones's explanatory note in *Collected Ghost Stories*, 438.

39. And is associated with scholarly work pursued outside the university context. See, for instance, the independent scholar Mr. Abney of "Lost Hearts," whose expertise is recognized by Cambridge professors but whose methods are highly questionable. *GSA*, 33.

40. Barker, "After M. R. James," 8.

41. *GSA*, 270.

42. *GSA*, 242.

43. *The Commonitory of Vincent of Lérins*, trans. John Jebb (Baltimore: Robinson, 1847), 64–65. Vincent, who died in the mid-fifth century, explicates 1 Timothy 6 in chapters 21–24; the work as a whole is devoted to the discernment of theological error.

44. In the view of Brian Cowlishaw, "Victorian Science and the Awful Unconscious," "the invented title suggests he studies what-writing-is, which indicates his investment in words, reading, writing, and investigation in general" (165). Others offer explanations of the fictional field that stress the tale's possible ontological implications, but I tend to agree with Mike Pincombe, "Homosexual Panic," 188, that the main parodic target here is the upstart and abstract nature of Parkins's chosen field. The manuscript of the story, now owned by the King's School, Canterbury, reveals that James changed Parkins's specialization from an original expertise in "morphology."

45. *GSA*, 222.

46. *GSA*, 200.

47. Burnstow is based on Felixstowe in Suffolk.

48. *GSA*, 189.

49. *GSA*, 183–84.

50. Pincombe, "Homosexual Panic,"188, argues that the tale itself "might well be seen as an example of homophobic bullying (though it is more complicated than that)"; Fielding, "Reading Rooms," 762, uses "Oh, Whistle" as an example of a tale expressing the "social phobia" of homosexuality. Darryl Jones, in his introduction to the 2011 edition of the *Collected Ghost Stories*, observes that "The bedsheet ghost . . . is an overdetermined

symbol: that is, the site where a number of anxieties converge to create an abundance of meaning. It simultaneously represents homosexual anxieties (the bed in which Mr Rogers is to sleep), and a fear of domesticity and *women* given nightmare form; and for James, these anxieties are related ones" (xxv).

51. The theme is pursued at length in a pair of articles by Terry W. Thompson: "James's Oh, Whistle, and I'll Come to You, My Lad," *Explicator* 59, no. 4 (2001): 193–95, and "'I Shall Most Likely Be Out on the Links': Golf as Metaphor in the Ghost Stories of M. R. James," *Papers on Language and Literature* 40 (2004): 340–52. Simon MacCulloch, "The Toad in the Study: M. R. James, H. P. Lovecraft, and Forbidden Knowledge," in Joshi and Pardoe, *Warnings to the Curious*, likewise emphasizes that "Parkins has tried strenuously to exclude from his awareness anything that might disturb the 'apple pie order' of his strictly rationalist, human-centred world view" (101–2).

52. *GSA*, 189.

53. The two idioms were frequently discussed together or (naturally) appeared side by side in etymological dictionaries. See the first volume of the 1888 edition of the *OED*, s.v. "apple-pie."

54. *GSA*, 216.

55. *GSA*, 188.

56. *GSA*, 210.

57. *GSA*, 188.

58. *GSA*, 188.

59. See Briggs, *Night Visitors*, 133–34; John Alfred Taylor, "'If I'm Not Careful': Innocents and Not-So-Innocents in the Stories of M. R. James," in Joshi and Pardoe, *Warnings to the Curious*, 197; Ron Weighell, "Dark Devotions: M. R. James and the Magical Tradition," in Joshi and Pardoe, *Warnings to the Curious*, 126; and Jacqueline Simpson, "That Whistle Again," *Ghosts & Scholars* 30 (2000): 26–27.

60. As early as Pope Clement V's bulls of 1312, Templars were accused of having fallen "execrabile facinus Sodomorum" (into the execrable crime of the Sodomites). Another bull, *Ad providam*, states that the Order is suppressed "propter magistrum et fratres ceterasque personas dicti Ordinis in quibuslibet mundi partibus consistens . . . que propter tristem et spurcidam eorum memoriam presentibus subticemus" (because of the abominable, even unspeakable, deeds of its master, brothers, and other persons of the Order in many places in the world . . . and we are silent as to detail here because the memory is so sad and unclean). The reception of this sexualized material (including the profuse and disturbing trial and confession records) is too complex for facile summary here, but of course there is no shortage of recapitulation of it in modern centuries.

61. *Robert Burns: Selections*, ed. John C. Weston (New York: Bobbs-Merrill, 1967), 241.

62. While folklore records long-standing regulations of the circumstances in which men in certain trades (from railwaymen, to sailors, to actors), and women in general, were forbidden to whistle, a peculiar association of the inability to whistle with effeminate or homosexual men existed in the early years of sexual pathology. The association seems to have emerged incidentally from the publication of case histories of male "sexual inverts" by pioneer sexologists such as Karl Heinrich Ulrichs (1825–1895), and was mentioned often between 1880 and 1920; representative examples can be found in Richard von Krafft-Ebing, *Psychopathia Sexualis*, trans. Charles Chaddock, 7th ed., (London: Rebman, 1894),

295, 354; and Havelock Ellis and John Addington Symonds, *Sexual Inversion* (London: Wilson and Macmillan, 1897), 51, 62, 64. In the much-revised 1901 Philadelphia edition of the latter, Ellis is more summary, stating that he is "quite satisfied" that an inability to whistle is "well marked among a considerable minority" of male homosexuals (177–78). My thanks to the anonymous reader for *Philological Quarterly* who directed this history to my attention.

63. See, for example, James Burnes, *Sketch of the History of the Knights Templars* (Edinburgh: Blackwood, 1837); Jeremy L. Cross, *The Templars' Chart, or Hieroglyphic Monitor* (New York, 1852); Theodore Gourdin, *Historical Sketch of the Order of Knights Templar* (Charleston, S.C.: Walker and Evans, 1855); and Anthony Oneal Haye, *The Persecution of the Knights Templars* (Edinburgh, 1865). In the closing chapter of *The New Knighthood: A History of the Order of the Temple* (Cambridge: Cambridge University Press, 1994), Malcolm Barber vividly sketches the afterlife of the Templars both in this kind of pseudo-chivalric fraternal organization and in various fictional works during that same time (317–28).

64. George Oliver made this claim after an excavation convinced him that Templar-sponsored immurement took place at Temple Bruer; see his *History of the Holy Trinity Guild at Sleaford. . . .* (Lincoln: Drury, 1837), 28n62. Three years after the publication of *Ghost Stories of an Antiquary*, Hope (1854–1919), a Cambridge man who, like James, had been mentored by Henry Bradshaw and J. W. Clark, took advantage of a chance opportunity to excavate Temple Bruer, "wish[ing] to test by excavations the truth (or otherwise) of [Oliver's] remarkable story." Hope, "The Round Church of the Knights Templars at Temple Bruer, Lincolnshire," *Archaeologia* 61 (1908): 185. He found Oliver's story to have no verifiable truth to it, assigning it to Oliver's "horror of the Templars and all their works" (188).

65. Léopold Delisle, *Mémoire sur les opérations financières des Templiers* (Paris: Imprimerie Nationale, 1889). James dedicated his catalogue and discussion in *The Ancient Libraries of Canterbury and Dover* (Cambridge: Cambridge University Press, 1903) to Delisle, in the same year he first read "Oh, Whistle" aloud to friends and colleagues at Cambridge.

66. Augustus Jessopp and Montague Rhodes James, eds., *The Life and Miracles of St William of Norwich, by Thomas of Monmouth* (Cambridge: Cambridge University Press, 1896), lxxviii. James's co-editor writes in another section of this book of "the enormous lying which prepared people to accept as true the unspeakable calumnies spread abroad against the Knights Templars in the 14th century" (xliv).

67. *GSA*, 206.

68. *GSA*, 189, 183, 208; the knightly implication of this last detail is noted in Pincombe, "Homosexual Panic," 190.

69. *GSA*, 183.

70. James, *Eton and King's*, 133.

71. Cox also notes this church in connection with the ruin of "Oh, Whistle." *Casting the Runes*, 313n61.

72. The original manuscript reading has apparently not been noted before now. On the history of the church, see Charles Henry Cooper, *Memorials of Cambridge* (Cambridge: Macmillan, 1866), 3:360–69; and W. T. Adams, *The Round Church of Cambridge: A Short History* (Cambridge: Cambridge University Press, 1930), 5–9.

73. The image is discussed in Stephen Taylor, *The Fylfot File* (Cambridge: Perfect Publishers, 2006), 57–59, which also observes that the design is present in a window in the Westminster College chapel in a grouping possibly intended to represent the Trinity (60). "Swastika" is fraught with connotations, of course, and Taylor's book is one of many that chart the variations and uses of the geometric design throughout human history (though of course in 1903 there could be no association with Nazism). The window, like most of those in the Round Church, was the work of Thomas Willement (1786–1871) and was installed as part of the extensive renovation of the structure by the Cambridge Camden Society in 1841 following a partial collapse of the aisle-vault, the older glass having been deliberately smashed by William Dowsing in 1644. Taylor describes the design as a "fylfot-cross," a term commonly used among antiquarians of the nineteenth century to specify a swastika design with crampons of shorter length than the arms of the cross.

74. Pfaff, *Montague Rhodes James*, 115. The Disney chair was established as the first of its kind in Great Britain in 1851 by the amateur John Disney (1779–1857), and Levine, *Amateur and the Professional*, 142, notes that the rather underfunded position was "filled by amateurs throughout the nineteenth century" but that the situation had begun to change by 1900.

75. Pfaff, *Montague Rhodes James*, 81.

76. *GSA*, 193.

77. My emphasis on disciplinary transgression here may be contrasted with that of Gabriel Moshenska, who writes in "James and the Archaeological Uncanny," "In light of his own interests and activities it would be too much to suggest that James himself considered archaeology a transgressive practice" (1198). Like many others, Moshenska tends to treat James's position vis-à-vis archaeology as wholly untroubled by the potential worry of amateurism, to the point where the uncanny effect is said to arise out of James's own lack of professional self-consciousness: "James' error, and it was a very productive error, was to confuse the 'ordinary and normal' settings of his own extraordinary life with those of everyone else's. For the medieval scholar and Provost of King's and Eton, as for his protagonists, the archaeological *was* the everyday" (1195).

78. Jacqueline Simpson, "The Riddle of the Whistle," *Ghosts & Scholars* 24 (1997): 55. In a letter to the editor, Bob Newman, *Ghosts & Scholars* 29 (1999): 55, decries such "ungainly shadowboxing" and offers a reading that takes each syllable as a complete word (two imperatives, an adverb, and a vocative): "Thief, blow twice, [then] lament." Such an imperative is as succinct as Tolkien's "speak, friend, and enter," but does not account for the obfuscation one expects in a riddle. Luke Thurston, in *Literary Ghosts,* offers two variations on this: "either 'Thief-whistle-twice-weep,' if we read it clockwise; or 'Thief-weep-twice-whistle' if anti-clockwise. But the total number of readings, the definite sum, can never be reached, since the signifying elements can be interconnected with endless variations of sense or hermeneutic 'spin'" (63).

79. *Collected Ghost Stories,* ed. Jones, 436.

80. See, however, my discussion of *furbis below.

81. As far as I can make out, the potential link between the two enigmatic elements of the whistle (the cruciform layout of the syllables, and the swastikas) has previously been noted only by Thurston (*Literary Ghosts*, 64, 72), who emphasizes its apparent implication of endlessly cycling through interpretive possibilities, so that it becomes a signal of the "semiotic torsion or dynamic disfiguring of legibility at work in the story" (64).

82. The last appearance of the original swastikas seems to have been in the "new edition" of *Ghost Stories of an Antiquary* published in 1919. James's *CGS* (1931) shows outline swastikas, without brackets (131). *Thirteen Ghost Stories* (Hamburg: Albatross Modern Continental Library, 1935), 40, is the same. *Best Ghost Stories of M. R. James* (Cleveland: World Publishing, 1944), 243, shows regularized swastikas solidly filled in. A Danish collection, *Otto beromte spogelseshistorier,* trans. Karen Vestergaard (Copenhagen: Winters, 1970), 35, changes the swastikas into plus signs (+). E. F. Bleiler's edition of *Ghost Stories of an Antiquary* (New York: Dover, 1971), 115, omits the swastikas entirely. Roden and Roden, in their edition *A Pleasing Terror*, 85, show outline swastikas without brackets, as do Joshi in *Count Magnus* (88), Cox in *Casting the Runes* (64), and Jones in *Collected Ghost Stories* (82), where it is simply noted that "the swastikas . . . are in this context an ancient symbol prevalent in Eastern religions, though also adopted by Christianity" (436). There is no recognition of the original form of the swastikas here or in any other edition of the stories I have been able to locate.

83. Note that the missing crampon on the top arm of the right-hand swastika seems unlikely to be significant but is rather some kind of printer's error, for it is present in the manuscript. The irony may be that James's swastikas have never appeared in their fully "correct" form, at least insofar as indicated in his own hand.

84. Further confirmation of this interpretation comes from the testimony of Henry Luxmoore (1841–1926), James's tutor at Eton and lifelong friend, who recalled hearing the story "Fur flebis" read at Christmas in 1903 (Cox, *Informal Portrait*, 136). It seems likely that Luxmoore's remembered title reflects a fragment of the "authorized" solution, or at least one that he guessed on that occasion.

85. MacCulloch, "Toad in the Study," 95. One wonders if this has anything to do with the consistent depiction of Parkins as an older man despite James's explicit description of him as "young"—not only in two separate BBC adaptations but in the original illustrations of *Ghost Stories of an Antiquary* produced by James's beloved friend James McBryde.

86. *GSA*, 196, 198, 202–5. The troubled night ends with a kind of ceraceous wet dream: "For about the first time in his orderly and prudent life he forgot to blow out the candle, and when he was called next morning at eight there was still a flicker in the socket and a sad mess of guttered grease on the top of the little table" (206).

87. *GSA*, 186–87.

88. *GSA*, 218.

89. *GSA*, 223–24.

90. The name seems thus at least triply significant, including in addition its connections to Felixstowe and Robert Burns.

91. *GSA*, 225.

92. Jane Suzanne Carroll, "A 'Dramar in Reel Life'—Freaky Dolls, M. R. James, and Modern Children's Ghost Stories," in Conrad O'Briain and Stevens, *Ghost Story from the Middle Ages*, 251.

CHAPTER 2

1. Quoted in *Collected Ghost Stories*, ed. Jones, 465.
2. Ibid., 403, 401.

3. Ibid., 405.
4. *GSA*, 169.
5. See Simon McKeown, "Recovering the *Codex Argenteus*: Magnus Gabriel De la Gardie, David Klöcker Ehrenstrahl, and Wulfila's Gothic Bible," *Lychnos* (2005): 9–28.
6. Rosemary Pardoe, "Who Was Count Magnus?," *Ghosts & Scholars* 33 (2001): 50–53.
7. *GSA*, 160.
8. *GSA*, 153.
9. *Edinburgh Review* 25 (1815): 541.
10. For a similar theme, see Ian Hesketh, "Diagnosing Froude's Disease: Boundary Work and the Discipline of History in Late-Victorian Britain," *History and Theory* 47 (October 2008): 373–95.
11. See Philip Elliot, "The Development of the Professions in Britain," chapter 2 of *The Sociology of the Professions* (New York: Herder and Herder, 1972), 14–57, esp. 55–56.
12. William Whyte, "The Intellectual Aristocracy Revisited," *Journal of Victorian Culture* 10, no. 1 (2005): 20. See also Noel Annan, "The Intellectual Aristocracy," in *Studies in Social History: A Tribute to G. M. Trevelyan*, ed. John Harold Plumb (New York: Longman, Green, 1955), 241–87; and Noel Annan, *The Dons: Mentors, Eccentrics, and Geniuses* (Chicago: University of Chicago Press, 1999).
13. See esp. A. J. Engel, *From Clergyman to Don: The Rise of the Academic Profession in Nineteenth-Century Oxford* (Oxford: Oxford University Press, 1983), 10–12.
14. Margaret F. Stieg, "The Emergence of the *English Historical Review*," *Library Quarterly* 46, no. 2 (1976): 122; David Cannadine, *The Decline and Fall of the British Aristocracy* (New York: Vintage, 1999), 393.
15. Acton's words here are taken from a letter he wrote Mandell Creighton, evaluating the first issue of the *English Historical Review*. Quoted in Doris S. Goldstein, "The Origins and Early Years of the English Historical Review," *English Historical Review* 101, no. 398 (1986): 13.
16. Hugh Paget, "The Early History of the Family of James of Jamaica," *Jamaican Historical Review* 1 (1948): 261. Paget writes, "no people have a better claim to be considered original Jamaicans than the descendants of the pioneer English colonising families"; "Of these pioneer families the family of James may be considered the oldest" (260). Paget devotes two separate passages to the family's most famous son, "the author of 'Ghost Stories of an Antiquary,'" who represented the culmination of the family's educational aspirations: "It is only fitting that the James family . . . should have produced one of the most eminent educationalists of modern times" (261, 272).
17. Pfaff, *Montague Rhodes James*, 2; Paget, "Family of James," 271.
18. Millicent Garrett Fawcett, *What I Remember* (London: Unwin, 1924), 16, quoted in Pfaff, *Montague Rhodes James*, 3.
19. Fitzwilliam Museum, Cambridge, James Notebook 6.vii.
20. CUL, MS Add. 7480/D6/284.
21. Sydney Rhodes James, *Seventy Years* (London: Williams & Norgate, 1926), 1.
22. *WTC*, 176.
23. CUL, MS Add. 7480/A1/9.
24. J. H. Clapham, "The Provost of Eton," *Cambridge Review* (9 October 1936), reprinted in *James: Praepositus necnon amicus*, 19.
25. Lubbock, *Memoir of Montague Rhodes James*, 19–21; see also Maisie Fletcher, *The Bright Countenance: A Personal Biography of Walter Morley Fletcher* (London: Hodder

and Stoughton, 1957), 64; Shane Leslie, *Mark Sykes: His Life and Letters* (New York: Cassell, 1923), 55 (quotation).

26. A. C. Benson, *From a College Window* (London: G. P. Putnam's Sons, 1906), 67.

27. M. R. James, *On the Abbey of S. Edmund at Bury* (Cambridge: Cambridge Antiquarian Society, 1895), 1.

28. Pierre Bourdieu, *Distinction: A Social Critique of the Judgement of Taste*, trans. Richard Nice (Cambridge: Harvard University Press, 1984), 28.

29. Browning's letter quoted in Cox, *Informal Portrait*, 213. On the films, see Tony Earnshaw, *Beating the Devil: The Making of Night of the Demon* (Bradford, UK: National Museum of Photography, Film, and Television, 2005).

30. See Daniel Martin, "Japan's *Blair Witch*: Restraint, Maturity, and Generic Canons in the British Critical Reception of *Ring*," *Cinema Journal* 48, no. 3 (2009): 47.

31. Ruth Hoberman, *Museum Trouble: Edwardian Fiction and the Emergence of Modernism* (Charlottesville: University of Virginia Press, 2011), 157. Hoberman writes, "The reading room's inclusiveness becomes a source of danger, allowing Karswell access to the professional network from which he has been excluded" (159). It should be noted, however, that the exchange does not take place in the main Reading Room but in the "Select Manuscript Room" (a photo of this room is found in Dennison, *Legacy of M. R. James*, back matter).

32. *MGSA*, 101.

33. McCorristine, "Academia, Avocation, and Ludicity," 59.

34. Mike Pincombe, "Class War in 'Casting the Runes,'" *Ghosts & Scholars M. R. James Newsletter* 9 (March 2006): 4–8.

35. See esp. Ron Weighell, "Dark Devotions: M. R. James and the Magical Tradition," in Joshi and Pardoe, *Warnings to the Curious*, 129–31.

36. Pfaff, *Montague Rhodes James*, 50; Cox, *Informal Portrait*, 62.

37. "I must say I don't think it was meant to be ill-natured . . . he was only trying his hand at a likeness in a jocose spirit." James to Browning, 4 August 1887, King's/OB/1/868/C. James's impersonations of Browning are noted in Cyril Alington, *Lionel Ford* (London: Society for Promoting Christian Knowledge, 1934), 15.

38. King's/OB/1/868/C.

39. Leslie, *Mark Sykes*, 55. The phrase is a pun on Monty's name with the old Eton tradition of *ad Montem* (discontinued by James's day), a raucous festival centered around the nearby earthwork of "Montem Mound."

40. E. F. Benson, *Our Family Affairs* (London: Cassell, 1920), 234.

41. Ian Anstruther, *Oscar Browning: A Biography* (London: John Murray, 1983), 9. For James's own take on this theme, see *Eton and King's*, 121: "Here was the key to the whole business: he never could be really interested in anything but his own concerns. If once he could have pushed past the figure (of O. B.) which loomed so large before him, he might have been a great man."

42. Cox, *Informal Portrait*, 62.

43. *MGSA*, 89.

44. *MGSA*, 119, 108, 91.

45. See Anstruther, *Oscar Browning*, 9–11; James, *Eton and King's*, 163. The pun on the O. B.'s OBesity is not my own; it was a widespread witticism and the basis for satiric verse by J. K. Stephen ("He may B 2 O.Bs"). Karswell's portrait is the spitting image of the popular image of the O. B., reproduced in memoir after memoir: "a grotesque, squat

figure, with large head and slightly gross clean-shaven features," in the recollection of Charles Tennyson in *Stars and Markets* (London: Chatto and Windus, 1957), 94.

46. Tennyson, *Stars and Markets*, 95; H. E. Wortham, *Victorian Eton and Cambridge: Being the Life and Times of Oscar Browning* (London: Arthur Barker, 1927), chap. 13.

47. *MGSA*, 91.

48. Anstruther, *Oscar Browning*, 167; James to his parents, 12 March 1889, CUL, MS Add. 7480/D6/308.

49. Anstruther, *Oscar Browning*, 167–68.

50. A. C. Benson, *Memories and Friends* (London: John Murray, 1924), 128, 140.

51. Anstruther, *Oscar Browning*, 158. Shane Leslie, *The Film of Memory* (London: Michael Joseph, 1938), 248, recalls: "In spite of a hurried and I am afraid mocking placard 'Vote for the O. B.,' the Fellows elected Monty James."

52. Wortham, *Victorian Eton and Cambridge*, 264–65.

53. Oscar Browning, *Memories of Later Years* (New York: D. Appleton, 1923), 114. Browning subtly frames this communication as disloyal (even a bit craven and cold) of James. Nevertheless, he does not count James among his "intriguers" and indeed credits his generous pension to "the pertinacity of the Provost."

54. James to Browning, 3 November 1907, King's/OB/1/868/C. James's discomfort is palpable in the language and even the handwriting of this letter, which concludes with a postscript: "He [Macauley] will also, by the way, should you wish it, be able to describe to you the attitude which I have adopted in the matter."

55. The story was published in 1911 in *More Ghost Stories of an Antiquary*, in the preface of which James states, "My stories have been produced (with one exception) at successive Christmas seasons." The exception is "Mr. Humphreys and His Inheritance," written to fill out the collection and occupying the final position in the volume. We know that the first story in the volume, "A School Story," was written for Christmas 1906, and "Casting the Runes" is the fourth story of the collection. If we assume that James lists his stories in the "successive" order in which they were produced (as he apparently also did in his first volume), then Christmas 1908 or 1909 seem the most likely dates for "Casting the Runes." As detailed in the introduction, the first audience would have consisted largely of present and past masters and graduates of Eton, who not only knew Browning personally but would not have appreciated the O. B.'s outspoken animosity toward their institution (from which he had been driven following scandal decades earlier). James emphasizes his own resentment of Browning's anti-Etonian sentiments in *Eton and King's*, 119.

56. In addition to numerous satires in Cambridge periodicals, Browning figures in a number of romans à clef that invariably emphasize the same character flaws that Karswell suffers from (minus the murderous black magic, of course). See "A. G.," in E. F. Benson's *David Blaize of King's* (New York: George H. Doran, 1924), which James read, and "Oliver Brownlow," in Shane Leslie, *The Cantab* (London: Chatto and Windus, 1926), which also features a thinly veiled portrait of James.

57. Browning, *Memories of Later Years*, 115.

58. *Long Shadows: Memoirs of Shane Leslie* (London: John Murray, 1966), 101.

59. Cox, *Informal Portrait*, 162; Browning to Charles Ryle Faye, 5 December 1920, CUL, MS Add. 7461/8, quoted in ibid.

60. It might be emphasized here that even those who objected to Browning's personality (and quality of scholarship) tended to recognize the value of his other contributions,

including the work he did to establish history as a university discipline and to promote teacher training at Cambridge. See Elisabeth Leedham-Green, *A Concise History of Cambridge* (Cambridge: Cambridge University Press, 1996), 173. For an account of Browning's progressive dedication to education reform, see Mark McBeth, "The Pleasure of Learning and the Tightrope of Desire: Teacher-Student Relationships and Victorian Pedagogy," in *Gender, Colonialism, and Education: The Politics of Experience*, ed. Joyce Goodman and Jane Martin (London: Woburn Press, 2002), 46–72.

61. See especially Leslie Howsam, *Past into Print: The Publishing of History in Britain, 1850–1950* (London: British Library, 2009); Rosemary Jann, "From Amateur to Professional: The Case of the Oxbridge Historians," *Journal of British Studies* 22, no. 2 (1983): 122–47. A. Lang, "'History as She Ought to Be Wrote,'" *Living Age*, 7th ser., 5, no. 223 (1899): 22, laments that the professionalization of history has rendered "the non-specialist (the abandoned 'popularizer') . . . a person of contemptible character."

62. *MGSA*, 125, 110.

63. Howsam, *Past into Print*, 57.

64. Ibid., 59.

65. Leslie Howsam, "Academic Discipline or Literary Genre? The Establishment of Boundaries in Historical Writing," *Victorian Literature and Culture* (2004): 530–33.

66. Goldstein, "Origins and Early Years," 13.

67. Ibid., 13–14; Stieg, "Emergence of the *English Historical Review*," 131–32.

68. Howsam, *Past into Print*, 61.

69. J. B. Bury, *An Inaugural Lecture* (Cambridge: Cambridge University Press, 1903), 42.

70. The former phrase is taken from the prefatory note to the first issue of the *English Historical Review* (January 1886): 5. The latter is from Robert Seely in 1883, quoted in Howsam, *Past into Print*, 50.

71. Henry Barclay Swete, "The Journal of Theological Studies," *Journal of Theological Studies* 1 (October 1899): 1.

72. Pfaff, *Montague Rhodes James*, 164.

73. "Oscar Browning would say, irritably rubbing a vaulted bald head with a short hand, 'James hates thought.'" Clapham, "Provost of Eton," 20. In *Eton and King's*, James notes, "I also owe [Browning] the pernicious distaste for theorists . . . which I can never hope to unlearn" (120).

74. M. R. James, "Some Remarks on 'The Head of John Baptist,'" *Classical Review* 31 (February 1917): 4. Harrison's response appeared in the following issue (31 [March 1917]: 63), where Harrison's colleague, Gilbert Murray, writes in her defense as well, offering that the "excessive hostility" of James's review is due to his ignorance of a field easily "misinterpreted by outsiders" (64). For a discussion of the affair sympathetic to Harrison, see Shelley Arlen, "'For the Love of an Idea': Jane Ellen Harrison, Heretic and Humanist," *Women's History Review* 5, no. 2 (1996): 179–82. Arlen rightly stresses the role that gender likely played in the nature of James's response, though Jacqueline Simpson (*Ghosts & Scholars M. R. James Newsletter* 12 [September 2007]: 33–35) makes the case that the facts justified James's critique.

75. Peter Novick, *That Noble Dream: The "Objectivity Question" and the American Historical Profession* (Cambridge: Cambridge University Press, 1988), 222.

76. Howsam, *Past into Print*, 119.

77. M. R. James, "The Christian Renaissance," in *The Cambridge Modern History*, vol. 1, ed. A. W. Ward et al. (Cambridge: Cambridge University Press, 1902), 585–619; M. R. James, "Latin Writings in England to the Time of Alfred," in *The Cambridge History of English Literature*, vol. 1, ed. A. W. Ward and A. R. Waller (Cambridge: Cambridge University Press, 1907), 65–87.

78. See Novick, *That Noble Dream*, 57–60.

79. *English Historical Review* 1 (June 1886): 4.

80. Jann, "From Amateur to Professional," 130.

81. *MGSA*, 98.

82. As documented in the chronological bibliography in Pfaff, *Montague Rhodes James*, 427–30.

83. See ibid., 427–38.

84. In a fascinating recent study of self-styled bibliomaniacs, Ina Ferris, *Book-Men, Book Clubs, and the Romantic Literary Sphere* (London: Palgrave Macmillan, 2015), argues that such organizations as the Roxburghe Club produced "unsettling recognition of alien trajectories within book and literary culture in uncomfortable proximity to its own" (6). In James's story draft "Merfield House," a gentleman hobbyist studies early modern drama: "in this department he stood high: but beyond editing a book for the Roxburghe Club, of which he was a member . . . he never published anything." *Ghosts & Scholars M. R. James Newsletter* 12 (September 2007): 14.

85. David Matthews, "Turtle Soup and Texts: From the Roxburghe Club to the Camden Society," chapter 4 of *The Making of Middle English, 1765–1910* (Minneapolis: University of Minnesota Press, 1999), 99. For a detailed history of the club, see Nicolas Barker, *The Roxburghe Club: A Bicentenary History* (London: Roxburghe Club, 2012), esp. 177–91 for James's contributions. One of the rules of the club is that each member must at some point present the others with an (often lavish) scholarly edition of his own production. As Barker notes, James was posthumously excused from the rule in 1936, his work as editor and "technical adviser" deemed adequate substitution (187).

86. Dennison, "Introduction," *Legacy of M. R. James*, 6.

87. John M. Kemble, "On Anglo-Saxon Runes," *Archaeologica* 28 (1840): 328.

88. Anna C. Paus, "Runes and Manuscripts," chapter 2 of *Cambridge History of English Literature*, 1:7–18.

89. See C. H. Talbot, ed. and trans., *The Anglo-Saxon Missionaries in Germany* (New York: Sheed and Ward, 1954), 10.

90. R. J. King, "Runes and Rune-Stones," *Fraser's Magazine*, new ser., 13 (June 1876): 750.

91. Simpson, "'Rules of Folklore,'" 15. In general, scholars since James's day have tended to be rather more cautious in positing an essential link between medieval runes and magic. See R. I. Page, *An Introduction to English Runes* (London: Methuen, 1973), 13–14.

92. Eiríkr Magnússon and William Morris, trans., *Völsunga Saga: The Story of the Volsungs and Niblungs, with Certain Songs from Elder Edda* (London: F. S. Ellis, 1870), 169. I cite here James's own copy, now in the Eton College Archives, Lpp.3.06. The original lines read, "einn veldr Óðinn ǫllǫ bolvi, / því at með sifiungom sacrúnar bar" (Odin is to blame for all the misfortune, as he brought runes of strife among those bound by ties of marriage). My translation. For the text, see Hans Kuhn, ed., *Edda: Die Lieder*

des Codex Regius Nebst Verwandten Denkmälern, vol. 1 (Heidelberg: Carl Winter, 1983), 157–58 (34.5–8).

93. *MGSA*, 133.

94. See Ian Wood, "Saint Wandrille and Its Hagiography," in *Church and Chronicle in the Middle Ages: Essays Presented to John Taylor*, ed. Ian Wood and G. A. Loud (London: Hambledon Press, 1991), 13: "In the Life of Wulfram there are several parallels with that of Willibrord, and the latter saint is even given a walk-on role." James visited St. Wulfram's church at Abbeville on several of his trips to France, once remarking that it "consist[s] of 2-large flamboyant towers and very little else." CUL, MS Add. 7480/D6/141.

95. *Vita Vulframni episcopi Senonici* [Life of Saint Wulfram] ed. W. Levison, in *Passiones Vitaeque Sanctorum Aevi Merovingici*, ed. B. Krusch and W. Levison, Monumenta Germaniae Historica, Scriptorum Rerum Merovingicarum V (Hannover: Hahn, 1910). The story is summarized in William Glaister, *Life and Times of S. Wulfram, Bishop and Missionary* (Grantham: Lawrence Ridge, 1878), 33–35.

96. *MGSA*, 88.

97. *MGSA*, 101.

98. *MGSA*, 97.

99. As Paus notes in "Runes and Manuscripts," 8.

100. The text and translation of this passage are from Eiríkr Magnússon, *Odin's Horse Yggdrasill (A Paper Read Before the Cambridge Philological Society, January 24, 1895)* (New York: E. & J. B. Young, 1895), 18. The Hávamál, in which "Odin's Rune Song" is found, was widely available in English translation by 1911 (the year "Casting the Runes" was published), including, for example, in Benjamin Thorpe, trans., *The Elder Edda of Saemund Sigfusson* (London: Norrœna Society, 1907). James, in a lecture delivered to the students of Shrewsbury School in November 1918, urged his audience to cultivate curiosity about such matters as "what the Song of Roland or the Elder Edda are really like." "M. R. James: Lectures and Addresses," CUL, MS Add. 7484/box 1/40.

101. George William Cox, *An Introduction to the Science of Comparative Mythology and Folklore* (London: Kegan Paul, 1881), 44.

102. Thorpe, *Elder Edda*, 46.

103. Paus, "Runes and Manuscripts," 8. Paus cites a passage in Alfred Holder's edition of *Saxonis Grammatici Gesta Danorum* (Strassburg, 1886), 79, in which Odin's attempt to kiss a young woman is rebuffed, for which indignity he gains revenge by touching her with a spell-inscribed piece of bark (*cortice carminibus adnotato contingens*).

104. *MGSA*, 120.

105. James recognizes the reader's desire to learn the identity of the individual magic runes: "As Harrington had said, the characters on it were more like Runes than anything else, but not decipherable by either man, and both hesitated to copy them, for fear, as they confessed, of perpetuating whatever evil purpose they might conceal. So it has remained impossible (if I may anticipate a little) to ascertain what was conveyed in this curious message or commission." *MGSA*, 123.

106. For more detailed accounts of these changes, see Page, *Introduction to English Runes*, 44–45; Michael P. Barnes, *Runes: A Handbook* (Woodbridge: Boydell Press, 2012), 38–39. The basic relationship between these runes was understood by James's day. See, for instance, Sir John Rhys, *Lectures on Welsh Philology* (London: Trübner, 1877), 360.

107. *MGSA*, 111–12.

108. *MGSA*, 112. As Edward Wagenknecht, *Seven Masters of Supernatural Fiction* (New York: Greenwood Press, 1991), points out, the mouth is the climactic horror, "by all means the most terrifying" moment in the story (61). For the sexual implications of this fright (in particular, the common interpretation of this mouth as a *vagina dentata*), see Dani Cavallaro, *The Gothic Vision: Three Centuries of Horror, Terror, and Fear* (London: Continuum, 2005), 67.

109. James had played an important role in tracing, historically, the Christian apocalyptic tradition, "in which various classes of sinners were represented as punished in a manner suitable to their offences," as he writes in *The Gospel According to Peter, and the Revelation of Peter*, with J. Armitage Robinson (London: C. J. Clay and Sons, 1892), 40. In the winter of 1886–87, there was discovered in an Egyptian tomb a portion of the Revelation (or Apocalypse) of Peter, a text that James had long devoted himself to reconstructing through fragments. In 1892 he lectured in Cambridge on his observations on the importance of the text to Christian and literary history, noting that it had indirectly influenced Dante's vision of hell, so that it "had had a share in moulding the greatest poem of the middle ages" (40).

110. Anthony Grafton, *The Footnote: A Curious History* (Cambridge: Harvard University Press, 1997), 8.

111. *MGSA*, 87.

112. See Robyn Warhol-Down, "Academics Anonymous: A Meditation on Anonymity, Power, and Powerlessness," *Symplokē* 16, nos. 1–2 (2008): 51–59, for reflections on this dynamic.

113. See David Shatz, "Peerless Review: The Strange Case of Book Reviews," chapter 4 of *Peer Review: A Critical Inquiry* (New York: Rowman & Littlefield, 2004), 109–20.

114. *MGSA*, 120; BL, MS Egerton 3141, fol. 13r.

115. BL, MS Egerton 3141, fol. 12r.

116. *MGSA*, 126, 109.

117. *MGSA*, 108.

118. A point emphasized in Brewster, "Casting an Eye," 47.

119. *MGSA*, 98.

120. Pincombe, "Class War," 5.

121. Quoted in Reba N. Soffer, *Discipline and Power: The University, History, and the Making of an English Elite, 1870–1930* (Stanford: Stanford University Press, 1995), 115, where Acton's hesitation to publish is discussed in detail.

122. *MGSA*, 107.

123. In BL, Egerton 3141, fol. 13r, we can see that James began writing a different number, then corrected his text to cite this particular volume: "Harley 30 3586."

124. CUL, MS Add. 7484/box 2/48, fol. 4r; Walter Map, *De nugis curialium*, ed. M. R. James, Anecdota Oxoniensia, Medieval and Modern Series 14 (Oxford: Clarendon Press, 1914); M. R. James, trans., *Walter Map's "De Nugis Curialium,"* Cymmrodorion Record Series 9 (London: Society of Cymmrodorion, 1923).

125. *MGSA*, 126.

126. M. R. James, "The Novels and Stories of J. Sheridan Le Fanu" (delivered to the Royal Institution of Great Britain on 16 March 1923), ed. Rosemary Pardoe in *Ghosts & Scholars* 7 (1985): 27. James considered this ghost story possibly the best of all time. "Some Remarks on Ghost Stories," 170.

127. Quoted in Pfaff, *Montague Rhodes James*, 255.

128. The epigraph is from "The Shepheardes Calender, Julye," in Edmund Spenser, *The Shorter Poems*, ed. Richard A. McCabe (London: Penguin, 1999), 102, lines 231–32.

129. Ibid., 97, lines 45–48.

130. Ibid., 96, lines 13–14.

131. *WTC*, 98, 99, 100.

132. *WTC*, 108. The phrase has inspired the name of a smartphone application that allows for the "augmented reality" of present-day sites with archaeological reconstructions. See http://www.dead-mens-eyes.org.

133. Sir Richard Fanshawe, *Il Pastor Fido: The Faithful Shepherd, With an Addition of divers other Poems* (London, 1664). The pastoral ode is found at 209–14.

134. Robert Macfarlane, in "The Eeriness of the English Countryside," *Guardian*, 10 April 2015, too detects "the pinnacle of the English pastoral" in James's landscape descriptions, using "A View from a Hill" as a starting point to argue that "the English eerie is on the rise. A loose but substantial body of work is emerging that explores the English landscape in terms of its anomalies rather than its continuities, that is sceptical of comfortable notions of 'dwelling' and 'belonging,' and of the packagings of the past as 'heritage,' and that locates itself within a spectred rather than a sceptred isle." James, of course, had a hungry eye for the underbelly of English heritage: for his "Rats" (1929), the stone base of a former gibbet at Thetford Heath inspires "just such another" discovered by Mr. Thomson as he strolls the countryside in the bright afternoon.

135. The range runs north–south along the border with Worcestershire.

136. James, *Seventy Years*, 143–44.

137. Readers may be interested to compare the description of the "fine pinnacled central tower" with "four big pinnacles at the corners" of the fictional Fulnaker priory church with that of Great Malvern Priory church (*WTC*, 114). In a work indebted to the "invaluable advice of Dr. M. R. James" (vii, 31), Anthony Charles Deane, *A Short Account of Great Malvern Priory Church* (London: G. Bell and Sons, 1914), stresses this feature of the fabric: "Altogether admirable also is the design of the central tower with its union of grace and strength" (41). Fanshawe would likely agree. "What a fine tower!" he exclaims, spotting Fulnaker through Baxter's binoculars (*WTC*, 107). For other attempts to localize the inspiration of this church and the surrounding landscape, see Martin Byrom, "A Wander Round Withybush," *Ghosts & Scholars* 19 (1995): 32–33; and Rosemary Pardoe and Darroll Pardoe, "The Herefordshire of 'A View from a Hill,'" *Ghosts & Scholars M. R. James Newsletter* 6 (September 2004). My point, of course, is not to dismiss other such potential topographical links, but to argue for a broader literary significance of setting a pastoral story in this corner of the countryside.

138. James first read this poem at the age of twenty, as he wrote to his parents in letters dated 30 and 31 May 1883 (CUL, MS Add. 7480/D6/196–97): "I have begun that book one always finds mentioned in English Histories—Langland's Vision of Piers Plowman. It is very interesting but the worst of it is that he wrote it three times and you have to read all three texts if you want to know it properly."

139. W. W. Skeat, ed., *The Vision of William Concerning Piers the Plowman, Part II*, B-Text (London: N. Trüber for the Early English Text Society, 1869), 1 (prologue, lines 1–16). Skeat provides this paraphrase: "One summer season, clothed as a hermit, I went abroad in the world to hear wonders. On Malvern hills, a strange thing befell me. Being

tired of wandering, I rested me by a bourne's side, where I fell asleep. Then dreamt I a wondrous dream, that I was in a strange wilderness, and saw on the east side of it a tower on a toft, and beneath it a deep dale with a dungeon."

140. See Roden and Roden's note in *A Pleasing Terror*, 325; and James, *Eton and King's*, 258–59.

141. *First Report of the Royal Commission on Public Records* (London, 1912), 3.

142. Philippa Levine, *The Amateur and the Professional: Antiquarians, Historians, and Archaeologists in Victorian England, 1838–1886* (Cambridge: Cambridge University Press, 1986), 105, 106.

143. *First Report of the Royal Commission*, 32–33.

144. Levine, *Amateur and the Professional*, 132–33.

145. James, *Eton and King's*, 258.

146. *Third Report of the Royal Commission on Public Records* (London, 1919), 2.

147. Unsigned review of *Third Report of the Royal Commission*, *American Historical Review* 25 (July 1920): 722.

148. *Third Report of the Royal Commission*, 38; Hubert Hall, "The Royal Commission on Public Records: A Study of the Archives in War-Time," *History* 3 (July 1918): 98.

149. *Report of the Royal Commission on Oxford and Cambridge Universities* (London: His Majesty's Stationery Office, 1922), 95. For a summary of the commission's work, see Christopher N. L. Brooke, *A History of the University of Cambridge*, vol. 4, *1870–1990* (Cambridge: Cambridge University Press, 1993), 341–69.

150. Thomas William Heyck, "The Idea of a University in Britain," *History of European Ideas* 8, no. 2 (1987): 209.

151. Brooke, *History of the University*, 342; Pfaff, *Montague Rhodes James*, 367.

152. *WTC*, 102.

153. Sir Walter Scott, *The Antiquary*, ed. Nicola J. Watson (Oxford: Oxford University Press, 2002), 40.

154. Ibid., 43.

155. Ibid., 363.

156. *WTC*, 105.

157. Barker, "After M. R. James," 8–9.

158. *WTC*, 103.

159. Bury, *Inaugural Lecture*, 32, 22.

160. Paul R. Deslandes, *Oxbridge Men: British Masculinity and the Undergraduate Experience, 1850–1920* (Bloomington: Indiana University Press, 2005), 25. For an example of James using this idiom in a quite similar context (as two gentlemen survey a haunted landscape), see the story draft "The Game of Bear," *Ghosts & Scholars M. R. James Newsletter* 12 (September 2007): 11.

161. M. R. James wrote to A. F. Scholfield, 29 October 1925, "By the way [A. E. Housman] said something to me which implied there was something wrong with the optics of a late story of mine called a View from a Hill. And there may be, but if these things happen, what are you going to do about it?" CUL, MS Add. 7894, fol. 113v.

162. Arthur Quiller-Couch, *On the Art of Writing: Lectures Delivered in the University of Cambridge, 1913–14* (Cambridge: Cambridge University Press, 1916), 175–76.

163. Hans Robert Jauss, "The Alterity and Modernity of Medieval Literature," *New Literary History* 10, no. 2 (1979): 181–227.

164. *WTC*, 115–16.

165. *WTC*, 129.

166. Laura Kendrick, "Games Medievalists Play: How to Make Earnest of Game and Still Enjoy It," *New Literary History* 40, no. 1 (2009): 45.

167. CUL, MS Add. 7484/box 2/48, fol. 2r.

168. Christopher Cherry, "How Can We Seize the Past?," *Philosophy* 64 (1989): 67.

169. Nicholas Watson, "Desire for the Past," in *Maistresse of My Wit: Medieval Women, Modern Scholars*, ed. Louise D'Arcens and Juanita Feros Ruys (Turnhout: Brepols, 2004), 149–88; and Nicholas Watson, "The Phantasmal Past: Time, History, and the Recombinative Imagination," *Studies in the Age of Chaucer* 32 (2010): 1–37. See also Thomas A. Prendergast and Stephanie Trigg, "The Negative Erotics of Medievalism," in *The Post-Historical Middle Ages*, ed. Elizabeth Scala and Sylvia Federico (New York: Palgrave Macmillan, 2009), 117–37; and, also by Prendergast and Trigg, "What Is Happening to the Middle Ages?," *New Medieval Literatures* 9 (2007): 215–29; and the response of Carolyn Dinshaw in the same volume, "Are We Having Fun Yet? A Response to Prendergast and Trigg," 231–41.

170. Cherry, "How Can We Seize the Past," 70, 77, 76.

171. Ibid., 70.

172. Louise Fradenburg, "'So That We May Speak of Them': Enjoying the Middle Ages," *New Literary History* 28 (1997): 219. See also Fradenburg, *Sacrifice Your Love: Psychoanalysis, Historicism, Chaucer* (Minneapolis: University of Minnesota Press, 2002).

173. For Brown's second career in amateur astronomy, see the obituary by R. L. S. Bruce-Mitford in *Proceedings of the Suffolk Institute of Archaeology and History* 34 (1980): 71.

174. Quoted in Martin Carver, *Sutton Hoo: Burial Ground of Kings* (Philadelphia: University of Pennsylvania Press, 1998), 5. Compare Richards's discussion of Baxter (*WTC* 104, 114).

175. *WTC*, 112–13.

176. *WTC*, 137.

177. *WTC*, 113.

178. Cherry, "How Can We Seize the Past," 76, 77–78.

179. *WTC*, 102.

180. *Collected Ghost Stories*, ed. Jones, 459.

181. "... remembering that Ring of *Pope Borgia*, with other known Specimens of the Horrid Art of the Italian Poysoners of the last age." *GSA*, 94.

182. The anecdote is found, among other places, in William Jones, *Finger-Ring Lore* (London: Spottiswoode, 1877), 435–36.

183. See Joshi's edition *Haunted Dolls' House*, 285. For a somewhat different take on amateurism in the tale, see Hay, *Modern British Ghost Story*, 100.

184. Carolyn Dinshaw, *Getting Medieval: Sexualities and Communities, Pre- and Postmodern* (Durham: Duke University Press, 1999).

185. *WTC*, 114.

CHAPTER 3

1. See Pfaff, *Montague Rhodes James*, 89–90; Cox, *Informal Portrait*, 72–74.

2. Edward White Benson, *The Cathedral: Its Necessary Place in the Life and Work of the Church* (London: John Murray, 1878), 124.

3. See A. G. L. Haig, "The Church, the Universities, and Learning in Later Victorian England," *Historical Journal* 29 (1986): 187–201; Hugh McLeod, *Secularization in Western Europe, 1848–1914* (New York: St. Martin's Press, 2000).

4. McLeod, *Secularization in Western Europe*, 74. James himself often preached sermons, more than a hundred of which survive in CUL, MS Add. 7485.

5. Letter dated 2 April 1905, in *The Letters of H. E. Luxmoore*, ed. M. R. James and A. B. Ramsay (Cambridge: Cambridge University Press, 1929), 117. For analysis of how the particular dynamics of secularization at Cambridge factored into disciplinary formation, see Alison Wood, "Secularity and the Uses of Literature: English at Cambridge, 1890–1920," *Modern Language Quarterly* 75, no. 2 (2014): 259–77.

6. See *OED*, s.vv. "secular," "secularization."

7. Kathleen Davis, *Periodization and Sovereignty* (Philadelphia: University of Pennsylvania Press, 2008), 77. See also Davis's more recent "Timelines: Feudalism, Secularity, and Early Modernity," *South Asia: Journal of South Asian Studies* 38, no. 1 (2015): 69–83.

8. Johannes Fabian, *Time and the Other: How Anthropology Makes Its Object* (New York: Columbia University Press, 1983). Examples of this critique applied to and within medieval studies include John Dagenais and Margaret R. Greer, "Decolonizing the Middle Ages: Introduction," *Journal of Medieval and Early Modern Studies* 30 (Fall 2000): 431–47; Jeffrey Jerome Cohen, *The Postcolonial Middle Ages* (New York: St. Martin's Press, 2000); Carol Symes, "The Middle Ages Between Nationalism and Colonialism," *French Historical Studies* 34 (2011): 37–46.

9. Bruno Latour, *We Have Never Been Modern*, trans. Catherine Porter (Cambridge: Harvard University Press, 1993).

10. Reinhart Koselleck, *Futures Past: On the Semantics of Historical Time*, trans. Keith Tribe (Cambridge: MIT Press, 1985), 17.

11. After his dissertation on the Apocalypse of Peter (King's College, 1887), James edited and/or translated *The Psalms of Solomon* (1891), *The Testament of Abraham* (1892), and two series of *Apocrypha Anecdota* (1893, 1897). For a time thereafter, he shifted his energies to the manuscript catalogues for which he is best known in the academic world, but later editions and translations include the pseudepigraphical *Biblical Antiquities of Philo* (1917), *The Lost Apocrypha of the Old Testament* (1920), and his magnificent *Apocryphal New Testament* (1924) and *Latin Infancy Gospels* (1927). More than sixty additional items on apocryphal topics—among them reviews, brief notes and queries, introductory essays, and critical studies—further enrich the columns of his scholarly output on the subject.

12. M. R. James, *Apocrypha Anecdota* 1, Texts and Studies 2.3 (Cambridge: Cambridge University Press, 1893), viii.

13. M. R. James, "Useless Knowledge," ed. Rosemary Pardoe, *Ghosts & Scholars M. R. James Newsletter* 14 (September 2008): 8. As Pardoe notes, the paper (CUL, MS Add. 7484/box 2/27) was likely read at the Chitchat Society in May 1883.

14. Roger Luckhurst, "Pseudobibliographomania: A Warning to the Curious," plenary lecture delivered at "M. R. James and the Modern Ghost Story: A One-Day Conference at the Leeds Library," 28 March 2015. I would like to thank Professor Luckhurst for generously providing me with a copy of his lecture.

15. James, *Apocrypha Anecdota* 1, viii.

16. M. R. James, *The Apocryphal New Testament* (Oxford: Clarendon Press, 1924), xiii.

17. *GSA*, 12.
18. *GSA*, 28.
19. Stephanie Trigg, "Walking Through Cathedrals: Scholars, Pilgrims, and Medieval Tourists," *New Medieval Literatures* 7 (2005): 12. As Elizabeth Emery argues in *Romancing the Cathedral: Gothic Architecture in Fin-de-Siècle French Culture* (Albany: State University of New York Press, 2001), "At a time of increased secularization, diminishing Church power over society, and the abandonment of churches, the Gothic cathedral . . . exerted a fascinating attraction for people worried about social fragmentation, disappearing beliefs, and vanishing traditions" (4). In his "Lecture on Art in France and England, 1154–1272, probably to a class at Eton," CUL, MS Add. 7484/box 1/75, James remarks, "The gothic church has bonds of association, religious, racial, and personal, which set it on a higher plane than the Greek temple."
20. James had a long-standing rivalry with Sir Arthur Hamilton-Gordon (1829–1912) to see who could visit all the cathedrals of France first. For James's cathedral holidays, see Cox, *Informal Portrait*, 106–9; Pfaff, *Montague Rhodes James*, 111–12.
21. Pfaff, *Montague Rhodes James*, 115–18.
22. *Contemporary Review* 98 (January–June 1910): 449–60. The subtitle was removed for its publication in *MGSA*.
23. *MGSA*, 143.
24. Martin Hughes compares these plots in his "Murder of the Cathedral," 74–75.
25. See the first chapter ("Who Will Be the New Bishop?") of Anthony Trollope, *Barchester Towers* (London: Trollope Society, 1995), 1–8.
26. *MGSA*, 11.
27. *MGSA*, 163.
28. *MGSA*, 166.
29. James refers to *The Dream of the Rood* as an example of "the really native product" and the "best worth reading" of early English literature in his chapter in *Cambridge Medieval History*, ed. J. B. Bury (Cambridge: Cambridge University Press, 1922), 537.
30. Albert S. Cook, ed., *The Dream of the Rood* (Oxford: Clarendon Press, 1905), 1, line 10. For purposes of citation, it is appropriate here to use an edition of the poem available to James, and all citations are to this edition. Translations are mine, unless otherwise indicated.
31. Ibid., 3, lines 28–33.
32. Ibid., 4, line 48. In a surviving lecture on medieval art (CUL, MS Add. 7484/box 2/49), James remarks that the "carved stone crosses of Northumbria testify to a ripeness and vigour such as the south could not show till a later time."
33. Translated in Albert S. Cook and Chauncey B. Tinker, eds., *Select Translations from Old English Poetry* (Boston: Ginn and Co., 1902), 103.
34. *MGSA*, 152–53. The 1901 *OED* entry for "holy" (James A. H. Murray, ed., *A New English Dictionary on Historical Principles*, vol. 5, s.v. "holy") notes that the word's "earlier application to heathen deities is found in ON. [Old Norse], but app. not in OE."
35. Cook, *Dream of the Rood*, xliii.
36. Ibid., xliii–xlvii.
37. *Collected Ghost Stories*, ed. Jones, 400.
38. *MGSA*, 167.
39. Cook, *Dream of the Rood*, 1.

40. One particularly characteristic of, but not limited to, the sexually suggestive double-entendre subgenre: *heo on mec gripeð* (she takes ahold of me) (Riddle 26, line 7b); *ful oft mec gesiþas sendað æfter hondum* (very often companions pass me around in their hands) (Riddle 31, line 5); *hwilum up ateah / folmum sinum* (at times [she] took [me] up in her hands) (Riddle 62, lines 2b–3a), etc. Frederick Tupper Jr., ed., *The Riddles of the Exeter Book* (London: Ginn and Co., 1910), 18, 23, 44. Numbering of the individual Exeter Riddles varies from edition to edition; numbers used in this chapter follow Tupper's system.

41. Ibid., 20 (Riddle 26, lines 9b–11a).

42. Ibid., 19 (Riddle 24, line 12).

43. Ibid., 64 (Riddle 92, lines 1–2, 4b–5a).

44. Ibid., 50 (Riddle 73, lines 1–8).

45. Even James's supernatural cat seems infused with enigmatography. Haynes describes its statuette thus: "One is an exquisitely modelled figure of a cat, whose crouching posture suggests with admirable spirit the suppleness, vigilance, and craft of the redoubted adversary of the genus *Mus.*" This carving comes to life, stalking Haynes as he wanders the corridors of his lodging late at night, lying in wait to trip him up on the stairs. Compare this to Aldhelm's cat enigma, which describes a *pervigil* (thoroughly vigilant) feline who boasts that, at night, *insidiis tacite dispono scandala mortis* (I silently set stumbling blocks as a deadly trap). The riddle ends with an etymological puzzle: *Gens exosa mihi tradebat nomen habendum* (A despised *gens* [race, kind] has given me the name I bear). The trick is to answer not with the Latin word *cattus* but with the rather more unusual *muriceps*, which means "mouse catcher," a reference of course to the cat's adversarial relationship with, as James's Haynes puts it, "the genus *Mus.*" James was an expert on Aldhelm, providing lengthy commentary on the author's works in chapter 5 ("Latin Writings in England to the Time of Alfred") of the *Cambridge History of English Literature*, vol. 1, ed. A. W. Ward and A. R. Waller (Cambridge: Cambridge University Press, 1907), 72–79, and in his *Two Ancient Scholars: St. Aldhelm and William of Malmesbury* (Glasgow: Jackson, Wylie and Co., 1931).

46. *MGSA*, 146.

47. Cook, *Dream of the Rood*, 4, line 44.

48. Elsewhere, Haynes's accomplice, the disgraced maid Jane Lee (who conspires in tampering with the stair-rod) complains that "all seems to go cross with us," and she demands blackmail money, "otherwise steps will have to be took." *MGSA*, 159. It is perhaps also possible to suspect wordplay on *stairs* and σταυρός, the word used in the Gospels for the cross of Christ's crucifixion; James was quite capable of, and prolific in, such puns. At any rate, the pattern also neatly dovetails with medieval typological tradition, in which the Holy Rood was seen as prefigured by the heavenly *scalam* (ladder, flight of stairs) that Jacob witnesses in Genesis.

49. See Charles D. Wright, "The Blood of Abel and the Branches of Sin: *Genesis A, Maxims I,* and Aldhelm's *Carmen de uirginitate*," *Anglo-Saxon England* 25 (December 1996): 7–19.

50. Quoted and translated in ibid., 15. James's translation of the Acts of Thomas (3:32) reads: "I am he that kindled and inflamed Cain to kill his own brother, and on mine account did thorns and thistles grow up in the earth" (Satan is the speaker). See James, *Apocryphal New Testament*, 379.

51. Wright, "Blood of Abel," 17. Another possible medieval representation of this tree is to be seen in the Pierpont Morgan Library, MS M. 638, which James co-edited for the Roxburghe Club in 1927. See Sydney C. Cockerell, Montague Rhodes James, and Charles J. Ffoulkes, eds., *A Book of the Old Testament Illustrations of the Middle of the Thirteenth Century* (Cambridge: Cambridge University Press for the Roxburghe Club, 1927), fol. 2a. (The explanatory notes for the image call attention to the treelike growths "springing from the ground" at the spot of Abel's slaughter, but do not refer directly to the tradition.)

52. Wright, "Blood of Abel," 10, 15n41.

53. The allusive reimagining of *The Dream of the Rood* in the service of such a theme might be deemed appropriate, given the poem's potential association with medieval "staurolatry" (worship of the Holy Cross), as Cook suspects. *Dream of the Rood*, lvii.

54. *MGSA*, 149.

55. *MGSA*, 161.

56. Cook, *Dream of the Rood*, 3, lines 35–36.

57. Ibid., 4, line 43.

58. Ibid., lii.

59. *MGSA*, 162.

60. *MGSA*, 161.

61. *MGSA*, 144.

62. For a useful overview, see Chris Brooks, *The Gothic Revival* (London: Phaidon Press, 1999).

63. *WTC*, 14. The author Horace Walpole (1717–1797) famously rebuilt the house at Strawberry Hill (near Richmond, west London) in an ostentatious neo-Gothic style.

64. To borrow a metaphor from Kathleen Biddick, *The Shock of Medievalism* (Durham: Duke University Press, 1998), 25.

65. See Brooks, *Gothic Revival*, 247, 137.

66. Chris Miele, "Real Antiquity and the Ancient Object: The Science of Gothic Architecture and the Restoration of Medieval Buildings," in *The Study of the Past in the Victorian Age*, ed. Vanessa Brand (Oxford: Oxbow Books, 1998), 112.

67. *CGS*, preface.

68. *MGSA*, 149–50.

69. *MGSA*, 153. As Hughes points out, "It is difficult to see what could have come from this enthusiasm on the part of a dedicated administrator with a restless passion for work other than reconstruction: and reconstruction at that time would have had to be Gothic." "Murder of the Cathedral," 78.

70. *MGSA*, 167.

71. "The Residence at Whitminster" concludes with the suspicion that the habitation of the title conceals a supernatural "Jack-in-the-box, awaiting some future occupant of the residence of the senior prebendary."

72. Commentators have often linked lamia mythology with the events of the story, often emphasizing its traditional threat to children (although the creature of the tale is "downright fatal" only to older residents). In his edition *The Haunted Dolls' House and Other Ghost Stories*, S. T. Joshi remarks that "a *lamia* is a monster out of Roman popular mythology, often thought to devour children" (276n14). Similarly, Michael Cox, in his edition of *Casting the Runes*, explains, "A lamia was a witch or demon supposed to suck the blood of children" (330n219). Darryl Jones, in his 2011 edition of the *Collected Ghost*

Stories, explains, "The lamia was a Greek succubus or night demon who devoured children, and gained particular cultural currency in the nineteenth century as a vampiric femme fatale" (452). Jacqueline Simpson takes a different approach, relating features of the haunting to various motifs of Danish folklore, including, for example, "the red-eyed church-dwelling ghost" that "appears in a widespread migratory legend." "'Rules of Folklore,'" 15. Perhaps the most prolonged look into lamia lore is Peter Bell, "The Lamia and the Screech-Owl: Some Thoughts on 'An Episode of Cathedral History,'" *Ghosts & Scholars M. R. James Newsletter* 16 (October 2009). A speaker's list of James's accomplishments for an honorary degree at Oxford in 1927 supposedly concluded with the words "ne dicam Lamiarum monstra et terricula, in lucem protulit." See James's obituary in the *Times* (London), 13 June 1936.

73. *TG*, 92.

74. The English here is that of the Cambridge King James translation used in the story (but see below, n. 77).

75. Or perhaps "métagraph." See Gerard Genette, *Paratexts: Thresholds of Interpretation*, trans. Jane E. Lewin (Cambridge: Cambridge University Press, 1997), 149.

76. The renowned Hebrew scholar Joseph Addison Alexander, in *The Earlier Prophecies of Isaiah* (New York: Putnam, 1846), 568–72, provides a detailed inventory of translations up to his own time.

77. To take these citations in reverse, the third is from Rosemary Pardoe, "The Demon in the Cathedral (a Jamesian Hoax)," *All Hallows* 1 (1989): 25–26; the second is from Roden and Roden's edition *A Pleasing Terror*, 264n15; the first is to be found as a reader's marginal gloss in the digitized copy of *A Thin Ghost and Others* (1919), currently available on Google books. I include this last example to emphasize that James has indeed left a challenge of translation that many of his readers have taken up. Numerous variations on all three of these might be cited. Many of those who have located the lamia's residence in the future have relied on the King James translation ("the screech owl also shall rest there"), which version is cited elsewhere in the tale for a different line ("the satyr shall cry to his fellow") but which is neither based on the Vulgate nor known for its faithfulness to verb tenses in the original. Notice, too, that translations glossing the line often flip between "there" (the literal sense of *ibi*) and "here" (a translation apparently influenced by the common epitaph formula "Here lies . . ."). As James leaves *ibi cubavit lamia* untranslated, however, it seems best to take him as much as possible at his (or at least that of Lyall's Vulgate's) literal word: "There a lamia has lain."

78. Sullivan, *Elegant Nightmares,* summarizes the story as involving "a vampire posing as a saintly relic in a fifteenth-century cathedral altar-tomb" (78).

79. Maisie Fletcher, *The Bright Countenance: A Personal Biography of Walter Morley Fletcher* (London: Hodder and Stoughton, 1957), 112–13.

80. Quoted by Cox in his edition of *Casting the Runes*, 143n19.

81. See his preface to *CGS*. James's descriptions of the architecture and fabric of English and French cathedrals, chapels, abbeys, and parish churches appear in some thirty-four books and articles; among the more notable are *The Sculptures in the Lady Chapel at Ely* (London: Nutt, 1895); *The Verses Formerly Inscribed on Twelve Windows in the Choir of Canterbury Cathedral* (Cambridge: Cambridge Antiquarian Society, 1901); *Notes of Glass in Ashridge Chapel* (Grantham: Leatton and Eden, 1906); *The Sculptured Bosses in the Cloisters of Norwich Cathedral* (Norwich: Goose, 1911); the chapter "Sculpture,

Glass, Painting," in *Medieval France: A Companion to French Studies*, ed. Arthur Tilley (Cambridge: Cambridge University Press, 1922), 388–434; *St. George's Chapel, Windsor: The Woodwork of the Choir* (Windsor: St. George's Chapel, 1933); and of course *Abbeys* (London: Great Western Railway, 1925); and *Suffolk and Norfolk: A Perambulation of the Two Counties* (London: Dent, 1930), the last of which is suffused with architectural anecdotes of every kind.

82. M. R. James, "The Edwin Drood Syndicate," *Cambridge Review* (30 November and 7 December 1905), reprinted in *Hunted Down: The Detective Stories of Charles Dickens*, ed. Peter Haining (London: Peter Owen, 1996), 210–23 (citations are to Haining's volume).

83. Cox, *Informal Portrait*, 178–79; James, *Eton and King's*, 215–16.

84. James, "Edwin Drood Syndicate," 212–16.

85. M. R. James, "About Edwin Drood" (review), *Cambridge Review* (9 March 1911), reprinted in Andrew Lang and M. R. James, *About Edwin Drood* (Edinburgh: Tragara Press, 1983), 16–24 (see esp. 20–22); see also James, *Eton and King's*, 215.

86. James, "Edwin Drood Syndicate," 219.

87. *TG*, 78.

88. Dickens's story appeared in his journal *All the Year Round* 16 (December 1866): 20–25, quoted lines at 21. James particularly admired "The Signal-Man," praising it as "a ghost story proper." "Some Remarks on Ghost Stories," 170.

89. Unique among English cathedrals, the walled choir of Rochester formed "in effect an eastern church"; "the long walled choir, the old choir of the monks ... could only be assigned to the clergy, and could not be opened to the nave." Richard John King, *Handbook to the Cathedrals of England (Southern Division)*, 3rd ed. (London: John Murray, 1903) (originally published 1862), 585–86. On the matter of the choir reduction, see James Storer, *History and Antiquities of the Cathedral Churches of Great Britain*, vol. 4 (London: Rivingtons, 1819), plate 7.

90. William H. St. John Hope (1854–1919) spent four years in Rochester compiling his *Architectural History of the Cathedral Church and Monastery of St. Andrew at Rochester* (London: Mitchell and Hughes, 1900); his capacious knowledge and keen ability to extrapolate based on observation make him something of an architectural counterpart to James, and the two men are of one voice on matters of nineteenth-century "restoration" (as Hope's frequent ironic use of the term in quotation marks indicates). Cox notes that James, "appealing to the authority of Ruskin, insisted that ancient buildings belonged to the men who built them: 'it was only our duty to preserve them for posterity if we could do so without altering them. Restoration was unjustifiable, reparation was beneficial'" (*Informal Portrait*, 43), and this Ruskinian attitude is explored in detail in Hughes, "Murder of the Cathedral"; and Françoise Dupeyron-Lafay, "Les cathédrales de Montague Rhodes James," in *La Cathédrale*, ed. Joëlle Prungnaud (Villeneuve d'Ascq: Université Charles-de-Gaulle, 2001), 203–14.

91. *Some Account of an Ancient Tomb, etc. etc. etc., Discovered at Rochester Cathedral, 1825, by L. N. Cottingham, Arch.* (London: Taylor, 1825). Both the tomb and the Wheel of Fortune are visible on the cathedral's panoramic tour, online at http://www.rochestercathedral.org/pano/.

92. *TG*, 87.

93. Hope, *Architectural History*, 111–20.

94. Ibid., 129–30.

95. John Thorpe, *Custumale Roffense, from the Original Manuscript in the Archives of the Dean and Chapter of Rochester: to which are added, Memorials of that Cathedral Church* (London: Nichols, 1788.)

96. *TG*, 79.

97. *TG*, 87.

98. *TG*, 79.

99. *TG*, 103.

100. This is how Joshi (*Haunted Dolls' House*, 274) summarizes the argument of Bill Read, "The Mystery of the Second Satyr," *Ghosts & Scholars* 31 (2000): 46–47. As Read explains, "Unless the occupant of the tomb had remarkable powers of telekinesis, this diversion was a remarkable coincidence. However, if there was a second creature already at liberty in the cathedral, then it is an obvious suspect" (47). As I argue, however, there is no need to assume either a second creature or a coincidence.

101. *TG*, 92. Jones, in his edition of the *Collected Ghost Stories*, wonders if the creature in "An Episode" is calling after the fiend from "Canon Alberic's Scrap-Book": "Could 'Canon Alberic's demon be the fellow to whom this satyr cries, 'as if it were calling after someone that wouldn't come'?" Jones further seems to imply that these two monsters may be mates: "Thus, importantly, 'Cathedral History's demon is *female* (as opposed to its male counterpart in 'Canon Alberic'" (452).

102. *GSA*, 223.

103. John 20:6–7, *Biblia sacra iuxta vulgatam versionem*, 3rd ed., ed. Robert Weber, 2 vols., paginated consecutively (Stuttgart: Deutsche Bibelgesellschaft, 1983), 1695.

104. Matthew 27:64, ibid., 1573.

105. Matthew 28:2, ibid. In an undated Easter sermon (CUL, MS Add. 7485/39), James focuses on this imagery as it is echoed in Psalm 73 and adopted for Easter services in the Latin liturgy: "They thought of the earthquake and the stone rolled away from the sepulchre, & they imagined the hushed silence that fell upon all things when God arose."

106. Like any medievalist, James would be very familiar with this genre (he cites, for instance, the Coventry Plays in his *Guide to the Windows of King's College Chapel, Cambridge* [London, 1899], 26), but more generally his interest in drama and its history was lifelong, including his own performances in Cambridge productions of Greek drama in the original language (see Pfaff, *Montague Rhodes James*, 53–54; Cox, *Informal Portrait*, 65–67). An analogous initiative to perform the entire cycle of Chester Mystery Plays occurred in 1906–7, a project controversial for religious reasons: "opposition was led by the Dean of the Chapter, who recoiled at what seemed to him the blasphemous medieval practice of representing sacred subjects on the stage." See David Mills, "Replaying the Medieval Past: Revivals of Chester's Mystery Plays," *Studies in Medievalism* 7 (1995): 185.

107. James Orchard Halliwell, *Ludus Coventriæ: A Collection of Mysteries* (London: Printed for the Shakespeare Society, 1841), 348 (glosses mine).

108. Quoted in Alfred Heales, "Easter Sepulchres: Their Object, Nature, and History," *Archaeologia* 42 (1868): 280. Heales notes another recorded performance in which "commeth sodenly a flash of fire wherewith they are all afraid and fall downe; and then up startes the man, and they begin to sing 'Alleluia' on all hands" (283).

109. *TG*, 101.

110. *TG*, 103.

111. *TG*, 103. Edward G. Tasker and John Beaumont, eds., *Encyclopedia of Medieval Church Art* (London: B. T. Batsford, 1993), notes: "In the thirteenth century there appeared

a representation of the Resurrection in Western art which became universal in the fifteenth century. Christ with the cross staff in His left hand and His right hand raised in blessing, steps out of a chest tomb onto a prostrate soldier. This form may reflect the influence of the Mystery Plays and the Easter Sepulchres some of which, as at Hawton, had the sleeping soldiers at their base and some of which were actual tombs" (67). Hundreds of depictions of this moment from the fifteenth century alone (the best known of which include paintings by Piero della Francesca, Mantegna, Bellini, Raphael, Perugino, and Dieric Bouts), as well as glass and sculptural programs involving it, can be found across Europe.

112. John Matthews Manly, ed., *Specimens of the Pre-Shakespearean Drama*, vol. 1 (London: Ginn and Co., 1897), 166–67.

113. *TG*, 104.

114. Matthew 27:66, *Biblia sacra*, 1573.

115. *TG*, 94.

116. Lucy Toulmin Smith, *York Plays: The Plays Performed by the Crafts or Mysteries of York.* . . . (Oxford: Clarendon Press, 1885), 352.

117. Halliwell, *Ludus Coventriæ*, 341 (glosses mine).

118. Ibid., 349 (glosses mine).

119. The soldier complains, "He sett his foote upon my backe, / That everye lith beganne to crake; / I would not abyde suche another shake / For all Jerusalem." Thomas Wright, ed., *The Chester Plays: A Collection of Mysteries* (London: Printed for the Shakespeare Society, 1847).

120. David Bevington, *Medieval Drama* (Boston: Houghton Mifflin, 1975), 240.

121. Heales, "Easter Sepulchres," 273 and passim.

122. E. K. Chambers, *The Mediaeval Stage*, 2 vols. (Oxford: Clarendon Press, 1903), 2:14.

123. *TG*, 80.

124. Heales, "Easter Sepulchres," 288.

125. *TG*, 79.

126. Quoted in Chambers, *Mediaeval Stage*, 2:310.

127. Quoted in translation in Francis Bond, *The Chancel of English Churches* (London: Humphrey Milford, 1916), 236. Heales, "Easter Sepulchres," 289, notes of this sepulcher, "This tomb was only removed (quite unnecessarily) at a recent date."

128. Bond, *Chancel of English Churches*, 236.

129. Ibid., 220.

130. *TG*, 87.

131. H. P. Lovecraft, *Dagon and Other Macabre Tales* (Sauk City, Wisc.: Arkham House, 1965), 433.

132. *TG*, 106.

133. Cox's note in *Casting the Runes*, 330n219.

134. As documented most fully in O. B. Hardison Jr., "Darwin, Mutations, and the Origin of Medieval Drama," chapter 1 of *Christian Rite and Christian Drama in the Middle Ages* (Baltimore: Johns Hopkins University Press, 1965), 1–34. In the decades since James's day, the assumptions underlying this research have been repeatedly called into question, so that we read in David Bevington's standard work, *Medieval Drama* (1975), "The evidence seems to contradict a once well-established scholarly hypothesis of dramatic growth, which assumed that the *Visitatio* grew first into a complex Resurrection play and then served as a model for the subsequent development of other kinds of drama" (31).

135. John Matthews Manly, "Literary Forms and the New Theory of the Origin of Species," *Modern Philology* 4, no. 4 (1907): 7.

136. Chambers, *Mediaeval Stage*, 2:32, 35, 73, 3.

137. Ibid., 2:180.

138. See Pfaff, *Montague Rhodes James*, 57–58.

139. *TG*, 79.

140. *TG*, 80.

141. Isaiah 34:10–14, King James translation.

142. Franz Delitzsch, *Biblical Commentary on the Prophecies of Isaiah*, trans. James Martin (Edinburgh: Clark, 1867), 72.

143. *MGSA*, 148.

144. Whether "it is possible for an archdeacon to be saved?" See Conrad O'Briain, "'Gates of Hell,'" 50. The question, which implies an answer in the negative, is found in a letter by John of Salisbury to Nicholas de Sigillo.

145. On this point, James is anything but subtle, having Haynes (for example) startled by supernatural terror just as he hears Psalm 109 sung: "Set thou an ungodly man to be ruler over him and let Satan stand at his right hand." His refurbishing of *The Dream of the Rood*, which reveals the future judgment of Haynes, is embellished with portentous signs ("when the wind blows high") and is envisioned by a sort of artisan-turned-prophet named "John Austin," a name that suspiciously recalls some of the foremost figures in the apocalyptic tradition: the legendary John of Patmos (author of the book of Revelation) and Saint Augustine. In characteristic fashion, though, James arranges these suggestive signs in ways that do not *quite* add up. For instance, much emphasis is placed on the exact timing of Haynes's era of organizing the archdeaconry, which is projected to take precisely three years ("The estimate appears to have been an exact one") and reaches completion on 30 August 1816, followed by a period of exactly seventeen months and twenty-seven days (painfully chronicled in Haynes's diary) until his demise on 26 February. As James was well aware, three years, seven months (not *seventeen*), and twenty-seven days is a traditional calculation for the length of the reign of the Antichrist. See M. R. James, *The Lost Apocrypha of the Old Testament* (New York: Macmillan, 1920), 82.

146. See, for example, Conrad O'Briain, "'Gates of Hell,'" 57: "medieval architecture has been separated from its spiritual and cultural source and the cathedral from its purpose."

CHAPTER 4

1. Quoted in Pfaff, *Montague Rhodes James*, 327. Pfaff provides a detailed account of this project (325–30), which is also the subject of Jayne Ringrose, "The Legacy of M. R. James in Cambridge University Library," in Dennison, *Legacy of M. R. James*, 23–36.

2. Quoted in Pfaff, *Montague Rhodes James*, 328.

3. Ibid., 329.

4. CUL, MS Add. 9329/5/1, quoted in Ringrose, "Legacy of M. R. James," 33.

5. Correspondence concerning the work and a methodical notebook (compiled by underlibrarian of manuscripts B. F. C. Atkinson) listing the manuscripts sent to and returned by James are kept in the manuscripts department of Cambridge University Library under shelfmarks MS Add. 9329 and 7894–95. The notes James actually produced

are also kept in the department, and some have been integrated into the library's online catalogue.

6. "The Experiment: A New Year's Eve Ghost Story," *Morning Post* (London), 31 December 1931. Citations are from Darryl Jones's edition of the *Collected Ghost Stories*.

7. "An experiment most ofte proved true, to find out tresure hidden in the ground, theft, manslaughter, or anie other thynge. Go to the grave of a ded man, and three tymes call hym by his nam at the hed of the grave, and say. Thou, N., N., N., I conjure the, I require the, and I charge the, bi thi Christendome that thou takest leave of the Lord Raffael and Nares and then askest leave this night to come and tell me trewlie of the tresure that lyith hid in such a place. Then take of the earth of the grave at the dead bodyes hed and knitt it in a lynnen clothe and put itt under thi right eare and sleape theruppon: and wheresoever thou lyest or slepest, that night he wil com and tell thee trewlie in waking or sleping."

8. *Collected Ghost Stories*, ed. Jones, 396.

9. CUL, MS Add. 9329/4 (the Atkinson Notebook), p. 4.

10. James, *Eton and King's*, 200–201.

11. Quoted in Pfaff, *Montague Rhodes James*, 330.

12. Ibid., 325.

13. *Collected Ghost Stories*, ed. Jones, 391, 394–95.

14. Rosemary Pardoe, "'The Experiment': Story Notes," *Ghosts & Scholars M. R. James Newsletter* 3 (January 2003): 22.

15. *Collected Ghost Stories*, ed. Jones, 393–94 (bracketed insertion mine).

16. For more on this letter, see Patrick J. Murphy and Fred Porcheddu, "Robert Thornton, the Alliterative *Morte Arthure*, and Cambridge University Library MS Dd.11.45," *Modern Philology* 114 (August 2016): 130–47.

17. *Collected Ghost Stories*, ed. Jones, 391.

18. James, "Some Remarks on Ghost Stories," 172.

19. For a useful overview of the subject of time and medievalism studies, see Stephanie Trigg, "Medievalism and Theories of Temporality," in *The Cambridge Companion to Medievalism*, ed. Louise D'Arcens (Cambridge: Cambridge University Press, 2016), 196–209.

20. See Kathleen Davis, *Periodization and Sovereignty* (Philadelphia: University of Pennsylvania Press, 2008), 5, for a related sense of the medieval as a "mobile category."

21. For an influential and rollicking take on the subject, see Umberto Eco, "Dreaming of the Middle Ages," in *Travels in Hyperreality*, trans. William Weaver (London: Harcourt Brace Jovanovich, 1986), 61–72.

22. See Theodor E. Mommsen, "Petrarch's Conception of the 'Dark Ages,'" *Speculum* 17, no. 2 (1942): 226–42.

23. Fred C. Robinson, "Medieval, the Middle Ages," *Speculum* 59, no. 4 (1984): 745–56; David Matthews, "From Mediaeval to Mediaevalism: A New Semantic History," *Review of English Studies*, new ser., 62 (2011): 695–715.

24. As James writes of two dabblers in black magic in "The Fenstanton Witch," "And how came it that they were on an enterprise which one associates, not always correctly, with the darkest mediaevalism and the most defective civilisation?" See James, *Pleasing Terror*, 417–25, and the corrected text provided in *Ghosts & Scholars M. R. James Newsletter* 4 (August 2003): 23.

25. Nicholas Watson, "The Phantasmal Past: Time, History, and the Recombinative Imagination," *Studies in the Age of Chaucer* 32 (2010): 3.

26. John Dagenais and Margaret R. Greer, "Decolonizing the Middle Ages: Introduction," *Journal of Medieval and Early Modern Studies* 30 (Fall 2000): 434.

27. Dinshaw, *How Soon Is Now*, 6.

28. For Dinshaw's discussion of James's parody of *Mandeville's Travels*, see ibid., 95–98. See also her "Temporalities," in *Middle English*, ed. Paul Strohm, Oxford Twenty-First Century Approaches to Literature (Oxford: Oxford University Press, 2007), 107–23; and her "All Kinds of Time," *Studies in the Age of Chaucer* 35 (2013): 3–25. Margery Kempe (along with her editor Hope Emily Allen) is important to Dinshaw's analysis; for a related study of Julian of Norwich, see Nicholas Watson, "Desire for the Past," in *Maistresse of My Wit: Medieval Women, Modern Scholars*, ed. Louise D'Arcens and Juanita Feros Ruys (Turnhout: Brepols, 2004), 149–88.

29. Christopher Stray, *Classics Transformed: Schools, Universities, and Society in England, 1830–1960* (Oxford: Clarendon Press, 1998), 132.

30. James, *Eton and King's*, 270.

31. James, *Letters to a Friend*, 108–9.

32. Quoted in Cox, *Informal Portrait*, 125, 220.

33. Quoted in ibid., 132–33.

34. Byron Rogers, "Whistle and I'll Come to You," *Times* (London), 22 May 1980, 19.

35. *MGSA*, 42; *TG*, 147.

36. Pfaff, *Montague Rhodes James*, 104.

37. Elizabeth Scala, "The Gender of Historicism," in *The Post-Historical Middle Ages*, ed. Elizabeth Scala and Sylvia Federico (New York: Palgrave Macmillan, 2009), 196–98.

38. J. B. Bury, *An Inaugural Lecture* (Cambridge: Cambridge University Press, 1903), 31–32.

39. *GSA*, 175.

40. Simon McKeown, "Recovering the *Codex Argenteus*: Magnus Gabriel De la Gardie, David Klöcker Ehrenstrahl, and Wulfila's Gothic Bible," *Lychnos* (2005): 11.

41. "If the present examination of the MSS. had been conducted by a member of the foundation of the College concerned, the allusion to Bishop Bateman would have been more respectful." Anonymous review of James's descriptive catalogue of the manuscripts of the library of Trinity Hall, in the *Athenæum*, no. 5176 (9 November 1907), 582. In a drafted response dated 15 November 1907, James protests that his assessment of the fourteenth-century bishop's books was accurate, noting that apart from "the sentimental interest which could have attached to them as the gifts of the founder, they would have been as little valuable as any manuscript can be." Eton College Archives, M. R. James Miscellanies, vol. I/2/1.

42. Dennison, "Introduction," *Legacy of M. R. James*, 8.

43. See, for example, Judith Halberstam, *In a Queer Time and Place* (New York: New York University Press, 2005); Elizabeth Freeman, *Time Binds: Queer Temporalities, Queer Histories* (Durham: Duke University Press, 2010).

44. Freeman, *Time Binds*, xv.

45. Leslie Stephen, *Sketches from Cambridge* (London: Macmillan, 1865), 89.

46. *Collected Papers of Henry Bradshaw* (London: C. J. Clay and Sons, 1889), 384.

47. D. G. Hogarth, *Authority and Archaeology: Sacred and Profane* (London: Charles Scribner's Sons, 1899), vi–vii, xii.

48. Britton J. Harwood, "The Ideological Use of Chaucer: The Examples of Kittredge and Donaldson," in *Medievalism in the Modern World: Essays in Honour of Leslie J. Workman*, ed. Richard Utz and Tom Shippey (Turnhout: Brepols, 1998), 391.

49. David Matthews, "What Was Medievalism? Medieval Studies, Medievalism, and Cultural Studies," in *Medieval Cultural Studies: Essays in Honour of Stephen Knight*, ed. Ruth Evans, Helen Fulton, and David Matthews (Cardiff: University of Wales Press, 2006), 16. For a useful overview of the presentist/pastist conundrum, see Louise D'Arcens, "Presentism," in *Medievalism: Key Critical Terms*, ed. Elizabeth Emery and Richard Utz (Cambridge: D. S. Brewer, 2014), 181–88.

50. Jeffrey Jerome Cohen, *Medieval Identity Machines*, Medieval Cultures 35 (Minneapolis: University of Minnesota Press, 2003), 21.

51. David Matthews, *Medievalism: A Critical History* (Cambridge: D. S. Brewer, 2015), emphasizes that "the moment of a retrieval, and the moment of recognition of a middle age, amount to almost the same thing" (2). Brian Stock, "The Middle Ages as Subject and Object: Romantic Attitudes and Academic Medievalism," *New Literary History* 5 (1974): 527–47, similarly argues that the disappearance of the period coincides with its entry into the academy (after a short delay), "to perpetuate *per monumentum* what is finally ceasing to exist *in vita*" (544).

52. *MGSA*, 7.

53. See Cohen, *Medieval Identity Machines*, 3–11; Dinshaw, *How Soon Is Now*, 9.

54. Pfaff, "James on the Cataloguing of Manuscripts," 111.

55. Ina Ferris, "Printing the Past: Walter Scott's Bannatyne Club and the Antiquarian Document," *Romanticism* 11, no. 2 (2005): 148.

56. *GSA*, 146. Cox notes that James particularly valued the state trial papers for the way they uniquely testify to "the unadorned common speech of Englishmen." *Casting the Runes*, 333n255.

57. M. R. James, ed., *Henry the Sixth: A Reprint of John Blacman's Memoir with Translation and Notes* (Cambridge: Cambridge University Press, 1919), xvi.

58. M. R. James, *The Ancient Libraries of Canterbury and Dover: The Catalogues of the Libraries of Christ Church Priory and St. Augustine's Abbey at Canterbury and of St. Martin's Priory at Dover* (Cambridge: Cambridge University Press, 1903), xxi.

59. M. R. James, *The Western Manuscripts in the Library of Trinity College, Cambridge*, vol. 4 (Cambridge: Cambridge University Press, 1904), v.

60. Talbot Jennings, "The Collected Ghost Stories of M. R. James: An Inquiry into Sources," manuscript dated 9 February 1963, now held in the Lilly Library collections in Bloomington, Indiana; Ron Weighell, "Dark Devotions: M. R. James and the Magical Tradition," in Joshi and Pardoe, *Warnings to the Curious*, 127; Martin Hughes, "A Maze of Secrets in a Story by M. R. James," *Durham University Journal* 85, no. 1 (1993): 81–93. Along these lines, the most compelling account of "James Wilson's secret"—to borrow the title of an article by Rosemary Pardoe and Jane Nicholls in *Ghosts & Scholars* 24 (1997): 45–47—interprets Humphreys's ancestor as a follower of a Gnostic sect, the Cainites, who viewed the Creator God of the Old Testament as enemy and deceiver of humankind (and thus also saw Old Testament villains such as Cain as counterintuitive heroes). As Pardoe and Nicholls (following Hughes) argue, such an interpretation may clarify much of the

sinister imagery of the tale, including the inverted globe at the center of the maze. I do not at all wish to dismiss the value of these insights; in fact, I would argue that my reading of the story, which emphasizes threats of temporal inversion, accords with them well.

61. James to Arthur Hort, 3 January 1912, quoted in *Collected Ghost Stories*, ed. Jones, 445.

62. M. R. James, "John Humphreys," ed. Rosemary Pardoe, *Ghosts & Scholars M. R. James Newsletter* 11 (March 2007): 14.

63. Ibid., 13; *MGSA*, 229.

64. M. R. James, *Apocrypha Anecdota* 2, Texts and Studies 5, ed. J. Armitage Robinson (Cambridge: Cambridge University Press, 1897), 168. A similar bleeding of such language beyond manuscript culture is found in James's story draft "Marcilly-le-Hayer," in which telling words are "palimpsested over the door." See *Ghosts & Scholars M. R. James Newsletter* 10 (September 2006): 33–34.

65. *MGSA*, 232, 256, 234, 273, 244–45, 19.

66. M. R. James, *A Descriptive Catalogue of the Manuscripts in the Library of Gonville and Caius College*, vol. 2 (Cambridge: Cambridge University Press, 1908), viii.

67. *MGSA*, 227–28, 218, 221, 243, 240.

68. *MGSA*, 268.

69. *MGSA*, 269–71.

70. *MGSA*, 240. The verb "to pore" (with its potential for porous wordplay) seems prominent in the story: aside from Cooper's phrase, we might notice that the inverted globe is "pored over," while Humphreys's vision of the infernal hole is compared to a child "por[ing] over" the surface of a windowpane. The word has specific associations for James. In a lecture on the "transmission of classical literature," James writes, "[Most scholars] are content to know that ancient MSS exist and to leave the closer study of them to those possibly eccentric and certainly remote scholars who feel an interest in poring over them—for I find that poring is the verb which is conventionally [used]." CUL, MS Add. 7484/box 1/46.

71. James, *Eton and King's*, xii.

72. For more on this incident, see chapter 2.

73. James to Gwendolen McBryde, 31 July 1915, in James, *Letters to a Friend*, 57.

74. *MGSA*, 246.

75. CUL, MS Add. 7484/box 2/4.

76. Such institutional rhythms are comically sounded in "After Dark in the Playing Fields" when several clock towers, including Lupton's Tower in the Eton School Yard, rudely announce the ominous arrival of midnight.

77. Rita McWilliams Tullberg, *Women at Cambridge* (Cambridge: Cambridge University Press, 1998), 115–16.

78. Jones, introduction to *Collected Ghost Stories*, xiv, citing King's/PP/MRJ/F/1.

79. Cited in Tullberg, *Women at Cambridge*, 110.

80. Ibid., 69.

81. Ibid., 146.

82. Pfaff, *Montague Rhodes James*, 127.

83. CUL, MS Add. 7484/box 2/62.

84. A. C. Benson, *From a College Window* (London: G. P. Putnam's Sons, 1906), 81. In the original, Benson conceals James under the pseudonym "Perry."

85. Paul R. Deslandes, *Oxbridge Men: British Masculinity and the Undergraduate Experience, 1850-1920* (Bloomington: Indiana University Press, 2005), 59.

86. Tullberg, *Women at Cambridge*, 132, 104, 108, 161, 176. Of course, probably the most famous account of a woman refused access to Cambridge libraries comes at the beginning of Virginia Woolf's *A Room of One's Own* (New York: Harcourt, Brace, 1929).

87. Charlotte Brewer, "Walter William Skeat (1835-1912)," in *Medieval Scholarship*, vol. 2, *Literature and Philology*, ed. Helen Damico (New York: Garland, 1998), 142, quoted in Tullberg, *Women at Cambridge*, 73.

88. David McKitterick, *Cambridge University Library: A History* (Cambridge: Cambridge University Press, 1986), 22.

89. *MGSA*, 47, 64, 68.

90. *MGSA*, 83; King's/PP/MRJ/A/6.

91. Quoted in Tullberg, *Women at Cambridge*, 152.

92. *MGSA*, 61.

93. For a translation, see *The Mishnah*, trans. Herbert Danby (Oxford: Oxford University Press, 1933).

94. Ibid., 3.4.

95. William J. Conybeare and John S. Howson, *The Life and Epistles of St. Paul*, vol. 2 (London: Longman, Brown, Green, and Longmans, 1852), 256.

96. *WTC*, 52, 59. In the first published critical essay on James's fiction, Mary Butts's "The Art of Montagu [sic] James," *London Mercury* 29 (February 1934): 306-17, reprinted in Joshi and Pardoe, *Warnings to the Curious*, 53-65, Butts notes that "Mr. Poschwitz, the Jew dealer, who stole the prayer books from Brockstone chapel, died by the most hideous death it is possible for the mind to conceive" (64).

97. Thompson, H. Y., MSS, 1917-1922, Lilly Library, Indiana University, collection no. LMC 1334. See also Pfaff, *Montague Rhodes James*, 194.

98. Augustus Jessopp and Montague Rhodes James, eds., *The Life and Miracles of St William of Norwich, by Thomas of Monmouth* (Cambridge: Cambridge University Press, 1896). To his "extreme pleasure," James discovered the only surviving copy of this text in 1889, after having been "instrumental in procuring" its manuscript for Cambridge University Library (1). A section of James's introduction in the watershed edition represents a first detailed attempt to detect whatever historical truth might lie behind the text. Although much of what James suggests is sound enough (exposing the absurdity of Jews' engaging in ritual murder "in *their corporate capacity*" (lxxvii, emphasis James's), his analysis also strangely overreaches at times—in untenable ways that transpose responsibility for the deadly myth back onto an ultimately Jewish source. Rather than emphasize the culpability of Thomas of Monmouth or the Christian community, for example, James lays most blame on the lies of his chief "informant," Theobald, a monk and converted Jew who (according to Thomas) claimed knowledge of a vast Jewish conspiracy of ritual murder: "we must look upon Theobald of Cambridge, as responsible for the blood of thousands of his fellow-countrymen" (lxxii). (By contrast, James's co-editor, Jessopp, chalks up Thomas's own contributions not to malice but to "an age of measureless credulity": see xiv.) James goes so far as to speculate groundlessly that Theobald himself might have murdered William, motivated by "a mad hatred of a dominant system, or a reversion to half-forgotten practices of a darker age" (lxxix). Gavin I. Langmuir, "Historiographic Crucifixion," in *Les juifs en regard de l'histoire: Mélanges en honneur de*

Bernhard Blumenkranz, ed. Gilbert Dahan (Paris: Picard, 1985), 109–27, concludes that James "seems to have wanted to exonerate Christians by any loophole he could find, even one that defied the only evidence he had, since it says that Theobald had been at Cambridge when the crime was committed" (119). For Langmuir's own influential assignment of responsibility (largely to Thomas of Monmouth himself), see his "Thomas of Monmouth: Detector of Ritual Murder," *Speculum* 59, no. 4 (1984): 820–46. John M. McCulloh, "Jewish Ritual Murder: William of Norwich, Thomas of Monmouth, and the Early Dissemination of the Myth," *Speculum* 72, no. 3 (1997): 698–740, presents an alternative account of how the myth originated. In a fascinating analysis, Anna Wilson, "*Similia similibus*: Queer Time in Thomas of Monmouth's Life and Miracles of St William of Norwich," *Exemplaria* 28, no. 1 (2016): 46–71, argues that the critical tendency to treat the text as a historical whodunit (arguably a trend initiated by James himself) obscures the vita's own investments in nonlinear temporalities (49).

99. CUL, MS Add. 7485/46.

100. Andrew P. Scheil, *The Footsteps of Israel: Understanding Jews in Anglo-Saxon England* (Ann Arbor: University of Michigan Press, 2004), 52.

101. Edward Wheatley, "'Blind' Jews and Blind Christians: Metaphorics of Marginalization in Medieval Europe," *Exemplaria* 14, no. 2 (2002): 354–55.

102. Romans 11:10.

103. *MGSA*, 58–59, 79.

104. *MGSA*, 80.

105. William Chase Green, trans., *City of God Against the Pagans*, vol. 6 (Cambridge: Harvard University Press, 1960), 49 (18.46).

106. Steven F. Kruger, *The Spectral Jew: Conversion and Embodiment in Medieval Europe*, Medieval Cultures 40 (Minneapolis: University of Minnesota Press, 2006), 3 and passim. For more on supersessionary concepts of time, see esp. Kathleen Biddick, *The Typological Imaginary: Circumcision, Technology, History* (Philadelphia: University of Pennsylvania Press, 2003). For an alternative "topological" view of how medieval Christians viewed Judaic temporalities, see Isabel Davis, "'Ye That Pasen by þe Weiye': Time, Topology, and the Medieval Use of Lamentations 1.12," *Textual Practice* 25 (2011): 437–72.

107. Kruger, *Spectral Jew*, 171–75, 177–83.

108. *MGSA*, 81.

109. Antony Oldknow, "Concerns for Women in 'The Tractate Middoth' by M. R. James," *Readerly/Writerly Texts* 9, nos. 1–2 (2001): 155, 148.

110. For instance, see Tim Martin's review of Mark Gatiss's 2013 dramatization of the story for the BBC. *Telegraph*, 25 December 2013, http://www.telegraph.co.uk/culture/tvandradio/tv-and-radio-reviews/10536086/The-Tractate-Middoth-BBC-Two-review.html (accessed 9 August 2016).

111. In seeking to understand such metaphors, we can of course easily lose sight of the very real "deadly work that a culture performs upon its spectral others," as Kruger, *Spectral Jew*, 12, rightly cautions.

112. Gray's pseudonym is borrowed from the name of Ingulf (d. 1109), an abbot of Crowland Abbey to whom a forged fifteenth-century chronicle was falsely attributed. The perils of being gulled by the Pseudo-Ingulphus became proverbial for nineteenth-century historians.

113. James, *Eton and King's*, 159.

114. Eton College Archives, Lp.2.24 (p. 159). Leslie's marginalia names the supposedly disgraced bursar, Thomas Brocklebank, who apparently did indeed die in 1878 (though not at the age of seventy). I have not been able to locate further information about this scandal, if it did take place. Tipped into the last page of this same copy of *Eton and King's* is a second scrap of writing that identifies James as Leslie's source for the Brocklebank identification, which he reportedly conveyed on Founder's Day at Eton, 1935. As the quotation indicates, Leslie seems to have subsequently consulted A. F. Scholfield, a friend of James's and the university librarian involved in the CUL manuscript catalogue discussed at the beginning of this chapter.

115. See Cox's note in *Casting the Runes*, 237n202.

116. *London Daily Post*, 17 February 1736.

117. Alexander Pope, *The Dunciad*, 3.187–89.

118. *Impartial Memorials of the Life and Writings of Thomas Hearne, M.A., by Several Hands* (London, 1736), 60; *Gentleman's Magazine* 64 (1788), 197.

119. *Impartial Memorials*, 26. In *The Wanderings and Homes of Manuscripts* (published in 1919, the same year as "Mr. Poynter"), James warmly credits Hearne for our knowledge of the lost library at Glastonbury: "We have its catalogue admirably reproduced by Thomas Hearne, at a time (early in the eighteenth century) when it was rare to find anyone who would take the trouble to make a faithful copy of such a record, with all its erasures and alterations" (62).

120. *TG*, 51, 60, 61.

121. *TG*, 67–68.

122. *TG*, 69–70. The parallels between the biblical Absalom and Everard are multiple. Both are long-haired, beautiful, vain, and rebellious against indulgent parents. Both may be interpreted as effeminate and sexually suspect (as Chaucer in *The Miller's Tale* portrays the dainty and fastidious Absolon—a character who, when enraged, viciously sodomizes a rival with a hot poker). Both end up dead in ditches (2 Samuel 18:17): *et tulerunt Absalom et proiecerunt eum in saltu in foveam grandem* (and they carried Absalom and threw him into a great pit in the woods). And in 2 Samuel 14:25–26, Absalom, like Everard, creates a memorial for himself (for more on this point, see chapter 5).

123. *MGSA*, 256.

124. *TG*, 58.

125. Thomas Hearne, *Remarks and Collections*, ed. C. E. Doble, D. W. Rannie, and H. E. Salter, 11 vols., Oxford Historical Society Publications, first series (Oxford: Clarendon Press, 1885–1918/1921). There is some uncertainty concerning the actual publication date of the last volume in this edition. On the original spine of the copy of the volume I have consulted, the publication date is given as 1918, the year before *A Thin Ghost* was published. However, the title page of the book lists 1921 (a delay that may have had to do with the war). If James did not have access to a print copy of the final volume of the Oxford editions by 1919, however, he still very possibly may have consulted all of the diaries in manuscript at the Bodleian (Rawlinson K). His research would have made such consultation likely enough, perhaps even professionally unavoidable.

126. *TG*, 58.

127. Hearne, *Remarks and Collections*, 6:265, 7:215, 9:28, 10:21, 5:259, 9:246, 8:185.

128. Language echoed in ibid., 2:332.

129. *TG*, 69–70.

130. Hearne, *Remarks and Collections*, 5:228.

131. For more on Hearne's relationship with Arthur Charlett, see Theodor Harmsen, "Bodleian Imbroglios, Politics, and Personalities, 1701–1716: Thomas Hearne, Arthur Charlett, and John Hudson," *Neophilologus* 82 (1998): 149–68.

132. Hearne, *Remarks and Collections*, 6:27, 6:48, 7:120.

133. Ibid., 4:253–54, 4:212, 8:217, 5:281, 4:401, 4:254, 5:86, 6:206–7, 8:65, 9:36.

134. *TG*, 54.

135. Rendcomb, the Warwickshire home of Denton, must lie near this border, for his aunt remarks, "Who did you say wrote them? Old Mr. Poynter, of Acrington? Well, of course, there is some interest in getting together old papers about this neighborhood." *TG*, 59.

136. Hearne, *Remarks and Collections*, 11:133.

137. Ibid., 10:70. Graham Midgley, *University Life in Eighteenth-Century Oxford* (New Haven: Yale University Press, 1996), 88–89, discusses Poynter's case.

138. *The Diaries of Thomas Wilson, D.D., 1731–37 and 1750*, ed. C. L. S. Linnell (London: Society for Promoting Christian Knowledge, 1964), 81–82. The entry is for 30 November 1732. The next day's entry reads: "This morning Pointer had the assurance to walk along under the wall when 40 people were there. They are certainly under the power of the devil, who has 'em at his will. They [sic] did I hear Wildair's Clerk brazen it out in the face of the Recorder, when the plainest proof in the world was given of him of sodomy. I am told the Warden and Fellows have ordered Pointer to leave the College. But they should indite and bring him to condeign punishment, how shall we otherwise free ourselves from the guilt and Judgments that hang over us" (82).

139. *TG*, 70.

140. Hearne, *Remarks and Collections*, 7:151 and passim.

CHAPTER 5

1. CUL, MS Add. 7484/box 1/40. James drives the message home more than once: "I bid you therefore to be curious: be interested."

2. Other examples include a sermon from 1926 (CUL, MS Add. 7485/53): "I should dearly like you—indeed I seriously ask you—to shake off that want of curiosity," "that fatal dismal ["dreary" in superscript] want of curiosity." The advice is echoed in published work, such as his *Wanderings and Homes of Manuscripts* (New York: Macmillan, 1919), the stated purpose of which is "rousing curiosity": "The moral is: Be inquisitive" (3, 95). Many other examples might be cited.

3. M. R. James, foreword to Maisie Fletcher, *Bright Countenance: A Personal Biography of Walter Morley Fletcher* (London: Hodder and Stoughton, 1957), 9–10.

4. See Pfaff, *Montague Rhodes James*, 91; Cox, *Informal Portrait*, 52, 61–62, 86, and passim.

5. This was the reply of the Regius Professor of Hebrew at Oxford in 1877 to a German professor who had, "with unseemly pride in his long list of publications, criticized the English university for its lack of serious scholarship." Reba N. Soffer, *Discipline and Power: The University, History, and the Making of an English Elite, 1870–1930* (Stanford: Stanford University Press, 1995), 14.

6. Pfaff, *Montague Rhodes James*, 242.

7. James, *Eton and King's*, 261–65. By no means was Cambridge deserted, however. Many soldiers were stationed there, and the cricket field for King's College was used as the site of a hospital for the war wounded. Hope Bagenal, in *Letters to a Niece*, ed. Rachel Bagenal (Oxford: Oxford Polytechnic, 1983), 19–21, gives an account of being invited to tea (and told a ghost story) by James in 1916 while convalescing at the hospital for war wounds suffered in the Battle of the Somme.

8. Quoted in Cox, *Informal Portrait*, 191.

9. Alban Goderick Arthur Hodges to John Saltmarsh, 8 July 1970, King's/PP/Misc. 69/3 (a.k.a. MRJ/X/1/2).

10. See Cox, *Informal Portrait*, 185–95; Pfaff, *Montague Rhodes James*, 240–47; M. R. James, *To Cambridge Men Serving in the War: Extract from the Address Delivered by the Vice-Chancellor, Dr James, on Resigning Office, Oct. 1, 1915* (Cambridge: Cambridge University Press, 1915?); M. R. James, *Address at the Unveiling of the Roll of Honour of the Cambridge Tipperary Club, July 12, 1916* (Cambridge: Cambridge University Press, 1918).

11. A detailed record of these deliberations (running to some 350 pages) is found in the minute book of the Eton War Memorial Fund (Eton College Archives, Misc. EWMF 01 01). The minutes reveal the central role played in this effort by James and his inner circle of friends, including Luxmoore, A. C. Ainger, A. B. Ramsay, and Walter Durnford.

12. An account of the 1921 unveiling of the frieze (over which James presided) is found in *Eton College Chronicle*, no. 1796 (6 January 1922). For the decision to include the initials of the housemasters, see the minute book, p. 139 (the eleventh meeting of the council, 18 November 1919).

13. Eton College Archives, COLL/P6/12/2a (quotations at p. 7).

14. Reviewing James's proposals, however, Luxmoore objected, "I regret the medievalism." In his opinion, "50 years hence the medieval attitude will seem an affectation of no value as a record even symbolic of a 20th century armageddon." See ibid., P6/12/32, 34. (Luxmoore's letter can be dated to late 1917 by an apology appended to his remarks, asking James to forgive him for breaking the tradition of his annual Christmas visit. A sense of wartime duty had compelled this decision in 1917: "What? Shall I pass a Xmas without . . . the walk in the Backs & the talk with ghosts & the sense of friendship [?]" See *The Letters of H. E. Luxmoore*, ed. M. R. James and A. B. Ramsay (Cambridge: Cambridge University Press, 1929), 219.

15. See Stefan Goebel, *The Great War and Medieval Memory: War, Remembrance, and Medievalism in Britain and Germany, 1914–1940* (Cambridge: Cambridge University Press, 2007), 56–58.

16. Ibid., 3.

17. The latter quotation is from James, *Address at the Unveiling*, 2. The former words are from a sermon delivered the day before Saint George's Day, almost certainly in 1917, at the Round Church in Cambridge, which would date its delivery to the day before James's memo to the Memorial Council, cited above. On 21 March 1917, James wrote to Gordon Carey, who was serving on the front in France, "Arthur Benson & I have been recently preaching in the Round Church—not simultaneously. . . . The solitary idea I have so far is that it will be the Eve of St George's Day" (King's/PP/MRJ/F/4). At least two drafts of the sermon survive, CUL, MS Add. 7483/15, and CUL, MS Add. 7485/71.

18. *TG*, 62, 71.

19. As both the minute book and James's memo cited above attest, plans for the memorial tapestries were already well under way by early 1917, nearly two years before "Poynter" was published, though they were not completed and installed in Lower Chapel until 1923. Part of the delay, apparently, involved an effort to train disabled soldiers to help weave the tapestries (see the minute book, p. 150).

20. As E. L. Risden stresses in his discussion of monuments in the context of medievalism studies. See his "Monument," in *Medievalism: Key Critical Terms,* ed. Elizabeth Emery and Richard Utz (Cambridge: D. S. Brewer, 2014), 157–63.

21. Goebel, *Great War and Medieval Memory,* 42.

22. Cox, *Informal Portrait,* 203–4; Pfaff, *Montague Rhodes James,* 247.

23. Bob Bushaway, "Name upon Name: The Great War and Remembrance," in *Myths of the English,* ed. Roy Porter (Cambridge: Polity Press, 1992), 162n10.

24. Pfaff, *Montague Rhodes James,* 406.

25. See James, *Letters to a Friend,* 127.

26. A program printed for the unveiling of the memorial provides a date of 2 January 1921. Ipswich, National Archives, Suffolk Records Office, ref. HD 1064, http://www.nationalarchives.gov.uk (accessed 10 June 2014). A letter in Eton College Archives (COLL/P6/02/13/7) reveals that James stayed at The White Lion in April 1921.

27. Vincent Baddeley, "The Provost and the Scroll," *Times* (London), 19 June 1936, 17.

28. As noted by the author on a visit with Fred Porcheddu to Aldeburgh in July 2013. The memorial's inscription, apart from the pluralizing of pronouns and verbs to suit this context, is essentially the same as James's words for the scroll, which can be found in Pfaff, *Montague Rhodes James,* 247.

29. *WTC,* 146.

30. Roden and Roden, in their edition *A Pleasing Terror,* 342n9 and 345n21, describe dates deleted from the manuscript that set the events of the story in 1916 and 1917. Rosemary Pardoe, "The Manuscript of 'A Warning to the Curious,'" *Ghosts & Scholars* 32 (2001): 49, speculates that upon reflection James may have "felt uncomfortable with a war-time date."

31. *WTC,* 151, 164. Trench coats figured prominently in Great War memorials; see Catherine Moriarty, "'Remnants of Patriotism': The Commemorative Representation of the Greatcoat after the First World War," *Oxford Art Journal* 27 (2004): 291–309. James's own most controversial war memorial design makes use of this motif. The striking (and not always admired) stained-glass window that James designed circa 1922 for the Eton War Memorial Chapel (the northern-side chapel within College Chapel) is dominated by a large red cross segmented into panels depicting medieval and contemporary soldiers. The soldiers in the lower panel are in modern military dress, including trench coats. For discussion of the design, see Pfaff, *Montague Rhodes James,* 337–38.

32. Charles Mackintosh to James, 30 May 1926, CUL, MS Add. 7481, M149.

33. For the "density" of memory traces left by war, see Jay Winter and Emmanuel Sivan, "Setting the Framework," in *War and Remembrance in the Twentieth Century,* ed. J. M. Winter and Emmanuel Sivan (Cambridge: Cambridge University Press, 1999), 6–39.

34. See, for example, Cavaliero, "Limitations of the Ghost Story," 137–38; *Collected Ghost Stories,* ed. Jones, 459–61; Scott Brewster, "The Pursuit of Knowledge: M. R. James, 'A Warning to the Curious,'" in *A New Companion to the Gothic,* ed. David Punter (Hoboken: Wiley-Blackwell, 2012), 492–93; Moshenska, "James and the Archaeological Uncanny," 1196–97.

35. McCorristine, "Academia, Avocation, and Lucidity," 58; Simon MacCulloch, "The Toad in the Study: M. R. James, H. P. Lovecraft, and Forbidden Knowledge," in Joshi and Pardoe, *Warnings to the Curious*, 84; Lane, "Fright Nights," 106. MacCulloch argues that "A Warning" is the "climactic statement" of the theme that "desire for knowledge" tends to "degenerate into a desire for possession" (84, 81).

36. Briggs, *Night Visitors*, 137; Brewster, "Pursuit of Knowledge," 492. See also Moshenska, "James and the Archaeological Uncanny," 1199, where Paxton is paired with the black magician/antiquary Baxter from "A View from a Hill" as one of two Jamesian protagonists who are particularly "culpable" and so deserving of their gruesome fates.

37. See Pincombe, "Homosexual Panic," 194, where Pincombe summarizes in rather starker terms the position he takes in "'No Thoroughfare': The Problem of Paxton in 'A Warning to the Curious,'" *Ghosts & Scholars* 32 (2001): 42–46. In the earlier essay, Pincombe notes that it "is tempting to see Paxton as a kind of traitor" (43), but the later summary states more definitively that "Paxton's curiosity is tantamount to treason, then, in the anxious days of the Great War" (193).

38. *WTC*, 139, 140–41.

39. Steve Duffy, "Introduction," in James, *Pleasing Terror*, xxi.

40. *WTC*, 138.

41. James, *Eton and King's*, 262.

42. *WTC*, 139, 140, 144. The troops stationed at Aldeburgh were in fact in the spiritual care of James's own brother Sydney, then serving as chaplain to the forces, who records the assignment in his memoir. His flock included "a mixed lot of troops, then called Provisional Battalions, spread about over Norfolk and Suffolk, mainly along the coast." Questioning some of these soldiers one day, Sydney notes their general contingency plan in case of invasion: "Line the beach and fire at the Huns." See Sydney Rhodes James, *Seventy Years* (London: Williams & Norgate, 1926), 197–98.

43. Frederick Klaeber, ed., *Beowulf and the Fight at Finnsburg* (Boston: Health, 1922), lines 2241b–43. Given the focus of this chapter, I thought it appropriate to take all citations of *Beowulf* from this landmark edition, published just three years before "A Warning," and the translations provided (my own unless otherwise indicated) rely on Klaeber's glossary. James himself never published research on *Beowulf*, though he would often find occasion to discuss it in unpublished academic lectures. See, e.g., CUL, MS Add. 7484/box 1/65 (this text, a lecture in James's hand on the history of the book, is unlisted in the CUL paper catalogue). His contribution to the first volume of *The Cambridge History of English Literature*, ed. A. W. Ward and A. R. Waller (Cambridge: Cambridge University Press, 1907), 65–87, covers a subject (Latin writings in England to the time of Alfred) explicitly linked to H. Munro Chadwick's chapter in that volume, "Early National Poetry" (19–40), which deals extensively with *Beowulf*. The third volume of the *Cambridge Medieval History* (to which James did not contribute) was delayed by the war. In 1916, it was decided to exclude "enemy alien contributors," a decision that damaged the quality of the project's scholarship as well as the livelihoods of some German scholars. In 1923, James himself contributed to a private subscription to award one such impoverished scholar £10 in compensation. See P. A. Linehan, "The Making of the *Cambridge Medieval History*," *Speculum* 57, no. 3 (1982): 463, 465n8.

44. See Simpson, "'Rules of Folklore,'" 13.

45. James, in his guide *Suffolk and Norfolk* (London, 1930), 11, echoing the text of "A Warning," relates that in 1687, "a silver crown, reputed to have been Redwald's, was

dug up, and (it is painful to relate) was melted down almost at once, so that we know nothing of its quality"; the ultimate source of the anecdote is probably the fourth (1772) edition of Edmund Gibson's translation of Camden's *Britannia*, 1:369. It is worth noting, as James does in *Suffolk and Norfolk* (10–11), that in Bede's *Ecclesiastical History* Redwald is a very memorable apostate, having conducted a kind of "hybrid worship" (in James's words) that included maintaining both heathen and Christian altars in the same chapel (possibly at Rendlesham). Redwald also quite cravenly and treacherously decides (though his queen later dissuades him) to betray his guest, Edwin of Northumbria (later venerated as a saint), in a sequence that includes some of the most famous passages in all of Bede's history. Such observations may complicate the idea of Redwald's crown as a relic of national fortitude. For the connection of Welsh folklore to James's crowns, see Rosemary Pardoe, "The Three Fortunate Concealments," *Ghosts & Scholars M. R. James Newsletter* 16 (October 2009): 30–31. A useful summary of James's coronal lore is found in Jennifer Westwood and Jacqueline Simpson, *The Lore of the Land: A Guide to England's Legends, from Spring-Heeled Jack to the Witches of Warboys* (London: Penguin, 2005), 682–83.

46. CUL, MS Add. 7484/box 2/49, fol. 11r: "Upon this parchment tag was sketched by a fifteenth century hand a crowned male head. And, by it, were written the words Here, here. . . . to me absolutely convincing proof that this is a Bury Bible." The anecdote is also related in ibid., box 1/65.

47. Quoted in Allen J. Frantzen, *Bloody Good: Chivalry, Sacrifice, and the Great War* (Chicago: University of Chicago Press, 2004), 69.

48. Ibid., 66–69; on Bury, see Pfaff, *Montague Rhodes James*, 136–40. James knew Harley 2278 well: see, e.g., his *On the Abbey of S. Edmund at Bury* (Cambridge: Cambridge Antiquarian Society, 1895), 136; and his "Bury St Edmunds Manuscripts," *English Historical Review* 42 (1926): 259. James was even involved in an attempt to excavate Edmund's bones at Bury, a project initiated after a rival set of relics (purportedly spirited away to France in 1216) were claimed to be Edmund's ("the Papists are foisting [them] upon us," James wrote his father in the summer of 1901; see CUL, MS Add. 7480/D6/450). James wrote a letter to the *Times* in opposition to this claim and helped supervise the excavations, which were not brought to full completion. See Pfaff, *Montague Rhodes James*, 139–40.

49. *WTC*, 147.

50. See Rupert Leo Scott Bruce-Mitford, "The Snape Boat-Grave," in his *Aspects of Anglo-Saxon Archaeology: Sutton Hoo and Other Discoveries* (London: Gollancz, 1974), 114–40; and William Filmer-Sankey, "Snape Anglo-Saxon Cemetery: The Current State of Knowledge," in *The Age of Sutton Hoo: The Seventh Century in North-Western Europe*, ed. M. O. H. Carver (Woodbridge: Boydell Press, 1992), 39–51.

51. *WTC*, 154. Westwood and Simpson, in *Lore of the Land*, note that the details of intaglios and cameos are "almost certainly anachronistic." Presumably this conclusion is reached on a basis similar to that of Filmer-Sankey, "Snape Anglo-Saxon Cemetery," 42, which notes that the Snape ring is "probably Frankish," observing that "Germanic settings of Roman intaglios are reasonably common on the continent but unknown in Anglo-Saxon England."

52. William Filmer-Sankey and Tim Pestell, *Snape Anglo-Saxon Cemetery: Excavations and Surveys, 1824–1992* (Ipswich: Suffolk County Council, 2001), 5.

53. Goebel, *Great War and Medieval Memory*, 150, 152.

54. Edwards, "'A Warning to the Curious' and *Beowulf*," 284. Edwards limits his brief notice to arguing that James "draws on the motif of guarded, forbidden treasure in the

poem." The observation is important and long overdue, but the broad narrative parallel, on its own, may not fully convince, for the motif—in its very general guise—is something of a staple in the tradition of the antiquarian ghost story. For instance, A. C. Benson's story "The Red Camp" tells of a young man digging up treasure from a Roman barrow, raising a shadowing specter of revenge, for "a curse would rest upon one that did disturb" the gold. See Benson, *The Hill of Trouble and Other Stories* (London: I. Pitman, 1906), 81–127. A superficially similar discovery is the basis of James's children's story *The Five Jars*, 26–28.

55. Thurston, *Literary Ghosts*, 57–58.

56. Paxton's plan to visit Sweden might serve as another nod to *Beowulf*, as most of the credible candidates for the hero's "Geatish" homeland (Västergötland, Östergötland, and the island of Gotland) are in Sweden (Klaeber, *Beowulf*, xlvi). But the detail also recalls the memory of James McBryde, illustrator of both James's first stories and McBryde's own *The Troll-Hunt*, a whimsical fantasy in cartoons narrating James's adventures with McBryde and Will Stone in Scandinavia in 1899 and 1900. Both of James's younger traveling companions would die tragically within a few years of the trip, losses that many regard as central events in James's life.

57. *WTC*, 142.

58. Klaeber, *Beowulf*, 572b–73.

59. *WTC*, 167, 159.

60. *WTC*, 142, 152, 162.

61. *GSA*, 196.

62. *WTC*, 162. Jones, in his edition of the *Collected Ghost Stories*, 461n352, identifies the reference in "A Warning" as the same as in "Oh, Whistle," but here the Valley of Death is the more likely reference. In a manuscript sermon to a youthful audience on Empire Day in 1917 or 1918, James explicitly compared Christian's experiences in the Valley of the Shadow of Death to the uncertainty of the outcome of the Great War, the bewilderment of personal loss, and—above all—the central role of prayer in finding one's way along a narrow and winding path surrounded by unseen perils: "The point is that we have got to keep going." CUL, MS Add. 7484/box 1/4.

63. Klaeber, *Beowulf*, lines 2448b–49.

64. Ibid., liv.

65. Ibid., lines 2247–52a.

66. *WTC*, 171.

67. *WTC*, 148–49.

68. Klaeber, *Beowulf*, lines 2267–68b.

69. The identification of the "last survivor" with the monster guarding the hoard seems to break the pattern, but as Klaeber's 1922 edition notes, "Regarding the story of the last survivor, it has been suggested that, according to the original notion, the man provided in the cave a burial place for himself as well as his treasures, and was then transformed into a dragon (cp. the story of Fáfnir)" (199, note on lines 2231ff.).

70. *WTC*, 164. The point is repeated on pp. 154, 156, and 166.

71. Klaeber, *Beowulf*, lines 3052b, 3053b–54a.

72. For a recent assessment of the issue, see William Cooke, "Who Cursed Whom, and When? The Cursing of the Hoard and Beowulf's Fate," *Medium Aevum* 76 (2007): 207–24.

73. Klaeber, *Beowulf*, 214, cites the characterization of the Norwegian scholar Sophus Bugge (1833–1907) and refers to no fewer than fourteen other sources that had weighed

in on the pair of lines by 1922. By the time of most recent iteration of Klaeber's edition (R. D. Fulk, Robert E. Bjork, and John D. Niles, eds., *Klaeber's Beowulf*, 4th ed. [Toronto: University of Toronto Press, 2008], 266–67), the note on these two lines had swollen to nearly two pages of tiny print, concluding with the phrase "*Embarras de richesse*." Howell D. Chickering Jr., in *Beowulf: A Dual-Language Edition* (Garden City, N.Y.: Anchor Books, 1977), remarks, "Surely before the century is out someone will have written an entire book on the textual criticism of these two lines" (375).

74. Klaeber, *Beowulf*, 214, cites this translation of the Dutch Anglo-Saxonist Pieter Cosijn (1840–1899). My intent here is not to endorse this reading but to present it as one available to James in 1925. By contrast, Fulk, Bjork, and Niles, *Klaeber's Beowulf*, 266, favors "He had not by any means sought out (or expected?) a curse on gold, rather the owner's favor."

75. Klaeber, *Beowulf*, 214. Fulk, Bjork, and Niles likewise note that many interpretations (appearing both before and after the publication of "A Warning to the Curious") assume that "these verses somehow exempt Beowulf from the effects of the curse." *Klaeber's Beowulf*, 266.

76. Klaeber, *Beowulf*, 214.

77. Ibid., 277, s.v. "*āgend*."

78. *WTC*, 148.

79. As Stewart Evans points out in "M. R. James and Local Names," *Ghosts & Scholars M. R. James Newsletter* 27 (April 2015): 23–25, "Ager" is a family name used in the Great Livermere area of James's upbringing. It was even, in legal cases during James's lifetime, associated with other locals of the "Mothersole" family, the name chosen for the witch in "The Ash-Tree." Recognition that James employs real-world names in his fiction, however, does not empty these selections of potential significance. It seems fairly clear that "Mothersole," for example, resonates thematically in the context of the tale (the monstrous Mothersole is the mother of kitten-sized spiders), and similarly, "Ager" may well be a local name that James recognized as a suitable modern version of the medieval owner-*agend*. Certainly, James stresses the antiquity of the name ("it's a very old name in these parts") in a way that suggests that we consider it a significant Old English survival.

80. *WTC*, 150.

81. James seems to have regarded the misquotation (spuriously attributed to the Duke of Wellington) that the Battle of Waterloo was "won on the playing fields of Eton" as something of an inglorious embarrassment. As he explained to the assembly at Shrewsbury School days after the Armistice of 1918, "the man with the best intentions is in no less danger than the inconsiderate. The class of transgression I mean—to take the most hackneyed of all instances—is that of him who reminds Eton publicly that a certain battle was won—or that it was fought—in the playing fields. This last misstatement we don't hear so often now—perhaps because a knowledge of the elements of geography is more widely spread." If Ager's name were connected to Agar's Plough by way of this cliché, there would likely be irony involved.

82. *WTC*, 175; Klaeber, *Beowulf*, line 2407.

83. Pincombe, "Homosexual Panic," 194.

84. Klaeber, *Beowulf*, xci. See also especially Sam Newton, *The Origins of Beowulf and the Pre-Viking Kingdom of East Anglia* (Cambridge: D. S. Brewer, 1993).

85. Alfred Hiatt, "*Beowulf* Off the Map," *Anglo-Saxon England* 38 (2009): 34.

86. William Taylor in 1816 and D. H. Haigh in 1861, respectively, quoted in ibid., 35.

87. Quoted in Robert E. Bjork, "Nineteenth-Century Scandinavia and the Birth of Anglo-Saxon Studies," in *Anglo-Saxonism and the Construction of Social Identity*, ed. Allen Frantzen and John D. Niles (Gainesville: University Press of Florida, 1997), 116.

88. T. A. Shippey, "Introduction," in *Beowulf: The Critical Heritage*, ed. T. A. Shippey and Andreas Haarder (London: Routledge, 1998), 55. The dynamic is discussed at the conclusion of Eleanor N. Adams, *Old English Scholarship in England from 1566-1800* (New Haven: Yale University Press, 1917), 110-11, which James reviewed favorably in the *Cambridge Review* (1 November 1917).

89. There is no doubt that James saw wartime duty as a very clear-cut issue. As he said in a 1919 sermon at King's, "Then came the exodus of our youth. They took leave of us and went out not knowing whither they went, seeing only that for honour's sake they must go, and glad that the issue was so plain." CUL, MS Add. 7484/box 1/1. Yet it is possible to overstate the stridency of James's patriotism. For instance, in 1915 the headmaster of Eton, Edward Lyttelton, provoked a national uproar with a sermon in which he advocated for a more "charitable" English response to German aggression. As senior fellow, James was chairman of the Eton committee charged with censuring Lyttelton for his remarks. As the minutes record, James was overruled in an attempt to soften the language of the committee's official resolution, and in his letter to Lyttelton noted "how sorry I am that it has fallen to me to be the channel of such a communication." See Eton College Archives, COLL/P6/7/10-11. For more on this incident, see Andrew Robinson, "Eton's Great War Scandal," *History Today* 33 (November 1993): 14-20.

90. *WTC*, 174.

91. W. P. Ker, *The Dark Ages* (New York: C. Scribner's, 1911), 253.

92. J. R. R. Tolkien, "The Monsters and the Critics," *Proceedings of the British Academy* 22 (1936): 245-95.

93. W. P. Ker, *Epic and Romance* (London: Macmillan, 1922), 165, 167; Ker, *Dark Ages*, 253.

94. Quoted in Cox, *Informal Portrait*, 191.

95. *WTC*, 173.

96. Suzannah Biernoff, "The Rhetoric of Disfigurement in First World War Britain," *Social History of Medicine* 24, no. 3 (2011): 670, 668, 678.

97. K. S. Inglis, "The Homecoming: The War Memorial Movement in Cambridge, England," *Journal of Contemporary History* 27, no. 4 (1992): 583-605, esp. 596-98.

98. For more on Shipley and this story, which was retitled upon its first publication in 1895, see the introduction.

99. Inglis, "Homecoming," 596, 599-601; Cox, *Informal Portrait*, 106, 135.

100. James, *Address at the Unveiling*, 3-4, 6.

101. Quoted in Cox, *Informal Portrait*, 190.

102. George Philip Krapp and Elliott van Kirk Dobbie, eds., *The Exeter Book* (New York: Columbia University Press, 1936), 136, lines 79b-80a. These memorable words are echoed in *Beowulf*, where the hero makes his final boast and insists on fighting the monster alone: "Nelle ic beorges weard / oferfleon fotes trem, ac unc furður sceal / weorðan æt wealle, swa unc wyrd geteoð" (Nor am I willing to retreat one footstep from the guardian of the barrow, but here by the wall it must go between us as fate decides).

103. Apart from other works cited above, see especially George L. Mosse, *Fallen Soldiers: Reshaping the Memory of the World Wars* (New York: Oxford University Press, 1990); J. M. Winter, *Sites of Memory, Sites of Mourning: The Great War in European*

Cultural History (New York: Cambridge University Press, 1995), esp. chapter 4, "War Memorials and the Mourning Process"; Alex King, *Memorials of the Great War in Britain: The Symbolism and Politics of Remembrance* (Oxford: Berg, 1998); J. M. Winter, *Remembering War: The Great War Between Memory and History in the Twentieth Century* (New Haven: Yale University Press, 2006), esp. chapter 6, "War Memorials: A Social Agency Interpretation."

104. Reinhart Koselleck, "War Memorials: Identity Formations of the Survivors," in *The Practice of Conceptual History: Timing History, Spacing Concepts*, trans. Todd Samuel Presner et al. (Stanford: Stanford University Press, 2002), 294.

105. *WTC*, 175.

AFTERWORD

1. James, "Some Remarks on Ghost Stories," 169.
2. Preface to *MGSA*, v.
3. James, "Some Remarks on Ghost Stories," 171.
4. Ibid., 170.
5. *TG*, 23.
6. James, introduction to Collins, *Ghosts and Marvels*, vii.
7. James, "Some Remarks on Ghost Stories," 172.
8. *CGS*, viii.
9. James, "Ghosts—Treat Them Gently!"
10. James, "Some Remarks on Ghost Stories," 171.

SELECTED BIBLIOGRAPHY

ARCHIVAL MATERIAL AND STORY MANUSCRIPTS

British Library (BL)
MS Egerton 3141 (autograph manuscript of "Casting the Runes")

Cambridge University Library (CUL)
Holdings include lectures, addresses, toasts, sermons, original plays, notes, drafts, and miscellaneous academic papers in James's hand; extensive correspondence (including seventy letters, many illustrated, from James McBryde to James and one [M120b] from James to McBryde on the subject of illustrating the stories, MS Add. 7481, M57–M123); the minutes of the Chitchat Society; James's "Greek New Testament Diary"; the autograph manuscripts of the abandoned story drafts "Speaker Lenthall's Tomb" and "The Fenstanton Witch."

Eton College Archives
Holdings include notes, drafts, correspondence, and other extensive materials relating to James's provostship at Eton; copies of books owned by James with marginalia in his hand and miscellanea tipped in; and five autograph story manuscripts: "The Mezzotint," "The Treasure of Abbot Thomas," "Martin's Close," "Mr. Humphreys and His Inheritance," and "The Uncommon Prayer-Book."

The Fitzwilliam Museum, Cambridge
Holdings include many detailed notebooks on manuscripts and other medieval subjects as well as two holograph versions of "The Rose Garden" and an untitled (and previously unnoted) precursor to "Martin's Close" (James Notebook 6.vi).

King's College, Cambridge (King's)
Holdings include a large amount of archival material selected and deposited by James's executors in 1947: correspondence (including one letter from James to James McBryde); photographs and sketches; material relating to his provostship at King's College; manuscript essays on Sheridan Le Fanu; and autograph manuscripts of "Canon Alberic's Scrap-Book," "Lost Hearts," "Number 13," "A School Story," "The Tractate Middoth," "An Episode of Cathedral History," "The Story of a Disappearance and an Appearance," "Count Magnus" (fragment of a draft), chapters 5–8 of *The Five Jars,* and four other abandoned story drafts.

The King's School, Canterbury
Autograph manuscript of "Oh, Whistle, and I'll Come to You, My Lad" in the Walpole Library

The Lilly Library, Indiana University, Bloomington
Holdings include correspondence and an autograph manuscript of "The Ash-Tree," for more on which, see Stephen Hopkins, Patrick J. Murphy, and Fred Porcheddu, "The Manuscript of M. R. James's 'The Ash-Tree,'" *Notes & Queries*, new ser., 61, no. 4 (2014): 583–85.

Pierpont Morgan Library, New York
Autograph manuscript of "A Warning to the Curious"

EDITIONS OF GHOST STORIES AND OTHER IMAGINATIVE WRITINGS

James, M. R. *Casting the Runes and Other Ghost Stories*. Edited by Michael Cox. Oxford World's Classics. Oxford: Oxford University Press, 2009.
———. *The Collected Ghost Stories*. Edited by Darryl Jones. Oxford: Oxford University Press, 2011.
———. *The Collected Ghost Stories of M. R. James*. London: Edward Arnold, 1931.
———. *Count Magnus and Other Ghost Stories*. Vol. 1 of *The Complete Ghost Stories of M. R. James*. Edited by S. T. Joshi. New York: Penguin, 2005.
———. "The Experiment: A New Year's Eve Ghost Story." *Morning Post* (London), 31 December 1931.
———. *The Five Jars*. London: Edward Arnold, 1922.
———. *Ghost Stories of an Antiquary*. London: Edward Arnold, 1904.
———. *The Haunted Dolls' House and Other Ghost Stories*. Vol. 2 of *The Complete Ghost Stories of M. R. James*. Edited by S. T. Joshi. New York: Penguin, 2006.
———. "The Malice of Inanimate Objects." *Masquerade*, June 1932, 29–32.
———. *More Ghost Stories of an Antiquary*. London: Edward Arnold, 1911.
———. *A Pleasing Terror: The Complete Supernatural Writings*. Edited by Christopher Roden and Barbara Roden. Ashcroft, British Columbia: Ash-Tree Press, 2001.
———. *A Thin Ghost and Others*. London: Edward Arnold, 1919.
———. "A Vignette." *London Mercury*, November 1936, 18–22.
———. *Wailing Well*. Stanford Dingley: Mill House Press, 1928.
———. *A Warning to the Curious and Other Ghost Stories*. London: Edward Arnold, 1925.

JAMES ON SUPERNATURAL FICTION

James, M. R. "Ghost Story Competition." *Spectator*, 27 December 1930, 1008–9.
———. "Ghosts—Treat Them Gently!" *Evening News* (London), 17 April 1931.
———. "Introduction." In V. H. Collins, *Ghosts and Marvels: A Selection of Uncanny Tales from Daniel Defoe to Algernon Blackwood*, v–xiii. Oxford: Oxford University Press, 1924.
———, ed. *Madam Crowl's Ghost and Other Tales of Mystery*, by Joseph Sheridan Le Fanu. London: George Bell & Sons, 1923.

Selected Bibliography

———. "Some Remarks on Ghost Stories." *Bookman* 77 (December 1929): 169–72.
———. "Stories I Have Tried to Write." *Touchstone*, 30 November 1929, 46–47.

BIOGRAPHIES, MEMOIRS, AND SELECTED CRITICISM

For a comprehensive bibliography of James's scholarly writings, see below Pfaff, *Montague Rhodes James*, 427–38.

Barker, Nicolas. "After M. R. James." *Book Collector* 19 (1970): 7–20.
Brewster, Scott. "Casting an Eye: M. R. James, at the Edge of the Frame." *Gothic Studies* 14 (Autumn 2012): 20–54.
Briggs, Julia. "Ghost Stories." In *A New Companion to the Gothic*, edited by David Punter, 176–85. Oxford: Wiley-Blackwell, 2012.
———. *Night Visitors: The Rise and Fall of the English Ghost Story*. London: Faber, 1977.
Cavaliero, Glen. "M. R. James: The Limitations of the Ghost Story." In *The Supernatural and English Fiction*, chapter 4. Oxford: Oxford University Press, 1995.
Chabon, Michael. "The Other James." In *Maps and Legends: Reading and Writing Along the Borderlands*, 109–20. New York: Harper Perennial, 2008.
Conrad O'Briain, Helen. "'The Gates of Hell Shall Not Prevail Against It': Laudian Ecclesia and Victorian Culture Wars in the Ghost Stories of M. R. James." In *The Ghost Story from the Middle Ages to the Twentieth Century: A Ghostly Genre*, edited by Helen Conrad O'Briain and Julie Anne Stevens, 47–60. Dublin: Four Courts Press, 2010.
Cowlishaw, Brian. "'A Warning to the Curious': Victorian Science and the Awful Unconscious in M. R. James's Ghost Stories." *Victorian Newsletter* 94 (Fall 1998): 36–42. Reprinted in Joshi and Pardoe, *Warnings to the Curious*, 162–76.
Cox, Michael. *M. R. James: An Informal Portrait*. Oxford: Oxford University Press, 1983.
Dennison, Lynda, ed. *The Legacy of M. R. James: Papers from the 1995 Cambridge Symposium*. Donington: Shaun Tyas, 2001.
Dinshaw, Carolyn. *How Soon Is Now? Medieval Texts, Amateur Readers, and the Queerness of Time*. Durham: Duke University Press, 2012.
Edwards, A. S. G. "M. R. James's 'A Warning to the Curious' and *Beowulf*." *Notes & Queries* 60, no. 2 (2013): 284.
Fielding, Penny. "Reading Rooms: M. R. James and the Library of Modernity." *Modern Fiction Studies* 46, no. 3 (2000): 749–71.
Gaselee, Stephen. "Montague Rhodes James." *Proceedings of the British Academy* 22 (1936): 418–33.
Hay, Simon. *A History of the Modern British Ghost Story*. New York: Palgrave Macmillan, 2011.
Hughes, Martin. "Murder of the Cathedral: A Story by M. R. James." *Durham University Journal* 87, no. 1 (1995): 73–98.
James, M. R. *Eton and King's: Recollections, Mostly Trivial, 1875–1925*. London: Williams & Norgate, 1926.
———. *Letters to a Friend, by M. R. James*. Edited by Gwendolen McBryde. London: Edward Arnold, 1956.

Joshi, S. T. *The Weird Tale*. Austin: University of Texas Press, 1990.

Joshi, S. T., and Rosemary Pardoe, eds. *Warnings to the Curious: A Sheaf of Criticism on M. R. James*. New York: Hippocampus Press, 2007.

Kraft, Robert A. "Reviving (and Refurbishing) the *Lost Apocrypha* of M. R. James." In *Things Revealed: Studies in Early Jewish and Christian Literature in Honor of Michael E. Stone*, edited by Esther G. Chazon, David Satran, and Ruth A. Clements, 37–51. Leiden: Brill, 2004.

Lane, Anthony. "Fright Nights: The Horror of M. R. James." *New Yorker*, 13 and 20 February 2012, 105–8.

Leslie, Shane. "Montague Rhodes James." *Quarterly Review* 304 (1966): 45–56.

Lubbock, S. G. *A Memoir of Montague Rhodes James*. With a list of his writings by A. F. Scholfield. Cambridge: Cambridge University Press, 1939.

McCorristine, Shane. "Academia, Avocation, and Lucidity in the Supernatural Fiction of M. R. James." *Limina: A Journal of Historical and Cultural Studies* 13 (2007): 54–65.

"Montague Rhodes James." *Eton College Chronicle* 2380 (18 June 1936): 165–72.

Montague Rhodes James: Praepositus necnon amicus, 1862–1936. Cambridge: Cambridge University Press, 1936.

Moshenska, Gabriel. "M. R. James and the Archaeological Uncanny." *Antiquity* 86, no. 334 (2012): 1192–1201.

Pardoe, Rosemary, ed. *Ghosts & Scholars*, 1979–2001. http://www.users.globalnet.co.uk/~pardos/Biblio.html.

———, ed. *The Ghosts & Scholars M. R. James Newsletter*, 2001–present. http://www.users.globalnet.co.uk/~pardos/Biblio.html.

Pardoe, Rosemary, and Jane Nicholls. "James Wilson's Secret." *Ghosts & Scholars* 24 (1997): 45–48.

Penzoldt, Peter. *The Supernatural in Fiction*. London: Neville, 1952.

Pfaff, Richard W. *Montague Rhodes James*. London: Scolar Press, 1980.

———. "M. R. James on the Cataloguing of Manuscripts: A Draft Essay of 1906." *Scriptorium* 31 (1977): 103–18.

Pincombe, Mike. "Homosexual Panic and the English Ghost Story: M. R. James and Others." In Joshi and Pardoe, *Warnings to the Curious*, 184–96.

———. "'No Thoroughfare': The Problem of Paxton in 'A Warning to the Curious.'" *Ghosts & Scholars* 32 (2001): 42–46.

Simpson, Jacqueline. "'The Rules of Folklore' in the Ghost Stories of M. R. James." *Folklore* 108 (1997): 9–18.

Smith, Andrew. *The Ghost Story, 1840–1920: A Cultural History*. Manchester: Manchester University Press, 2010.

Sullivan, Jack. *Elegant Nightmares: The English Ghost Story from Le Fanu to Blackwood*. Athens: Ohio University Press, 1978.

Thompson, Terry W. "Revenge of the Matriarchy: M. R. James's 'The Ash-Tree.'" *English Language Notes* 41 (June 2004): 64–70.

Thurston, Luke. *Literary Ghosts from the Victorians to Modernism: The Haunting Interval*. New York: Routledge, 2012.

INDEX

Absolom (biblical rebel), 141, 159, 169, 229 n. 122
academics as a university profession, 6–8, 17–19, 29, 54, 56, 62–66
Acton, Lord (1834–1902), 54, 56–57, 72–73, 204 n. 15, 210 n. 121
  Cambridge Histories initiated by, 65
Acts of Thomas. *See* apocrypha
Ælfric of Eynsham (c.950–c.1010), *Life of St. Edmund*, 174
Ainger, A.C. (1841–1919), 13, 21, 193 n. 73, 231 n. 11
alchemy, 58, 72
Alcuin (735–804), *Life of Willibrord*, 67, 209 n. 94
Aldeburgh, 55, 170–75, 183, 232 n. 28, 233 n. 42
Aldhelm, 60, 98
  Carmen de uirginitate, 101
  Enigmata, 98, 198 n. 24, 216 n. 45
Alfred Jewel, 98
"Ali Baba and the Forty Thieves," 22
amateurism, 8, 26, 28–29, 54, 82–87, 202 n. 77. *See also* antiquarianism
Anglo-Saxon Chronicle, 57
Antichrist, 90, 123, 222 n. 145
antiquarianism, 15–20, 28–32, 39–40, 51, 82–87, 137–40
  associated with nonnormative sexualities, 16, 31
  class restrictions of, 54
  compared with university professionals, 17, 194–94 n. 88
  focused on local or trivial interests, 16, 81
  lack of specialization of, 15–16, 29
  networks of, 54, 58
  reputation of, 15–16
antiquaries. *See* antiquarianism

anti-Semitism, 151–55, 227–28 n. 98, 228 n. 111
  and supersessionary logic, 151–55, 227–28 n. 98, 228 n. 106
Apocalypse of Peter. *See* apocrypha
apocrypha, 71, 91–92, 101, 214 n. 11
  Acts of Thomas, 101, 216 n. 50
  Apocalypse of Peter, 210 n. 109, 214 n. 11
  Testament of Solomon, 92, 189–90 n. 21, 190 n. 30
archives, access to, 77–79
Aristophanes, *The Birds*, 20
Arnold, Matthew (1822–1888), 81
Ashridge Park, 31
Asquith Commission (1919–1922), 19, 79

Bateman, Bishop William (d. 1355), 224 n. 41
Beaumont, Francis (1584–1616). *See* Beaumont, Francis and John Fletcher
Beaumont, Francis, and John Fletcher, *Bonduca*, 80
Bede, the Venerable, 60, 153, 234 n. 45
Benson, A. C. (1862–1925), 13–14, 192–93 n. 65, 193 nn. 67–68, 193 n. 73, 231 n. 17
  ghost stories of, 196 n. 107, 235 n. 54
Benson, E. F. (1876–1940), 88, 195 n. 100, 196 n. 107
  David Blaize of King's, 206 n. 56
Benson, E. W. (1829–1896), 88
Benson, R. H. (1871–1914), 196 n. 107
Beowulf, 172–83, 233 n. 43, 234–35 n. 54, 235 n. 56, 235 n. 69, 235–36 nn. 73–75, 237 n. 102
Bible, books of
  Genesis, 92, 100–101, 216 n. 48
  Isaiah, 92, 106–7, 112, 121–22

Bible, books of (*cont'd*)
   Psalms, 92, 220 n. 105, 222 n. 145
   Revelation, 33, 199 n. 32, 222 n. 145
   2 Samuel, 229 n. 120
   2 Thessalonians, 90, 122–23
   1 Timothy, 38, 199 n. 43
   Zechariah, 33
Blacman, John (1407/8–1485), memoir of Henry VI, 139
blood libel, 151, 227–28 n. 98
Boccaccio, Giovanni, 66
Bodleian Library, 157, 229 n. 125
Borgia family, 86, 213 n. 181–82
Bosanquet, R. C. (1871–1935), 191–92 n. 43
Bradshaw, Henry (1831–1886), 137, 148, 201 n. 64
British Empire Exhibition (1924–1925), 16
British Museum, reading rooms of, 58, 73, 205 n. 31
Brocklebank, Thomas (d. 1878), 229 n. 114
Brown, Basil (1888–1977), 84, 87, 213 n. 173
Browning, Oscar (1837–1923), 60–64, 205 n. 37, 205 n. 41, 205–6 n. 45, 206 nn. 53–56, 206–7 n. 60, 207 n. 73
Brussels reliquary, 97
Burns, Robert (1759–1796), 42, 203 n. 90
Bury, John Bagnell (1861–1927), 17, 64, 81, 135, 145
Bury St. Edmunds, 11, 175, 234 n. 46, 234 n. 48
Bury St. Edmunds Abbey, manuscripts in the library of, 57
Byland Abbey Ghost Stories, 24

Cain, 141
   legendary tree of, 100–101, 217 n. 51, 225–26 n. 60
Cainites, 225–26 n. 60
Cambridge Camden Society, 103
Cambridge History of English Literature, 25, 65, 67, 198 n. 24
Cambridge Medieval History, 233 n. 43
Cambridge University, 9, 81, 93
   celibacy of college fellows at, 12, 88
   degrees for women at, 19, 145–55
   ordination rates of graduates of, 88
   reforms of, 18–19 (*see also* Asquith Commission)
   Tripos examinations of, 18, 146
Cambridge University Library, 35, 125–27, 147–50, 222–23 n. 5, 227 n. 98, 229 n. 114
   James's unpubublished manuscript catalogue of, 125–29, 222 n. 1, 222–23 n. 5
Canterbury Cathedral, 107, 123
Carey, Gordon Vero (1886–1969), 167, 231 n. 17
cartularies, 73
cathedrals, Gothic, 215 n. 20
   restoration of, 94
   significance of, 93–94, 215 n. 19, 222 n. 146
Cerne Abbas Giant, 15, 194 n. 76
Chambers, E. K. (1866–1954), 120, 122
Charlett, Arthur (1655–1722), 160, 230 n. 131
Chaucer, *Miller's Tale*, 229 n. 120
Chester Mystery Plays, 116, 220 n. 106, 221 n. 119. *See also* mystery plays
Chitchat Society, 9, 21–22, 73, 91, 191 n. 41, 195 n. 100
Chore (biblical rebel), 141
Church of the Holy Sepulchre ("Round Church"), Cambridge, 44, 47, 231 n. 17
Church of the Holy Sepulchre, Jerusalem, 44
Classical Review, 69
Clark, J. W. (1833–1910), 201 n. 64
Clement V, Pope (1264–1314), 200 n. 60
Cobbold, Felix (1841–1909), 156
Codex Argenteus. *See* manuscripts
Codex D (Codex Bezae). *See* manuscripts
Codex Gigas ("Devil's Bible"). *See* manuscripts
Coleridge, Samuel Taylor, 76
Comparative Mythology, 64, 69
Cory, William Johnson (1823–1892), 166, 192–93 n. 65
Cottingham, Lewis (1787–1847), 109–10
Coventry Plays, 114, 116, 220 n. 106

Index

Crowley, Aleister (1875–1947), 60
cryptograms. *See Riddles*

Dante, 71, 210 n. 109
Darwin, Charles (1809–1882), 194 n. 80
  Origin of the Species, 119
  theories applied to literary study, 120–21
Delisle, Léopold (1826–1910), 43
Dennistoun, James (1803–1855), 5
Depositio crucis ceremony, 117
Dickens, Charles, 4
  Dombey and Son, 42
  Great Expectations, 176
  Mystery of Edwin Drood, 105, 108–9, 111, 121, 124
  Pickwick Papers, 195 n. 104
  "The Signal-Man," 109, 219 n. 88
dilettantism. *See* antiquarianism, amateurism
disciplinary specialization, 10, 15, 26, 29
Disney Chair of Archaeology, 45, 202 n. 74
Disney, John (1779–1857), 202 n. 74
Drag Me to Hell (2009 film), 58
drama, liturgical, 117–21
Dream of the Rood, 25, 96–102, 122, 215 n. 29, 217 n. 51, 222 n. 145
Durnford, Walter (1847–1926), 21, 231 n. 11

Easter sepulchers, 117–21, 220 n. 108, 221 n. 111, 221 n. 127
Edwin of Northumbria (fl. 616–633), 234 n. 45
Egeria (4c. pilgrim), 148
Egeria (Roman deity), 147–48
Elder Edda. *See Poetic Edda*
Eleanor Crosses, 168
English Historical Review, 63–65
enigmas. *See* riddles
Erasmus, 29
error
  anxieties of, 17, 26, 28–51, 54
  role in James's fiction, 29–51
  significance to medieval studies, 28, 197 n. 3

Eton College, 11–12, 180, 205 n. 39, 226 n. 76, 236 n. 81
Eton War Memorial Chapel (within College Chapel), 232 n. 31
Eton War Memorial Council, 168, 231 nn. 11–12, 231 n. 17. *See also* war memorials
Eusebius, 98
Exeter Book. *See* manuscripts
Exeter Riddles, 98–100, 216 n. 40
  Riddle 24, 98–99
  Riddle 26, 98, 216 n. 40
  Riddle 31, 216 n. 40
  Riddle 62, 216 n. 40
  Riddle 73, 99–100
  Riddle 90, 33, 198 n. 24
  Riddle 92, 99

Fanshawe, Sir Richard (1608–1666), 76
  translation of Guarini's *Il pastor fido* of, 76
  translation of Fletcher's *Faithful Shepherdess* of, 76
Felixstowe, 44, 199 n. 47, 203 n. 90
Fitzwilliam Museum, 10, 30, 55
Fletcher, John (1579–1625), *The Faithful Shepherdess*, 76. *See also* Beaumont, Francis and John Fletcher
fylfots, 44, 47–49, 202 n. 73, 202 n. 81, 203 nn. 82–83

Gaselee, Stephen (1882–1943), 14, 30
Gentleman's Magazine, 157
George V, 169
Ghosts & Scholars, 4
Giblin, L. F. (1872–1951), 195–96 n. 106
Girton College, 146
Gnosticism, 225–26 n. 60
Gothic Revival, 7, 94, 102–5, 119, 122–23, 217 n. 63
Gray, Arthur (1852–1940), under pseudonym "Ingulphus," *Tedious Brief Tales of Granta and Gramarye*, 155, 196 n. 107
Great Livermere, 11, 52, 175, 236 n. 79
Great Malvern Priory Church, 76, 82, 211 n. 137

Great War, The, 12, 19, 78–79, 164–87, 231 n. 7, 233 n. 42, 237 n. 89
  memorials of, 19, 26, 164, 168–71, 182–84, 231 nn. 11–12, 231 n. 17, 232 n. 19, 232 n. 26, 232 n. 28, 232 n. 31
Greek, required at Cambridge, 79
Guarini, Giovanni Battista (1538–1612), *Il pastor fido*, 76

Hamilton-Gordon, Sir Arthur (1829–1912), 215 n. 20
Harrison, Jane Ellen (1850–1928), 64, 74, 144, 207 n. 74
Headlam, Walter (1866–1908), 10
Hearne, Thomas (1678–1735), 15, 139, 156–64, 229 n. 119
  edition of Leland's *Collectanea*, 156
  diaries (*Remarks and Collections*) of, 156, 159–64
Henry VI, 133, 139
Henslow, John Stevens (1796–1861), 119
Hereford Cathedral, 103, 107, 124
Herefordshire, 76
history, "scientific," 17, 64–65, 81, 137, 194–95 n. 88
  contrasted with popular historical writings 17, 59, 62–66, 207 n. 61
Hogarth, D. G. (1862–1927), 45, 137
homosociality, 38, 41, 50–51
Hope, W. H. St. John (1854–1919), 43, 110–11, 219 n. 90
Housman, A. E. (1859–1936), 212 n. 161
Hutchinson, F. E. (1871–1947), 22

Ingulf (d. 1109), 228 n. 112
Ingulphus (pseudonym), 228 n. 112. See also Gray, Arthur (1852–1940)

Jackson, Henry (1839–1921), 108
Jaime I of Aragon (1208–1276), 154
Jamaican Historical Review, 55
James, Caroline Pope (d. 1870), 56
James family, 54, 204 n. 16
  educational ties to Eton of, 55
  Jamaican plantations of, 11, 54–56, 204 n. 16
  slave ownership of, 54–56

James, Montague Rhodes (1862–1936)
  administrative work of, 19
  antiquarian persona and identity of, 17, 20
  apocrypha, studies of, 214 n. 11
  bachelorhood of, 12
  background in archaeology, 45
  cathedral architecture, studies of, 218–19 n. 81
  decision not to be ordained, 88
  devotion to educational institutions of, 133–37
  director of the Fitzwilliam Museum, 6, 19
  doctorate of, 18
  education of, 11–12
  lectureship of, 19
  manuscript catalogues of, 1–2, 6, 26, 30, 121, 125–28, 136, 140, 142, 164, 214 n. 11
  memory of, 57
  opposition to degrees for women of, 19, 145–148, 154
  Order of Merit, awarded, 189 n. 3
  perceived childishness of, 12, 133–35
  perceived dilettantism of, 8, 29
  professional identity of, 8, 10, 16
  provostship of: Eton, 1, 13, 19, 55, 168; King's College, 1, 19, 61, 168, 206 n. 51
  roles as teacher and mentor of, 19, 166–67
  roles during and after the Great War of, 19, 164–184, 231 n. 7, 231 nn. 11–12, 231 n. 17, 232 n. 19, 232 n. 28, 232 n. 31
  sermons of, 214 n. 4, 231 n. 17
  sexuality of, 12–14
  theatrical performances of, 20, 220 n. 106
  vice-chancellorship of Cambridge University, 1, 167–68
  view of curiosity of, 165–66, 230 nn. 1–2
James, Montague Rhodes (1862–1936), ghost stories of
  affective power of, 2–3, 185–87
  allusive quality of, 22–23

anti-Semitic implications of, 151–55, 227 n. 96
characteristic features of, 2–3
critical reception of, 3–4, 8–9
formal qualities of, 3, 23, 173
influences of, 4
manuscript cataloguing, as a thematic concern of, 125–64
medievalism of, 22–25, 186–87
nature of the ghosts depicted in, 9, 25
original audience of, 20–23, 155, 168, 195 n. 104, 203 n. 84, 206 n. 55, 231 n. 14
original performances of, 13–14, 20, 44, 62, 155, 195 n. 105, 196 n. 108, 203 n. 84
overlap with academic interests of, 18, 125–31
parodic style of, 22, 132, 198 n. 19
potential incongruity with academic professionalism, 17–18, 32, 190 n. 29
relationship to folklore of, 23–24
"reticence" of, 23, 185–87
sexual implications of, 14–15, 41, 161–64, 199–200 n. 50, 210 n. 108, 229 n. 122
James, Montague Rhodes (1862–1936), books of ghost stories
Ghost Stories of an Antiquary (1904), 12–13, 27, 30, 32, 47, 52, 201 n. 64, 203 nn. 82–86, 204 n. 16
More Ghost Stories of an Antiquary (1911), 190 n. 30, 191 n. 41, 206 n. 55
A Thin Ghost and Others (1919), 156, 218 n. 77, 229 n. 125
A Warning to the Curious and Other Ghost Stories (1925), 171
Collected Ghost Stories (1931), 76, 126, 170, 203 n. 82
James, Montague Rhodes (1862–1936), individual ghost stories of
"After Dark in the Playing Fields," 226 n. 76
"The Ash-Tree," 86, 213 n. 181, 236 n. 79
"Canon Alberic's Scrap-Book" ("A Curious Book"), 2, 4, 9–10, 92, 182, 190 n. 30, 191 n. 41, 220 n. 101

"Casting the Runes," 10, 57– 74, 83, 85, 87, 205 n. 31, 206 nn. 55–56, 209 n. 105, 210 n. 108, 210 n. 123
"Count Magnus," 52–54, 56, 135–36, 190 n. 24
"The Diary of Mr. Poynter," 15, 156–64, 169, 229 n. 119, 229 n. 120, 230 n. 135, 232 n. 19
"An Episode of Cathedral History," 22, 94, 103–24, 196 n. 108, 220 nn. 100–101
"An Evening's Entertainment," 14–15, 55
"The Experiment," 126–32
"The Fenstanton Witch," 155, 223 n. 24
"The Game of Bear," 212 n. 160
"The Haunted Dolls' House," 16
"Lost Hearts," 199 n. 39
"The Malice of Inanimate Objects," 98
"Marcilly-le-Hayer," 226 n. 64
"The Mezzotint," 16.
"Mr. Humphreys and His Inheritance," 134, 140–45, 153, 206 n. 55, 225–26 n. 60, 226 n. 70
"Martin's Close," 138–39
"Merfield House," 208 n. 84
"A Neighbor's Landmark," 24
"Number 13," 25, 138, 196 n. 106
"Oh, Whistle, and I'll Come to You, My Lad," 4, 10, 14, 31, 40–52, 113, 166–84, 193 n. 73, 194 n. 80, 199 n. 44, 199–200 nn. 50–51, 201 n. 71, 202 n. 78, 203 nn. 82–86, 235 n. 62
"Rats," 211 n. 134
"The Residence at Whitminster," 14, 186, 217 n. 71
"The Rose Garden," 23–24, 134, 147
"A School Story," 11, 133, 138, 206 n. 55
"Stalls of Barchester Cathedral," 94–104, 122–24, 216 n. 45, 216 n. 48, 217 n. 69
"The Story of a Disappearance and an Appearance," 22, 195 n. 104
"The Tractate Middoth," 148–55
"The Treasure of Abbot Thomas," 31–40, 198 n. 18, 198 n. 21, 198–99 n. 30, 199 n. 33, 199 n. 36

James, Montague Rhodes (1862–1936), individual ghost stories of (cont'd)
"Two Doctors," 134
"The Uncommon Prayer-Book," 138, 151, 227 n. 96
"A View from a Hill," 57–58, 74–87, 211 n. 134, 211 n. 137, 212 n. 161, 213 n. 174, 213 n. 183, 233 n. 36
"A Vignette," 52
"Wailing Well," 192 n. 52
"A Warning to the Curious," 26, 166–84, 232 n. 30, 233 nn. 35–37, 233 n. 43, 234–35 n. 54, 235 n. 56, 235 n. 62, 235 n. 69

James, Montague Rhodes (1862–1936), other imaginative works of
Alex Barber, 22, 195–96 n. 106
Auditor and Impresario, 196 n. 106
The Dismal Tragedy of Henry Blew Beard, Esq., 22, 196 n. 106
The Five Jars, 235 n. 54

James, Montague Rhodes (1862–1936), academic and other publications of
Address at the Unveiling of the Roll of Honour of the Cambridge Tipperary Club, July 12, 1916, 183
apocrypha, translations and editions of, 214 n. 11
cathedral architecture, scholarship on, 218–19 n. 81
Descriptive Catalogue of the Latin Manuscripts in the John Rylands Library at Manchester, 190 n. 30
Descriptive Catalogue of the Manuscripts in the Library of Trinity Hall, 224 n. 41
Eton and King's, 127–28, 133, 155, 167, 173, 229 n. 114
Notes of Glass in Ashridge Chapel, 31, 39, 48
"Twelve Medieval Ghost Stories," 24
The Wanderings and Homes of Manuscripts, 5, 136, 197 n. 9, 229 n. 119

James, Grace (1860–1940), 191 n. 41
James, Herbert (1822–1909), 55, 234 n. 48
James, Sydney Rhodes (1855–1934), 55, 76, 193 n. 68, 233 n. 42

James, William Rhodes I (fl. c. 1700), 55.
James, William Rhodes IV (1786–1842), 55–56
Johannes Trithemius (1462–1516)
Steganographia, 36
John of Salisbury (c. 1120–1180), 222 n. 144
Johnson, William. *See* Cory, William Johnson
Journal of Theological Studies, 64–65
Julian of Norwich (1342–c.1416), 133

Kemble, John M. (1807–1857), 67
Kempe, Margery (c. 1373–c.1438), 133
Ker, W. P. (1855–1923), 181
King James Bible, 218 n. 77
King's College, Cambridge, 12, 16, 18, 51, 54, 60–62, *See also* Cambridge University
legendary haunting of, 155–56
King's College Choir School, 11
Kristensen, Evald Tang (1843–1929), 23

lamia (mythology), 106–7, 112, 119, 121–22, 217–18 n. 72, 218 n. 77
Lambeth Palace Library, manuscripts of, 55
Langland, William (c. 1325–c. 1390)
Vision of Piers Plowman, 76–77, 81–82, 211–12 nn. 138–39
Leland, John (c.1506–1552)
Collectanea, 156
Le Fanu, Sheridan (1814–1873), 4
Carmilla, 107
"The Familiar," 74, 210 n. 126
Lee, Christopher (1922–2015), 20
Leigh, Augustus Austen (1840–1905), 61
Leslie, Shane (1885–1971), 146, 156, 229 n. 114
The Cantab, 56
Lewis, C. S. (1898–1963), 190 n. 29
London Mercury, 52
Lovecraft, H. P., 3, 9, 119
Lowe, John (c.1385–1467), 111, 118–19
Lubbock, Percy (1879–1965), 13–14, 21, 193 nn. 67–68, 193 n. 73

Lubbock, Samuel Gurney (1873–1958), 20–21, 195 n. 106
Luxmoore, H. E. (1841–1926), 11, 21, 156, 166, 192 n. 65, 203 n. 84, 231 n. 14
Lydgate, John (ca. 1370–ca. 1451), 175
"Banners of St. Edmund," 175
Lyell, Charles (1797–1875), 119
Lyttelton, Edward (1855–1942), 237 n. 89

magic, 14, 25, 37, 73
Magnus Gabriel De la Gardie (1622–1686), 5, 53, 135, 190 n. 24
Maitland, F.W. (1850–1906), 73
Malden, R. H. (1879–1951), *Nine Ghosts*, 196 n. 107
Malvern Hills, 76
Mandeville's Travels, 133
Manuscripts
  Cambridge, University Library MS Dd.11.45, 126–27, 129–31, 223 n. 7
  Cambridge, University Library MS Nn.2.41 ("Codex D," "Codex Bezae"), 16
  Exeter, Exeter Cathedral Library MS 3501 ("The Exeter Book"), 33, 98
  London, British Library, Harley 2278, 175, 234 n. 48
  London, British Library, Harley 3586, 73, 210 n. 123
  London, British Library, Royal 15. A. xx, 24
  Manchester, John Rylands Library, Latin MS 105, 190 n. 30
  New York, Pierpont Morgan Library, MS M. 638, 217 n. 51
  Stockholm, Kungliga Biblioteket, MS A. 148 ("Codex Gigas"/"Devil's Bible"), 5, 9, 190 nn. 23–24
  Uppsala, Uppsala Universitetsbibliotek, DG 1 ("Codex Argenteus"), 5, 53, 135, 190 n. 23
Manly, John Matthews (1865–1940), 120
Map, Walter (ca. 1140–ca. 1210), 73, 82, 195 n. 100
  De nugis curialium, 25, 73
McBryde, Gwendolen (1878–1958), 144

McBryde, James (1874–1904), 12–13, 192–93 nn. 64–66, 235 n. 54
  illustrations of *Ghost Stories of an Antiquary* by, 203 n. 85
  The Troll-Hunt, 235 n. 54
McKenzie, Robert Tait (1867–1938), 182
medieval studies, 6, 28
  as an occupational vocation, 28, 54, 56, 58, 78–79
  scholarly networks of, 58
  university training for, 15
medievalism, 6–7, 25–27, 90, 186–87, 191 n. 31
memorial scroll, 169, 232 n. 28
memorials. See war memorials
Middle Ages as a temporal category, 132–33, 223 n. 20
Middoth, Tractate (section of the Talmud), 149–51
Morte Arthure, alliterative 130–31
mystery plays, 22, 105, 113–24, 220 n. 106, 221 n. 111, 221 n. 134
  and evolutionary theory, 120–21

Nachmanides (1194–1270), 150, 154
Newnham College, 146
Nicholas de Sigillo (fl. 1170), 222 n. 144
Njál's Saga, 60

Odin, 68–70, 208 n. 92, 209 n. 103
Old English Hexateuch, 101
Owen, Henry (1844–1919), 77, 79

Parry, Robert Lloyd, 20
pastoral literature, 26, 74–77, 79–87, 211 n. 134
peer review, 26, 59, 71–72, 74
periodization, 89–90, 132, 225 n. 51
Petrarch, 132
Pilgrim's Progress, 50, 177, 235 n. 62
Poetic Edda, 68
  Hávamál, 69–70, 209 n. 100
Pope, Alexander (1688–1744)
  The Dunciad, 157
Poynter, John (1668–1754), 15, 160–63, 230 n. 138

professionalism, 9, 39, 54, 71–74, 77–78, 82–87, 94
Public Record Office, 78
Public Record Office Act (1838), 77–78
publishing, academic 59, 62–66
Pugin, A. W. N. (1812–1852), 103
Punch and Judy, 22

Queen Mary's Dolls' House, 16
Quem quaeritis ceremony, 117–20, 221 n. 134
Quiller-Couch, Arthur (1863–1944), 81

Radbod (d. 719), 67–68
Ramsay, Agnata Frances (1867–1931), 146
Ramsay, Allen Beville (1872–1955), 21–22, 196 n. 108, 231 n. 11
Redwald (fl. c.599–c.624), 233–34 n. 45
Rendlesham, 174–75, 234 n. 45
Richmond, Oliffe Legh (1881–1977), 13–14, 20–21, 193 n. 68
riddles, 31–40, 97–100, 198 n. 24, 198 n. 29. *See also* Exeter Riddles
Ridgeway, William (1858–1926), 18, 147
Ringu (1998 film), 58
Rites of Durham, 118
Rochester Cathedral, 107–11, 124, 219 nn. 89–91
  Gothic Revival at, 109–11
Round Church. *See* Church of the Holy Sepulchre, Cambridge
Roxburghe Club, 65–66, 80, 208 nn. 84–85
Royal Commission on Public Records, 77–79
  and the Great War, 78–79
Royal Commission on Oxford and Cambridge. *See* Asquith Commission
runes, 25–26, 58–60, 66–74, 208 n. 91, 209 nn. 105–6
  "casting of," 67–69
  runic alphabets, 70–71
Ruskin, John (1819–1900), 219 n. 90
Ruthwell Cross, 97

Saint-Bertrand-de-Comminges, 2, 5, 92–93, 106, 182, 191 n. 41

St. Augustine of Hippo, 222 n. 145
St. Edmund, 172, 174–76, 234 n. 46, 234 n. 48
St. George, 168, 183, 231 n. 17
St. Martin's Priory, 73
St. Wulfram's Church, Abbeville, 68, 209 n. 94
Salisbury Cathedral, 103, 107, 123
Saxo Grammaticus, 70, 209 n. 103
Sayers, Dorothy (1893–1957), 18
Scholfield, A. F. (1884–1969), 125, 156, 212 n. 161, 229 n. 114
Scot, Michael (d. ca. 1235), 190 n. 30
Scott, Sir George Gilbert (1811–1878), 102–3, 110
Scott, Sir Walter (1771–1832), *The Antiquary*, 63, 79–80, 82
secularization, 88–95, 120–24, 214 n. 5
Shakespeare
  Macbeth, 183
  The Merchant of Venice, 152
de Sheppey, John (c.1300–1360), 110–11, 119
Shipley, Arthur (1861–1927), 9–10, 182, 191 n. 41
Shrewsbury School, 165
Skeat, W. W. (1835–1912), 148
slave trade, 54–55
Smith, Owen Hugh (1869–1958), 21, 195 n. 104
Snape, Anglo-Saxon burial mounds at, 172, 175, 234 n. 51
Spenser, Edmund, *The Shepheardes Calendar*, 74–75, 81
state trial papers, 225 n. 56
Steinfeld Abbey, 31
Stephen, Leslie (1832–1904), 137, 194 n. 80
Stephens, George (1813–1895), *Old-Northern Runic Monuments of Scandinavia and England*, 67
Stone, W. J. (d. 1901), 195–96 n. 106, 235 n. 56
Strachey, Lytton (1880–1932), 11, 134
Strawberry Hill, gothic revival style of, 16, 102, 217 n. 63
Sturgis, Howard (1855–1920), 13, 193 n. 68, 193 n. 73

Sutton Hoo ship burial, 84
Swain, E. G. (1861–1938), 195 n. 102, 195 n. 106
  Stoneground Ghost Tales, 146, 196 n. 107
swastikas. *See* fylfots
Symphosius, 98
  Aenigmata, 198 n. 29

Talmud, 153–54. See also *Middoth, Tractate* (section of the Talmud)
Tatham, H. W. F. (1861–1909), *Footprints in the Snow,* 196 n. 107
Tatwine, 98
Templar, Knights, 40, 42–44, 50, 200 n. 60, 201 nn. 63–64, 201 n. 66
temporalities, 26, 73–74, 82–87, 128–64, 228 n. 98, 228 n. 106
Temple Bruer, 43
Temple Grove, 11, 21
Testament of Solomon. *See* apocrypha
Thetford Heath, 211 n. 134
Thomas of Monmouth (fl. 1149–1172), *Life and Miracles of St. William of Norwich,* 151, 227–28 n. 98
Thompson, Henry Yates (1838–1928), 151
Thorpe, John (1715–1792), 111
Tolkien, J. R. R. (1892–1973), 181, 190 n. 29, 202 n. 78
Tourneur, Jacques, *Night of the Demon,* 58
"transpersonal replicability," 64–65, 81
Trollope, Anthony (1815–1882), *Barchester Towers,* 95
typology, 216 n. 48

Ulrichs, Karl Heinrich (1825–1895), 200 n. 62

Vincent of Lérins, 39, 199 n. 43
Visitatio sepulchri. See Quem quaeritis ceremony.

Vita Vulframni, 68
Völsunga Saga, 68, 208 nn. 92–93
Vulgate Bible, 37–38, 106, 113, 115, 218 n. 77, 229 n. 120

Waldstein, Charles (1856–1927), 9, 18, 191–92 n. 43
Walpole, Horace (1717–1797), 217 n. 63
Walpole, Hugh (1884–1941), 14, 193 n. 73
Wanderer, The (Old English poem), 183
war memorials, 231 n. 11–12, 232 n. 19, 232 n. 26, 232 n. 28, 232 n. 31. *See also* Great War, memorials of
Weyer, Johann (1515–1588), *De praestigiis daemonum,* 190 n. 30
whistling, incapability of, considered a mark of homosexuals, 200–201 n. 62
White Lion (Aldeburgh hotel), 170, 176, 232 n. 26
Whitting, Fred (1834–1911), 156
Willement, Thomas (1786–1871), 202 n. 73
Wilson, Thomas (1703–1784), 162, 230 n. 138
women
  at Cambridge denied degrees, 19, 79, 145–48, 154
  at Cambridge denied access to libraries, 148–55, 227 n. 86
Woolf, Virginia (1882–1941), *A Room of One's Own,* 227 n. 86
World War I. *See* Great War
Wormsley Priory, 73
Wraxall, Sir Nathaniel William (1751–1831), 53
Wulfram of Sens, 68, 209 n. 94
Wyatt, James (1746–1813), 103

Yggdrasil, 70
York Mystery Plays, 114–16. *See also* mystery plays